체크 포인트 토익

CHECKPOINT TOEIC

하명호 지음

KM 경문사

체크 포인트 토익

지은이 하명호
펴낸이 조경희
펴낸곳 경문사
펴낸날 2025년 2월 21일 1판 1쇄
등 록 1979년 11월 9일 제1979-000023호
주 소 04057, 서울특별시 마포구 와우산로 174
전 화 (02)332-2004 팩스 (02)336-5193
이메일 kyungmoon@kyungmoon.com

값 19,000원

ISBN 979-11-6073-319-8

머리말

TOEIC 시험은 단순한 영어 평가를 넘어, **글로벌 커리어와 학업을 위한 필수 역량**이 되었습니다. 하지만 방대한 시험 범위와 다양한 문제 유형은 많은 학습자에게 부담으로 다가오기도 합니다. 이 책은 그러한 고민을 해결하고, **효율적이며 체계적인 학습법을 제공**하기 위해 설계되었습니다. 총 16장으로 구성된 이 책은 학습자가 **TOEIC 문법과 독해를 체계적으로 학습**할 수 있도록 도와줍니다.

왜 이 책인가요?

➡ 문법과 독해의 자연스러운 연결

Checkpoint와 연습문제를 활용해 **문법 기초를 탄탄하게 다진 후**, Part 6과 Part 7 문제 풀이로 자연스럽게 확장합니다.

➡ 기초부터 실전까지

초급 학습자도 이해할 수 있는 **자세한 개념 설명과 난이도별 문제 구성**을 통해, 영어 실력을 체계적으로 향상할 수 있습니다.

➡ 실전 감각 극대화

최신 TOEIC 시험 경향을 반영한 **실전 문제 풀이 훈련**으로 철저한 시험 대비가 가능합니다.

➡ 효율적인 학습 전략 제공

문제 풀이 속도를 높이고 **시간 관리 능력을 강화하는 전략과 실전 팁**을 제공합니다.

이 책은 단순히 TOEIC 점수를 높이는 것을 넘어 **영어 실력의 확실한 도약**을 이루기 위해 설계되었습니다.

이 책과 함께 TOEIC 준비를 시작하세요.

목표를 향해 도전하며, **성공적인 학습 여정**을 시작해 보세요!

TOEIC 문법과 독해 전략

이 책은 TOEIC 시험 대비를 위한 **체계적이고 효과적인 학습 도구**로, 총 16장으로 구성되어 있습니다. **초급부터 고급 학습자까지 활용**할 수 있도록, 문법을 중심으로 **명확하고 논리적인 설명을 제공**합니다. 또한, 실전 문제 풀이를 통해 **실제 시험 환경을 경험하며 문제 풀이 감각**을 익힐 수 있도록 설계되었습니다.

책의 구성

구성	설명
문법 파트	TOEIC에서 **자주 출제되는 핵심 문법 항목**을 체계적으로 정리하여, 명확한 개념 설명과 다양한 예문을 통해 학습자가 **쉽고 효과적으로 이해할 수 있도록 구성**되었습니다. 또한, **Checkpoint 섹션과 연습문제**를 통해 개념을 점검하고 실력을 강화할 수 있습니다.
독해와 응용 파트	TOEIC **Part 6 & 7 문제 유형을 집중 분석**하여, 독해 실력을 **체계적으로 향상**시킬 수 있도록 구성되었습니다. **문맥과 문장 흐름을 파악하는 능력을 강화**하며, 난이도별 문제를 제공하여 실전 감각을 익힐 수 있습니다.

책의 특징

구성	설명
체계적인 Checkpoint 제공	각 장마다 **핵심 문법 포인트와 예제**를 포함하여 학습자가 개념을 명확히 이해하고 **스스로 실력을 점검**할 수 있도록 구성되었습니다.
문법과 독해의 자연스러운 연결	문법 학습을 기반으로 **Part 6 & 7 문제 풀이로 자연스럽게 확장**하여, **실전 문제 해결 능력**을 효과적으로 키울 수 있습니다.
초급부터 고급까지 맞춤형 학습	**기초 학습자를 위한 필수 개념 정리**부터, **고급 학습자를 위한 심화 문제 및 응용 학습**까지 폭넓게 활용할 수 있습니다.
실전 대비 최적화	최신 TOEIC 출제 경향을 반영한 문제를 제공하여, **실전 환경 적응력**을 높이고 **자신감을 강화**할 수 있도록 구성되었습니다.
Part 6 & 7 문제 풀이 훈련	유형별 풀이 전략과 연습문제를 통해 **독해 능력과 실전 문제 해결력을 향상**시킬 수 있습니다.

이 책의 목표

- 이 책을 통해 학습자는 **TOEIC에서 필수적인 핵심 문법을 정확히 이해**하고, **실전 문제 풀이 능력을 효과적으로 향상**시킬 수 있습니다.
- **목표 점수 달성**뿐만 아니라, **영어 실력을 한 단계 더 향상**시키는 데 큰 도움이 될 것입니다.

차례

Chapter

01

문장의 유형과 동사의 종류

1. 1형식 문형

(부사/부사구/부사절), 주어 + 동사 + (부사/부사구/부사절)

1형식 문형의 구조는 기본적으로 주어와 완전자동사로 이루어져 있고, 부사/부사구/부사절이 선택적으로 문장의 앞이나 뒤에 올 수 있다. 주어 자리에는 명사(구), 대명사, To부정사, 동명사, 명사절이 올 수 있다.

✔ CheckPoint 1. 1형식 동사

▶ 생사 동사: live, die, exist(존재하다)
▶ 왕래 발착 동사: come, arrive, appear(나타나다), go, leave, depart(출발하다), disappear(사라지다)
▶ 상승과 하락 동사: increase(증가하다), rise(오르다), decrease(감소하다), decline(감소하다, 쇠퇴하다)
▶ 기타: work, stand, study

Some ancient creatures no longer **exist** on Earth.
몇몇 고대 생물들은 더 이상 지구에 존재하지 않는다.
The flight **departs** from Gate 5 at 2 p.m.
항공편은 오후 2시에 5번 게이트에서 출발한다.
The price of gasoline **increased** last month.
지난달에 휘발유 가격이 올랐다.
The company's profits **declined** due to poor management.
회사의 수익은 부실한 경영으로 인해 감소했다.

토익 연습문제

1. The species __________ in the wild, but it is rarely seen by humans.
(A) increases
(B) exists
(C) declines
(D) departs

2. The flight __________ at the airport 30 minutes late due to bad weather.
(A) rose
(B) stood
(C) arrived
(D) worked

2. 2형식 문형

(부사/부사구/부사절), 주어 + 동사 + 주격보어 + (부사/부사구/부사절)

2형식 문형의 구조는 기본적으로 주어 + 불완전자동사 + 주격보어로 이루어져 있고, 부사/부사구/부사절 역시 문장의 앞이나 뒤에 선택적으로 올 수 있다. 주격보어 자리에는 명사나 형용사가 올 수 있는데, 명사가 오면 주어와 동격관계를 나타내고, 형용사가 오면 주어를 보충 설명하므로 보(충)어라고 한다.

✔ CheckPoint 2. 2형식 동사

▶ 지각, 인상, 감각 동사: appear(~처럼 보이다), seem, look, sound, smell, taste, feel
▶ 계속 동사 (~인 상태를 유지하다): remain, stay, keep
▶ 상태 변화 동사 (~하게 되다): become, go, get, turn
▶ 판단 동사 (~으로 판명되다): prove, turn out

The suggestion **sounds reasonable** to the team.
그 제안은 팀에게 합리적으로 들린다.

They **remained silent** during the discussion.
그들은 토론 중에 침묵을 지켰다.

The room **turned cold** when the heater stopped working.
난방기가 작동을 멈추자 방이 차가워졌다.

The strategy **turned out better** than expected.
그 전략은 예상보다 더 나은 것으로 밝혀졌다.

토익 연습문제

1. The manager __________ calm despite the unexpected situation.
   (A) remained
   (B) disappeared
   (C) appeared
   (D) started

2. The new software __________ easy to use and highly efficient.
   (A) operates
   (B) seems
   (C) sounds
   (D) remains

3. 3형식 문형

(부사/부사구/부사절), 주어 + 동사 + 목적어 + (부사/부사구/부사절)

3형식 문형의 구조는 기본적으로 주어 + 완전타동사 + 목적어로 이루어져 있고, 부사/부사구/부사절 역시 문장의 앞이나 뒤에 선택적으로 올 수 있다. 목적어 자리에는 주어 자리처럼 명사(구), 대명사, To부정사, 동명사, 명사절이 올 수 있다.

✔ CheckPoint 3. 3형식 동사

▶ 대부분의 영어 문장은 3형식 동사로 구성되어 있다.

The company **announced the new policy** during the meeting.
회사는 회의 중에 새로운 정책을 발표했다.

The manager **reviewed it** thoroughly before making a decision.
매니저는 결정을 내리기 전에 그것을 철저히 검토했다.

He **decided to take** a break after the project.
그는 프로젝트 후에 휴식을 취하기로 결정했다.

We **finished preparing** the documents this morning.
우리는 오늘 아침에 서류 준비를 마쳤다.

The instructor **explained that the test would be postponed.**
강사는 시험이 연기될 것이라고 설명했다.

토익 연습문제

1. The committee approved ________ during the meeting.
   (A) the proposal
   (B) carefully
   (C) quickly
   (D) efficiently

2. The team ________ the new schedule after the meeting.
   (A) discussed
   (B) arrived
   (C) increased
   (D) included

4. 4형식 문형

(부사/부사구/부사절), 주어 + 동사 + 간접목적어 + 직접목적어 + (부사/부사구/부사절)

4형식 문형의 구조는 기본적으로 주어 + 수여동사 + 간접목적어 + 직접목적어로 이루어져 있고, 부사/부사구/부사절 역시 문장의 앞이나 뒤에 선택적으로 올 수 있다.

✔ CheckPoint 4. 4형식 동사

▶ 주어 + 수여동사 + 간접목적어 + 직접목적어 (4형식)
⇒ 주어 + 수여동사 + 직접목적어 + 전치사 + 간접목적어 (3형식)

▶ 전치사 to를 사용하는 동사: bring, give, offer, send, show

▶ 전치사 for를 사용하는 동사: buy, make, order

▶ 전치사 of를 사용하는 동사: ask

He **offered** the clients a new proposal.
⇒ He **offered** a new proposal **to** the clients.
그는 고객들에게 새 제안을 제공했다.

The boss **ordered** the employees lunch.
⇒ The boss **ordered** lunch **for** the employees.
상사는 직원들을 위해 점심을 주문했다.

The director **asked** the board members their opinion.
⇒ The director **asked** an opinion **of** the board members.
그 감독은 이사회 구성원들에게 의견을 요청했다.

토익 연습문제

1. The company __________ the marketing team a budget proposal for the next quarter.
   (A) bought
   (B) gave
   (C) removed
   (D) designed

2. The manager __________ the team the necessary resources to complete the project.
   (A) sent
   (B) ordered
   (C) decreased
   (D) transferred

5. 5형식 문형

(부사/부사구/부사절), 주어 + 불완전타동사 + 목적어 + 목적보어 + (부사/부사구/부사절)

5형식 문형의 구조는 기본적으로 주어 + 불완전타동사 + 목적어 + 목적보어로 이루어져 있고, 부사/부사구/부사절 역시 문장의 앞이나 뒤에 선택적으로 올 수 있다. 목적보어 자리에는 명사, 형용사, to부정사, 분사가 올 수 있지만, to부정사를 목적보어로 취하는 문제가 압도적으로 많이 나온다.

✔ CheckPoint 5. 5형식 동사

- ▶ 지각동사(feel, hear, listen to, see, watch) + 목적어 + 목적보어(동사원형/현재분사/과거분사)
- ▶ 사역동사(have, let, make, help) + 목적어 + 목적보어(동사원형/과거분사)
- ▶ 5형식 동사 + 목적어 + 목적보어(to부정사)
  advise(충고하다), allow(허락하다), ask(요청하다), cause(~을 야기하다), enable(~할 수 있게 하다), encourage(격려하다), expect(기대하다), force(강요하다), invite(초대하다), remind 상기시키다), require(요구하다), tell(말하다)

They **heard** the manager **announce** the new policy.
그들은 매니저가 새로운 정책을 발표하는 것을 들었다.

I **had** the technician **fix** the computer.
나는 기술자가 컴퓨터를 고치게 했다.

The program **enabled** the staff **to work** more efficiently.
그 프로그램은 직원들이 더 효율적으로 일할 수 있게 했다.

The manager **required** us **to finish** the project by Friday.
매니저는 우리가 금요일까지 프로젝트를 끝내도록 요구했다.

☞ 지각동사의 목적보어 자리에 오는 동사원형과 현재분사의 차이점

동사원형은 전체 동작이나 완전한 동작을 지각한 경우이고, 현재분사는 진행 중인 동작의 일부를 지각한 경우이다.

I saw him leave the room.
나는 그가 방을 떠나는 것을 (처음부터 끝까지) 보았다.

I saw him leaving the room.
나는 그가 방을 떠나고 있는 중인 것을 보았다.

토익 연습문제

1. We saw the interns __________ the meeting room after the presentation.
(A) leave
(B) being left
(C) left
(D) to leave

2. The professor made the students __________ the report by the deadline.
(A) to complete
(B) completed
(C) completing
(D) complete

3. The manager encouraged the team __________ innovative ideas for the project.
(A) develop
(B) developing
(C) to develop
(D) developed

토익 종합 실전문제

1. The factory __________ around the clock to meet the high demand for products.
   (A) increases
   (B) works
   (C) departs
   (D) rises

2. The number of users has steadily __________ due to new competition.
   (A) declined
   (B) worked
   (C) reduced
   (D) disappeared

3. The building __________ empty for several years before it was renovated.
   (A) increased
   (B) remained
   (C) disappeared
   (D) started

4. The new policy has __________ a controversial topic among employees.
   (A) designed
   (B) included
   (C) become
   (D) removed

5. The employees were instructed to __________ calm during the emergency situation.
   (A) stay
   (B) leave
   (C) disrupt
   (D) arrive

6. After months of neglect, the fruit has __________ bad and cannot be eaten.
   (A) started
   (B) stayed
   (C) disappeared
   (D) gone

7. She tends to __________ nervous before giving a presentation.
   (A) decrease
   (B) get
   (C) run
   (D) improve

8. The supervisor instructed __________ to follow the new safety procedures.
   (A) effectively
   (B) them
   (C) yesterday
   (D) clearly

9. The team agreed __________ additional resources for the project.

(A) allocate
(B) allocating
(C) to allocate
(D) allocated

10. The employees suggested __________ a more flexible work schedule.

(A) to implement
(B) implementing
(C) implemented
(D) implement

11. The CEO mentioned __________ the company would expand overseas next year.

(A) what
(B) to
(C) that
(D) if

12. The CEO __________ an important task of the assistant to ensure the event runs smoothly.

(A) analyzed
(B) designed
(C) removed
(D) asked

13. The clerk __________ the customer a refund for the damaged product.

(A) organized
(B) transferred
(C) gave
(D) replaced

14. The company __________ a generous compensation package to its employees.

(A) transferred
(B) designed
(C) offered
(D) delivered

15. She bought a gift __________ her colleague to celebrate his promotion.

(A) to
(B) for
(C) with
(D) about

16. The manager __________ a meal for the entire team after the late meeting.

(A) gave
(B) asked
(C) sent
(D) ordered

17. The manager had the document __________ by the assistant before the meeting.
(A) review
(B) reviewing
(C) reviewed
(D) to review

18. The instructor reminded the students __________ the safety rules during the lab session.
(A) follow
(B) following
(C) to follow
(D) followed

19. The manager allowed the team __________ additional resources for the project.
(A) to access
(B) accessing
(C) access
(D) accessed

20. The CEO asked the employees __________ a detailed report by the end of the week.
(A) prepare
(B) preparing
(C) to prepare
(D) prepared

21. The employees were encouraged __________ part in the training program.
(A) take
(B) taking
(C) taken
(D) to take

22. The students were required __________ the assignment before the deadline.
(A) submit
(B) submitting
(C) to submit
(D) submitted

23. The project team was expected __________ significant progress by the end of the quarter.
(A) to achieve
(B) achieving
(C) achieve
(D) achieved

24. The participants were ______ to ask questions during the presentation.
(A) allow
(B) allowed
(C) allows
(D) allowing

PART 6

Questions 1–4 refer to the following email.

Dear Team,

As we prepare to welcome several new employees next week, I want to provide an update on the orientation schedule and tasks. Firstly, the orientation will begin on Monday at 9:00 AM in the main conference room. As a reminder, all department heads 1________ to give brief presentations about their respective teams. Please ensure that your presentations are ready and that you arrive on time. Secondly, the HR team will conduct the general onboarding session. This session will cover the company's policies, benefits, and 2________. It is essential that all new employees attend this session to fully understand the company's expectations and guidelines. Lastly, remember to assign a mentor for each new employee. These mentors will help guide them through the first few weeks, answer any questions, and 3________ with their integration into the team. Thank you all for your cooperation. Let's ensure a smooth onboarding process and make the new employees feel welcome. 4________.

Best regards,
HR Manager, Martha Sullivan

1. (A) expect
   (B) expected
   (C) are expected
   (D) are expecting

2. (A) work-life balance
   (B) customer satisfaction
   (C) annual reviews
   (D) meeting protocols

3. (A) assisting
   (B) assisted
   (C) assist
   (D) assistance

4. (A) Please keep the onboarding schedule flexible
   (B) Looking forward to working together
   (C) The orientation will last the entire day
   (D) Let me know if you need further clarification

PART 7

Questions 1-4 refer to the following announcement.

To: All employees
From: Facilities Management
Date: September 12
Subject: Upcoming Office Renovations

Dear Team,

This is to inform you that our office will undergo renovations starting from October 1 and continuing until the end of the month. The renovations are part of our efforts to improve the workspace and create a more comfortable and efficient environment for all employees.

During this time, certain sections of the building, including the third and fourth floors, will be temporarily closed. Please note that while the work is ongoing, there may be occasional noise disruptions, particularly during the daytime. We apologize for any inconvenience this may cause and appreciate your understanding.

To accommodate everyone, we have arranged for alternative workspaces on the first and second floors. Employees whose offices are affected by the renovations will be notified in advance and provided with details regarding their temporary workstations. If you have any concerns or special requests related to your workspace during the renovation period, please contact the Facilities Management team directly.

We appreciate your cooperation and look forward to unveiling the newly renovated areas soon.

Best regards,
Facilities Management Team

1. When will the renovations begin?
   (A) On September 12
   (B) On September 30
   (C) On October 1
   (D) At the end of October

2. Where will employees work if their offices are affected by the renovations?
   (A) On the third floor
   (B) On the fourth floor
   (C) In off-site offices
   (D) In temporary spaces on the first and second floors

3. What should employees do if they have concerns about their workspace during the renovation period?
   (A) Speak with their manager
   (B) Contact the Facilities Management team
   (C) Work from home
   (D) Wait for further instructions

4. What can be inferred about the third and fourth floors during the renovation?
   (A) Employees will not be able to access these areas.
   (B) They will be converted into new office spaces.
   (C) They will be used as storage for construction materials.
   (D) Employees will need to work overtime to accommodate the changes.

Chapter

02

동사의 시제

1. 동사의 변화

① 규칙변화 동사: 동사원형 + (e)d

▶ love: loved

▶ study: studied

▶ play: played

▶ stop: stopped

▶ picnic: picnicked

He **studied** hard for the exam and passed with excellent marks.
그는 시험을 위해 열심히 공부했고, 우수한 성적으로 통과했다.

They **played** soccer after work to relieve stress.
그들은 스트레스를 풀기 위해 퇴근 후 축구를 했다.

The company **stopped** producing the outdated model last year.
그 회사는 작년에 구형 모델 생산을 중단했다.

We **picnicked** in the park last weekend and enjoyed the nice weather.
우리는 지난 주말에 공원에서 피크닉을 했고, 좋은 날씨를 즐겼다.

② 불규칙변화 동사

▶ A-A-A형: cut-cut-cut

▶ A-B-A형: come-came-come

▶ A-B-B형: buy-bought-bought

▶ A-B-C형: sing-sang-sung

The company **cut** costs by reducing unnecessary expenses.
그 회사는 불필요한 비용을 줄여서 비용을 절감했다.

He **came** to the meeting on time despite the heavy traffic.
그는 교통이 막혔음에도 불구하고 회의에 제시간에 도착했다.

They **bought** new office equipment to improve productivity.
그들은 생산성을 높이기 위해 새로운 사무 장비를 샀다.

The band **sang** several popular songs at the company event last night.
그 밴드는 어젯밤 회사 행사에서 여러 인기곡을 불렀다.

2. 동사의 시제

① 기본 시제: 현재, 과거, 미래

✔ CheckPoint 1. 현재 시제

▶ 반복 되풀이되는 습관이나 동작
▶ 불변의 진리
▶ 일반적이거나 과학적인 사실
▶ 일정표 (영화 상영시간, 버스/기차/비행기 운행 시간, 등)
▶ 가까운 미래 (왕래 발착 동사 + 미래 시제 부사/부사구)
▶ 시간과 조건의 부사절 (미래시제 대신 현재시제 사용)

The team **meets** in the conference room every Monday.
팀은 매주 월요일에 회의실에서 만난다.

Blood **carries** oxygen to different parts of the body.
혈액은 몸의 다양한 부분에 산소를 운반한다.

The train **leaves** the station at 9:30 AM every weekday.
기차는 매주 평일 오전 9시 30분에 역을 떠난다.

When the meeting ends, we **will discuss** the next steps.
회의가 끝나면 우리는 다음 단계를 논의할 것이다.

☞ 명사절과 형용사절에서는 미래시제를 그대로 사용

The CEO **wants** to know **if the sales team will meet their target.**
CEO는 영업팀이 목표를 달성할 수 있을지 알고 싶어 한다.

The laptop that you will use is in the storage room.
네가 사용할 노트북은 보관실에 있다.

토익 연습문제

1. Every Saturday, she ______ her friends at the café.
   (A) meet
   (B) meets
   (C) meeting
   (D) met

2 The bus __________ the terminal at 8:15 AM every weekday.
   (A) will leave
   (B) leaves
   (C) leaving
   (D) left

3 When the meeting ______, we will discuss the new policy.
   (A) start
   (B) starts
   (C) starting
   (D) started

✔ CheckPoint 2. 과거 시제

▶ 과거의 동작이나 상태: last (weekend, year, night,...), in the past, in 연도나 세기, ago, yesterday,

▶ 과거의 습관

▶ 주절과 종속절의 두 사건의 순서가 명확한 경우 과거완료 대신 사용 가능

The company **launched** a new product **last year**.
그 회사는 작년에 신제품을 출시했다.

In the past, employees **were** required to submit reports by hand.
과거에는 직원들이 보고서를 손으로 제출해야 했다.

We **used to** hold annual meetings in person.
우리는 매년 대면으로 회의를 열곤 했다.

She **finished** the report **before** the meeting **started**.
그녀는 회의가 시작되기 전에 보고서를 끝냈다.

토익 연습문제

1. In 2015, the company ______ its most successful product.
   (A) launch
   (B) launched
   (C) launches
   (D) launching

2 We ______ the new policy during the meeting yesterday.
   (A) discuss
   (B) discusses
   (C) discussing
   (D) discussed

3. They ______ the contract before they met with the client.
   (A) signed
   (B) sign
   (C) signing
   (D) signs

✔ CheckPoint 3. 미래 시제

▶ 미래를 나타내는 부사/부사구: tomorrow, in the (near) future, next (time, year, month), soon, before long(머지않아), this coming Monday(다가오는 월요일), as of(~부터) + 미래 시제, starting (from)(~부터) + 미래 시제

Before long, the company **will implement** a new policy.
머지않아 그 회사는 새로운 정책을 시행할 것이다.

The training session **will begin this coming Monday**.
교육 세션은 다가오는 월요일에 시작될 것이다.

As of next week, the new regulations **will be** in effect.
다음 주부터 새로운 규정이 발효될 것이다.

Starting next month, we **will offer** discounts on all products.
다음 달부터 우리는 모든 제품에 할인을 제공할 것이다.

토익 연습문제

1. Starting next week, the company ______ a new software system to improve productivity.
   (A) implements
   (B) will implement
   (C) implemented
   (D) implementing

2. This coming Friday, the CEO __________ the annual performance review meeting.
   (A) hosts
   (B) hosted
   (C) hosting
   (D) will host

3. As of next month, the marketing team __________ a new advertising campaign.
   (A) launches
   (B) launched
   (C) will launch
   (D) launching

② 완료시제: 현재완료, 과거완료, 미래완료

✔ CheckPoint 4. 현재완료

▶ 과거에 일어난 일이 현재까지 영향을 미치거나, 과거의 경험이 현재와 관련이 있을 때 사용하는 시제로, 보통 “have/has + 과거분사” 형태로 구성된다.
▶ 완료 (already, just, yet, recently),
▶ 경험 (ever, never, two times, once, before)
▶ 결과 (have lost, have missed, have gone)
▶ 계속 (for, in, since, over)

☞ 현재완료의 계속 용법일 경우 형태는 다르지만, 내용상 의미가 동일하므로 주절에 현재완료형이나 현재완료 진행형을 모두 사용 가능하다. 단, 정적 동사가 있으면 현재완료형만 사용 가능하다. 정적 동사는 감정동사 (like, love, hate), 인식동사 (know, believe, understand), 상태(존재)동사 (be, exist, resemble, stand), 소유동사 (have, possess, own, belong to), 지각동사(see, hear)가 있다.

We **have recently launched** a new marketing campaign.
우리는 최근에 새로운 마케팅 캠페인을 시작했다.

☞ recently는 과거와 현재완료 시제에 모두 사용 가능하지만, 특정 과거 시점에 일어난 사건을 강조할 경우에는 과거 시제를 사용하고, 과거부터 현재까지의 연속성 또는 현재와 연결된 사건을 강조할 경우에는 현재완료 시제를 사용한다.

I **have never worked** with such a demanding client before.
나는 전에 이렇게 까다로운 고객과 일해 본 적이 없다.

I **have missed** the deadline, so we need to request an extension.
나는 마감일을 놓쳐서 연장을 요청해야 한다.

We **have worked/ have been working** on this project **for six months.**
우리는 6개월 동안 이 프로젝트를 진행해 왔다.

☞ 시간과 조건의 부사절에서는 미래완료 대신 현재완료를 사용

They **will start** the presentation **when** everyone **has taken** their seats.
모두가 자리에 앉으면 프레젠테이션을 시작할 것이다.

If you **have finished** the report by tomorrow, we **will send** it to the client.
네가 내일까지 보고서를 끝내면, 우리는 그것을 고객에게 보낼 것이다.

토익 연습문제

1. He ______ on this project for three months.
   (A) have worked
   (B) has worked
   (C) was working
   (D) worked

2. Employee satisfaction has improved since the company __________ flexible working hours.
   (A) introduces
   (B) introduced
   (C) introducing
   (D) has introduced

3. The marketing team ______ the campaign successfully over the past month.
   (A) launches
   (B) launched
   (C) is launching
   (D) has launched

✔ CheckPoint 5. 과거완료

▶ 과거의 특정 시점이나 사건 이전에 벌어진 동작이나 상태를 나타내는 시제로, 과거의 두 가지 사건 중 하나가 다른 하나보다 먼저 일어났음을 강조할 때 사용되고, 보통 "had + 과거분사" 형태로 구성된다.

▶ 완료, 경험, 결과, 계속

By the time the meeting began, she **had already reviewed** all the documents.
회의가 시작되었을 때쯤 그녀는 이미 모든 문서를 검토했었다.

They **had tried** several times to fix the issue **before they called the technician**.
그들은 기술자를 부르기 전에 여러 번 문제를 고치려 했었다.

The presentation **was** successful because he **had prepared** thoroughly.
그는 철저히 준비했었기 때문에 발표는 성공적이었다.

She **had worked** at the company for five years **before she got promoted**.
그녀는 승진하기 전에 5년 동안 그 회사에서 일을 했었다.

토익 연습문제

1. They ______ the contract before the meeting started.
   (A) signed
   (B) had signed
   (C) were signing
   (D) signs

2. By the time the CEO arrived, the team ______ the presentation.
   (A) prepares
   (B) prepared
   (C) had prepared
   (D) is preparing

3. The team ______ the design changes for three weeks before the client approved them.
   (A) reviews
   (B) reviewed
   (C) had been reviewing
   (D) has reviewed

✔ CheckPoint 6. 미래완료

▶ 미래의 특정 시점까지 완료될 동작이나 상태를 나타내는 시제로, 미래 시점 이전에 발생한 사건의 결과가 미래까지 영향을 미친다는 것을 강조하고, 보통 "will have + 과거분사" 형태로 구성된다.

▶ 완료, 경험, 결과, 계속

We **will have launched** the new product **by next quarter.**
우리는 다음 분기쯤이면 신제품을 출시할 것이다.

We **will have attended** ten conferences **by the end of this year.**
우리는 올해 말쯤이면 10개의 회의에 참석했을 것이다.

They **will have reached** their sales target **by next month.**
그들은 다음 달쯤이면 판매 목표를 달성할 것이다.

By next month, she **will have lived** in New York since she moved there in 2015.
다음 달쯤이면 그녀는 2015년에 이사한 후 계속 뉴욕에 살게 될 것이다.

토익 연습문제

1. By the time the seminar ends, the team ______ all the necessary data.
   (A) will have gathered
   (B) gathers
   (C) will gather
   (D) has gathered

2. The company ______ its expansion plan by the end of the next quarter.
   (A) announces
   (B) announced
   (C) will announce
   (D) will have announced

3. By the time she retires, she ______ numerous awards for her contributions to the company.
   (A) receives
   (B) has received
   (C) will have received
   (D) will receive

토익 종합 실전문제

1. The CEO __________ for Singapore next week to attend the business summit.
(A) departs
(B) departed
(C) departing
(D) will depart

2. The meeting __________ at 9:00 AM sharp and ends by 11:00 AM.
(A) starting
(B) started
(C) starts
(D) will start

3. The CEO wants to ask if the project __________ completed on time.
(A) is
(B) was
(C) will be
(D) has been

4. The meeting that you ______ to attend is scheduled for Monday.
(A) will need
(B) need
(C) needed
(D) needing

5. The team ______ hard to finish the project on time last month.
(A) work
(B) works
(C) worked
(D) working

6. She had finished the presentation before the meeting __________.
(A) starting
(B) starts
(C) started
(D) has started

7. The team __________ the client's feedback two weeks ago.
(A) reviews
(B) reviewed
(C) has reviewed
(D) reviewing

8. He ______ in Paris for three years before moving to London last year.
(A) live
(B) lives
(C) living
(D) lived

9. Starting from January, the HR team ______ a new policy for employee benefits.

(A) introduced

(B) introduces

(C) will introduce

(D) introducing

10. The manager ______ a meeting with the clients this coming Monday.

(A) has

(B) had

(C) is having

(D) will have

11. The new rules will come into effect __________ next month.

(A) before long

(B) at

(C) by

(D) as of

12. The construction of the new office building __________ in the near future.

(A) will begin

(B) began

(C) begins

(D) has begun

13. The employee ______ multiple training sessions since joining the company.

(A) attends

(B) attended

(C) has attended

(D) is attending

14. Sales have increased significantly since the marketing team __________ a new strategy.

(A) implements

(B) has implemented

(C) implemented

(D) implement

15. The marketing team has been conducting surveys ______ the past two weeks.

(A) in

(B) over

(C) for

(D) since

16 The team ______ the software for six months to meet the deadline.

(A) develops

(B) developed

(C) had developed

(D) has been developing

17. The employees have been working on the proposal ______ yesterday.
(A) for
(B) since
(C) in
(D) over

18. I will give you an update as soon as we ______ more information.
(A) have gathered
(B) has gathered
(C) gathered
(D) are gathering

19. The manager ______ the upcoming changes with the team recently.
(A) discusses
(B) discussing
(C) has discussed
(D) had discussed

20. She ______ the report thoroughly before submitting it to the manager.
(A) had reviewed
(B) reviews
(C) was reviewing
(D) reviewed

21. The report was rejected because the team ______ to include critical details.
(A) forgot
(B) was forgetting
(C) forgets
(D) had forgotten

22. The project ______ behind schedule for several months before the new manager took over.
(A) had been
(B) has been
(C) was
(D) will be

23. By the time the system crashed, the IT team ______ on the issue since the morning.
(A) has worked
(B) had been working
(C) worked
(D) is working

24. We ______ this research project for two years by the time it is published.
(A) have worked on
(B) works on
(C) worked on
(D) will have worked on

PART 6

Questions 1-4 refer to the following memo.

Upcoming Team Building Workshop

Dear Team,

As part of our efforts to enhance teamwork and collaboration, we are pleased to announce an upcoming team building workshop scheduled for next month. This workshop aims to strengthen our team dynamics and improve our overall efficiency. To facilitate, we have organized a series of interactive sessions designed to foster better communication and problem-solving skills. The workshop 1________ on the 15th of next month at our conference center. Please mark your calendars and make sure to attend as this will be an important opportunity for us to grow as a team. During the workshop, 2________. These activities will help us understand each other's strengths and improve our collective performance.

If you have any dietary restrictions or other special needs, please inform the HR department 3________ so that we can make the necessary arrangements. We want to ensure that everyone has a comfortable and productive experience.

Finally, we will be sending out detailed information about the workshop schedule and agenda closer to the date. 4________, please feel free to reach out if you have any immediate questions or concerns.

Thank you for your attention and cooperation.

Best regards,

The HR Team

1. (A) takes place
   (B) will take place
   (C) will be taken place
   (D) is taken place

2. (A) we will analyze the company's financial reports
   (B) a guest speaker will deliver a motivational talk
   (C) we will be engaging in various team activities that are both fun and educational
   (D) all team leaders will present their quarterly performance updates

3. (A) after the event
   (B) on the day of the workshop
   (C) during the session
   (D) before the workshop

4. (A) In this case
   (B) Until then
   (C) Therefore
   (D) As a reminder

PART 7

Questions 1-4 refer to the following email.

To: allstaff@sunnydayresorts.com
From: Sarah Lee s.lee@sunnydayresorts.com
Date: September 9
Subject: Annual Staff Retreat Information

Dear Team,

I am pleased to announce that our Annual Staff Retreat will take place on October 15-16 at the Blue Lagoon Resort. This year, we have planned a series of activities to promote teamwork and relaxation. As always, we encourage all employees to attend this retreat, as it is a great opportunity to connect with colleagues and recharge.

The retreat will start at 9:00 AM on October 15 with a team-building workshop led by a professional facilitator. Lunch will be provided, followed by an afternoon of outdoor activities such as hiking and canoeing. Please remember to bring comfortable clothing and shoes for these activities. Dinner will be a barbecue by the beach, with a bonfire and social time afterward.

On October 16, we will have a morning yoga session at 8:00 AM, followed by a leadership seminar. The retreat will conclude with lunch and a closing address from our CEO, Mr. Thompson, at 1:00 PM.

Please confirm your attendance by replying to this email by September 30. If you have any dietary restrictions or require special accommodations, let us know as soon as possible.

Looking forward to seeing you there!

Best regards,
Sarah Lee
Event Coordinator, Sunny Day Resorts

1. When is the last day to confirm attendance for the retreat?
   (A) September 9
   (B) October 15
   (C) September 30
   (D) October 16

2. What is planned for the first day of the retreat after lunch?
   (A) Outdoor activities
   (B) A team-building workshop
   (C) A leadership seminar
   (D) The CEO's closing address

3. What should employees bring for the activities?
   (A) A laptop
   (B) A beach towel
   (C) Formal attire
   (D) Comfortable clothing and shoes

4. What is one possible reason the company organizes the retreat annually?
   (A) To evaluate employee performance
   (B) To promote teamwork and relaxation
   (C) To introduce new company policies
   (D) To conduct training sessions for leadership

Chapter

03

능동태와 수동태

1. 태의 구조와 시제

① 능동태와 수동태의 기본 구조

▶ 능동태는 문장의 주어가 동작을 수행하는 주체이다.

▶ 수동태는 문장의 주어가 동작을 받는 대상이다.

▶ 수동태는 주로 3, 4, 5형식 문장에서 사용되며, 행위자는 "by + 행위자" 형태로 나타낼 수 있다.

능동태: The manager(주어) approved(동사) the proposal(목적어).
매니저가 그 제안을 승인했다.
수동태: The proposal(주어) was approved(be동사 + 과거분사) by the manager(by + 행위자).

✔ CheckPoint 1. 능동태와 수동태의 시제

▶ 다양한 시제의 능동태 문장을 수동태 문장으로 변경할 수 있다.

The manager **reviews** the report. (현재)
⇒ The report **is reviewed** by the manager.
The manager **reviewed** the report. (과거)
⇒ The report **was reviewed** by the manager.
The manager **will review** the report. (미래)
⇒ The report **will be reviewed** by the manager.
The manager **has reviewed** the report. (현재 완료)
⇒ The report **has been reviewed** by the manager.
The manager **is reviewing** the report. (현재 진행)
⇒ The report **is being reviewed** by the manager.

토익 연습문제

1. The final decision ______ by the board before the end of the meeting.
   (A) was made
   (B) made
   (C) will make
   (D) is making

2. The building ______ when the earthquake struck.
   (A) was repairing
   (B) was being repaired
   (C) has been repaired
   (D) will be repaired

2. 타동사의 수동태

✔ CheckPoint 2. 4형식 동사의 수동태

▶ 4형식 동사는 간접목적어와 직접목적어로 구성되어 있어 수동태도 2개 존재한다.
▶ 직접목적어가 수동태의 주어가 되면 뒤에 남은 간접목적어 앞에 전치사를 추가한다.
전치사 to를 사용하는 동사: award, bring, give, offer, send, show
전치사 for를 사용하는 동사: buy, make, order
전치사 of를 사용하는 동사: ask

The supervisor **showed** the team(간접목적어) the new plan(직접목적어). (4형식)
감독관이 팀에게 새로운 계획을 보여주었다.
⇒ The team **was shown** the new plan by the supervisor. (3형식)
The supervisor **showed** the new plan(직접목적어) to the team(간접목적어). (3형식)
⇒ The new plan **was shown to** the team by the supervisor. (1형식)

토익 연습문제

1. The researcher ______ a grant for her study by the committee.
(A) awarded
(B) was awarded
(C) has awarded
(D) were awarded

2. The new design ______ to the client by the team leader.
(A) was showing
(B) showed
(C) was shown
(D) has shown

3. The team ______ several important questions by the consultant regarding the upcoming project.
(A) was asked
(B) asked
(C) is asking
(D) had asked

CheckPoint 3. 5형식 동사의 수동태

- ▶ 지각동사의 목적어가 수동태의 주어가 되면 목적보어 앞에 to부정사를 추가한다.
- ▶ 지각동사/사역동사의 목적어 이후에서 수동태 변환이 이루어지면 목적보어 자리에 과거분사가 남는다.
- ▶ to부정사를 목적보어로 취하는 5형식 동사(advise, allow, ask, cause, enable, encourage, expect, force, invite, remind, require, tell)가 수동태로 변환되면 목적보어인 to부정사가 남는다.
- ▶ 형용사/현재분사/과거분사를 목적보어로 취하는 5형식 동사(make, find, keep, leave, consider)가 수동태로 변환되면 목적보어인 형용사/현재분사/과거분사가 남는다.

I **saw** him **deliver** the presentation.
나는 그가 발표하는 것을 보았다.
⇒ He **was seen to deliver** the presentation.
⇒ I **saw** the presentation **delivered** by him.
The manager **had** the contractor **fix** the air conditioning system.
매니저는 계약업자에게 에어컨 시스템을 수리하게 했다.
⇒ The manager **had** the air conditioning system **fixed** by the contractor.
The new system **allowed** users **to access** data remotely.
새로운 시스템은 사용자들이 데이터를 원격으로 접근할 수 있도록 허용했다.
⇒ Users **were allowed to access** data remotely by the new system.
The supervisor **considered** the new system **efficient.**
감독관은 새로운 시스템이 효율적이라고 여겼다.
⇒ The new system **was considered efficient** by the supervisor.

토익 연습문제

1. The lawyer saw the documents ______ by the client.
   (A) sign
   (B) signed
   (C) signing
   (D) to sign

2. All employees were advised ______ the new policy by the HR department.
   (A) to follow
   (B) following
   (C) follow
   (D) followed

✔ CheckPoint 4. 목적어가 명사절인 문장의 수동태

▶ 사유나 사고 동사(believe, consider, expect, report, say, suppose, think)들은 목적어로 명사절을 취할 수 있다.

▶ 사유나 사고 동사들은 2가지 유형의 수동태로 변환될 수 있다.

They **believe** that the company will launch a new product. (3형식)
그들은 회사가 신제품을 출시할 것이라고 믿는다.

⇒ **It is believed** that the company will launch a new product. (1형식)

They **believe** the company **to launch** a new product. (5형식)

⇒ The company **is believed to launch** a new product. (2형식)

토익 연습문제

1. It ______ that the report contains critical information.
   (A) is thinking
   (B) thinks
   (C) thought
   (D) is thought

2. The merger ______ successful by all stakeholders.
   (A) considers
   (B) is considered
   (C) has considered
   (D) had considered

3. The new regulations are believed ______ a significant impact on the company's operations.
   (A) to have
   (B) to have had
   (C) to be
   (D) to have been

3. 수동태의 관용표현

✔ CheckPoint 5. 수동태를 포함하는 관용표현

be absorbed in	~에 몰두하다	be excited about	~에 대해 기대하다
be accustomed to	~에 익숙하다	be exposed to	~에 노출되다
be amazed by	~에 놀라다	be focused on	~에 집중하다
be annoyed at	~에 짜증이 나다	be impressed by	~에 감동받다
be associated with	~와 관련이 있다	be interested in	~에 관심이 있다
be based on	~에 기초하다	be involved in	~에 참여하다
be blamed for	~에 대해 비난받다	be known by	~으로 판단되다
be centered on	~에 중심을 두다	be known for	~로 알려지다
be committed to	~에 전념하다	be opposed to	~에 반대하다
be composed of	~로 구성되다	be prepared for	~을 위해 준비되다
be concerned about	~에 대해 걱정하다	be provided with	~이 제공되다
be conflicted over	~에 대해 갈등을 느끼다	be punished for	~에 대해 벌을 받다
be confused about	~에 대해 혼란스러워하다	be puzzled over	~에 대해 어리둥절해하다
be controlled by	~에 의해 통제되다	be related to	~와 관련이 있다
be covered with	~로 덮여 있다	be satisfied with	~에 만족하다
be damaged by	~에 의해 손상되다	be scared of	~을 무서워하다
be debated over	~에 대해 논의되다	be skilled at/in	~에 능숙하다
be disappointed at	~에 실망하다	be surprised at	~에 놀라다
be engaged in	~에 종사하다	be worried about	~에 대해 걱정하다
be equipped with	~이 갖춰져 있다		

The manager **was blamed for** the failure of the project.
매니저는 프로젝트 실패에 대해 비난받았다.

The discussion **was centered on** the company's future plans.
논의는 회사의 향후 계획에 중점을 두었다.

The policy changes **were** heavily **debated over** the past few months.
정책 변경 사항은 지난 몇 달 동안 크게 논의되었다.

Workers **are** frequently **exposed to** loud noise and heavy machinery.
근로자들은 자주 큰 소음과 무거운 기계에 노출된다.

The quality of a product **is known by** the materials used in its production.
제품의 품질은 그것의 생산에 사용된 재료들로 판단된다.

The team **was puzzled over** the unexpected drop in sales last quarter.
팀은 지난 분기 매출이 예상 밖으로 감소한 것에 대해 어리둥절해했다.

The new intern **is** highly **skilled at** using graphic design software.
신입 인턴은 그래픽 디자인 소프트웨어를 매우 능숙하게 사용한다.

토익 연습문제

1. Many experts are ______ by the rapid advancements in artificial intelligence technology.
   (A) blamed
   (B) confused
   (C) amazed
   (D) satisfied

2. The company's new project is ______ on developing eco-friendly products.
   (A) focused
   (B) opposed
   (C) concerned
   (D) conflicted

3. The environmental damage caused by the factory was ______ with toxic chemicals.
   (A) equipped
   (B) known
   (C) covered
   (D) blamed

토익 종합 실전문제

1. The report ______ before the deadline by the team leader.
(A) submits
(B) submitted
(C) will be submitted
(D) has been submitted

1. Several documents ______ by the manager right now.
(A) are being reviewed
(B) are reviewed
(C) is reviewing
(D) will review

3. The final presentation ______ by the team before the project deadline.
(A) has been completed
(B) was completed
(C) is completed
(D) will have been completed

4. The CEO ______ the marketing team a significant budget increase to boost the new product launch.
(A) had bought
(B) was asked
(C) made
(D) was made

5. A detailed invoice ______ to the client by the accounting department.
(A) sent
(B) was sent
(C) sending
(D) sends

6. Detailed instructions ______ the team by the manager.
(A) were given to
(B) was given to
(C) gave
(D) give to

7. Several challenging questions ______ the students by the professor.
(A) were asked of
(B) was asked to
(C) are asked
(D) will be asked

8. A custom-built desk ______ for the employee by the manager, but it arrived later than expected.
(A) was ordered
(B) were ordered
(C) has been ordered
(D) was being ordered

9. The CEO had the new marketing strategy ______ by the consultants.
(A) implement
(B) implemented
(C) implementing
(D) to implement

10. The employees ______ to meet the quarterly goals despite the challenges by the company.
(A) are expected
(B) is expected
(C) expected
(D) have been expected

11. The team was ______ to complete the task before the deadline by the manager.
(A) asking
(B) asked
(C) to ask
(D) asks

12. Customers ______ to track orders through the new app by the company.
(A) was enabled
(B) enabled
(C) were enabled
(D) will be enabling

13. The participants ______ to submit their feedback after the seminar by the instructor.
(A) were reminding
(B) were reminded
(C) is reminded
(D) reminded

14. The employees were forced ______ on weekends by the company to meet the deadline.
(A) work
(B) to be worked
(C) to work
(D) working

15. The research results ______ to be reliable.
(A) is believed
(B) are believed
(C) believe
(D) have been believed

16. It ______ that the budget will be approved next week.
(A) has supposed
(B) will be supposed
(C) is supposed
(D) was supposed

17. It ______ that the candidate will have secured sufficient votes by the end of the election.
(A) will have expected
(B) had expected
(C) is expected
(D) was expected

18. The suspect is believed ______ the country before the investigation began.
(A) to have been left
(B) to leave
(C) leaving
(D) to have left

19. The technology is said ______ a breakthrough in renewable energy production over the past few years.
(A) to achieve
(B) to have achieved
(C) to be achieving
(D) to have been achieving

20. The project is expected ______ before the end of the fiscal year, despite the delays.
(A) to complete
(B) to be completed
(C) to have completed
(D) to be completing

21. The organization is ______ in multiple initiatives to promote environmental sustainability.
(A) impressed
(B) involved
(C) conflicted
(D) blamed

22. The team is ______ about the potential risks involved in the project.
(A) conflicted
(B) controlled
(C) puzzled
(D) concerned

23. The employees were ______ over the sudden decision to change the company's direction.
(A) involved
(B) puzzled
(C) committed
(D) blamed

24. The new marketing strategy is ______ on reaching younger consumers through social media.
(A) absorbed
(B) amazed
(C) centered
(D) involved

PART 6

Questions 1–4 refer to the following announcement.

Dear Employees,

We would like to inform you of a change in the office hours that will take effect starting next month. As discussed in the last meeting, the new working hours will be from 8:00 AM to 5:00 PM, Monday through Friday. This adjustment 1________ to better accommodate client needs and improve overall workflow efficiency.
Additionally, we are introducing a flexible work schedule option. Employees who prefer to start their day earlier or later can discuss scheduling options with their direct supervisors. Furthermore, the 2________ working hours when all employees 3________ be in the office will remain from 10:00 AM to 3:00 PM.
We understand that changes in routine can be challenging, but we believe these adjustments will contribute to a better work-life balance. Moreover, 4________.
If you have any questions or concerns regarding the new office hours or flexible schedule options, please feel free to reach out to HR. Once again, we appreciate your cooperation as we transition to these new hours.
Thank you for your understanding and continued dedication.

Sincerely,
Management

1. (A) made
   (B) has made
   (C) has been made
   (D) had been made

2. (A) core
   (B) shared
   (C) extended
   (D) limited

3. (A) expect to
   (B) is expected to
   (C) were expected to
   (D) are expected to

4. (A) These changes will help streamline operations and improve collaboration across teams.
   (B) These changes will allow employees to take more vacation days.
   (C) These changes do not align with the company's long-term goals.
   (D) These changes could intensify conflicts within teams.

PART 7

Questions 1–4 refer to the following email.

Dear Team,

I am excited to announce that our Annual Sales Conference will be held from March 20 to March 22 at the Grand Riverside Hotel in downtown Chicago. This year's theme is "Innovating for the Future," where we will focus on the latest trends in customer engagement and sales strategies. As always, we expect full participation from all team members.

Key sessions will include presentations from industry leaders and workshops on new sales tools that will be implemented next quarter. Additionally, each regional team will have an opportunity to present its success stories from the past year, so please be prepared to share your achievements.

We will also be introducing our new customer relationship management (CRM) software, which is expected to significantly streamline our communication with clients. Training sessions on the new CRM will be mandatory for all sales personnel, and further details on these sessions will be provided at the conference.

For those traveling from outside Chicago, hotel accommodations will be arranged by the company. Please ensure that your travel plans are confirmed by February 28 to guarantee your room reservation. If you have any special dietary requirements or need assistance, contact the HR department no later than March 10.

Looking forward to seeing you all there!

Best regards,
Jessica Lee
Director of Sales

1. What is the main purpose of the email?
   (A) To announce a new sales campaign
   (B) To provide information about a training session
   (C) To invite team members to an upcoming conference
   (D) To request reports on regional performance

2. What is NOT mentioned as part of the conference activities?
   (A) Regional team presentations
   (B) Workshops on new sales tools
   (C) Training on CRM software
   (D) Guest presentations by clients

3. What should employees do by March 10 if they have specific dietary requirements?
   (A) Cancel their participation in the conference
   (B) Contact the HR department
   (C) Submit a detailed expense report
   (D) Register for CRM training sessions

4. What can be inferred about the CRM software?
   (A) It will be optional for most employees.
   (B) It will replace the current customer communication system.
   (C) It is currently being used by some teams.
   (D) It will be introduced at the regional offices after the conference.

Chapter

04

가정법

1. 가정법 현재
2. 가정법 미래
3. 가정법 과거
4. 가정법 과거완료
5. 혼합 가정법

◆ 토익 종합 실전문제

PART 6

PART 7

가정법은 실제로 일어나지 않은 상황을 가정하거나 상상할 때 사용하는 문법 구조로서 영어에서는 특히 "if" 조건절과 주절의 동사 형태를 통해 가정법이 표현된다. 가정법에는 가정법 미래, 가정법 과거, 가정법 과거완료의 세 가지 주요 유형이 있으며, 특정한 주장, 요구, 명령, 제안, 권고, 요청 등을 표현할 때는 가정법 현재라는 특수한 형태가 사용된다.

1. 가정법 현재

특정한 주장, 요구, 명령, 제안, 권고, 요청 등을 표현할 때 사용하는 문법 구조로서, 주로 현재 또는 미래에 대한 특정 행동이 필요하거나 바람직하다고 생각될 때 사용된다.

✔ CheckPoint 1. 가정법 현재의 구조

- ▶ 동사(insist, demand, require, command, order, propose, suggest, recommend) + that + 주어 + (should) + 동사원형 ~.
- ▶ 명사(insistence, suggestion, recommendation, decision) + that + 주어 + (should) + 동사원형 ~.
- ▶ 이성적 판단을 나타내는 형용사(important, essential, necessary, crucial, vital) + that + 주어 + (should) + 동사원형 ~.

The manager **insists** that the meeting **(should) start** on time.
매니저는 회의가 정시에 시작해야 한다고 주장한다.

He **orders** that the new policy **(should) be** implemented immediately.
그는 새로운 정책이 즉시 시행되어야 한다고 명령한다.

The **suggestion** that the meeting **(should) be** rescheduled was accepted by everyone.
회의 일정이 다시 조정되어야 한다는 제안이 모두에게 받아들여졌다.

It is **important** that everyone **(should) be** present at the meeting.
모두가 회의에 참석해야 한다는 것이 중요하다.

It is **vital** that the software **(should) be** updated to prevent security issues.
보안 문제를 방지하기 위해 소프트웨어가 업데이트되어야 하는 것이 중요하다.

토익 연습문제

1. The doctor suggested that the patient _______ more exercise to improve his health.
   (A) doing
   (B) to do
   (C) does
   (D) do

2. The committee recommended that the new policy ______ by legal experts.
   (A) to be reviewed
   (B) is reviewed
   (C) be reviewed
   (D) was reviewed

3. It is crucial that every participant _______ the safety procedures before starting the activity.
   (A) understands
   (B) understand
   (C) understanding
   (D) understood

✔ CheckPoint 2. If 조건절에서의 직설법 사용

▶ If 조건절을 사용하여 미래의 불확실한 상황을 표현할 때는 직설법을 사용한다.
▶ 조건절은 현재 시제를 사용하고, 주절은 미래 시제(will/shall + 동사 원형)를 사용한다.
▶ 시간의 부사절(when, as soon as, before, after, while, until, once)과 조건의 부사절(if, unless) 에서는 미래시제 대신 현재시제를 사용한다.

After she **completes** her internship, she **will apply** for a full-time position.
그녀가 인턴십을 마친 후, 정규직에 지원할 것이다.
Once the contract **is** signed, we **will begin** the project immediately.
일단 계약서에 서명되면, 우리는 즉시 프로젝트를 시작할 것이다.
If the team **completes** the project ahead of schedule, they **will receive** a bonus.
팀이 일정을 앞당겨 프로젝트를 완료하면, 보너스를 받을 것이다.
Unless you **submit** the report by 5 PM, the project **will be** delayed.
네가 오후 5시까지 보고서를 제출하지 않으면, 프로젝트가 지연될 것이다.

토익 연습문제

1. If the project ______ on time, we will meet the deadline.
(A) is completed
(B) will be completed
(C) was completed
(D) had completed

2. If the documents ______ by the time the meeting starts, we will have to reschedule the discussion.
(A) won't be submitted
(B) aren't submitted
(C) didn't submit
(D) haven't submitted

3. As soon as the report is ready, we ______ it to the client.
(A) submit
(B) are submitted
(C) will submit
(D) has been submitted

2. 가정법 미래

미래에 일어날 가능성이 거의 없는 상황이나 실현 가능성이 희박한 순수한 가정을 나타낼 때 사용한다.

✔ CheckPoint 3. 미래에 일어날 가능성이 거의 없는 상황

▶ If + 주어 + should + 동사원형 ~, 주어 + will/can/may + 동사원형
▶ 도치 구조 ⇒ Should + 주어 + 동사원형 ~, 주어 + will/can/may + 동사원형

If the weather **should** worsen, we **will postpone** the outdoor event.
⇒ **Should** the weather worsen, we **will postpone** the outdoor event.
만약 날씨가 나빠진다면, 우리는 야외 행사를 연기할 것이다.
If the proposal **should** be approved by the board, we **can proceed** with the project.
⇒ **Should** the proposal be approved by the board, we **can proceed** with the project.
만약 제안서가 이사회에서 승인된다면, 우리는 프로젝트를 진행할 수 있다.

토익 연습문제

1. If the market conditions should change, we ______ our investment strategy.
(A) revise
(B) would revise
(C) will be revised
(D) will revise

2. Should the shipment be delayed, the production schedule ______.
(A) will be affected
(B) would be affected
(C) has been affected
(D) affects

3. ______ any delays should occur, we will have to reschedule the meeting.
(A) What
(B) Would
(C) If
(D) Could

✔ CheckPoint 4. 실현 가능성이 희박한 순수한 가정

▶ If + 주어 + were to + 동사원형 ~, 주어 + would/should/could/might + 동사원형
▶ 도치 구조 ⇒ Were + 주어 + to + 동사원형 ~, 주어 + would/should/could/might + 동사원형

If she **were to** apply for the job, she **might have** a good chance of getting it.
⇒ **Were** she **to** apply for the job, she **might have** a good chance of getting it.
만약 그녀가 그 직장에 지원한다면, 그녀는 그것을 얻을 가능성이 있을 것이다.

If the team **were to** win the championship, it **would be** a historic achievement.
⇒ **Were** the team **to** win the championship, it **would be** a historic achievement.
만약 그 팀이 챔피언십에서 우승한다면, 그것은 역사적인 업적이 될 것이다.

토익 연습문제

1. ______ the CEO were to approve the budget increase, the project would expand significantly.
(A) Should
(B) Were
(C) If
(D) Could

2 ______ the market to crash, many investors would face significant losses.
(A) Should
(B) Were
(C) If
(D) Had

3 Were they ______ a more efficient method, production costs could decrease significantly.
(A) discover
(B) discovering
(C) discovered
(D) to discover

3. 가정법 과거

현재 사실과 반대되는 상황을 가정할 때 사용한다.

✔ CheckPoint 5. 가정법 과거의 구조

▶ If + 주어 + 과거동사/were ~, 주어 + would/should/could/might + 동사원형
▶ 도치 구조 ⇒ Were + 주어 ~, 주어 + would/should/could/might + 동사원형
▶ Without = But for = If it were not for = Were it not for = If not for '만약 ~가 없다면'

If the presentation **were** ready, we **would start** the meeting.
⇒ **Were** the presentation ready, we **would start** the meeting.
발표가 준비되어 있다면, 우리는 회의를 시작할 것이다.

Without the updated software, our team **would struggle** to meet the project deadlines.
= **But for** the updated software, our team **would struggle** to meet the project deadlines.
= **If it were not for** the updated software, our team **would struggle** to meet the project deadlines.
= **Were it not for** the updated software, our team **would struggle** to meet the project deadlines.
= **If not for** the updated software, our team **would struggle** to meet the project deadlines.
최신 소프트웨어가 없다면, 우리 팀은 프로젝트 마감일을 맞추는 데 어려움을 겪을 것입니다.

토익 연습문제

1. If the weather __________ warmer, we might spend the day outside.
(A) are
(B) is
(C) be
(D) were

2 ____ the proposal simpler, more stakeholders would likely approve it.
(A) If
(B) Was
(C) Were
(D) Had

4. 가정법 과거완료

과거 사실과 반대되는 상황을 가정할 때 사용한다.

✔ CheckPoint 6. 가정법 과거완료의 구조

▶ If + 주어 + had P.P. ~, 주어 + would/should/could/might + have P.P.

▶ 도치 구조 ⇒ Had + 주어 + P.P. ~, 주어 + would/should/could/might + have P.P.

▶ Without = But for = If it had not been for = Had it not been for = If not for '만약 ~가 없었다면'

If the project **had been** completed on time, we **might have secured** the contract.

⇒ **Had** the project **been** completed on time, we **might have secured** the contract.

만약 프로젝트가 제시간에 완료되었다면, 우리는 그 계약을 따냈을지도 모른다.

Without the recent investments, the company **might have faced** bankruptcy.

= **But for** the recent investments, the company **might have faced** bankruptcy.

= **If it had not been for** the recent investments, the company **might have faced** bankruptcy.

= **Had it not been for** the recent investments, the company **might have faced** bankruptcy.

= **If not for** the recent investments, the company **might have faced** bankruptcy.

최근의 투자가 없었다면, 회사는 파산을 겪었을지도 모른다.

토익 연습문제

1. If the package ______ on time, the customer would not have complained.
   (A) arrived
   (B) has arrived
   (C) had arrived
   (D) had been arrived

2 If the shipment had arrived earlier, the event ______ as planned.
   (A) would proceed
   (B) could have proceeded
   (C) should be proceeded
   (D) might have been proceeded

5. 혼합 가정법

과거의 가정이 현재에 영향을 미치는 경우에 사용한다.

✔ CheckPoint 7. 혼합 가정법의 구조

▶ If + 주어 + had P.P. ~, 주어 + would/should/could/might + 동사원형

▶ 도치 구조 ⇒ Had + 주어 + P.P. ~, 주어 + would/should/could/might + 동사원형

▶ Without = But for = If it had not been for = Had it not been for = If not for '만약 ~가 없었다면'

If I **had taken** the job offer last year, I **would be** working in New York now.

⇒ **Had** I **taken** the job offer last year, I **would be** working in New York now.

만약 내가 작년에 그 일자리를 수락했더라면, 지금 뉴욕에서 일하고 있을 것이다.

Without his advice, we **might be** facing the same challenges.

= **But for** his advice, we **might be** facing the same challenges.

= **If it had not been for** his advice, we **might be** facing the same challenges.

= **Had it not been for** his advice, we **might be** facing the same challenges.

= **If not for** his advice, we **might be** facing the same challenges.

그의 조언이 없었다면, 우리는 같은 문제에 직면해 있을지도 모른다.

토익 연습문제

1. If they ______ more precautions, they might not be facing this crisis now.
   (A) take
   (B) took
   (C) have taken
   (D) had taken

2. ______ the weather been better, we would be holding the event outdoors now.
   (A) If
   (B) Had
   (C) Were
   (D) Should

토익 종합 실전문제

1. The instructor required that the students _______ their assignments on time.
(A) submit
(B) submitted
(C) be submitted
(D) are submitting

2. The CEO insisted that the meeting ______ until further notice.
(A) postponed
(B) be postponed
(C) was postponing
(D) postpones

3 The committee's suggestion that the annual report ______ released earlier was considered.
(A) be
(B) is
(C) is being
(D) was

4 The recommendation that the training program ______ was accepted by the board.
(A) will be extended
(B) would be extended
(C) be extended
(D) was extended

5 It is essential that every employee ______ aware of the new company policy.
(A) is
(B) are
(C) be
(D) to be

6 If the team ______ significant progress by the next meeting, we will need to reassess our strategy.
(A) hasn't made
(B) didn't make
(C) won't make
(D) doesn't make

7 ______ the project exceed its budget, additional funding will be required.
(A) Should
(B) Would
(C) If
(D) Can

8 Should the merger ______ through, the company will have to devise alternative strategies.
(A) do not go
(B) will not go
(C) be not go
(D) not go

9 Should any discrepancies ______ in the financial report, the auditors will initiate further investigation.
(A) be found
(B) find
(C) are found
(D) finding

10. .If the new product launch ______, the marketing strategy would need to be adjusted.
(A) were to delay
(B) were to be delayed
(C) was to be delayed
(D) was to delay

11. If she ____ a few more hours each week, she would complete her tasks on time.
(A) had worked
(B) were working
(C) works
(D) worked

12. If the company had more resources, it __________ able to expand its operations.
(A) was
(B) would be
(C) can be
(D) would have been

13. If it were not for the advanced training, the employees ______ able to handle the new software.
(A) aren't
(B) wouldn't be
(C) couldn't have been
(D) hasn't been

14. ______ it not for the supportive team members, the project would face more challenges.
(A) Was
(B) If
(C) Were
(D) But

15. If the product launch ______, the company could have lost a significant market share.
(A) delayed
(B) has been delayed
(C) had delayed
(D) had been delayed

16. Had they known about the risk, they ______ to continue with the project.
(A) would refuse
(B) might have refused
(C) should refuse
(D) could refuse

17. Had she __________ the opportunity, she would have taken it immediately.
(A) seen
(B) sees
(C) seeing
(D) see

18. Had it not been for the extra funding, the project ______ on time.
(A) would not be completed
(B) will not have been completed
(C) could be completed
(D) might not have been completed

19. ______ it not been for the prompt intervention, the issue would have escalated further.
(A) If
(B) Had
(C) Were
(D) Should

20. ______ the funding not been approved, the project would have been delayed.
(A) If
(B) Should
(C) Had
(D) Were

21. ______ the company adopted the new regulations earlier, it would not be facing legal issues now.
(A) If
(B) Should
(C) Without
(D) Had

22. Had the client ______ the proposal earlier, we would be finalizing the details now.
(A) accepted
(B) accepts
(C) accepting
(D) to accept

23. If it had not been for the new investors, the company ______ a more stable financial position now.
(A) would have achieved
(B) will be having
(C) might not be in
(D) would be in

24. Without the initial support from clients, the business ______ as successful today.
(A) might not have been
(B) would not be
(C) would not have thrived
(D) could have achieved

PART 6

Questions 1–4 refer to the following email.

To: All department managers
From: Mark Thompson, Project Lead
Subject: Project Timeline and Resource Allocation

Dear Team,

As we move forward with our current project, I wanted to take a moment to discuss the importance of meeting our deadlines. If we were to miss any critical milestones, it would impact the overall schedule, 1________ delaying the final delivery date. 2________ such setbacks, please ensure that your teams have the necessary resources.

Had it not been for the initial support from our main client, we 3________ in this advantageous position today. Therefore, 4________. If anyone needs additional resources or has specific concerns, please do not hesitate to contact me directly.

Thank you for your hard work and commitment. Let's make this project a success.

Best regards,
Mark Thompson

1. (A) especially
   (B) critically
   (C) potentially
   (D) gradually

2. (A) To prevent
   (B) Preventing
   (C) Prevention
   (D) To be prevented

3. (A) may not have been
   (B) would not be
   (C) can not be
   (D) would not have been

4. (A) we need to submit progress reports by the end of each month
   (B) we should do our utmost to maintain their confidence and meet their expectations
   (C) this will ensure that our team meets the client's standards
   (D) meeting deadlines requires consistent communication and clear planning

PART 7

Questions 1–5 refer to the following event schedule and internal e–mail.

Workshop: Professional Development Day
Date: October 25, 2024
Location: Grand Hall Conference Center

Schedule:
9:00 AM – 10:30 AM: Keynote Speech by CEO Mr. Robert Sanders
10:45 AM – 12:00 PM: Workshop 1: Leadership Skills Development
12:00 PM – 1:30 PM: Lunch Break (Catering provided)
1:30 PM – 3:00 PM: Workshop 2: Team Collaboration & Communication
3:15 PM – 4:45 PM: Workshop 3: Time Management Strategies
5:00 PM – 6:00 PM: Networking Session (Refreshments provided)
All employees are required to attend the event and must register by October 18. For registration, please visit the company portal or contact HR at hr@company.com.

Subject: Reminder: Professional Development Day
To: All Staff
From: HR Department
Date: October 20, 2024

Dear Team,
This is a reminder for the upcoming Professional Development Day event scheduled for October 25, 2024, at the Grand Hall Conference Center. As mentioned previously, this event will feature workshops on leadership, communication, and time management, along with a networking session. It's a great opportunity to develop key professional skills and connect with your colleagues.
Please ensure you are registered for the event by October 18. If you have not registered yet, kindly visit the company portal or contact the HR Department directly at hr@company.com. Additionally, lunch and refreshments will be provided during the event.
We look forward to seeing you there!

Best regards,
HR Team

1. When is the registration deadline for the Professional Development Day?
   (A) October 18
   (B) October 20
   (C) October 25
   (D) October 30

2. What is the main focus of the workshops on Professional Development Day?
   (A) Marketing strategies
   (B) Team-building exercises
   (C) Leadership, communication, and time management
   (D) Technical skills development

3. Which part of the event is scheduled to occur last?
   (A) Time Management Strategies workshop
   (B) Networking session
   (C) Lunch break
   (D) Keynote speech

4. How long is the time allocated for the networking session?
   (A) 1 hour
   (B) 1.5 hours
   (C) 2 hours
   (D) 45 minutes

5. What can be inferred about the importance of the workshops scheduled on Professional Development Day?
   (A) Attendance at the workshops may affect employees' evaluations.
   (B) The primary goal of the workshops is to build rapport among employees.
   (C) The company views the workshops as a critical learning opportunity for skill development.
   (D) The workshops are intended to prepare employees for upcoming leadership changes.

Chapter

05

To부정사

1. To부정사의 용법
2. To부정사의 의미상의 주어
3. To부정사의 시제
◆ 토익 종합 실전문제
PART 6
PART 7

To부정사는 준동사의 일종으로, "To + 동사원형"의 형태를 가지며, 문장에서 명사, 형용사, 부사의 역할을 한다.

1. To 부정사의 용법

① 명사적 용법

▶ To부정사가 명사처럼 주어, 보어, 목적어 자리에서 명사 역할을 한다.

▶ 의문사 + To부정사는 의문사 + 주어 + should + 동사원형과 같은 의미이다.

To finish this project on time is crucial.

= **It** is crucial **to finish** this project on time.

이 프로젝트를 제시간에 끝내는 것이 중요하다.

☞ To부정사가 주어로 사용될 때는 주어가 너무 길어지므로 실제 영어에서는 가주어(It)를 사용하는 경우가 더 많다.

The objective is **to increase** market share by 10%.

목표는 시장 점유율을 10% 증가시키는 것이다.

The company plans **to launch** a new product next month.

회사는 다음 달에 새로운 제품을 출시할 계획이다.

We need to decide **who to invite** to the conference.

= We need to decide **who we should invite** to the conference.

우리는 회의에 누구를 초대할지 결정해야 한다.

✔ CheckPoint 1. To부정사를 목적어로 취하는 동사

▶ agree, choose, decide, expect(기대하다, 예상하다), hope, plan(계획하다), pretend(~인 척하다), refuse(거절하다), seek(찾다, 추구하다), want

The company **expects to increase** sales by 20% this year.

회사는 올해 매출이 20% 증가할 것으로 기대하고 있다.

The department **plans to hire** more staff by the end of this year.

해당 부서는 올해 말까지 더 많은 직원을 고용할 계획이다.

He **pretended to know** the answer during the meeting.

그는 회의 중에 답을 알고 있는 척했다.

She **refused to sign** the agreement without further review.
그녀는 추가 검토 없이 계약서에 서명하는 것을 거부했다.

토익 연습문제

1. The manager decided ______ a new strategy to increase sales.
   (A) implement
   (B) to implement
   (C) implementing
   (D) implements

2. She refused ______ the contract under the current conditions.
   (A) sign
   (B) signed
   (C) signing
   (D) to sign

3. The company is planning ______ additional staff next quarter.
   (A) hire
   (B) to hire
   (C) hiring
   (D) hires

② 형용사적 용법

▶ To부정사가 명사를 뒤에서 수식하며, 해당 명사에 대한 추가 정보를 제공하거나 그 특성을 설명하는 역할을 한다.

✔ CheckPoint 2. To부정사를 목적어로 취하는 명사

▶ ability(능력), attempt(시도), chance(기회), decision(결정), desire(욕구, 바람), goal(목표), intention(의도), need(필요), opportunity(기회), plan(계획), promise(약속), proposal(제안), requirement(요구사항, 필요조건), responsibility(책임), right(권리), time, way, work

The manager has no **intention to approve** the request.
매니저는 그 요청을 승인할 의도가 없다.
The company has a strategic **plan to expand** into Asian markets.
회사는 아시아 시장으로 확장할 전략적 계획을 가지고 있다.
Meeting this deadline is a **requirement to secure** the contract.
이 기한을 맞추는 것은 계약을 확보하기 위한 요구사항이다.
You have the **right to access** this information.
당신은 이 정보를 열람할 권리가 있다.

토익 연습문제

1. We have a plan ______ our current services by the end of the year.
(A) improves
(B) improved
(C) to improve
(D) to be improved

2. The desire ______ a leadership role motivated her to take additional courses.
(A) to assume
(B) is assuming
(C) assumes
(D) assumed

3. We made an attempt ______ the contract negotiations last week.
(A) finalize
(B) finalized
(C) to finalize
(D) to be finalized

③ 부사적 용법

▶ To부정사가 부사처럼 동사, 형용사, 또는 다른 부사를 수식하고, 주로 목적, 결과, 원인 및 이유나 판단의 근거를 나타내기 위해 사용된다.

✔ CheckPoint 3. 목적

▶ so that S + may/can/will (not)
▶ in order that S + may/can/will (not)
▶ (so as) (not) toV
▶ in order (not) toV
▶ lest ~ (should)

The manager adjusted the schedule **so that** everyone **could** attend the meeting.
관리자는 모든 사람이 회의에 참석할 수 있도록 일정을 조정했다.
In order that we **may** meet the deadline, we need to increase our staff.
우리가 마감 기한을 맞출 수 있도록, 우리는 직원 수를 늘려야 한다.
She organized her schedule **(so as) to** have free time on the weekend.
그녀는 주말에 여유 시간을 갖기 위해 자신의 일정을 조정했다.
(In order) to improve our efficiency, we are updating our software systems.
우리의 효율성을 향상시키기 위해, 우리는 소프트웨어 시스템을 업데이트하고 있다.
She saves money **lest** she **should** face financial difficulties.
그녀는 재정적 어려움에 직면하지 않도록 돈을 저축한다.

토익 연습문제

1. The staff worked overtime ______ they could complete the project by the deadline.
(A) so as
(B) in order that
(C) to
(D) lest

2. She arrived early ______ not to miss the presentation.
(A) in order that
(B) lest
(C) so that
(D) so as

✔ CheckPoint 4. 결과

- ▶ so + 형용사/부사 + that S + V
- ▶ so + 형용사/부사 + as toV
- ▶ so + 형용사 + a(n) + 명사 + that S + V
- ▶ such + a(n) + 형용사 + 명사 + that S + V

The report was **so detailed that** it took me hours to review it.
그 보고서는 너무 상세해서 검토하는 데 몇 시간이 걸렸다.

The problem was **so complicated as to** require expert advice.
문제는 너무 복잡해서 전문가의 조언이 필요했다.

It was **so challenging a project that** we had to extend the deadline.
그 프로젝트는 너무 어려워서 우리는 마감일을 연장해야 했다.

They faced **such a difficult challenge that** they had to work together.
그들은 너무 어려운 도전에 직면해서 함께 일해야 했다.

토익 연습문제

1. The presentation was ______ that everyone understood the key points clearly.
   (A) such clear
   (B) so clear
   (C) such a clear
   (D) so clearly

2. The task was ______ difficult as to require additional support from the team.
   (A) so
   (B) such
   (C) too
   (D) very

3. The new policy is ______ a significant change that employees need time to adjust.
   (A) so
   (B) such
   (C) too
   (D) very

✔ CheckPoint 5. 원인 및 이유나 판단의 근거

▶ 원인: 감정의 형용사 + To부정사

▶ 이유나 판단의 근거: must be + 형용사 + To부정사

She is **happy to receive** the promotion after years of hard work.
그녀는 오랜 노력 끝에 승진을 하게 되어 기쁘다.

He **must be very smart to solve** the complex problem so quickly.
그가 그렇게 복잡한 문제를 그렇게 빨리 풀다니 정말 똑똑할 것이다.

토익 연습문제

1. She was happy ______ her name was mentioned during the ceremony.
   (A) hear
   (B) to hear
   (C) hearing
   (D) heard

2. He must be very tired ______ the project in just two days.
   (A) to finish
   (B) to be finished
   (C) finished
   (D) finishing

2. To부정사의 의미상의 주어

문장의 주어와 To부정사의 의미상의 주어가 동일하면 의미상의 주어를 생략하고, 일반인 (we, you, they, people)이 To부정사의 의미상의 주어이면 생략 가능하다.

✔ CheckPoint 6. To부정사의 의미상의 주어: For + 목적격

▶ 형용사 difficult, easy, hard, impossible, possible, necessary는 It ~ for ~ toV 구문을 사용하여 To부정사의 의미상의 주어를 나타낸다.

▶ To부정사의 목적어를 문장의 주어로 이동하는 것도 가능하지만, 영어에서는 It ~ for ~ toV 구문이 일반적으로 더 선호된다.

It was **impossible for them** to finish the project on time.
⇒ The project was impossible for them to finish on time.
그들이 제시간에 프로젝트를 끝내는 것은 불가능했다.

It is **possible for us** to complete the task by the deadline.
⇒ The task is possible for us to complete by the deadline.
우리가 그 일을 마감일까지 완료하는 것은 가능하다.

토익 연습문제

1. It was difficult for him ______ the presentation in such a short time.
   (A) to prepare
   (B) preparing
   (C) prepare
   (D) prepared

2. It is necessary for students ______ the assignments before the deadline.
   (A) submitting
   (B) submit
   (C) to submit
   (D) submits

3. It is impossible ______ to sign the contract without approval.
   (A) them
   (B) for them
   (C) of them
   (D) they

✔ CheckPoint 7. To부정사의 의미상의 주어: Of + 목적격

▶ 사람의 성질이나 성격을 나타내는 형용사 clever, considerate, foolish, generous, good, kind, rude, thoughtful, wise는 It ~ of ~ toV 구문을 사용하여 To부정사의 의미상의 주어를 나타낸다.

▶ To부정사의 목적어를 문장의 주어로 이동할 수 없다.

It was **kind of him** to help us with the project.

⇒ We were kind of him to help with the project. (x)

그가 우리 프로젝트를 도와준 것은 친절했다.

It is **rude of you** to interrupt others while they are speaking.

⇒ Others are rude of you to interrupt while they are speaking. (x)

다른 사람이 말하고 있을 때 끼어드는 것은 무례한 일이다.

토익 연습문제

1. It was generous of her ______ so much money to the charity.
   (A) to donate
   (B) donate
   (C) donating
   (D) donated

2. It was foolish of him ______ the warning signs.
   (A) ignoring
   (B) to ignore
   (C) ignored
   (D) to be ignored

3. It was considerate ______ to bring extra materials for the presentation.
   (A) her
   (B) for her
   (C) of her
   (D) from her

3. To 부정사의 시제

✔ CheckPoint 8. 단순 부정사

▶ 주절과 종속절의 시제가 동일하면 복문을 단문으로 변경할 때 단순 부정사 (toV)를 사용한다.
▶ 주절과 종속절의 주어가 동일하면 종속절의 주어를 생략한다.
▶ 주절과 종속절의 주어가 다르면 종속절의 주어를 for + 목적격으로 변경하여 사용한다.

She promised that **she would finish** the report by tomorrow.
⇒ She promised **to finish** the report by tomorrow.
그녀는 내일까지 보고서를 끝내겠다고 약속했다.

It is possible that **we complete** the project by Friday.
⇒ It is possible **for us to complete** the project by Friday.
우리가 금요일까지 프로젝트를 완료하는 것이 가능하다.

토익 연습문제

1. They planned ______ the event by the end of the week.
(A) organize
(B) organized
(C) organizing
(D) to organize

2. The manager decided ______ the new strategy.
(A) implementing
(B) to implement
(C) implemented
(D) implement

3. It is important ______ to follow the new safety guidelines.
(A) employees
(B) them
(C) for employees
(D) of employees

✔ CheckPoint 9. 완료 부정사

▶ 주절보다 종속절의 시제가 한 시제 앞서면 복문을 단문으로 변경할 때 완료 부정사 (to have P.P.)를 사용한다.

▶ 주절과 종속절의 주어가 동일하면 종속절의 주어를 생략한다.

▶ 주절과 종속절의 주어가 다르면 종속절의 주어를 for + 목적격으로 변경하여 사용한다.

She claimed that **she had completed** the task before the deadline.

⇒ She claimed **to have completed** the task before the deadline.

그녀는 마감일 전에 작업을 완료했다고 주장했다.

It is beneficial that **students have participated** in the project.

⇒ It is beneficial **for students to have participated** in the project.

학생들이 그 프로젝트에 참여한 것이 유익하다.

토익 연습문제

1. She admitted ______ a mistake in the report.
   (A) to make
   (B) to have made
   (C) to making
   (D) making

2. He claimed ______ the project before the deadline.
   (A) to finishing
   (B) finishing
   (C) to finish
   (D) to have finished

3. They reported the company ______ the sales target last quarter.
   (A) to exceed
   (B) to have exceeded
   (C) exceeding
   (D) exceeded

토익 종합 실전문제

1. The company is seeking ______ a strategic partnership with local businesses.
(A) to form
(B) forming
(C) form
(D) forms

2. They decided ______ additional resources for the project.
(A) allocate
(B) to allocate
(C) allocating
(D) allocated

3. The employee agreed ______ additional responsibilities in exchange for a promotion.
(A) to take
(B) taking
(C) taken
(D) takes

4. The company's decision ______ a new branch in Europe has been well-received by the shareholders.
(A) opening
(B) opens
(C) to open
(D) to be opened

5. The customer has the right ______ a refund if the product is defective.
(A) request
(B) requesting
(C) to request
(D) to be requested

6. There is a need ______ better communication between departments.
(A) establish
(B) to establish
(C) establishing
(D) established

7. The opportunity ______ a global team is a valuable experience for any employee.
(A) leading
(B) leads
(C) to be led
(D) to lead

8. She kept the backup copies of the documents ______ they should get lost.
(A) so as to
(B) so that
(C) in order not to
(D) lest

9. The company provided additional training ______ its employees can enhance their skills.
(A) so that
(B) so as to
(C) lest
(D) to

10. ______ improve customer satisfaction, the company has implemented a new feedback system.
(A) So as
(B) To
(C) So that
(D) In order

11. ______ expand its business globally, the company is looking for new partnerships.
(A) So as
(B) In order to
(C) In order that
(D) Lest

12. ______ increase market share, the company plans to launch a new product.
(A) So that
(B) In order
(C) In order that
(D) So as to

13. It was ______ difficult a decision that the board had to discuss it for hours.
(A) such
(B) so
(C) so as
(D) as

14. The report was ______ detailed that it answered all the client's questions.
(A) so
(B) such
(C) too
(D) very

15. We are sorry ______ that the meeting has been postponed.
(A) inform
(B) informing
(C) to inform
(D) to be informed

16. They must be very dedicated ______ every weekend for this project.
(A) working
(B) work
(C) to be worked
(D) to work

17. It is possible ______ employees to follow the new guidelines.
(A) with
(B) of
(C) from
(D) for

18. It will be difficult ______ to achieve the sales target this month.
(A) for us
(B) of us
(C) about us
(D) on us

19. The task was easy for the team ______ in two days.
(A) complete
(B) to complete
(C) completed
(D) completing

20. All the company policies are hard for new employees ______ at once.
(A) understand
(B) understanding
(C) to understand
(D) to be understood

21. It was wise ______ to save a portion of her income for future investments.
(A) her
(B) for her
(C) of her
(D) to her

22. It was thoughtful of her ______ flowers after the meeting.
(A) send
(B) sending
(C) to be sent
(D) to send

23. It was clever ______ to fix the computer issue without professional help.
(A) of him
(B) for him
(C) him
(D) to him

24. They are expected ______ the project next month.
(A) to complete
(B) completing
(C) complete
(D) completed

PART 6

Questions 1–4 refer to the following advertisement.

New Fitness App Launch!

Are you looking to improve your health and fitness? We are excited to introduce our brand-new fitness app, FitLife, 1________ to help you reach your goals effectively. This app offers personalized workout plans, nutrition advice, and a community of fitness enthusiasts to keep you motivated.

2________, the app provides daily reminders and progress tracking to ensure you stay on top of your goals. It is perfect for beginners and advanced users alike.

The app is free to download, and you can access premium features by subscribing to the monthly membership. These premium features include personalized training sessions, advanced meal planning, and 24/7 access to fitness coaches.

If you're interested, 3________. Don't miss out! Download FitLife today so that you can begin your fitness journey right away!

For any questions or support, feel free to contact us at support@fitlife.com.

Thank you for choosing FitLife, and we look forward to supporting you in achieving your fitness goals!

4________ improve your health and fitness, FitLife is here to help you every step of the way!

1. (A) designing
   (B) designed
   (C) designs
   (D) to design

2. (A) Additionally
   (B) As a result
   (C) Otherwise
   (D) Nevertheless

3. (A) you can upgrade to a premium membership for advanced features
   (B) the app includes reminders to keep you on track with your goals
   (C) sign up now to receive a 14-day free trial of our premium features
   (D) this app is designed to track your fitness progress automatically

4. (A) In order to
   (B) So as
   (C) In order that
   (D) So that

PART 7

Questions 1–4 refer to the following letter.

To: Ms. Jessica Thompson
From: Emily Parker, Customer Service Manager
Date: September 10
Subject: Inquiry about Product Refund

Dear Ms. Thompson,

Thank you for contacting us regarding your recent purchase. We regret to hear that the product you received did not meet your expectations.

We have reviewed your request for a refund, and we are happy to inform you that your request has been approved. The refund amount of $120 will be credited to your original payment method within 5-7 business days. Please note that it may take additional time for your bank to process the transaction.

If you would like to exchange the product for another item, we would be happy to assist you. In that case, please return the product in its original packaging, and we will arrange the exchange. Alternatively, you may visit our store to explore other products.

Should you have any further questions or concerns, feel free to contact us via email or phone at your convenience. We appreciate your understanding and look forward to serving you again in the future.

Best regards,
Emily Parker
Customer Service Manager

1. Why did Ms. Thompson contact customer service?
   (A) To inquire about a delayed delivery
   (B) To request a refund for a product
   (C) To ask about product availability
   (D) To change her payment method

2. When will Ms. Thompson receive her refund?
   (A) Immediately after returning the product
   (B) After the product is exchanged
   (C) Within 2-3 business days
   (D) Within 5-7 business days

3. What option is offered to Ms. Thompson besides a refund?
   (A) A product exchange
   (B) A store credit
   (C) A full refund with a discount coupon
   (D) A repair service for the product

4. What can be inferred about Ms. Thompson's experience with the product?
   (A) She was satisfied with its quality.
   (B) She found the product defective or unsuitable.
   (C) She wanted to purchase an additional product.
   (D) She planned to use the product for a special event.

Chapter

06

분사

분사는 준동사의 일종으로, 현재분사와 과거분사로 나뉘고, 문장에서 주로 형용사 역할을 하여 명사를 수식하거나 보어로 사용된다.

1. 분사의 용법

① 한정용법: 현재분사나 과거분사가 형용사처럼 명사의 앞이나 뒤에서 명사를 수식하는 용법이다.

✔ CheckPoint 1. 현재분사 + 명사

approaching deadline	다가오는 마감일	ongoing project	진행 중인 프로젝트
challenging task	도전적인 과제	operating costs	운영비용
changing trends	변화하는 추세	participating members	참여하는 회원들
declining sales	감소하는 판매	promising candidate	유망한 후보자
developing technology	발전 중인 기술	remaining seats	남아 있는 좌석
exciting opportunity	흥미로운 기회	remaining time	남은 시간
expanding business	확장되는 사업	rising prices	상승하는 가격
growing market	성장하는 시장	rising unemployment	증가하는 실업률
improving performance	향상되는 성과	running program	실행 중인 프로그램
increasing demand	증가하는 수요	supporting evidence	뒷받침하는 증거
leading company	선도적인 회사	supporting role	지원 역할
leading expert	일류 전문가	surrounding area	주변 지역
missing child	실종된 아이	traveling expenses	여행 경비
missing documents	분실된 서류	upcoming event	다가오는 행사
moving truck	이사 트럭	welcoming committee	환영 위원회
ongoing negotiations	진행 중인 협상		

Completing this **challenging task** will require careful planning.
이 도전적인 과제를 완료하려면 신중한 계획이 필요하다.

Declining sales have prompted the company to reconsider its strategy.
감소하는 판매는 회사가 전략을 재고하게 만들었다.

Increasing demand for eco-friendly products is shaping the market.
친환경 제품에 대한 증가하는 수요가 시장을 형성하고 있다.

The office is searching for the **missing documents**.
사무실에서는 분실된 서류를 찾고 있다.
The company is trying to reduce its **operating costs**.
회사는 운영비용을 줄이려고 노력하고 있다.

토익 연습문제

1. The ______ prices of food are making it difficult for many families.
   (A) missing
   (B) rising
   (C) promising
   (D) remaining

2. The team is working late to meet the ______ deadline for the project.
   (A) growing
   (B) approaching
   (C) exciting
   (D) rising

3. The ______ opportunity to expand the business must not be missed.
   (A) exciting
   (B) missing
   (C) declining
   (D) remaining

✔ CheckPoint 2. 과거분사 + 명사

approved plan	승인된 계획	limited offer	한정된 제안
assigned task	할당된 업무	limited time	제한된 시간
attached file	첨부된 파일	locked door	잠긴 문
broken equipment	고장 난 장비	marked price	표시된 가격
canceled order	취소된 주문	printed materials	인쇄된 자료
chosen candidate	선택된 후보자	qualified applicant	자격을 갖춘 지원자
chosen method	선택된 방법	reduced price	할인된 가격
completed form	작성된 양식	required documents	필요한 서류
connected device	연결된 장치	required reading	필수 읽기 자료
damaged goods	손상된 상품	reserved seat	예약된 좌석
damaged property	손상된 재산	returned merchandise	반품된 상품
detailed report	상세한 보고서	revised version	수정된 버전
established company	설립된 회사	scheduled meeting	예정된 회의
expected outcome	예상된 결과	selected items	선택된 품목
experienced professional	경험이 풍부한 전문가	unlimited access	무제한 접근
experienced staff	경험이 많은 직원	updated information	갱신된 정보
expired contract	만료된 계약	updated schedule	갱신된 일정
extended warranty	연장된 보증	written consent	서면 동의
informed decision	정보에 근거한 결정	written instructions	서면 지시 사항

He submitted a **detailed report** on the project's progress.
그는 프로젝트 진행에 대한 상세한 보고서를 제출했다.

We hired an **experienced professional** to manage the project.
우리는 프로젝트를 관리하기 위해 경험이 풍부한 전문가를 고용했다.

The **expired contract** needs to be renewed as soon as possible.
만료된 계약은 가능한 빨리 갱신되어야 한다.

The store is offering a **reduced price** on all winter clothing.
매장은 모든 겨울 의류에 대해 할인된 가격을 제공하고 있다.

The **returned merchandise** must be in its original packaging.
반품된 상품은 원래 포장 상태여야 한다.

토익 연습문제

1. The ______ candidate will start the job next month.
   (A) written
   (B) chosen
   (C) damaged
   (D) locked

2. The technician quickly fixed the ______ equipment.
   (A) broken
   (B) assigned
   (C) completed
   (D) published

3. The ______ file contains the latest updates on the project.
   (A) experienced
   (B) canceled
   (C) damaged
   (D) attached

② 서술용법: 분사가 주격보어나 목적보어 자리에서 주어나 목적어를 보충 설명하는 용법이다.

✔ CheckPoint 3. 주어 + 동사 + 목적어 + 목적보어(형용사/현재분사/과거분사)

▶ make, find, keep, leave, consider

The company decided to **make** the new software **available** to all employees.
회사는 모든 직원들이 새 소프트웨어를 사용할 수 있도록 결정했다.

The project manager **found** the team **exhausted** after the long meeting.
프로젝트 매니저는 긴 회의 후에 팀이 지쳐 있는 것을 알게 되었다.

The software update **keeps** the system **running** smoothly.
소프트웨어 업데이트는 시스템이 원활하게 작동하도록 유지한다.

They **left** the contract **unsigned** until further notice.
그들은 추가 통지가 있을 때까지 계약을 미완성 상태로 두었다.

The committee **considered** the proposal **valuable** for the company's growth.
위원회는 그 제안이 회사 성장에 가치 있다고 간주했다.

토익 연습문제

1. The CEO kept the announcement ______ until the final details were confirmed.
   (A) secret
   (B) secretly
   (C) secrets
   (D) to secret

2. The supervisor made the deadline ______ to ensure the project's success.
   (A) strictly
   (B) strictness
   (C) strict
   (D) strictest

3. The teacher left the assignments ______ for the students to complete at home.
   (A) finishes
   (B) finish
   (C) finishing
   (D) unfinished

2. 분사구문

문장의 간결성 원칙을 준수하기 위해 부사절(시간, 조건, 양보, 이유) + 주절로 구성된 복문을 부사구 + 주절의 단문으로 변경하기 위해 사용한다.

✔ CheckPoint 4. 분사구문의 시제

- ▶ 주절과 종속절의 시제가 동일하면 복문을 단문으로 변경할 때 단순 분사구문(동사원형 + ing)을 사용한다.
- ▶ 주절보다 종속절의 시제가 한 시제 앞서면 완료 분사구문(having + p.p.)을 사용한다.
- ▶ 주절과 종속절의 주어가 동일하면 종속절의 주어를 생략하고, 다르면 생략하지 않는다.

If **you follow** the guidelines carefully, **you will improve** your performance.
⇒ **Following** the guidelines carefully, you will improve your performance.
지침을 신중히 따르면, 성과가 향상될 것이다.

Since **the equipment is** outdated, **we need** to replace it immediately.
⇒ **The equipment being** outdated, we need to replace it immediately.
장비가 구식이라서, 우리는 즉시 그것을 교체해야 한다.

Although **they had finished** the work, **they did not submit** the report.
⇒ **Having finished** the work, they did not submit the report.
그들은 작업을 끝냈지만, 보고서를 제출하지 않았다.

After **the team had finished** the project, **the manager praised** their hard work.
⇒ **The team having finished** the project, the manager praised their hard work.
팀이 프로젝트를 마친 후, 매니저는 그들의 노고를 칭찬했다.

토익 연습문제

1. ______ the new software, the employees found it easier to manage their tasks.
   (A) Using
   (B) Used
   (C) Being used
   (D) Having used

2. The deadline ______, the project was rushed to completion.
   (A) approaching
   (B) having approached
   (C) approached
   (D) was approaching

✔ CheckPoint 5. 분사구문의 태와 부정

▶ 능동형 분사구문은 동사원형 + ing을 사용한다.

▶ 수동형 분사구문은 Being + p.p. 또는 Having been + p.p.을 사용한다. 다만, 대부분의 경우 Being이나 Having been을 생략하고, 과거분사만 사용한다.

▶ 부정어는 분사 앞에 위치시킨다.

While **the engineers tested** the system, **they identified** several issues.

⇒ **Testing** the system, the engineers identified several issues.

엔지니어들이 시스템을 테스트하는 동안, 몇 가지 문제를 발견했다.

When **she was given** the assignment, **she started** working on it immediately.

⇒ **(Being) given** the assignment, she started working on it immediately.

그녀는 과제를 받았을 때, 즉시 작업을 시작했다.

After **the contract had been signed**, **the project** officially **started**.

계약이 체결된 후, 프로젝트가 공식적으로 시작되었다.

⇒ **The contract (having been) signed**, the project officially started.

Because **the documents were not signed**, **the contract did not become** valid.

서류에 서명이 되지 않았기 때문에, 계약은 유효하지 않았다.

⇒ **The documents not (being) signed**, the contract did not become valid.

토익 연습문제

1. ______ the results, the manager made a significant decision.
   (A) Analyzing
   (B) Having analyzed
   (C) Analyzed
   (D) Was analyzing

2. The issues ______ by the customers, the product design was improved.
   (A) being reported
   (B) having reported
   (C) reported
   (D) having been reported

3. ______ the necessary precautions, the experiment posed significant risks.
   (A) Taking
   (B) Taken
   (C) Not taking
   (D) Not taken

토익 종합 실전문제

1. Due to the ______ demand for our product, we are expanding our production line.
(A) increasing
(B) supporting
(C) challenging
(D) remaining

2. The ______ members need to sign in at the registration desk.
(A) remaining
(B) participating
(C) supporting
(D) declining

3. The team is working hard to complete the ______ project.
(A) moving
(B) supporting
(C) changing
(D) ongoing

4. The ______ candidate has experience in both marketing and sales.
(A) leading
(B) missing
(C) challenging
(D) promising

5. The team is focused on completing the ______ task before the deadline.
(A) promising
(B) exciting
(C) challenging
(D) growing

6. The marketing team is working hard to identify the ______ trends in the market.
(A) changing
(B) challenging
(C) remaining
(D) approaching

7. The company is investing in new technology to stay ahead in the ______ market.
(A) remaining
(B) operating
(C) supporting
(D) growing

8. The ______ contract must be renewed before the end of the month.
(A) increasing
(B) expired
(C) delayed
(D) experienced

9. The company decided to offer a ______ price on all clearance items.
(A) limited
(B) increased
(C) reduced
(D) required

10. All ______ documents must be submitted before the end of the week.
(A) ignored
(B) limited
(C) damaged
(D) required

11. Making an ______ decision requires careful analysis of all available data.
(A) extended
(B) informed
(C) canceled
(D) delayed

12. The report includes a ______ version of the product specifications.
(A) broken
(B) canceled
(C) revised
(D) damaged

13. Employees with a premium membership enjoy ______ access to the company's online resources.
(A) unlimited
(B) increased
(C) challenging
(D) expanding

14. The customer requested a refund due to receiving ______ goods.
(A) assigned
(B) extended
(C) expanding
(D) damaged

15. The recent policy change left many employees ______ and seeking clarification.
(A) confuse
(B) confusing
(C) confused
(D) confusion

16. After the presentation, the client found the proposal to be ______ and signed the contract.
(A) satisfy
(B) satisfied
(C) satisfying
(D) satisfaction

17. The committee found the report ______ and requested further clarification.

(A) unclear

(B) clearly

(C) clear

(D) clearest

18. The recent upgrade made the software ______ to all users across the company.

(A) access

(B) accessing

(C) accessed

(D) accessible

19. The team left the office ______ and ready for the next day's work.

(A) clean

(B) cleaned

(C) cleaning

(D) cleaner

20. ______ the new system, they were able to complete their tasks more efficiently.

(A) To implement

(B) Implemented

(C) Implementing

(D) Having implemented

21. ______ all relevant information, the analyst provided a detailed report.

(A) Collecting

(B) Collected

(C) Has collected

(D) Having collected

22. The event ______, the venue was quickly cleaned and prepared for the next occasion.

(A) ended

(B) having ended

(C) ending

(D) having been ended

23. The project ______, the team celebrated their success.

(A) having been completed

(B) having completed

(C) completing

(D) was completed

24. ______ the updates, the manager was unaware of the issues.

(A) Not receiving

(B) Not received

(C) Not having received

(D) Having not received

PART 6

Questions 1–4 refer to the following announcement.

Dear Employees,

We are excited to inform you that our company will be relocating to a new office building next month. This move is part of our 1________ to provide a better working environment and accommodate our growing team. The new office is equipped with modern facilities, including spacious meeting rooms, collaborative workspaces, and a state-of-the-art cafeteria.

In addition, we are confident that this move will greatly enhance our workplace culture and boost productivity. The official moving date is set for the 15th of next month. Please be sure to pack your personal belongings and label them clearly for the move. We have arranged professional movers to assist with the transition.

Additionally, each department will be assigned specific times for moving to minimize disruption. 2________. If you have any questions or concerns, feel free to reach out to the HR department.

We understand that moving can be a stressful process, but we believe that this relocation will provide many benefits for the company and all employees. Lastly, we appreciate your cooperation and patience during this time. The new office location will be easily 3________ by public transportation, and parking spaces will be available for 4 ________ who drive.

We look forward to welcoming you to the new office and are excited for this new chapter in our company's journey.

Sincerely,

Management Team

1. (A) ongoing efforts
(B) established procedures
(C) increased efficiency
(D) temporary measures

2. (A) We expect a smooth transition during the move.
(B) Detailed instructions will be provided closer to the moving date.
(C) It is important to follow the packing guidelines.
(D) All employees are encouraged to assist with the moving process.

3. (A) accessible
(B) necessary
(C) productive
(D) convenient

4. (A) this
(B) that
(C) these
(D) those

PART 7

Questions 1–4 refer to the following article.

The Benefits of Remote Work for Employee Well-being

In recent years, more companies have begun offering remote work options to their employees. Remote work allows employees to perform their job duties from a location other than the office, often from their home. This arrangement offers numerous benefits for both employees and employers.

One significant advantage is the improvement in work-life balance. Without the need to commute, employees can save time and use it to spend more time with their families or engage in personal hobbies. This flexibility can lead to higher job satisfaction and reduced stress levels.

Moreover, remote work can lead to increased productivity. Studies show that employees who work remotely tend to take fewer sick days and often work longer hours than their in-office counterparts. The quiet environment of home allows for more focus and fewer distractions, which contributes to higher efficiency.

However, remote work is not without its challenges. Some employees may feel isolated and miss the social interaction that comes with working in an office. Additionally, managing time and avoiding burnout can be difficult without a clear separation between work and personal life.

Overall, while remote work has its drawbacks, the potential benefits make it a valuable option for many businesses and their employees.

1. What is one significant advantage of remote work mentioned in the article?
   (A) Employees can take more vacation days.
   (B) Employees can spend more time with their families.
   (C) Employers provide better office equipment for remote work.
   (D) Remote workers receive higher salaries.

2. According to the article, why can remote work lead to higher productivity?
   (A) Employees can work fewer hours.
   (B) Employees have access to better technology.
   (C) Employees can focus better in a quieter environment.
   (D) Employees receive additional training.

3. What is a potential problem of remote work mentioned in the article?
   (A) Remote workers lack social interaction.
   (B) Remote workers feel more stressed.
   (C) Remote workers can manage their time effectively.
   (D) Remote workers have limited access to technology.

4. What can be inferred about the role of employers in remote work?
   (A) They should help employees stay connected.
   (B) They should pay less to remote workers.
   (C) They should pay for workers' internet bills.
   (D) They should ask employees to visit the office sometimes.

Chapter

07

동명사

동명사는 준동사의 일종으로, "동사원형 + ing"의 형태를 가지며 문장에서 명사 역할을 한다.

1. 동명사의 용법

동명사는 명사처럼 주어, 보어, 목적어 자리에서 명사 역할을 한다.

Applying for the job early increases your chances of getting hired.
일찍 지원하는 것이 채용될 확률을 높인다.

Their main focus is **improving customer satisfaction**.
그들의 주된 초점은 고객 만족을 향상시키는 것이다.

The manager suggested **implementing a new strategy** to improve sales.
매니저는 매출을 개선하기 위해 새로운 전략을 시행할 것을 제안했다.

The company is committed to **reducing its environmental impact**.
그 회사는 환경 영향을 줄이는 데 전념하고 있다.

✔ CheckPoint 1. 동명사를 목적어로 취하는 동사

▶ admit, avoid, appreciate, deny, enjoy, finish, give up, mind, postpone, quit, recommend, stop, suggest

He **admitted making** a mistake in the report.
그는 보고서에서 실수를 저질렀음을 인정했다.

The company **gave up developing** the new product due to budget constraints.
그 회사는 예산 제약으로 인해 신제품 개발을 포기했다.

She doesn't **mind working** late as long as she gets the weekend off.
그녀는 주말에 쉴 수만 있다면 늦게까지 일하는 것을 신경 쓰지 않는다.

She **quit working** at the company to start her own business.
그녀는 자신의 사업을 시작하기 위해 회사에서 일을 그만두었다.

토익 연습문제

1. The manager suggested __________ a new approach to solving the issue.
   (A) implementing
   (B) to implement
   (C) implemented
   (D) implements

2. They stopped __________ for directions while heading to the client's office.
   (A) ask
   (B) asking
   (C) to ask
   (D) asked

3. The company postponed __________ the product until next year.
   (A) launch
   (B) launching
   (C) to launch
   (D) launched

✔ CheckPoint 2. 의미 차이 없이 To부정사와 동명사를 모두 목적어로 취하는 동사

▶ attempt, begin, continue, start

The engineer **attempted to fix/fixing** the issue before the deadline.
그 엔지니어는 마감 전에 문제를 해결하려고 시도했다.

The team **began to work/working** on the new project last week.
팀은 지난주에 새 프로젝트를 작업하기 시작했다.

They **continued to monitor/monitoring** the progress of the project closely.
그들은 프로젝트의 진행 상황을 계속 면밀히 모니터링했다.

She **started to organize/organizing** the files for the meeting.
그녀는 회의를 위해 파일을 정리하기 시작했다.

✔ CheckPoint 3. To부정사와 동명사를 목적어로 취할 때 의미 차이가 있는 동사

▶ remember, forget, regret + to부정사: 미래에 할 일
▶ remember, forget, regret + 동명사: 과거에 한 일
▶ try + to부정사(~위해 노력하다) / try + 동명사(시험 삼아 ~를 해보다)

He **remembered to send** the email before the deadline.
그는 마감 전에 이메일을 보내야 할 것을 기억했다.

He **remembered sending** the email yesterday.
그는 어제 이메일을 보낸 것을 기억했다.

We **regret to inform** you that your application was not successful.
귀하의 지원서가 통과되지 않았음을 알려드리게 되어 유감입니다.

He **regrets** not **taking** the job offer last year.
그는 작년에 그 일자리를 수락하지 않은 것을 후회한다.

They are **trying to improve** the system.
그들은 시스템을 개선하려고 노력 중이다.

He **tried restarting** the computer to fix the issue.
그는 문제를 해결하기 위해 컴퓨터를 재부팅해 보았다.

토익 연습문제

1. He regrets __________ the decision to leave the company last year.
   (A) make
   (B) to make
   (C) making
   (D) made

2. I remembered __________ my keys before leaving the house.
   (A) to be taken
   (B) taking
   (C) take
   (D) taken

3. They are trying __________ the system to make it more efficient.
   (A) improve
   (B) to improve
   (C) improving
   (D) improved

✔ CheckPoint 4. 동명사와 명사의 차이점

▶ 동명사는 "동사원형 + ing"의 형태로, 문장에서 명사 역할을 하지만 동사적 성질을 가지고 있어 동사의 유형에 따라 보어와 목적어를 가질 수 있고, 부사의 수식도 받을 수 있다.
▶ 명사는 관사, 전치사, 소유격 뒤에 위치할 수 있지만 목적어를 취할 수 없다.

They succeeded in **finding a solution** to the problem.
그들은 문제의 해결책을 찾는 데 성공했다.

He admitted **regretting deeply his decision** to leave the company.
그는 회사를 떠나기로 한 결정을 깊이 후회한다고 인정했다.

The discovery **of new evidence** changed the course of the investigation.
새로운 증거의 발견은 수사의 방향을 바꾸었다.

The manager's decision surprised everyone in the meeting.
매니저의 결정은 회의에 있는 모든 사람을 놀라게 했다.

토익 연습문제

1. The committee is focused on __________ new strategies to enhance productivity.
(A) develop
(B) developed
(C) developing
(D) development

2. Their __________ of the new system has significantly improved operational efficiency.
(A) adapting
(B) adapted
(C) to adapt
(D) adaptation

3. The company's __________ of remote working policies is crucial to maintaining employee satisfaction.
(A) adopted
(B) adopting
(C) to adopt
(D) adoption

2. 동명사의 시제

✔ CheckPoint 5. 단순 동명사와 완료 동명사

▶ 주절과 종속절의 시제가 동일하면 복문을 단문으로 변경할 때 단순 동명사(V + ing)를 사용한다.
▶ 주절보다 종속절의 시제가 한 시제 앞서면 완료 동명사(having + P.P.)를 사용한다.
▶ 주절과 종속절의 주어가 동일하면 종속절의 주어를 생략하고, 다르면 생략하지 않는다.

She suggested **starting** the project earlier than planned.
그녀는 계획보다 일찍 프로젝트를 시작할 것을 제안했다.
⇒ 원 문장 She suggested that she should start the project earlier than planned를 보면 주절과 종속절의 시제가 동일한 단순 동명사(starting)이고, 또 주절과 종속절의 주어가 동일하므로 종속절의 주어는 생략되었다.

The team appreciated the client **having provided** feedback early.
팀은 고객이 피드백을 일찍 제공한 것에 대해 고마워했다.
⇒ 원 문장 The team appreciated that the client had provided feedback early을 보면 주절보다 종속절의 시제가 한 시제 앞서는 완료 동명사(having provided)이지만 주절과 종속절의 주어가 다르므로 종속절의 주어(the client)는 생략되지 않았다.

토익 연습문제

1. The employees suggested __________ more training sessions to improve their skills.
   (A) holding
   (B) hold
   (C) having held
   (D) holds

2. The consultant admitted __________ a mistake during the financial analysis.
   (A) making
   (B) make
   (C) having made
   (D) makes

3. The company acknowledged ________ innovative solutions to improve customer satisfaction.
   (A) having implemented
   (B) implementing
   (C) implemented
   (D) implements

3. 동명사의 의미상의 주어

✔ CheckPoint 6. 동명사의 의미상의 주어

▶ 문장의 주어와 동명사의 의미상의 주어가 동일하면 후자의 주어를 생략한다.
▶ 일반인(we, you, they, people)이 동명사의 의미상의 주어이면 생략 가능하다.
▶ 문장의 주어와 동명사의 의미상의 주어가 다를 경우, 생물이나 인칭 대명사가 동명사의 의미상의 주어일 때는 목적격이 자연스럽지만, 소유격이 문법적으로 더 적절하고 공식적인 표현으로 간주된다.
▶ 무생물이 동명사의 의미상의 주어일 때는 소유격을 사용할 수 있지만 일반적으로 목적격을 사용하는 것이 더 일반적이며 자연스럽다.

They started **(their) working** on the project last week.
그들은 지난주에 프로젝트 작업을 시작했다.
We are looking forward to **his/him joining** the team.
우리는 그가 팀에 합류하는 것을 기대하고 있다.
The company's starting of the project was delayed until next month.
그 회사의 프로젝트 시작이 다음 달로 미뤄졌다.
The company delayed **the project starting** until next month.
그 회사는 프로젝트 시작을 다음 달로 미뤘다.

토익 연습문제

1. The director was impressed by __________ taking responsibility for the error.
   (A) they
   (B) theirs
   (C) their
   (D) themselves

2. We are confident about __________ the company's performance this year.
   (A) improving
   (B) our improving
   (C) his improving
   (D) your improving

4. 동명사의 관용표현

✔ CheckPoint 7. 동명사를 포함하는 관용표현

be busy (in) + 동명사	~하느라 바쁘다
be on the point of + 동명사	막 ~하려고 하다
be worth + 동명사	~할 가치가 있다
by 소유격 own + 동명사	스스로 ~하다
cannot help + 동명사	~하지 않을 수 없다
feel like + 동명사	~하고 싶다
have difficulty (trouble, problem, a hard time) (in) + 동명사	~하는 데 어려움을 겪다
it is no use + 동명사	~해봤자 소용없다
on(upon) + 동명사	~하자마자
spend 시간/돈 + 동명사	(시간/돈)을 ~하는 데 쓰다
there is no + 동명사	~하는 것은 불가능하다

She was **on the point of quitting** her job.
그녀는 직장을 그만두려던 참이었다.

The proposal **is worth discussing** at the next meeting.
그 제안은 다음 회의에서 논의할 만한 가치가 있다.

We **had trouble setting up** the new equipment.
우리는 새로운 장비를 설치하는 데 어려움을 겪었다.

Upon finishing the training, participants will receive a certificate of completion.
교육을 마치면 참가자들은 수료증을 받게 됩니다.

토익 연습문제

1. The company spent a significant amount of time __________ the market trends.
   (A) analyze
   (B) analyzing
   (C) analyzed
   (D) to analyze

2. There is no __________ the importance of communication in this project.
   (A) deny
   (B) to deny
   (C) denying
   (D) denied

✔ CheckPoint 8. 전치사 to를 포함하는 동명사 관용표현

be accustomed to + 동명사	~에 익숙하다
be addicted to + 동명사	~에 중독되다
be close to + 동명사	~에 가까워지다
be committed to + 동명사	~에 전념하다
be dedicated to + 동명사	~에 헌신하다
be devoted to + 동명사	~에 전념하다, 헌신하다
be opposed to + 동명사	~에 반대하다
be susceptible to + 동명사	~에 취약하다, 영향을 받기 쉽다
be used to + 동명사	~에 익숙하다
contribute to + 동명사	~에 기여하다
lead to + 동명사	~로 이어지다, 초래하다
look forward to + 동명사	~을 기대하다
object to + 동명사	~에 반대하다

She **is accustomed to preparing** detailed reports on a regular basis.
그녀는 정기적으로 상세한 보고서를 작성하는 데 익숙하다.

He **is committed to improving** the company's performance.
그는 회사의 성과를 개선하는 데 전념하고 있다.

The software **is susceptible to crashing** when overloaded.
그 소프트웨어는 과부하가 걸리면 다운되기 쉽다.

The employees **are used to communicating** with clients.
직원들은 고객들과 소통하는 데 익숙하다.

☞ be used to + 동사원형

They use the machine to manufacture automotive parts.
수동태 ⇒ The machine is used to manufacture automotive parts.
그 기계는 자동차 부품을 제조하는 데 사용된다.

토익 연습문제

1. The company is dedicated to __________ new energy-efficient technologies.
   (A) develop
   (B) developed
   (C) developing
   (D) to develop

2. The team looks forward to __________ the results of the new marketing strategy.
   (A) analyze
   (B) analyzing
   (C) analyzed
   (D) to analyze

3. The new policy contributed to __________ a more efficient workflow within the organization.
   (A) establish
   (B) establishing
   (C) established
   (D) to establish

토익 종합 실전문제

1. They stopped __________ the project after receiving feedback from the client.
(A) discuss
(B) discussing
(C) to discuss
(D) discussed

2. The company gave up __________ the new product due to budget cuts.
(A) develop
(B) developing
(C) to develop
(D) developed

3. The team avoided __________ the sensitive topic during the meeting.
(A) discuss
(B) to discuss
(C) discussing
(D) discussed

4. He forgot __________ the documents to the meeting this morning.
(A) bring
(B) bringing
(C) to bring
(D) brought

5. They tried __________ the new software to see if it would solve the problem.
(A) to install
(B) install
(C) installed
(D) installing

6. He remembered __________ the tickets for the concert, so we were able to get in.
(A) buy
(B) to buy
(C) buying
(D) bought

7. The CEO's __________ to expand the business was met with strong support from the board of directors.
(A) deciding
(B) decision
(C) decided
(D) decide

8. The manager was responsible for __________ the new policy across all departments.
(A) implement
(B) implemented
(C) implementing
(D) implementation

9. The team's __________ of the client's needs helped improve the project's outcome.
(A) understanding
(B) understood
(C) to understand
(D) understands

10. The director approved __________ additional resources to meet the growing demand.
(A) allocating
(B) allocated
(C) to allocate
(D) allocation

11. The team emphasized the importance of __________ clear communication between departments.
(A) maintain
(B) maintaining
(C) to maintain
(D) maintenance

12. The director denied __________ the confidential information to unauthorized parties.
(A) sharing
(B) share
(C) having shared
(D) to share

13. The client insisted on __________ all the necessary documents before the deadline.
(A) submitted
(B) submitting
(C) submit
(D) having submitted

14. The CEO regrets __________ the opportunity to collaborate with the partner company.
(A) missing
(B) missed
(C) miss
(D) having missed

15. We appreciate __________ conducting the survey in such a short time.
(A) they
(B) their
(C) them
(D) themselves

16. Upon __________ the meeting, they immediately began working on the project.
(A) to finish
(B) finishing
(C) finished
(D) finish

17. The engineers had trouble __________ the malfunction in the new system.

(A) to identify
(B) identify
(C) identifying
(D) identified

18. The CEO emphasized that it was no use __________ about the budget cuts after the decision was finalized.

(A) complain
(B) complaining
(C) to complain
(D) complained

19. The manager could not help __________ the team's performance after they exceeded all expectations.

(A) praising
(B) to praise
(C) praise
(D) praised

20. The director was on the point of __________ the merger deal when the company received a better offer from a competitor.

(A) sign
(B) signed
(C) to sign
(D) signing

21. The company is susceptible to __________ due to external factors such as market fluctuations.

(A) fail
(B) failing
(C) to fail
(D) failed

22. They are opposed to __________ any further changes to the project plan.

(A) make
(B) made
(C) making
(D) to make

23. They are devoted to __________ high-quality healthcare services to the community.

(A) provide
(B) provides
(C) providing
(D) provided

24. The scientist is close to __________ a major breakthrough in cancer research.

(A) make
(B) making
(C) to make
(D) made

PART 6

Questions 1–4 refer to the following information.

Dear Employees,

To ensure clarity and consistency, we are providing updated information 1________ the company's travel reimbursement process. When submitting reimbursement requests, employees are required to include detailed receipts and a completed expense report. 2________. For trips involving air travel, booking flights through the company's approved travel agency is mandatory to qualify for reimbursement. Additionally, employees are encouraged to use the corporate credit card for paying expenses during business trips. This helps streamline the reimbursement process and avoids any unnecessary confusion. Please note that reimbursement claims must be submitted 3________ 30 days of completing your trip. Claims submitted after this period will not be processed, unless there are exceptional circumstances, which must be approved by your department manager. For more details or assistance, please contact the Finance Department.
Thank you for 4________ these guidelines.

Sincerely,
Finance Team

1. (A) in
   (B) to
   (C) regarding
   (D) at

2. (A) The company will reimburse only business-related expenses.
   (B) Employees should submit their claims via email.
   (C) All reimbursement requests must include a project code.
   (D) Missing documents may result in delays in processing claims.

3. (A) by
   (B) within
   (C) after
   (D) for

4. (A) adhering to
   (B) consulting
   (C) respecting
   (D) considering

PART 7

Questions 1–4 refer to the following announcement.

Training & Development Opportunities for 2024

As part of our commitment to improving career development, we are excited to announce new training programs starting in January 2024. These programs are designed based on employee feedback from the latest Employee Engagement Survey. Below is a schedule of available training sessions:

- Leadership Development (January 15-17, 2024): Aimed at current managers and employees aspiring to take on leadership roles.
- Inter-departmental Communication Workshop (February 5-6, 2024): Focused on improving communication and collaboration between teams.
- Advanced Technical Skills Training (March 10-12, 2024): Covering advanced skills in project management, data analysis, and software development.
- Work-Life Balance Strategies (April 2, 2024): A one-day session on managing work-life balance more effectively.

All training sessions will be held in our main conference room. To register, please visit our internal portal or contact the HR Department.

We hope you take advantage of these opportunities!

1. When will the Leadership Development training take place?
   (A) January 15-17, 2024
   (B) February 5-6, 2024
   (C) March 10-12, 2024
   (D) April 2, 2024

2. What is the main focus of the Inter-departmental Communication Workshop?
   (A) Leadership skills
   (B) Project management
   (C) Team communication and collaboration
   (D) Work-life balance

3. How can employees register for the training sessions?
   (A) By attending a meeting
   (B) By sending an email to HR
   (C) By visiting the internal portal or contacting HR
   (D) By filling out a paper form

4. Which of the following can be inferred about the training programs?
   (A) They are mandatory for all employees.
   (B) They were created based on employee feedback.
   (C) They require prior approval from department heads.
   (D) They focus exclusively on technical skills.

Chapter

08

명사

명사(Noun)는 문장의 기본 구성요소로, 사람, 장소, 사물, 동물, 생각, 개념, 상태 등을 나타내며, 문장에서 주어, 보어, 목적어로서 중요한 역할을 한다.

1. 명사의 역할 및 자리

① 명사의 역할

The CEO announced the merger during the press conference.
CEO는 기자 회견에서 합병을 발표했다.

The main concern was **the budget** of our department.
주요 관심사는 우리 부서의 예산이었다.

The board of directors appointed her **the head of the department**.
이사회는 그녀를 부서장으로 임명했다.

The team completed **the project** ahead of schedule.
팀은 일정보다 앞서 프로젝트를 완료했다.

The success **of the project** depends on the team's collaboration.
프로젝트의 성공은 팀의 협력에 달려 있다.

② 명사의 자리

✔ CheckPoint 1. 관사/소유격/형용사 + 명사

관사나 소유격은 특정 명사를 가리키거나 소유관계를 나타내고, 형용사는 명사를 수식하여 그 성질이나 상태를 설명한다.

The initial proposal was revised based on feedback.
초기 제안은 피드백을 바탕으로 수정되었다.

An efficient process was implemented to reduce costs.
효율적인 프로세스가 비용을 줄이기 위해 도입되었다.

The company's success depends on its employees.
회사의 성공은 직원들에게 달려 있다.

Their performance exceeded expectations.
그들의 성과는 기대를 초과했다.

☞ 명사와 동명사의 차이점

명사는 주어, 보어, 목적어 역할을 하지만 목적어를 수반하지 않는 반면, 동명사는 동사 원형에 -ing를 붙인 형태로, 명사처럼 주어, 보어, 목적어 역할을 하면서도 동사의 성질을 유지하므로 목적어를 수반할 수 있다.

The manager's **approval** was essential for the project.
매니저의 승인은 프로젝트에 필수적이었다.

The manager's **approving the request** made the team very happy.
매니저가 요청을 승인한 것이 팀을 매우 기쁘게 만들었다.

토익 연습문제

1. The manager's __________ was highly appreciated by the team.
   (A) approve
   (B) approving
   (C) approval
   (D) approved

2. __________ performance exceeded expectations.
   (A) Theirs
   (B) Their
   (C) Them
   (D) They

3. A __________ report is essential for the upcoming meeting.
   (A) precisely
   (B) precision
   (C) precise
   (D) precisions

2. 가산명사와 불가산명사

① 가산명사 (Countable Nouns): 셀 수 있는 명사로서, 단수형과 복수형이 있으며, 단수형일 때는 앞에 관사(a, an)를 사용하고, 복수형일 때는 보통 's'나 'es'를 붙인다.

ex) book → a book, two books

idea → an idea, many ideas

② 불가산명사 (Uncountable Nouns): 셀 수 없는 명사로서, 앞에 a나 an 같은 관사를 사용하지 않고, 복수형도 없다.

ex) information → an information (x), informations (x)

milk → a milk (x), milks (x)

✔ CheckPoint 2. 토익 시험에 자주 나오는 가산명사와 불가산명사

가산명사	불가산명사
account (계정)	access (접근)
application (신청서)	accounting (회계)
approval (승인)	advertising (광고)
approach (접근법)	advice (조언)
assignment (과제)	behavior (행동)
benefit (혜택)	clothing (의류)
brochure (소책자, 안내 책자)	compensation (보상)
candidate (후보자)	confirmation (확인)
certificate (증명서)	construction (건설)
challenge (도전)	confidence (자신감)
complaint (불만, 불평)	equipment (장비)
contract (계약)	evidence (증거)
decision (결정)	furniture (가구)
detail (세부사항)	information (정보)
document (문서)	knowledge (지식)
increase (증가)	luggage/baggage (수하물)
invoice (청구서)	machinery (기계류)
issue (이슈, 문제)	maintenance (유지)
job (직업)	merchandise (상품)
meeting (회의)	news (뉴스)
offer (제안)	operation (운영)

opportunity (기회)	participation (참여)
permit (허가증)	patience (인내)
plan (계획)	performance (성과)
problem (문제)	permission (허가)
project (프로젝트)	planning (계획, 계획 수립)
proposal (제안서)	pollution (오염)
report (보고서)	productivity (생산성)
requirement (요구사항)	progress (진행)
reservation (예약)	research (연구)
result (결과)	satisfaction (만족)
schedule (일정)	scenery (풍경)
statement (진술)	ticketing (발권)
survey (조사)	traffic (교통)
task (과제)	training (훈련)
ticket (티켓)	transportation (운송)
view (견해, 전망)	work (일, 작업)

The team decided to take **a new approach** to the problem.
팀은 문제에 대해 새로운 접근 방식을 취하기로 결정했다.

The company conducted **a survey** to assess customer satisfaction.
회사는 고객 만족도를 평가하기 위해 설문 조사를 실시했다.

The company increased its budget for online **advertising**.
그 회사는 온라인 광고 예산을 늘렸다.

The report contains vital **information** about the market trends.
그 보고서에는 시장 동향에 대한 중요한 정보가 포함되어 있다.

☞ certificate (가산 명사) / certification (불가산 명사)

certificate는 개별적인 증명서를 의미하는 가산 명사이고, certification은 특정 자격이나 인증 상태를 의미하는 불가산 명사이다.

He received **two certificates** after completing the courses.
그는 과정을 마치고 두 개의 증명서를 받았다.

This position requires **certification** in safety training.
이 직책은 안전 교육 자격 인증을 요구한다.

☞ permit (가산 명사) / permission (불가산 명사)

permit은 주로 특정한 허가증이나 면허증을 의미하는 가산 명사이고, permission은 허가나 승인이라는 개념 자체를 의미하는 불가산 명사이다.

You need **a building permit** to start construction on your property.
귀하의 부지에서 건설을 시작하려면 건축 허가증이 필요하다.

You need **permission** from your supervisor to access this file.
이 파일에 접근하려면 상사의 허가가 필요하다.

☞ plan (가산 명사) / planning (불가산 명사)

plan은 구체적인 계획이나 방안을 의미하는 가산 명사이고, planning은 계획을 세우는 과정이나 행위 자체를 의미하는 불가산 명사이다.

The team developed **a detailed plan** for the project.
팀은 프로젝트에 대한 상세한 계획을 세웠다.

Effective **planning** is essential for the success of any project.
효율적인 계획 수립은 모든 프로젝트의 성공에 필수적이다.

토익 연습문제

1. Please provide more __________ regarding the upcoming project.
   (A) informations
   (B) details
   (C) advices
   (D) researches

2. The consultant provided valuable __________ to help the team enhance their productivity.
   (A) advices
   (B) advice
   (C) advising
   (D) advisor

3. The job requires __________ in project management and risk assessment.
   (A) certificate
   (B) certificates
   (C) certified
   (D) certification

3. 복합명사 (Compound Noun)

복합명사는 두 개 이상의 단어가 결합하여 하나의 명사 역할을 하는 구조로서 주로 명사 + 명사로 구성되어 있다.

✔ CheckPoint 3. 토익 시험에 자주 나오는 복합명사

budget plan (예산 계획)	marketing campaign (마케팅 캠페인)
business strategy (사업 전략)	marketing strategy (마케팅 전략)
company policy (회사 정책)	meeting agenda (회의 안건)
conference room (회의실)	office supplies (사무용품)
contract negotiation (계약 협상)	performance appraisal (성과 평가)
corporate strategy (기업 전략)	product development (제품 개발)
customer feedback (고객 피드백)	product launch (제품 출시)
customer loyalty (고객 충성도)	product quality (제품 품질)
customer satisfaction (고객 만족)	project manager (프로젝트 매니저)
customer service (고객 서비스)	quality assurance (품질 보증)
data analysis (데이터 분석)	quality control (품질 관리)
delivery schedule (배송 일정)	return policy (반품 정책)
employee training (직원 교육)	risk assessment (위험 평가)
event planning (행사 기획)	sales department (영업 부서)
expense report (비용 보고서)	sales forecast (판매 예측)
inventory management (재고 관리)	service agreement (서비스 계약)
job opening (채용 공고)	staff meeting (직원회의)
market analysis (시장 분석)	supply chain (공급망)
market research (시장 조사)	training session (교육 세션)

The **contract negotiation** took longer than expected.
계약 협상은 예상보다 오래 걸렸다.

Effective **inventory management** can significantly reduce costs.
효과적인 재고 관리는 비용을 크게 줄일 수 있다.

The annual **performance appraisal** will be conducted next month.
연례 성과 평가는 다음 달에 실시될 것이다.

Make sure to review the **return policy** before making a purchase.
구매하기 전에 반품 정책을 검토하십시오.

토익 연습문제

1. The finance team submitted the __________ for next quarter to the board of directors.
   (A) budget plan
   (B) project manager
   (C) customer satisfaction
   (D) return policy

2. The company invested heavily in __________ to improve product standards.
   (A) service agreement
   (B) quality assurance
   (C) marketing campaign
   (D) office supplies

3. The team prepared a __________ to address potential risks in the project.
   (A) job opening
   (B) risk management
   (C) product launch
   (D) sales forecast

✔ CheckPoint 4. 토익 시험에 자주 나오는 형용사 + 명사 구조

annual report (연례 보고서)	legal requirement (법적 요구 사항)
competitive advantage (경쟁 우위)	limited budget (한정된 예산)
detailed plan (상세한 계획)	major issue (주요 문제)
effective solution (효과적인 해결책)	new product (신제품)
efficient system (효율적인 시스템)	official statement (공식 성명)
environmental impact (환경 영향)	operational cost (운영비용)
financial report (재무 보고서)	overall performance (전체성과)
global market (세계 시장)	potential risk (잠재적 위험)
global trends(세계적 추세)	public relations (대외 홍보)
high demand (높은 수요)	recent development (최근 발전)
initial investment (초기 투자)	significant improvement (상당한 개선)
innovative idea (혁신적인 아이디어)	strategic plan (전략적 계획)
internal audit (내부 감사)	successful outcome (성공적인 결과)
key factor (핵심 요소)	technical support (기술 지원)

The company's technology gives it a **competitive advantage** in the market.
그 회사의 기술은 시장에서 경쟁 우위를 제공한다.

The **initial investment** for the project was substantial.
그 프로젝트의 초기 투자는 상당했다.

We need to find a solution that fits within our **limited budget.**
우리는 한정된 예산 내에서 해결책을 찾아야 한다.

The new process has led to a **significant improvement** in efficiency.
새로운 프로세스는 효율성에 상당한 개선을 가져왔다.

토익 연습문제

1. The finance department is working on the __________ for the upcoming fiscal year.
   (A) potential risk
   (B) annual report
   (C) public relations
   (D) competitive advantage

2. To minimize expenses, the company is focusing on reducing __________.
   (A) efficient system
   (B) high demand
   (C) operational costs
   (D) global market

3. The company implemented an __________ to enhance the efficiency of its manufacturing process.
   (A) internal audit
   (B) innovative idea
   (C) initial investment
   (D) effective solution

✔ CheckPoint 5. 사람명사와 사물/추상명사

▶ 문맥에 따라 사람명사와 사물/추상명사를 적절히 구별하고 사용하는 것이 중요하므로, 사람명사와 사물/추상명사를 구별하는 능력이 필요하다.

사람명사	사물/추상명사
applicant(지원자)	application(신청서, 지원)
assistant(보조자)	assistance(도움, 보조)
attendant(참석자, 수행원)	attendance(참석, 출석)
competitor(경쟁자)	competitiveness(경쟁력)
consultant(상담가, 컨설턴트)	consultation(상담, 협의)
consumer(소비자)	consumption(소비)
contractor(계약자, 도급업자)	contract(계약)
donor(기부자)	donation(기부, 기증)
employee(직원)	employment(고용, 직업)
executive(경영진, 임원)	execution(집행, 실행)
expert(전문가)	expertise(전문지식)
facilitator(촉진자, 진행자)	facilitation(촉진, 진행)
founder(설립자)	foundation(설립)
inspector(검사자)	inspection(검사)
interviewer(면접관)	interview(면접, 인터뷰)
investor(투자자)	investment(투자)
manager(관리자)	management(경영, 관리)
manufacturer(제조업자)	manufacturing(제조업, 생산)
moderator(조정자, 사회자)	moderation(조정, 중재)
negotiator(협상자)	negotiation(협상, 협의)
organizer(조직자)	organization(조직, 단체)
participant(참가자)	participation(참여, 참가)
performer(공연자)	performance(공연, 성능)
planner(계획자)	planning(계획 (수립))
producer(생산자)	production(생산)
provider(공급자)	provision(공급, 제공)
recipient(수령자)	reception(수령, 환영)
representative(대표자)	representation(대표, 표현)
resident(거주자)	residence(거주)
subscriber(구독자)	subscription(구독)
supervisor(감독자)	supervision(감독, 관리)
supplier(공급자)	supply(공급, 비축)

tenant(세입자)	tenancy(임대, 임대 기간)
translator(번역가)	translation(번역)
visitor(방문객)	visit(방문)

Our main **competitor** has just released a new product.
우리 주요 경쟁자가 새 제품을 출시했다.

The **contractor** completed the project ahead of schedule.
계약자는 일정을 앞당겨 프로젝트를 완료했다.

Her **expertise** in digital marketing is highly valued by the company.
디지털 마케팅에 대한 그녀의 전문지식은 회사에서 매우 가치 있게 여겨진다.

The project was completed under the **supervision** of an experienced manager.
프로젝트는 경험이 풍부한 관리자의 감독 하에 완료되었다.

토익 연습문제

1. The success of the project depends heavily on the ___________ of all team members.
   (A) participate
   (B) partnership
   (C) participant
   (D) participation

2. The HR department provides career development ___________ to all new employees.
   (A) assistance
   (B) assistant
   (C) applicant
   (D) attendance

3. The ___________ suggested a few strategies to improve customer engagement.
   (A) consumer
   (B) consumption
   (C) consultation
   (D) consultant

토익 종합 실전문제

1. The __________ of the new policy has been delayed.
(A) implement
(B) implementation
(C) implementing
(D) implemented

2. The CEO's __________ to invest in new technologies was well received by the board.
(A) decision
(B) decide
(C) decided
(D) deciding

3. The marketing team developed an __________ strategy to increase customer engagement.
(A) effective
(B) effectively
(C) effect
(D) effectiveness

4. The company conducted extensive __________ to understand customer needs.
(A) research
(B) researches
(C) researching
(D) researcher

5. The CEO emphasized the importance of thorough __________ in all future projects.
(A) plan
(B) planning
(C) plans
(D) planned

6. In order to meet the project deadline, the team must finalize all __________ by the end of this week.
(A) assignment
(B) assign
(C) assignments
(D) assigned

7. Upon successful completion of the program, students will receive two __________ for their achievements.
(A) certifications
(B) certificate
(C) certificates

8. You must obtain a __________ from the local government to hold an event in this park.
(A) permission
(B) permitting
(C) permit
(D) permissions

9. The marketing team presented several __________ for the product launch event.
(A) plan
(B) planned
(C) planning
(D) plans

10. Employees need __________ from their manager to take additional leave days.
(A) permit
(B) permission
(C) permitted
(D) permits

11. All new employees must complete __________ within the first month of their employment.
(A) event planning
(B) inventory management
(C) employee training
(D) customer feedback

12. The sales department analyzed last quarter's __________ to improve future performance.
(A) risk assessment
(B) sales forecast
(C) data analysis
(D) expense report

13. The sales team has prepared a detailed __________ for the new product release.
(A) project manager
(B) marketing campaign
(C) inventory management
(D) budget plan

14. The team conducted a detailed __________ to forecast trends for the upcoming fiscal year.
(A) performance appraisal
(B) data analysis
(C) training session
(D) risk assessment

15. The company updated its __________ to include new regulations regarding product returns and refunds.
(A) return policy
(B) customer satisfaction
(C) market research
(D) expense report

16. The CEO approved an updated __________ to adapt to recent changes in the market.
(A) sales department
(B) employee training
(C) project manager
(D) corporate strategy

17. The CEO highlighted the importance of addressing __________ to prevent project delays.
(A) competitive advantage
(B) major issues
(C) limited budget
(D) operational cost

18. The finance team conducted an __________ to identify unnecessary expenses and reduce costs.
(A) official statement
(B) internal audit
(C) annual report
(D) strategic plan

19. The company is analyzing the __________ of launching a new product line to increase market share.
(A) potential risks
(B) legal requirements
(C) limited budget
(D) recent developments

20. The team conducted a thorough analysis of the __________ in international markets.
(A) internal audits
(B) operational costs
(C) global trends
(D) efficient systems

21. Due to recent technological advancements, the company has gained a __________ in the industry.
(A) legal requirement
(B) limited budget
(C) major issue
(D) competitive advantage

22. The __________ of the facilities is scheduled for next month to ensure safety standards.
(A) inspector
(B) inspection
(C) investment
(D) execution

23. The __________ reviewed the terms of the new contract thoroughly before signing.
(A) contractor
(B) contract
(C) competition
(D) presenter

24. Our company's __________ in product quality has contributed to its reputation.
(A) foundation
(B) competitor
(C) competitiveness
(D) manufacturer

PART 6

Questions 1–4 refer to the following advertisement.

GreenWave Solar Panels

Are you ready to power your home with future energy? GreenWave is excited to introduce our new solar panels, 1________ to help you save on electricity bills and lower your carbon footprint. With the latest technology, our panels perform at their best—even on cloudy days!

With GreenWave Solar, 2________. Our panels come with a 30-year guarantee for top efficiency and need very little maintenance. Whether you're a homeowner or a business owner, switching to solar power has never been easier.

For a 3________, we're offering a discount on installation fees for all new customers. Plus, we provide free 4________ to help you find the best setup for maximum savings and efficiency.

Why wait? Start your journey to a brighter, more sustainable future with GreenWave Solar Panels. Contact us today to begin your path to eco-friendly energy!

1. (A) make
   (B) making
   (C) made
   (D) to make

2. (A) you're contributing to a healthier planet with every solar panel installed
   (B) each panel is designed to withstand harsh weather conditions
   (C) our products come with a customer satisfaction guarantee
   (D) you're not just buying panels; you're choosing a cleaner future

3. (A) limited time
   (B) available choice
   (C) complete offer
   (D) select group

4. (A) assistance
   (B) consultations
   (C) guidelines
   (D) operations

PART 7

Questions 1-5 refer to the following job advertisement and e-mail exchange.

Position: Sales Representative
Location: San Francisco, CA
Company: Global Tech Solutions

Global Tech Solutions is seeking an experienced Sales Representative to join our expanding team. The successful candidate will be responsible for developing new business opportunities, managing client relationships, and achieving sales targets.
Responsibilities include:

- Identifying and contacting potential clients
- Developing and delivering sales presentations
- Negotiating contracts and closing deals
- Providing after-sales support

Qualifications:

- Minimum of 3 years of sales experience, preferably in the technology industry
- Excellent communication and negotiation skills
- Strong organizational and time management abilities

Interested candidates should send their resume and cover letter to recruitment@globaltechsolutions.com by October 1.

From: David Chen (Client)
To: Sarah Moore (Sales Representative, Global Tech Solutions)
Date: September 10
Subject: Follow-up on Product Demonstration

Dear Sarah,
Thank you for the product demonstration last week. I was impressed by the features of your software and believe it could be a valuable addition to our company. Before making a final decision, I would like to clarify a few points regarding pricing and post-purchase support.

Could you please provide me with a detailed breakdown of the pricing structure, including any potential discounts for bulk purchases? Additionally, could you explain the types of support services available after the purchase?
I look forward to hearing from you soon.

Best regards,
David Chen

1. What is one of the responsibilities of the Sales Representative at Global Tech Solutions?
   (A) Managing after-sales support teams
   (B) Closing deals with clients
   (C) Developing new software features
   (D) Organizing team-building events

2. What is the deadline to apply for the Sales Representative position?
   (A) September 10
   (B) September 30
   (C) October 1
   (D) October 15

3. What additional information does David Chen request from Sarah Moore?
   (A) A breakdown of the pricing structure
   (B) A new product demonstration
   (C) References from other clients
   (D) A list of available products

4. According to the job advertisement, how much sales experience is required for the Sales Representative position?
   (A) At least 1 year
   (B) At least 3 years
   (C) At least 5 years
   (D) No specific experience is required

5. What is the primary purpose of David Chen's email to Sarah Moore?
   (A) To express satisfaction with the product demonstration
   (B) To ask about the job application process
   (C) To inquire about pricing and support options
   (D) To schedule another product demonstration

Chapter

09

대명사

1. 인칭 대명사
2. 재귀 대명사
3. 지시 형용사/대명사
4. 부정 형용사/대명사

◆ 토익 종합 실전문제

PART 6

PART 7

대명사(Pronouns)는 명사의 반복을 피하거나 명사를 대신하여 문장을 자연스럽게 만드는 역할을 하며, 용도와 형태에 따라 인칭 대명사, 재귀 대명사, 지시 대명사, 부정 대명사로 나뉜다.

1. 인칭 대명사

인칭 대명사는 사람이나 사물을 가리키는 대명사로, 주격, 목적격, 소유격 및 소유대명사 역할을 한다.

인칭	수/성	주격 (~은, ~는, ~이, ~가)	목적격 (~을, ~를)	소유격 (~의)	소유대명사 (~의 것)
1인칭	단수	I	me	my	mine
	복수	we	us	our	ours
2인칭	단수	you	you	your	yours
	복수	you	you	your	yours
3인칭	단수/남성	he	him	**his**	**his**
	단수/여성	she	her	her	hers
3인칭	단수/사물	it	it	**its**	**x**
	복수	they	them	their	theirs

She completed the project ahead of the deadline.
그녀는 기한 전에 프로젝트를 완료했다.

They have submitted their proposals to the board.
그들은 이사회에 제안서를 제출했다.

His report was very detailed and informative.
그의 보고서는 매우 상세하고 유익했다.

Its performance has improved significantly.
그것의 성능이 크게 향상되었다.

The company hired **me** as a project manager.
회사는 나를 프로젝트 매니저로 고용했다.

The CEO met with **him** to discuss the new strategy.
CEO는 새로운 전략을 논의하기 위해 그를 만났다.

✔ CheckPoint 1. 소유격과 소유대명사

▶ 소유대명사는 소유격 + 명사의 축약된 형태로, 소유를 나타내며, 뒤에 명사를 수반하지 않는다.
▶ 소유대명사는 주어, 보어, 목적어 자리에 온다.

The manager has finalized his report. **Mine (= my report)** will be completed by the end of the day.
매니저는 그의 보고서를 완료했다. 내 것은 오늘 안에 완료될 것이다.
The team has submitted their project proposal. **Ours (= our project proposal)** is still under review.
팀은 그들의 프로젝트 제안서를 제출했다. 우리의 것은 아직 검토 중이다.

토익 연습문제

1. This laptop is mine, and that one is __________.
   (A) you
   (B) your
   (C) yours
   (D) yourself

2. She has completed her assignment, but __________ needs more time.
   (A) hers
   (B) her
   (C) mine
   (D) our

3. Their presentation was excellent, and __________ received high praise from the board.
   (A) hers
   (B) mine
   (C) my
   (D) theirs

2. 재귀 대명사

재귀 대명사는 주어와 동일한 사람이나 사물을 지칭할 때 사용되며, myself, yourself, himself, herself, itself, ourselves, yourselves, themselves가 있고, 크게 재귀용법과 강조용법으로 나눌 수 있다.

✔ CheckPoint 2. 재귀용법과 강조용법

▶ 재귀용법은 재귀 대명사가 주어와 동일한 대상을 가리킬 때 필수적으로 사용되며, 생략할 수 없다. 재귀 목적어라고도 부른다.

▶ 강조용법은 재귀 대명사가 주어 또는 목적어를 강조하기 위해 사용되며, 강조의 의미가 필요하지 않다면 생략할 수 있다.

She introduced **herself(O)** to the new team members.
그녀는 새 팀원들에게 자신을 소개했다.

The manager blamed **himself(O)** for the project's failure.
매니저는 프로젝트 실패에 대해 자신을 탓했다.

The CEO himself reviewed the financial report.
CEO 자신이 재무 보고서를 검토했다.

The developers fixed the software bugs **themselves**.
개발자들이 스스로 소프트웨어 버그를 수정했다.

The manager reviewed **the report itself** before submitting it to the board.
매니저는 이사회에 제출하기 전에 그 보고서 자체를 검토했다.

토익 연습문제

1. The marketing department ___________ designed the entire campaign.
   (A) itself
   (B) himself
   (C) herself
   (D) themselves

2. She often finds ___________ working late into the night to meet deadlines.
   (A) himself
   (B) herself
   (C) themselves
   (D) itself

✔ CheckPoint 3. 재귀 대명사의 관용표현

by oneself (= on one's own)	혼자서, 스스로
for oneself	혼자 힘으로, 자신을 위해
of itself	저절로
in itself	그 자체로, 본질적으로
beside oneself	제정신이 아닌, 매우 흥분한
keep to oneself	혼자 지내다, 다른 사람과 잘 어울리지 않다
come to oneself	정신을 차리다, 의식을 되찾다

She completed the entire project **by herself** without any help.
그녀는 아무런 도움 없이 혼자서 전체 프로젝트를 완료했다.

He learned how to manage the new software **on his own.**
그는 혼자서 새 소프트웨어를 관리하는 법을 배웠다.

She took it upon herself to learn the new skills **for herself.**
그녀는 혼자 힘으로 새로운 기술을 배우기로 결심했다.

The machine stopped **of itself** after running continuously for twelve hours.
기계는 12시간 동안 연속으로 가동된 후 저절로 멈췄다.

The proposal is not bad **in itself**, but it needs some improvements.
그 제안 자체는 나쁘지 않지만, 약간의 개선이 필요하다.

☞ by oneself와 for oneself의 차이점

by oneself는 "혼자서"라는 의미로, 어떤 일을 독립적으로 수행하는 행동 자체를 강조하는 반면, for oneself는 "혼자 힘으로" 또는 "자신을 위해"라는 의미로, 행동이 자기 자신을 위한 것이며, 스스로의 힘으로 이루어졌다는 점을 강조한다.

토익 연습문제

1. The manager decided to handle the situation __________, without involving any other departments.
   (A) in itself
   (B) for himself
   (C) by himself
   (D) of itself

2. The designer's idea was innovative __________, but it needed some refinement to be implemented.
   (A) for itself
   (B) beside itself
   (C) by itself
   (D) in itself

3. 지시 형용사/대명사

① 지시형용사는 명사 앞에 위치하여 특정한 사람이나 사물을 지시한다. this와 that은 단수명사를, these와 those는 복수명사를 수식한다. 그리고 this와 these는 말하는 사람에게 가까운 사람이나 사물을 가리키고, that과 those는 멀리 있는 사람이나 사물을 가리킨다.

This document must be signed by the end of the day.
이 문서는 오늘 안에 서명되어야 한다.

That office building was recently renovated.
저 사무실 건물은 최근에 리모델링되었다.

These contracts require approval from the manager.
이 계약들은 매니저의 승인이 필요하다.

Those reports were submitted last week.
저 보고서들은 지난주에 제출되었다.

② 지시 대명사는 대화나 글 속에서 특정한 사람, 사물 또는 개념을 가리킬 때 사용한다. this와 that은 단수를, these와 those는 복수를 지시한다. 그리고 this와 these는 말하는 사람에게 가까운 대상들을 가리키고, that과 those는 멀리 있는 대상들을 가리킨다.

This is the final version of the report.
이것이 보고서의 최종 버전이다.

These are the items that need to be delivered today.
이것들은 오늘 배송되어야 하는 항목들이다.

That was a challenging project to complete.
저것은 완료하기 어려운 프로젝트였다.

Those are the forms you need to fill out.
저것들이 당신이 작성해야 하는 양식들이다.

☞ those가 관계절, 분사 및 전치사구에 의해 후치 수식을 받으면 '~한 사람들'이라는 의미로 사용된다.

Those who attended the seminar found it very informative.
세미나에 참석한 사람들은 그것이 매우 유익하다고 생각했다.

Those (who are) working on the project should submit their reports by Monday.
프로젝트에 참여하는 사람들은 월요일까지 보고서를 제출해야 한다.

Those (who are) interested in the project should contact the manager by Friday.
프로젝트에 관심 있는 사람들은 금요일까지 매니저에게 연락해야 한다.

Those in the marketing department will attend the workshop tomorrow.
마케팅 부서에 있는 사람들은 내일 워크숍에 참석할 것이다.

✔ CheckPoint 4. 비교구문에서의 지시 대명사

▶ 지시 대명사는 비교구문에서 두 대상을 비교할 때, 반복을 피하고 문장의 간결함을 유지하기 위해 사용된다.

▶ that은 단수명사를, those는 복수명사를 대신한다.

The speed of the new processor is faster than **that** of the older model.
새 프로세서의 속도가 이전 모델의 그것보다 더 빠르다.

The features of the updated software are more advanced than **those** of the older versions.
업데이트된 소프트웨어의 기능이 이전 버전들의 그것들보다 더 발전되었다.

토익 연습문제

1. The customer service provided by this company is better than _____ of its competitors.
   (A) those
   (B) that
   (C) these
   (D) this

2. The production costs for these new models are lower than _____ of the previous versions.
   (A) these
   (B) those
   (C) this
   (D) that

3. The technology used in these devices is more advanced than _____ used in older models.
   (A) these
   (B) those
   (C) this
   (D) that

4. 부정 형용사/대명사

① 부정 형용사는 문장에서 명사를 수식하여 특정되지 않은 대상이나 수량을 나타내는 형용사로, some, any, another, other, the other 등이 있다.

✔ CheckPoint 5. 부정 형용사의 유형과 용례

단어	용법	의미
some	긍정문이나 권유나 요청을 나타내는 의문문에 사용. 복수 (가산) 명사나 불가산 명사 수식	몇몇의, 약간의
any	부정문, 의문문, 조건문이나 강조의 의미를 나타내는 긍정문에 사용. 단수, 복수 (가산) 명사나 불가산 명사 수식	어떤, 아무런
another	단수 (가산) 명사 수식	또 다른 하나
other	복수 (가산) 명사나 불가산 명사 수식	다른
the other	단수 (가산) 명사 수식	(둘 중) 나머지 하나

Some employees have already completed the training program.
몇몇 직원들은 이미 교육 프로그램을 완료했다.

We don't have **any** time left to complete the project.
프로젝트를 완료할 시간이 전혀 남지 않았다.

The manager suggested **another** solution to the problem.
매니저는 그 문제에 대한 또 다른 해결책을 제안했다.

We need **other** information to make an informed decision.
우리는 정보에 입각한 결정을 내리기 위해 다른 정보가 필요하다.

One of the conference rooms is booked, but **the other** room is still available.
회의실 중 하나는 예약되었지만, 나머지 하나의 방은 아직 사용 가능하다.

토익 연습문제

1. We need to schedule _____ meeting to discuss the remaining issues.
   (A) some
   (B) another
   (C) other
   (D) any

2. The manager suggested _____ ways to improve the process efficiency.
   (A) another
   (B) this
   (C) the other
   (D) some

② 부정 대명사는 불특정한 사람, 사물 등을 대신하여 문장에서 주어, 목적어 등으로 사용될 수 있고, one, another, others, the other(s), each other, one another 등이 있다.

✔ CheckPoint 6. 부정 대명사의 유형과 용례

단어	용법	의미
one	단수 (가산) 명사를 대신함	(불특정한) 하나
another	단수 (가산) 명사를 대신함	(불특정한) 또 다른 하나
others	복수 (가산) 명사를 대신함	(불특정한) 다른 사람들/사물들
the other	단수 (가산) 명사를 대신함	(둘 중) 나머지 하나
the others	복수 (가산) 명사를 대신함	(특정한) 나머지 사람들/사물들
each other	둘 이상의 대상을 서로 가리킴	(둘 사이) 서로
one another	셋 이상의 대상을 서로 가리킴	(셋 이상 사이) 서로

She had one cup of coffee and ordered **another**.
그녀는 커피 한 잔을 마시고 또 다른 한 잔을 주문했다.
Some employees prefer working from home, while **others** like to work in the office.
일부 직원들은 재택근무를 선호하는 반면, 다른 직원들은 사무실에서 일하는 것을 좋아한다.
One of the printers is broken, but **the other** is working fine.
프린터 중 하나는 고장 났지만, 나머지 하나는 잘 작동한다.
Two team members are on vacation; **the others** are working on the project.
팀원 두 명은 휴가 중이고, 나머지 팀원들은 프로젝트를 진행하고 있다.
The team members share information freely with **one another**.
팀원들은 서로 자유롭게 정보를 공유한다.

토익 연습문제

1. One of the two team members is working remotely, but _____ is in the office.
   (A) another
   (B) others
   (C) the others
   (D) the other

2. Several clients have submitted their feedback, but _____ have not responded yet.
   (A) the other
   (B) others
   (C) another
   (D) the others

✔ CheckPoint 7. 특정 명사의 일부나 전체를 나타내는 부정 대명사의 유형과 용례

some of the/소유격 + 복수 (가산) 명사	복수 동사
all of the/소유격 + 복수 (가산) 명사	복수 동사
many of the/소유격 + 복수 (가산) 명사	복수 동사
most of the/소유격 + 복수 (가산) 명사	복수 동사
any of the/소유격 + 복수 (가산) 명사	복수 동사
(a) few of the/소유격 + 복수 (가산) 명사	복수 동사
one of the/소유격 + 복수 (가산) 명사	단수 동사
either of the/소유격 + 복수 (가산) 명사	단수 동사
neither of the/소유격 + 복수 (가산) 명사	단수 동사
each of the/소유격 + 복수 (가산) 명사	단수 동사
some of the/소유격 + 불가산 명사	단수 동사
all of the/소유격 + 불가산 명사	단수 동사
much of the/소유격 + 불가산 명사	단수 동사
most of the/소유격 + 불가산 명사	단수 동사
any of the/소유격 + 불가산 명사	단수 동사
(a) little of the/소유격 + 불가산 명사	단수 동사

All of the documents are required to be submitted by Friday.
모든 문서는 금요일까지 제출해야 한다.

A few of the products were damaged during shipping.
제품 중 몇 개가 배송 중에 손상되었다.

Each of the team members is responsible for their tasks.
팀원들 각자는 자신의 임무에 책임이 있다.

Some of the information is outdated and needs to be updated.
정보의 일부가 오래되어 업데이트가 필요하다.

A little of the budget has been allocated for the new project.
예산의 일부가 새로운 프로젝트에 할당되었다.

토익 연습문제

1. Each of the strategies _____ carefully analyzed before implementation.
   (A) were
   (B) are
   (C) is
   (D) have been

2. Some of the documents _____ still missing, and the team needs to locate them as soon as possible.
   (A) is
   (B) are
   (C) was
   (D) has been

3. Most of the information provided in the report _____ accurate, but a few details require verification.
   (A) were
   (B) is
   (C) are
   (D) being

토익 종합 실전문제

1. The manager has approved his budget plan, and ________ will be submitted next.
(A) me
(B) my
(C) ours
(D) our

2. Their project is progressing well, while ________ has encountered some delays.
(A) my
(B) mine
(C) theirs
(D) our

3. The project plan submitted by our team was detailed and thorough. However, ________ received more positive feedback from the client.
(A) their
(B) theirs
(C) our
(D) ours

4. The company executives ________ made the final decision on the merger.
(A) itself
(B) himself
(C) themselves
(D) ourselves

5. The team members divided the tasks among ________ to meet the deadline.
(A) itself
(B) himself
(C) herself
(D) themselves

6. He should familiarize _____ with the new software before the training session begins.
(A) themselves
(B) himself
(C) ourselves
(D) yourself

7. He prefers to keep _____ during company events and rarely engages in conversations with colleagues.
(A) himself
(B) in itself
(C) beside himself
(D) to himself

8. The device shut down _____ after operating continuously for several hours.
(A) beside itself
(B) for itself
(C) of itself
(D) by itself

9. To achieve his goals, he resolved to work on the project _____, without relying on anyone else.
(A) of itself
(B) in itself
(C) by himself
(D) beside himself

10. The company has offered additional training to _____ working in the sales department.
(A) one
(B) that
(C) those
(D) this

11. _____ in charge of the project must submit a weekly report to the manager.
(A) Those
(B) This
(C) That
(D) One

12. The revenue generated by our top product line is double _____ of any other line.
(A) those
(B) this
(C) that
(D) these

13. The results of the study were more conclusive than _____ of earlier research.
(A) this
(B) that
(C) these
(D) those

14. We need _____ time to finalize the report before the deadline.
(A) other
(B) another
(C) some
(D) any

15. Could you bring me _____ copy of the document? I misplaced mine.
(A) some
(B) the other
(C) another
(D) other

16. There are three candidates for the position. Two have been interviewed, and _____ will be interviewed tomorrow.
(A) another
(B) the others
(C) one
(D) the other

17. The first meeting was very productive, and we hope _____ will be the same.
(A) the other
(B) another
(C) others
(D) the others

18. The two departments have been working closely with _____ to improve efficiency.
(A) each other
(B) another
(C) others
(D) the others

19. The company provided laptops to some employees and tablets to _____.
(A) others
(B) the other
(C) another
(D) each other

20. Some departments have submitted their budget reports on time, but _____ still need to finalize theirs.
(A) another
(B) the other
(C) other
(D) the others

21. One of the candidates _____ the necessary experience, while the others lack it.
(A) have
(B) having
(C) has
(D) are

22. Either of the solutions _____ likely to resolve the issue, so you can choose either one.
(A) are
(B) is
(C) have
(D) were

23. Much of the research data _____ outdated and needs to be updated.
(A) were
(B) have
(C) are
(D) is

24. _____ the information provided in the reports is essential for the upcoming presentation.
(A) Some
(B) Most
(C) Any
(D) All

PART 6

Questions 1-4 refer to the following memo.

Dear Team,

We are pleased to inform you that we will soon be implementing a new project management tool to support our operations. This software is tailored to streamline processes and improve team efficiency. 1________ with the transition, we have scheduled a series of training sessions over the next two weeks. The initial session is set for this Friday at 10 AM in the main conference room. We strongly encourage everyone to attend, as these sessions will cover the key features of the software essential for your daily tasks. Please remember to bring your laptops, as you'll have a chance to try out the software in a hands-on session. Additionally, 2________. If you cannot attend any of the sessions, please inform your department head 3________. We will work to arrange additional sessions or provide online resources for 4________ unable to join. Thank you for your cooperation as we adopt this new tool. We are confident that it will enhance our productivity and make project management smoother for everyone.

Best regards,
Management Team

1. (A) Assisting
   (B) To be assisted
   (C) To assist
   (D) Assisted

2. (A) a user manual will be provided to guide you through the software's basic functions
   (B) a quick reference guide will be available to help you learn key features
   (C) training materials will cover essential tasks and troubleshooting tips
   (D) we will provide a video tutorial on advanced features

3. (A) in advance
   (B) on time
   (C) at the latest
   (D) as expected

4. (A) this
   (B) that
   (C) these
   (D) those

PART 7

Questions 1–5 refer to the following announcement and e-mail.

Subject: Updated Company Meeting Schedule
Date: September 10
To: All Employees
From: HR Department

Dear Team,

Please note the following changes to our weekly meeting schedule:

Team Leaders Meeting

Every Monday at 9:00 AM (previously 10:00 AM)
Location: Conference Room B

All Staff Meeting

Every Wednesday at 11:00 AM
Location: Main Auditorium

Project Review Meeting

Every Friday at 3:00 PM
Location: Project Room 1

All employees are expected to attend the All Staff Meeting on Wednesdays. If you cannot attend one or more of the other meetings, please notify your manager in advance.

Thank you,
HR Department

From: Sarah Kim (Project Manager)
To: Paul Johnson (Team Leader)
Date: September 11
Subject: Project Review Meeting

Hi Paul,

I wanted to confirm that the Project Review Meeting scheduled for this Friday at 3:00 PM will be held in Project Room 1, as noted in the updated company meeting schedule. I also wanted to remind you to bring the latest project report, as we will need to review the current status and plan next steps.
Please let me know if you need any additional information before the meeting.

Best regards,
Sarah Kim
Project Manager

1. What change has been made to the Team Leaders Meeting?
   (A) It has been canceled
   (B) It will now be held in Conference Room A
   (C) The time has changed to 9:00 AM
   (D) The meeting will now take place every Wednesday

2. Where will the All Staff Meeting be held?
   (A) Conference Room B
   (B) Project Room 1
   (C) Main Auditorium
   (D) Project Room 2

3. What does Sarah Kim ask Paul Johnson to bring to the Project Review Meeting?
   (A) A new project proposal
   (B) The latest project report
   (C) A financial report
   (D) A client presentation

4. When will the Project Review Meeting take place?
   (A) Every Wednesday at 11:00 AM
   (B) Every Monday at 9:00 AM
   (C) Every Friday at 3:00 PM
   (D) Every Thursday at 4:00 PM

5. How does the e-mail expand on the information in the announcement?
   (A) It confirms a meeting location listed in the announcement
   (B) It requests feedback on the meeting's schedule
   (C) It provides additional details about a holiday meeting
   (D) It discusses changes to the company’s main conference room

Chapter

10

형용사

형용사(Adjective)는 명사나 대명사를 수식하여 그 의미를 구체화하거나 한정하는 역할을 하며, 명사 앞이나 보어 자리에 위치할 수 있다.

1. 형용사의 역할 및 자리

✔ CheckPoint 1. 형용사의 한정 용법

▶ 전치 수식: 형용사가 명사 앞에 위치하여 명사를 수식하는 경우
▶ 후치 수식: 형용사가 명사 뒤에서 명사를 수식하는 경우
선행사(명사) + (주격 관계대명사 + Be동사) + 형용사/현재분사/과거분사 + 전치사구

The company implemented an **innovative** strategy to increase market share.
회사는 시장 점유율을 늘리기 위해 혁신적인 전략을 도입했다.
They provided information (which is) **relevant to the project**.
그들은 프로젝트와 관련된 정보를 제공했다.
The employees (who are) **working on the new project** will attend the meeting.
새 프로젝트에서 일하고 있는 직원들이 회의에 참석할 것이다.
The report (which was) **prepared by the consultant** was very informative.
컨설턴트가 준비한 보고서는 매우 유익했다.

토익 연습문제

1. The workshop provided participants with _____ tips to improve productivity.
(A) usefulness
(B) useful
(C) use
(D) usage

2. The manager praised the team for their _____ performance in the recent project.
(A) impressive
(B) impress
(C) impressing
(D) impression

✔ CheckPoint 2. 형용사의 서술 용법

▶ 형용사가 주격보어나 목적보어로 사용되어 주어나 목적어의 상태를 보충 설명하는 역할을 한다.

The proposal seemed **reasonable** to everyone in the meeting.
그 제안은 회의에 참석한 모든 사람에게 합리적으로 보였다.

The manager considered the plan **acceptable**.
매니저는 그 계획이 받아들일 만하다고 여겼다.

The CEO found the results **encouraging**.
CEO는 그 결과를 고무적으로 여겼다.

The manager kept the team **motivated** throughout the project.
매니저는 프로젝트 내내 팀의 동기부여를 유지시켰다.

☞ 일부 형용사(afraid, alive, asleep, aware, fond, worth)는 서술 용법으로만 사용되며, 명사를 직접 수식하는 한정 용법으로는 사용되지 않는다.

The employees were **afraid** of being laid off during the company restructuring.
직원들은 회사 구조조정 동안 해고될까 봐 두려워했다.

The staff members are **aware** of the upcoming policy changes.
직원들은 다가오는 정책 변화에 대해 알고 있다.

토익 연습문제

1. The manager considered the new marketing strategy _____ for the current market trends.
   (A) suitability
   (B) suitable
   (C) suitably
   (D) suit

2. The CEO found the presentation _____ and informative.
   (A) interesting
   (B) interest
   (C) interests
   (D) interested

2. 형용사의 종류

형용사는 그 역할과 기능에 따라 수량 형용사, 지시 형용사, 서수 형용사로 분류될 수 있다.

① 수량형용사

수량형용사(Quantitative Adjectives)는 명사의 양이나 수를 나타내며, 가산명사와 불가산명사에 따라 다르게 사용된다.

✔ CheckPoint 3. 수량형용사의 종류

▶ 가산명사에만 사용하는 수량형용사

수량형용사	의미	예문
many	많은	many books
few	거의 없는 (부정적 의미)	few students
a few	약간의, 몇몇의 (긍정적 의미)	a few ideas
several	몇 가지의	several reasons
numerous	수많은	numerous opportunities
a number of	다수의, 많은	a number of problems
a majority of	대다수의	a majority of voters
a variety of	다양한	a variety of options
another	또 다른	another chance
each	각각의 (+ 단수명사)	each member
every	모든 (+ 단수명사)	every student
either	어느 하나의 (+ 단수명사)	either solution
neither	어느 쪽도 아닌 (+ 단수명사)	neither option
both	둘 다	both solutions

▶ 불가산명사에만 사용하는 수량형용사

수량형용사	의미	예문
much	많은	much time
little	거의 없는 (부정적 의미)	little information
a little	약간의, 조금의 (긍정적 의미)	a little patience
a great deal of	많은 양의	a great deal of effort
half	절반의, 반	half the equipment

▶ 가산명사와 불가산명사 모두 사용하는 수량형용사

수량형용사	의미	예문
some	몇몇의, 약간의	some books / some advice
any	어떤, 약간의	any problems / any water
most	대부분의	most workers / most furniture
all	모든	all students / all equipment
a lot of	많은	a lot of apples / a lot of sugar
lots of	많은	lots of tools / lots of work
plenty of	많은, 충분한	plenty of ideas / plenty of time

A few documents need to be revised before submission.
몇몇 문서들은 제출 전에 수정이 필요하다.

A majority of the attendees voted in favor of the proposal.
대다수의 참석자들이 그 제안에 찬성표를 던졌다.

There is **little time** left to finish the project.
프로젝트를 끝낼 시간이 거의 남지 않았다.

A great deal of information was collected during the survey.
설문조사 동안 많은 양의 정보가 수집되었다.

There is **a lot of work** to be done before the deadline.
마감 기한 전에 해야 할 일이 많이 있다.

There is **plenty of time** to complete the project.
프로젝트를 완료할 시간이 충분하다.

토익 연습문제

1. The survey revealed that _____ employees preferred remote work over office-based work.
   (A) many
   (B) much
   (C) a little
   (D) little

2. The team collected _____ information to make an informed decision about the project.
   (A) several
   (B) few
   (C) a few
   (D) plenty of

3. 형용사의 관용표현

형용사의 관용표현은 특정한 형용사와 결합하여 고유한 의미를 가지며, 자주 사용되므로 익혀두는 것이 중요하다.

✔ CheckPoint 4. 토익에 자주 출제되는 관용표현

be about to	막 ~하려고 하다	be impressed with	~에 감명을 받다
be absent from	~에 결석하다	be indifferent to	~에 무관심하다
be accessible to	~에 접근 가능하다	be interested in	~에 관심이 있다
be accustomed to	~에 익숙하다	be involved in	~에 관여하다
be afraid of	~을 두려워하다	be keen on	~에 열중하다
be anxious about	~에 대해 불안해하다	be known for	~로 유명하다
be aware of	~을 알고 있다	be late for	~에 늦다
be capable of	~할 수 있다	be opposed to	~에 반대하다
be committed to	~에 헌신하다	be prepared for	~에 준비되어 있다
be compatible with	~와 호환되다	be proud of	~을 자랑스러워하다
be confident about	~에 대해 자신이 있다	be related to	~와 관련이 있다
be concerned about	~에 대해 걱정하다	be relevant to	~와 관련이 있다
be consistent with	~와 일치하다	be responsible for	~에 책임이 있다
be critical of	~을 비판하다	be satisfied with	~에 만족하다
be dedicated to	~에 전념하다	be sensitive to	~에 민감하다
be delighted with	~에 기뻐하다	be similar to	~와 유사하다
be dependent on	~에 의존하다	be skilled in/at	~에 능력이 있다
be eligible for	~에 자격이 있다	be subject to	~하기 쉽다
be engaged in	~에 종사하다	be suitable to	~에 적합하다
be envious of	~을 부러워하다	be thankful for	~에 감사하다
be familiar with	~에 익숙하다	be tired of	~에 싫증나다
be fond of	~을 좋아하다	be willing to	기꺼이 ~하다
be hesitant to	~을 망설이다	be worried about	~에 대해 걱정하다

The manager **is about to** announce the new policy changes.
매니저가 곧 새로운 정책 변화를 발표하려고 한다.

The new software **is** easily **accessible to** all employees.
새로운 소프트웨어는 모든 직원들이 쉽게 접근할 수 있다.

She **is eligible for** the promotion due to her excellent performance.
그녀는 우수한 성과로 인해 승진 자격이 있다.

The CEO **was impressed with** the team's dedication to the project.
CEO는 팀의 프로젝트에 대한 헌신에 감명을 받았다.

The company **is keen on** expanding its operations overseas.
회사는 해외로 사업을 확장하는 데 열중하고 있다.

The schedule **is subject to** change depending on the circumstances.
일정은 상황에 따라 변경될 수 있다.

토익 연습문제

1. The manager seemed _____ to the concerns raised during the meeting.
   (A) impressed
   (B) indifferent
   (C) sensitive
   (D) delighted

2. The company is _____ of expanding its market to international clients.
   (A) confident
   (B) eligible
   (C) capable
   (D) subject

3. The employees are _____ for handling customer complaints efficiently.
   (A) response
   (B) responsive
   (C) responsible
   (D) responsibly

4. 혼동하기 쉬운 형용사

✔ CheckPoint 5. 토익에 자주 출제되는 혼동하기 쉬운 형용사

advisable	바람직한, 권장할 만한	advisory	자문의, 충고의
beneficent	선행을 베푸는	beneficial	유익한, 이로운
comparable	비교할 만한, 필적하는	comparative	비교의, 상대적인
complementary	보완적인	complimentary	무료의
comprehensible	이해할 수 있는	comprehensive	포괄적인, 종합적인
confident	자신감이 있는	confidential	기밀의
considerable	상당한, 중요한	considerate	사려 깊은, 배려하는
continual	반복되는, 빈번한	continuous	연속적인, 끊임없는
dependable	믿을 수 있는	dependent	의존적인
economic	경제의, 경제적인	economical	경제적인, 절약하는
favorable	호의적인, 유리한	favorite	가장 좋아하는
historic	역사적으로 중요한	historical	역사적인, 역사와 관련된
imaginary	상상의, 가상의	imaginative	상상력이 풍부한, 창의적인
impressed	감명 받은	impressive	인상적인
industrial	산업의, 공업의	industrious	부지런한, 근면한
informed	정통한, 잘 알고 있는	informative	유익한
literal	문자 그대로의	literary	문학의, 문학적인
personal	개인적인, 사적인	personnel	인사부, 직원
preventable	예방할 수 있는	preventive	예방적인
proficient	능숙한, 숙련된	profitable	이익이 되는, 유익한
prospective	전도유망한, 잠재적인	prosperous	번영하는
reliable	믿을 수 있는	reliant	의존적인
respectable	존경할 만한, 훌륭한	respective	각각의, 개별적인
responsible	책임이 있는	responsive	반응하는
sensible	분별 있는, 현명한	sensitive	민감한, 예민한
successful	성공적인	successive	연속적인, 잇따른
understandable	이해할 만한	understanding	이해심이 있는, 이해, 지식

It is **advisable** to consult with a legal expert before signing the contract.
계약서에 서명하기 전에 법률 전문가와 상담하는 것이 바람직하다.

The company requires all employees to sign a **confidential** agreement.
회사는 모든 직원이 기밀 협약에 서명할 것을 요구한다.

The project requires a **considerable** amount of resources.
이 프로젝트는 상당한 양의 자원이 필요하다.

The presentation was **impressive** and well-received by the audience.
발표는 인상적이었고 청중들에게 좋은 평가를 받았다.

The workshop was very **informative** and provided valuable insights.
워크숍은 매우 유익했고 귀중한 통찰을 제공했다.

The teams returned to their **respective** offices after the meeting.
팀들은 회의 후 각자의 사무실로 돌아갔다.

토익 연습문제

1. The new policy is designed to be _____ to the diverse needs of employees.
   (A) relevant
   (B) responsible
   (C) responsive
   (D) respective

2. The report provided a _____ analysis of the economic trends affecting the industry.
   (A) beneficial
   (B) comprehensive
   (C) comparative
   (D) considerate

3. The results of the experiment were both surprising and _____.
   (A) indifferent
   (B) industrious
   (C) impressed
   (D) impressive

토익 종합 실전문제

1. The team discussed the issues _____ for the successful completion of the project.
(A) relevance
(B) relevancy
(C) relevantly
(D) relevant

2. The committee discussed several topics _____ to the company's future plans.
(A) relates
(B) related
(C) relating
(D) relation

3. The engineers _____ the new design are confident in its success.
(A) develops
(B) development
(C) developed
(D) developing

4. The team _____ the results of the survey will present their findings at the conference.
(A) analyzes
(B) analysis
(C) analyzing
(D) analyzed

5. The equipment _____ in the warehouse is ready for shipment.
(A) storing
(B) stored
(C) storage
(D) stores

6. The new design made the team _____ about its potential success.
(A) excites
(B) excited
(C) exciting
(D) excitement

7. The feedback from customers has made the development team _____ about the new feature.
(A) confident
(B) confidence
(C) confidently
(D) confide

8. The report left the management team _____ about the financial forecast.
(A) concern
(B) concerned
(C) concerning
(D) concerns

9. The employees kept the office environment _____ during the busy season.
(A) organize
(B) organization
(C) organizing
(D) organized

10. The new manager implemented _____ changes to improve team productivity.
(A) much
(B) many
(C) little
(D) few

11. Only _____ employees attended the meeting, so the manager decided to reschedule it.
(A) little
(B) a little
(C) many
(D) few

12. There are _____ options available to address this issue, but we need to evaluate them carefully.
(A) several
(B) much
(C) a little
(D) few

13. There was _____ time left to complete the task, so the team had to work faster.
(A) little
(B) a little
(C) few
(D) some

14. _____ research has been conducted to understand the long-term effects of this treatment.
(A) Few
(B) A few
(C) Some
(D) Many

15. The employees are _____ of the potential risks associated with the new policy.
(A) aware
(B) suitable
(C) sensitive
(D) eligible

16. The CEO is _____ about the company's ability to meet its financial targets this year.
(A) satisfied
(B) impressed
(C) hesitant
(D) confident

17. The staff members were _____ to the changes in company policies.
(A) accustomed
(B) similar
(C) subject
(D) suitable

18. The schedule is _____ with the client's request, so no changes are needed.
(A) consistent
(B) consistency
(C) consist
(D) consistented

19. The new product design is _____ to the latest market trends, which makes it highly competitive.
(A) aware
(B) indifferent
(C) accustomed
(D) relevant

20. The team is _____ to complete the project within the given timeline despite the challenges.
(A) capable
(B) committed
(C) related
(D) sensitive

21. The team presented a _____ solution that addressed both efficiency and cost concerns.
(A) continual
(B) respective
(C) sensible
(D) sensitive

22. The manual provides _____ instructions for assembling the equipment.
(A) comprehensible
(B) comparative
(C) successive
(D) responsive

23. The manager stated that it would be _____ to review the contract thoroughly before signing it.
(A) advisory
(B) advisable
(C) complementary
(D) informed

24. The policy changes are expected to have a _____ impact on employee satisfaction.
(A) continuous
(B) beneficent
(C) beneficial
(D) dependent

PART 6

Questions 1–4 refer to the following memo.

Dear Team,

We are excited to announce updates to our training program designed to help new employees adapt quickly and contribute effectively to our company.
The program includes 1________ online and in-person sessions. These sessions provide clear guidance and practical tips for understanding the company's workflow and goals.
Additionally, managers are encouraged to be responsive to the specific needs of their team members during this transition.
Employees will also have access to resources that 2________ the company's current systems and policies.
Finally, 3________. Your insights are valuable and will help us make this training as 4________ as possible.
Thank you for your cooperation and commitment to professional growth.

Best regards,
HR Department

1. (A) only
   (B) both
   (C) either
   (D) neither

2. (A) are in alignment with
   (B) are dependent on
   (C) are in contrast to
   (D) are compatible with

3. (A) feedback from participants will be used to continuously improve the program
   (B) the program will end with a certification process for all employees
   (C) team members will not be required to complete any assessments
   (D) there will be no further changes to the training structure

4. (A) colorful
   (B) effective
   (C) optional
   (D) adaptable

PART 7

Questions 1–5 refer to the following announcement and employee review.

Subject: Office Renovation Notice
Date: September 1, 2024
To: All Employees
From: Facilities Management Team

Dear Team,

We are excited to inform you that starting September 15, we will begin renovations on the 3rd and 4th floors of our main office building. These renovations will improve the layout of our workspaces and upgrade the office equipment. The renovation work is expected to last six weeks, with a projected completion date of October 27, 2024.

During this period, employees working on the 3rd and 4th floors will be temporarily relocated to the 2nd floor. Please ensure that you pack up your personal belongings by September 12 to facilitate a smooth transition. More details on seating arrangements will follow in a separate email.

We apologize for any inconvenience this may cause and appreciate your cooperation during this time. Should you have any questions or concerns, feel free to contact the Facilities Management Team at **facilities@company.com.**

Best regards,
Facilities Management Team

Subject: My Experience with the Recent Office Renovation
Date: November 5, 2024
From: Sarah Kim, Marketing Department

The recent office renovation on the 3rd and 4th floors was a success, and I wanted to share my thoughts on the experience. The construction period lasted six weeks as expected, and though there were some initial inconveniences with the temporary relocation to the 2nd floor, the facilities team was helpful throughout the process. They made sure all employees had adequate seating and access to necessary resources.

The new layout of the 4th floor is fantastic. The open workspaces and updated equipment have improved our productivity, and the team is particularly happy with the new collaborative areas. Overall, the renovation was worth the temporary disruption.

I believe the renovation has created a much more efficient and pleasant working environment, and I would recommend future office renovations to follow a similar approach.

1. When did the renovation work on the 3rd and 4th floors begin?
   (A) September 1
   (B) September 12
   (C) September 15
   (D) October 27

2. How long did the renovation take?
   (A) Four weeks
   (B) Six weeks
   (C) Eight weeks
   (D) Two months

3. What does Sarah Kim highlight as a benefit of the renovation?
   (A) The new cafeteria
   (B) The new private offices
   (C) The improved lighting system
   (D) The open workspaces

4. Where were the employees temporarily relocated during the renovation?
   (A) To the 1st floor
   (B) To the 2nd floor
   (C) To the 5th floor
   (D) To a nearby building

5. According to the documents, what was a key feature of the renovated office?
   (A) New collaborative workspaces on the 4th floor
   (B) An upgraded cafeteria for employees
   (C) Expanded private offices for management staff
   (D) Improved parking facilities for visitors

Chapter

11

부사

부사(Adverbs)는 문장에서 다양한 위치에 올 수 있으며, 행동, 상태, 또는 다른 수식어의 성질을 구체적으로 설명하여 문장의 의미를 풍부하게 만들어준다.

1. 부사의 위치

부사는 문장에서 동사, 형용사, 부사 및 문장 전체를 수식할 수 있다.

The information is **readily** available online.
그 정보는 온라인에서 쉽게 구할 수 있다.

She handled the situation **quite effectively**.
그녀는 그 상황을 꽤 효과적으로 처리했다.

The team worked **extremely hard** to meet the deadline.
팀은 기한을 맞추기 위해 매우 열심히 일했다.

They finished the task **almost perfectly**.
그들은 거의 완벽하게 그 작업을 마쳤다.

Unfortunately, the shipment was delayed due to bad weather.
불행히도, 악천후로 인해 배송이 지연되었다.

✔ CheckPoint 1. 동사 수식

▶ Be동사와 조동사 뒤에 위치하거나 본동사 앞에 위치한다.
▶ 동사 (+ 목적어) 뒤에 위치한다.

The presentation was **clearly** well-received by the audience.
그 발표는 청중에게 명확하게 좋은 평가를 받았다.

The project must **certainly** be completed by the deadline.
그 프로젝트는 기한 내에 반드시 완료되어야 한다.

The company has **already** sent the revised contract.
회사는 이미 수정된 계약서를 보냈다.

The company **regularly** updates its policies to comply with regulations.
회사는 규정을 준수하기 위해 정책을 정기적으로 업데이트한다.

The company reviewed the proposal **thoroughly** before making a decision.
회사는 결정을 내리기 전에 제안서를 철저히 검토했다.

토익 연습문제

1. The researchers tested the new software _____ before releasing it to the public.
   (A) extensively
   (B) extensive
   (C) extension
   (D) extend

2. The project must _____ be reviewed by the legal team to ensure compliance with regulations.
   (A) carefully
   (B) careful
   (C) care
   (D) caring

3. The employee's performance evaluation was _____ conducted to ensure fairness.
   (A) thorough
   (B) thoroughness
   (C) thoroughlyness
   (D) thoroughly

2. 부사의 종류

부사의 종류에는 방법, 장소, 시간, 빈도, 정도 및 접속 부사 등이 있다.

✔ CheckPoint 2. 시간 부사

부사	의미	사용 시제	사용 구문	사용 위치
already	이미, 벌써	현재완료, 과거	긍정문, 의문문	조동사 뒤, 본동사 앞
still	아직도, 여전히	현재, 현재완료, 과거	긍정문, 의문문, 부정문	조동사 뒤, 본동사 앞, 부정어 앞
yet	아직, 이미, 벌써	현재완료	의문문, 부정문	문장의 뒤, 부정어 뒤
soon	곧, 머지않아	미래	긍정문, 의문문, 부정문	문장의 앞 또는 뒤
just	막, 방금	현재완료, 과거	긍정문, 의문문, 부정문	조동사 뒤, 본동사 앞
ago	이전에	과거	긍정문, 의문문, 부정문	시간 표현 뒤
once	한때, 한 번은	과거 (조건절: 미래)	긍정문, 의문문, 부정문	문장의 앞 또는 뒤

The team has **already** submitted the report.
팀은 이미 보고서를 제출했다.

The manager **still** hasn't approved the budget.
매니저는 아직도 예산을 승인하지 않았다.

The report hasn't been reviewed **yet**.
그 보고서는 아직 검토되지 않았다.

The company launched the product three years **ago**.
회사는 3년 전에 그 제품을 출시했다.

토익 연습문제

1. The team has _____ finalized the report and sent it to the client.
   (A) yet
   (B) still
   (C) already
   (D) ago

2. The company hasn't made any decisions about the new policy _____.
   (A) already
   (B) yet
   (C) soon
   (D) once

3. The new CEO will announce the company's long-term strategy _____.
   (A) soon
   (B) ago
   (C) still
   (D) once

✔ CheckPoint 3. 빈도나 정도 부사

▶ 빈도 부사는 행동이나 상태가 얼마나 자주 발생하는지를 나타내는 부사로서, 주로 Be동사와 조동사 뒤, 본동사 앞에 위치한다.

빈도부사	의미	빈도
always	항상	100%
usually	보통	80-90%
often	자주	60-70%
sometimes	때때로	40-50%
occasionally	가끔	20-30%
rarely	거의 ~않다	5% 이하
seldom	거의 ~않다	5% 이하
never	결코 ~않다	0%

▶ 정도 부사는 행동이나 상태의 강도나 정도를 나타내는 부사로서, 주로 Be동사와 조동사 뒤, 본동사 앞에 위치한다.

정도부사	의미	강도
totally	완전히	매우 강함
completely	완전히, 전적으로	매우 강함
very	매우, 아주	강함
quite	꽤, 상당히	강함
almost	거의	중간
slightly	약간	약함
barely	거의 ~않다, 겨우	매우 약함
hardly	거의 ~않다	매우 약함
scarcely	거의 ~않다	매우 약함

The manager is **sometimes** available for unscheduled meetings.
매니저는 때때로 비정기적인 회의에 참석할 수 있다.

We must **never** ignore safety regulations during inspections.
우리는 검사 중에 안전 규정을 결코 무시해서는 안 된다.

The manager **rarely** approves overtime requests.
매니저는 거의 초과 근무 요청을 승인하지 않는다.

The presentation was **completely** revised to meet the client's expectations.
프레젠테이션은 고객의 기대를 충족하기 위해 완전히 수정되었다.

They should **hardly** rely on outdated information for decision-making.
그들은 의사 결정을 위해 구식 정보를 거의 의존하지 말아야 한다.

The company **slightly** increased its advertising budget this quarter.
회사는 이번 분기에 광고 예산을 약간 늘렸다.

토익 연습문제

1. The company _____ conducts safety inspections to ensure compliance with regulations.
   (A) always
   (B) slightly
   (C) almost
   (D) completely

2. The marketing plan was _____ revised to align with the company's new goals.
   (A) rarely
   (B) completely
   (C) sometimes
   (D) very

3. The team can _____ complete urgent tasks when under pressure.
   (A) slightly
   (B) completely
   (C) very
   (D) sometimes

✔ CheckPoint 4. 접속 부사

▶ 접속 부사는 문장과 문장을 연결하여 그들 사이의 논리적 관계를 나타내는 역할을 하는 부사로서, 주로 완전한 문장을 연결할 때 사용되며, 주어진 상황에 따라 여러 가지 의미를 전달할 수 있다.

분류	접속 부사	의미
인과관계	therefore, accordingly, thus, consequently, as a result	따라서, 그러므로, 그 결과
대조(역접)	however, nevertheless, nonetheless, still, conversely, on the other hand	그러나, 그럼에도 불구하고, 반대로, 반면에
추가(부가)	moreover, furthermore, in addition, besides	게다가, 더욱이
예시	for example, for instance, in particular, specifically	예를 들어, 특히, 구체적으로
조건	otherwise, (or) else	그렇지 않으면, 달리
시간의 경과	meanwhile, then, subsequently, later	그 동안에, 그 다음에, 이어서, 나중에
요약	in summary, in conclusion, to sum up	요약하면, 결론적으로

The deadline was missed; **therefore**, the team had to submit a revised timeline.
기한을 놓쳤다; 따라서 팀은 수정된 일정을 제출해야 했다.

The product is expensive. **However**, it has received excellent reviews from customers.
제품은 비싸다. 그러나 고객들로부터 훌륭한 평가를 받았다.

The project was completed on time; **moreover**, it stayed well within the budget.
프로젝트는 제시간에 완료되었다; 게다가 예산 내에서 잘 마무리되었다.

The team must follow safety regulations; **or else**, the project will be delayed.
팀은 안전 규정을 따라야 한다; 그렇지 않으면 프로젝트가 지연될 것이다.

The team completed the project. **Subsequently**, they presented their findings to the board.
팀은 프로젝트를 완료했다. 이어서 그들은 결과를 이사회에 발표했다.

☞ 마침표(.)와 세미콜론(;)의 차이점

마침표는 두 문장을 명확히 분리하여 각각 독립된 생각을 표현할 때 사용하고, 세미콜론은 두 문장을 논리적으로 긴밀하게 연결하고, 의미적 연관성을 강조할 때 사용한다. 하지만 두 방법 모두 문법적으로 맞으며, 선택은 글쓴이의 의도와 문맥에 따라 달라질 수 있다.

토익 연습문제

1. The research data was analyzed thoroughly; _____, the team was able to identify key trends.
   (A) however
   (B) or else
   (C) nonetheless
   (D) consequently

2. The deadline was tight; _____, the team managed to complete the project on schedule.
   (A) however
   (B) thus
   (C) specifically
   (D) besides

3. You must follow the dress code at the company event; _____, you might be asked to leave.
   (A) accordingly
   (B) otherwise
   (C) in addition
   (D) conversely

3. 혼동하기 쉬운 부사

✔ CheckPoint 5. 혼동하기 쉬운 부사와 그 의미

단어	품사	의미	단어	품사	의미
hard	부사	열심히, 단단히	hardly	부사	거의 ~않다
late	부사	늦게	lately	부사	최근에
near	부사	가까이	nearly	부사	거의
high	부사	높이	highly	부사	매우, 대단히
close	부사	가깝게	closely	부사	면밀히, 철저히
just	부사	막, 방금, 정확히	justly	부사	공정하게, 정당하게
most	부사	가장	mostly	부사	대부분, 주로
also	부사	또한, 역시	as well	부사	또한, 게다가

She worked **hard** to complete the project before the deadline.
그녀는 마감 기한 전에 프로젝트를 완료하기 위해 열심히 일했다.

The new employee **hardly** understands the company's procedures yet.
새 직원은 아직 회사의 절차를 거의 이해하지 못한다.

The balloon floated **high** above the city, providing a stunning view.
풍선은 도시 위로 높이 떠올라 놀라운 전망을 제공했다.

The candidate is **highly** qualified for the position due to her extensive experience.
그 후보자는 풍부한 경험 덕분에 그 직책에 매우 적합하다.

The photographer stood **close** to the subject to capture the perfect shot.
사진작가는 완벽한 샷을 찍기 위해 피사체 가까이에서 섰다.

The analyst **closely** examined the financial report to identify any discrepancies.
분석가는 불일치를 확인하기 위해 재무 보고서를 면밀히 조사했다.

토익 연습문제

1. The new office building is _____ the city center, making it an ideal location for business.
   (A) nearly
   (B) near
   (C) closely
   (D) high

2. The workers climbed _____ onto the roof to complete the repairs.
   (A) closely
   (B) mostly
   (C) high
   (D) highly

3. The new manager is _____ regarded by her team for her excellent leadership skills.
   (A) close
   (B) lately
   (C) highly
   (D) high

✔ CheckPoint 6. 형용사와 부사의 형태가 같은 단어

단어	형용사	부사	단어	형용사	부사
hard	어려운, 단단한	열심히, 단단히	late	늦은	늦게
early	이른, 초기의	일찍, 이르게	high	높은	높이
close	가까운	가깝게	fast	빠른	신속히, 빨리
just	공정한	막, 방금, 정확히	near	가까운	가까이
right	옳은, 오른쪽의	바로, 정확히	most	대부분의	가장
well	건강한	잘	enough	충분한	충분히

He made the **right** decision by investing in the new project.
그는 새로운 프로젝트에 투자함으로써 옳은 결정을 내렸다.

The employee was standing **right** next to the door.
직원은 문 바로 옆에 서 있었다.

We have **enough** time to review the proposal before the meeting.
우리는 회의 전에 제안을 검토할 충분한 시간이 있다.

The report was detailed **enough** to address all the client's concerns.
보고서는 고객의 모든 우려를 해결하기에 충분히 상세했다.

토익 연습문제

1. The company faces a _____ challenge in meeting the growing demand for its products.
   (A) hard
   (B) most
   (C) close
   (D) late

2. The customer service representative responded _____ to resolve the client's issue.
   (A) late
   (B) most
   (C) fast
   (D) high

토익 종합 실전문제

1. The CEO announced the changes _____ to address the concerns raised by employees.
(A) publicly
(B) public
(C) publicity
(D) publicize

2. The team completed the project _____, ahead of the scheduled deadline.
(A) effectively
(B) early
(C) easily
(D) barely

3. The sales figures for this quarter were _____ higher than those of the previous quarter.
(A) significantly
(B) shortly
(C) rarely
(D) hastily

4. She has _____ returned from her business trip and is ready to start the next project.
(A) just
(B) soon
(C) still
(D) yet

5. The report hasn't been submitted _____ because the team is still collecting data.
(A) still
(B) just
(C) already
(D) yet

6. Three years _____, the company faced significant challenges, but it has since recovered remarkably.
(A) just
(B) soon
(C) ago
(D) already

7. The shipment _____ hasn't arrived at the warehouse, which is causing delays in production.
(A) yet
(B) just
(C) still
(D) already

8. The supervisor _____ approves vacation requests during busy seasons.
(A) never
(B) almost
(C) completely
(D) slightly

9. The feedback from the client was _____ helpful in improving the proposal.
(A) sometimes
(B) rarely
(C) very
(D) seldom

10. She could _____ finish the report before the deadline because of constant interruptions.
(A) hardly
(B) occasionally
(C) usually
(D) totally

11. The team leader can _____ provide guidance to junior employees when workloads increase.
(A) almost
(B) seldom
(C) slightly
(D) completely

12. The marketing campaign was highly successful; _____, the company decided to increase its budget for the next quarter.
(A) on the other hand
(B) moreover
(C) accordingly
(D) conversely

13. The factory increased production capacity; _____, the supply chain was unable to meet the growing demand.
(A) in addition
(B) conversely
(C) nonetheless
(D) as a result

14. You must complete the safety training before starting the project; _____, you will not be allowed to participate.
(A) nevertheless
(B) moreover
(C) subsequently
(D) otherwise

15. The team must finalize the presentation today; _____, they will miss the submission deadline.
(A) or else
(B) nonetheless
(C) as a result
(D) therefore

16. The new strategy has proven effective; it reduces costs and increases efficiency _____ .
(A) most
(B) mostly
(C) also
(D) as well

17. The instructions were so unclear that I could _____ understand what to do.
(A) hard
(B) hardly
(C) nearly
(D) carefully

18. The company's policy is designed to reward employees _____ for their contributions to the organization.
(A) highly
(B) justly
(C) hardly
(D) slightly

19. The supervisor monitored the workers _____ to ensure all safety protocols were followed.
(A) closely
(B) close
(C) nearly
(D) most

20. The team worked _____ to meet the tight deadline, showing great determination.
(A) hard
(B) hardly
(C) rarely
(D) nearly

21. She has been _____ praised for her innovative contributions to the project.
(A) slightly
(B) hardly
(C) high
(D) highly

22. The manager spoke clearly _____ to ensure everyone understood the instructions.
(A) enough
(B) hard
(C) near
(D) well

23. The _____ quality of the materials impressed the clients and ensured the success of the project.
(A) late
(B) highly
(C) high
(D) early

24. The technician ensured the equipment was installed _____ according to the safety guidelines.
(A) closely
(B) high
(C) late
(D) right

PART 6

Questions 1-4 refer to the following article.

Improving Workplace Communication

Effective workplace communication is crucial for fostering collaboration and 1________. Clear and concise communication helps employees understand their roles and responsibilities, reducing the risk of misunderstandings. Additionally, providing employees with regular updates on company goals and changes keeps everyone focused and motivated. Managers should also respond 2________ to employee feedback to show that their concerns are valued. Furthermore, organizations should encourage open communication through team meetings and feedback sessions. 3________. When employees feel heard, they are more likely to contribute ideas and express concerns, leading to a more 4________ work environment. To ensure the success of communication initiatives, companies must adopt strategies that are both practical and effective for their unique workplace culture.

1. (A) relaxation
   (B) confusion
   (C) productivity
   (D) retention

2. (A) promptly
   (B) nearly
   (C) fast
   (D) lately

3. (A) Regular updates are crucial for improving workplace morale.
   (B) Clear communication helps employees focus on their tasks.
   (C) This practice ensures transparency and builds trust among team members.
   (D) Employees are encouraged to provide feedback on a regular basis.

4. (A) inclusive
   (B) demanding
   (C) chaotic
   (D) exclusive

PART 7

Questions 1–5 refer to the following job posting and internal email.

Position: Marketing Manager
Location: New York, NY
Company: Apex Innovations

Apex Innovations, a leading technology company, is looking for a highly skilled Marketing Manager to join our team. The ideal candidate will be responsible for developing and executing marketing strategies to promote our new products and increase market share. The successful applicant will collaborate closely with the sales team, product developers, and external partners.

Responsibilities include:

- Creating and managing marketing campaigns
- Analyzing market trends and competitors
- Managing the marketing budget and ensuring a high ROI
- Coordinating with product teams to align marketing strategies with product launches
- Presenting campaign results to senior management

Qualifications:

- Bachelor's degree in marketing or a related field
- 5+ years of marketing experience
- Proven track record of successful marketing campaigns
- Strong communication and leadership skills

To apply, send your resume and cover letter to careers@apexinnovations.com by September 15.

From: James Lee (Marketing Director)
To: Marketing Department
Date: August 5
Subject: Team Meeting – OmegaX Product Launch

Dear Team,

As you all know, our highly anticipated OmegaX smartwatch is set to launch on August 20. I want to ensure that we are fully prepared for a successful release. We will hold a meeting on August 10 at 10:00 AM to finalize the details of the marketing campaign.

Agenda:

- Review current market trends and competitor analysis
- Discuss our marketing strategy for OmegaX
- Finalize the budget and resource allocation
- Assign tasks for the campaign execution

Please come prepared with your ideas on how we can maximize our impact. It's important that we collaborate effectively to make this product launch a success.

Best regards,

James Lee

Marketing Director, Apex Innovations

1. What is the deadline to apply for the Marketing Manager position at Apex Innovations?
   (A) August 10
   (B) August 20
   (C) September 15
   (D) August 5

2. What is one of the responsibilities of the Marketing Manager as listed in the job posting?
   (A) Creating and managing marketing campaigns
   (B) Managing customer service teams
   (C) Overseeing product development
   (D) Designing the OmegaX smartwatch

3. What will be discussed during the meeting on August 10, according to the internal email?
   (A) The hiring process for new employees
   (B) The launch of a new smartwatch
   (C) Product development strategies for next year
   (D) Plans for the OmegaX marketing campaign

4. According to the job posting, what qualification is required for the Marketing Manager position?

(A) A master's degree in business administration

(B) 5+ years of experience in marketing

(C) Previous work at a tech company

(D) Strong graphic design skills

5 How does the internal email relate to the job posting?

(A) It confirms that the OmegaX smartwatch will be delayed.

(B) It highlights the responsibilities of a future Marketing Manager.

(C) It outlines the duties of the current marketing team at Apex Innovations.

(D) It shows that the Marketing Manager role is no longer needed.

Chapter

12

전치사

전치사(Preposition)는 명사, 대명사, 명사구 앞에 위치해 다른 단어와의 관계를 나타내며, 항상 뒤에 목적어를 동반하여 전치사구(prepositional phrase)를 형성한다.

1. 시간(Time) 전치사

시간 전치사는 특정 시간, 기간, 시점 등을 나타낸다.

✔ CheckPoint 1. 시간 전치사의 종류

at	특정 시각, 시점	at 3 p.m., at midnight
on	날짜, 요일, 특정한 날	on Monday, on July 4th, on Christmas Day
in	월, 계절, 연도, 세기, 하루의 특정 부분	in March, in 1990, in the evening
by	~까지 (특정 시점 이전에 완료되는 일회성 행동이나 행위, 기한 강조)	by tomorrow, by next week
until/till	~까지 (특정 시점까지 지속되는 상태나 행동, 지속성 강조)	until midnight, till the end of the year
since	(특정 시점) 이래로, 부터	since 2000, since morning
for	~하는 동안 (숫자 기간)	for two hours, for five years
during	~하는 동안 (특정 기간이나 사건)	during the meeting, during the holiday
within	~이내에	within an hour, within the next two days
throughout	~하는 내내	throughout the year, throughout the day

The client meeting is scheduled **on Tuesday** afternoon.
고객 회의는 화요일 오후로 예정되어 있다.

Employees must complete their training **by next week.**
직원들은 다음 주까지 교육을 완료해야 한다.

The store will be open **until 10 p.m.** every Friday.
이 가게는 매주 금요일 밤 10시까지 영업한다.

All inquiries will be resolved **within 48 hours**.
모든 문의 사항은 48시간 이내에 해결될 것이다.

The company experienced steady growth **throughout the fiscal year**.
그 회사는 회계 연도 내내 꾸준한 성장을 경험했다.

토익 연습문제

1. The library will remain open ________ 9 p.m. on weekdays.
   (A) by
   (B) since
   (C) until
   (D) during

2. The employees have been working on the report __________ three hours without a break.
   (A) during
   (B) since
   (C) for
   (D) until

3. The new policy has been effective __________ January 1st.
   (A) during
   (B) since
   (C) for
   (D) by

2. 장소(Place) 전치사

장소 전치사는 대상의 특정 지점, 위치, 방향 등을 나타낸다.

✔ CheckPoint 2. 장소 전치사의 종류

at	특정 지점, 장소	at the bus stop, at the door
on	표면 위	on the table, on the wall
in	특정 공간 내부	in the room, in the park
over	~위에	over the bed
under	~아래에	under the bridge
above	~위에	above the clouds
below	~아래에	below the surface
near	~근처에	near the station, near the school
next to	~바로 옆에	next to the window
beside	~옆에	beside the bed, beside the road
between	~사이에 (둘 사이)	between the houses
among	~사이에 (셋 이상)	among the students
in front of	~앞에	in front of the building
behind	~뒤에	behind the door, behind the sofa
opposite	~맞은편에	opposite the bank
throughout	~의 전역에	throughout the city

The guest speaker will be seated **next to** the host during the event.
행사 동안 초청 연사는 진행자 바로 옆에 앉을 것이다.

The winner was selected **among** hundreds of talented candidates.
우승자는 수백 명의 재능 있는 지원자들 중에서 선정되었다.

The new branch office is located **opposite** the city park.
새 지점 사무실은 도시 공원 맞은편에 위치해 있습니다.

The new marketing campaign has been promoted **throughout** Asia.
새로운 마케팅 캠페인은 아시아 전역에 걸쳐 홍보되었다.

☞ over와 above의 차이점

over는 물체의 바로 위에 위치하거나 접촉 가능성이 있는 상황, 또는 물체가 표면 위로 움직이거나 덮는 경우에 사용하는 반면, above는 물체와의 접촉 없이, 단순히 더 높은 위치나 고정된 위치를 설명할 때 사용한다.

The company placed a protective cover **over** the new equipment.
회사는 새로운 장비 위에 보호 덮개를 씌웠다.

The company's new logo is displayed **above** the entrance of the building.
회사의 새 로고가 건물 입구 위에 표시되어 있다.

☞ under와 below의 차이점

under는 접촉 가능성, 가림, 지배나 통제를 강조하는 반면, below는 접촉 여부와 상관없이 단순히 더 낮은 위치나 수준을 강조한다.

The documents are **under** the stack of books on the manager's desk.
문서들은 매니저 책상 위 책 더미 아래에 있다.

The maintenance area is located **below** the main production floor.
유지보수 구역은 주요 생산 층 아래에 위치해 있다.

토익 연습문제

1. The promotional posters have been placed __________ the walls of the shopping center.
   (A) on
   (B) in
   (C) over
   (D) across

2. The office building is located __________ the river, offering a beautiful view for employees.
   (A) below
   (B) near
   (C) behind
   (D) under

3. The memorial plaque is mounted __________ the doorway of the museum.
   (A) over
   (B) in
   (C) on
   (D) above

3. 기타 주요 전치사

기타 주요 전치사로 이유, 목적, 양보, 주제, 수단, 제외, 부가 등이 있다.

✔ CheckPoint 3. 기타 주요 전치사의 종류

because of, due to, on account of	~때문에 (이유)
for	~을 위해 (목적, 용도)
despite, in spite of	~에도 불구하고 (양보)
about, concerning, on, regarding	~에 관하여 (주제)
via, by	~을 통해, ~에 의해 (수단)
except (for), without	~을 제외하고 (제외)
besides, in addition to	~외에도, ~에 더하여 (부가)

This tool was developed **for** simplifying the data analysis process.
이 도구는 데이터 분석 과정을 단순화하기 위해 개발되었다.

The presentation was **about** the company's future strategy.
발표는 회사의 미래 전략에 관한 것이었다.

The documents were sent **via** email to ensure quick delivery.
문서는 빠른 전달을 위해 이메일로 발송되었다.

All employees **except for** the interns are required to attend the training session.
인턴을 제외한 모든 직원은 교육 세션에 참석해야 한다.

토익 연습문제

1. The conference was postponed __________ the unexpected weather conditions.
   (A) in spite of
   (B) besides
   (C) because of
   (D) without

2. The training program includes a section __________ handling customer complaints.
   (A) regarding
   (B) because of
   (C) except
   (D) in addition to

3. __________ the unexpected changes in the schedule, the team completed the project on time.
   (A) Except for
   (B) In addition to
   (C) Despite
   (D) Regarding

4. 전치사의 관용표현

✔ CheckPoint 4. 전치사의 관용표현

at a loss	어찌할 바를 몰라
at a low cost	저렴한 가격으로
at no extra charge	추가 비용 없이
at risk	위험에 처한
at stake	위태로운
at work	근무 중
on a regular basis	정기적으로
on behalf of	~을 대신하여
on duty	근무 중
on purpose	고의로
on time	제시간에
in a timely manner	시기적절하게
in advance	미리, 사전에
in charge of	~을 담당하여
in favor of	~에 찬성하여
in progress	진행 중
by chance	우연히
by means of	~을 통해, ~을 수단으로
by mistake	실수로
with regard to	~에 관하여
with respect to	~에 관하여
with the help of	~의 도움으로
out of order	고장 난
out of stock	품절된
under control	통제된
without fail	반드시
beyond doubt	의심의 여지없이
across the board	전반적으로

The new system upgrade is provided **at no extra charge.**
새로운 시스템 업그레이드는 추가 비용 없이 제공된다.

The team meets **on a regular basis** to discuss project updates.
팀은 프로젝트 업데이트를 논의하기 위해 정기적으로 회의를 한다.

The proposal must be submitted **in a timely manner** for the project.
제안서는 프로젝트를 위해 시기적절하게 제출되어야 한다.

The manager is **in charge of** organizing the annual company retreat.
매니저는 연례 회사 야유회를 조직하는 것을 담당하고 있다.
The new product is currently **out of stock** due to high demand.
새 제품은 높은 수요로 인해 현재 품절되었다.

토익 연습문제

1. The factory's production process is currently __________ and will resume next week.
   (A) out of order
   (B) under control
   (C) out of stock
   (D) beyond doubt

2. The team leader is __________ coordinating the logistics for the upcoming event.
   (A) by chance
   (B) in favor of
   (C) at a loss
   (D) in charge of

3. The technician was able to repair the machine __________ the proper tools and equipment.
   (A) at a loss
   (B) with the help of
   (C) on duty
   (D) beyond doubt

토익 종합 실전문제

1. Employees must submit their reports __________ Friday at noon.
   (A) by
   (B) until
   (C) during
   (D) for

2. The company has experienced remarkable growth __________ the past five years.
   (A) during
   (B) since
   (C) within
   (D) for

3. All customer complaints will be addressed __________ 36 hours of submission.
   (A) until
   (B) by
   (C) within
   (D) for

4. The product has been in development __________ two years and is expected to launch this quarter.
   (A) within
   (B) for
   (C) during
   (D) since

5. The announcement has been delayed __________ further notice.
   (A) by
   (B) during
   (C) since
   (D) until

6. The employees have not received updates __________ the meeting was postponed last week.
   (A) during
   (B) until
   (C) since
   (D) by

7. The new shopping mall is being constructed __________ the city skyline, visible from miles away.
   (A) on
   (B) above
   (C) in
   (D) near

8. The team is seated __________ the conference table to discuss the new project proposal.
   (A) near
   (B) in front of
   (C) at
   (D) next to

9. The meeting room is located __________ the CEO's office and the main conference hall.
(A) among
(B) beside
(C) between
(D) near

10. The parking area is located __________ the office building for employees' convenience.
(A) above
(B) below
(C) on
(D) among

11. The security cameras are installed __________ the corners of the parking lot.
(A) on
(B) in
(C) below
(D) throughout

12. The manager praised the team __________ their outstanding performance during the project.
(A) on account of
(B) without
(C) except
(D) despite

13. The new policy was implemented __________ improving employee productivity.
(A) for
(B) in addition to
(C) in spite of
(D) about

14. The team successfully completed the project __________ the limited resources available.
(A) about
(B) in spite of
(C) via
(D) except

15. All employees are required to attend the meeting __________ the newly announced guidelines.
(A) via
(B) concerning
(C) despite
(D) beside

16. The final report was prepared __________ the manager's specific instructions.
(A) about
(B) except for
(C) in
(D) via

17. __________ the keynote speaker, all attendees are expected to arrive 30 minutes early.
(A) Without
(B) Except for
(C) Concerning
(D) About

18. __________ his excellent academic performance, the candidate also has extensive work experience.
(A) In addition to
(B) Except for
(C) Because of
(D) Regarding

19. The equipment will be replaced __________ to the customer.
(A) on time
(B) at no extra charge
(C) in advance
(D) under control

20. The company conducts performance evaluations __________ to ensure consistent employee development.
(A) on purpose
(B) on duty
(C) on a regular basis
(D) on time

21. The meeting room has been reserved __________ to accommodate all participants.
(A) in charge of
(B) on purpose
(C) in advance
(D) on duty

22. The company was able to secure the contract __________ their innovative approach to the project.
(A) with regard to
(B) in progress
(C) at a loss
(D) by means of

23. Customer inquiries must be addressed __________ to maintain satisfaction.
(A) in a timely manner
(B) at a low cost
(C) by chance
(D) under control

24. The safety protocols were revised __________ recent changes in government regulations.
(A) with respect to
(B) without fail
(C) on purpose
(D) out of the question

PART 6

Questions 1-4 refer to the following letter.

Dear Team,

I am writing to inform you about recent updates to the employee handbook, which will take effect starting next month. These changes are aimed at improving our workplace policies and ensuring a more supportive environment for everyone.
First, adjustments have been made to the vacation policy. Employees are now encouraged to submit their requests for time off at least two weeks 1________ to help managers plan schedules more effectively.
Second, 2________. The handbook outlines clear expectations for employees working from home, including availability hours and regular check-ins with supervisors.
Lastly, please take note of the updated section 3________ workplace safety protocols. All employees are required to review these updates and acknowledge them by signing the 4________ form.
Should you have any questions about the changes, feel free to reach out to your department head or the HR team. Thank you for your cooperation as we continue striving for a positive and productive work environment.

Sincerely,
Alex Johnson
HR Manager

1. (A) on time
   (B) in detail
   (C) in advance
   (D) by tomorrow

2. (A) adjustments are needed for the current vacation policy
   (B) a new section has been added to address remote work guidelines
   (C) additional benefits for remote workers have been announced
   (D) the remote work policy remains unchanged

3. (A) on
   (B) in
   (C) of
   (D) with

4. (A) accompanying
   (B) affixed
   (C) attached
   (D) limited

PART 7

Questions 1-5 refer to the following email, notice, and schedule.

To: All Employees
From: HR Department
Subject: Upcoming Training Session
Date: May 15

Dear Team,

We are pleased to announce that a mandatory training session on "Workplace Communication and Conflict Resolution" will be held next Friday in the main conference room. The training is part of our continuous effort to enhance teamwork and productivity across departments.

Details:

- Date: Next Friday
- Time: 10:00 AM - 1:00 PM
- Location: Main Conference Room

Please ensure that you attend this session, as it is a key component of our professional development program. If you have any scheduling conflicts, kindly inform your supervisor and the HR Department by the end of this week.
Thank you for your cooperation.

Best regards,
HR Department

Please be advised that the following maintenance work is scheduled for the conference facilities:

- **Main Conference Room:** Closed for technical checks from 6:00 PM on Thursday to 8:00 AM on Friday.
- **Small Conference Rooms (A & B):** Closed for repainting from Wednesday to Friday afternoon.

We apologize for any inconvenience this may cause and appreciate your understanding.

For urgent inquiries, please contact the Facilities Department at extension 1023.

Facilities Department

Weekly Conference Room Schedule

Day	Time	Room	Event	Notes
Thursday	3:00 PM	Small Conference A	Marketing Team Meeting	Ends at 5:30 PM
Friday	10:00 AM	Main Conference Room	Workplace Communication Training	Scheduled by HR Department
Friday	2:00 PM	Small Conference B	Project Kickoff Meeting	Check availability due to maintenance

1. What is the primary purpose of the email from the HR Department?
   (A) To provide details about a new workplace policy
   (B) To inform employees about a required training session
   (C) To request feedback on a recent event
   (D) To announce changes to the conference room schedule

2. According to the notice, what time will the Main Conference Room be available again after maintenance?
   (A) 8:00 AM on Friday
   (B) 10:00 AM on Friday
   (C) 1:00 PM on Thursday
   (D) 6:00 PM on Wednesday

3. Which event is directly affected by the maintenance schedule?
   (A) Marketing Team Meeting
   (B) HR Department Briefing
   (C) Workplace Communication Training
   (D) Project Kickoff Meeting

4. Why are employees asked to inform their supervisors by the end of this week?
   (A) To confirm their attendance at the training session
   (B) To report any issues with the conference room schedule
   (C) To reschedule missed events due to maintenance
   (D) To discuss workplace communication policies

5. What can be inferred about the Facilities Department?
   (A) They are responsible for organizing training sessions.
   (B) They prioritize technical checks over other tasks.
   (C) They handle inquiries about conference room maintenance.
   (D) They schedule weekly meetings in the Main Conference Room.

Chapter

13

형용사절

형용사절은 문장에서 명사나 대명사를 수식하여, 그 의미를 구체화하거나 추가적인 정보를 제공한다. 주로 관계대명사(who, whom, whose, which, that)나 관계부사(when, where, why)로 시작하며, 수식하는 명사의 뒤에 위치한다.

1. 관계대명사(Relative Pronouns)

관계대명사는 접속사와 대명사 역할을 동시에 하고, 일반적으로 불완전한 절이 뒤따른다. 관계대명사가 절의 주어로 사용되면 생략할 수 없지만, 목적어로 사용되면 생략할 수 있다.

✔ CheckPoint 1. 관계대명사의 종류

선행사	주격	목적격	소유격
사람	who	whom(who)	whose
사물	which	which	whose / of which
사람/사물/동물	that	that	-

The employee is very competent. + **The employee(주격)** was promoted last week.

⇒ **The employee** **who/that S** was promoted last week is very competent.

지난주에 승진한 직원은 매우 유능하다.

The candidate has extensive experience. + The company hired **the candidate(목적격)**.

⇒ **The candidate** **(whom/that)** the company hired **O** has extensive experience.

회사가 채용한 후보자는 광범위한 경험을 가지고 있다.

토익 연습문제

1. The strategy __________ was implemented helped increase productivity.
   (A) which
   (B) who
   (C) whose
   (D) whom

2. The employee __________ team achieved the highest sales will receive a bonus.
   (A) which
   (B) whose
   (C) who
   (D) whom

✔ CheckPoint 2. 관계대명사의 생략

▶ 선행사 + (주격 관계대명사 + be동사) + 형용사/ 현재분사/ 과거분사/ 전치사구 구조에서 주격 관계대명사와 be동사를 생략하여 형용사절을 더 간단하고 자연스럽게 표현할 수 있다.

The employee (who/that is) **responsible** for the project will attend the meeting.
프로젝트를 담당하는 직원이 회의에 참석할 것이다.

The woman (who/that is) **talking** to the manager is the new employee.
매니저와 이야기하고 있는 여자가 새로운 직원이다.

The documents (that/which are) **required** for the meeting should be submitted by tomorrow.
회의에 필요한 문서들은 내일까지 제출되어야 한다.

The documents (that/which are) **on the desk** need to be reviewed.
책상 위에 있는 문서들은 검토될 필요가 있다.

토익 연습문제

1. The car __________ parked outside belongs to the CEO.
   (A) that is
   (B) who
   (C) which
   (D) is

2. The engineer __________ the new software is very talented.
   (A) was designing
   (B) designed
   (C) designs
   (D) designing

3. The product __________ last year has been a great success.
   (A) launches
   (B) launching
   (C) launched
   (D) was launching

✔ CheckPoint 3. 전치사 + 관계대명사

▶ 전치사 + 관계대명사 구조는 공식적이고 격식을 차린 문장에서 사용되고, 관계대명사는 주로 whom(사람)이나 which(사물 또는 동물)를 사용한다.

▶ 이 구조는 전치사가 문장 끝에 오는 것을 피하거나, 문장 흐름을 더 자연스럽게 만들기 위해 사용된다.

The consultant provided detailed solutions. + We worked with **the consultant(목적격)**.

⇒ **The consultant** <u>**whom/that** we worked **with O**</u> provided detailed solutions.

⇒ **The consultant** <u>**with whom** we worked</u> provided detailed solutions.

우리가 함께 일한 컨설턴트가 상세한 해결책을 제시했다.

토익 연습문제

1. The company __________ I work is a global leader.
   (A) by which
   (B) for which
   (C) to which
   (D) with which

2. The foundation __________ the funds were received is renowned for its charitable work.
   (A) from which
   (B) to which
   (C) by which
   (D) with which

3. The conference __________ the new product was launched attracted a lot of media attention.
   (A) with which
   (B) on which
   (C) by which
   (D) at which

✔ CheckPoint 4. 관계대명사 that의 용례

▶ 사람, 사물, 동물이 선행사일 때 사용한다.
▶ 최상급, 서수, the only, the very 등 강조 표현이 오면 사용한다.
▶ 전치사와 함께 사용할 수 없으므로 which나 whom을 대신 사용한다.
▶ 쉼표(,)가 있는 계속적(비제한적) 용법에서 사용할 수 없으므로 which나 who를 대신 사용한다.
▶ 소유격으로 사용할 수 없으므로 whose를 대신 사용한다.

The customer that provided feedback received a prompt response.
피드백을 제공한 고객이 신속한 응답을 받았다.

This is **the most** effective strategy **that** we have ever implemented.
이것이 우리가 실행한 가장 효과적인 전략이다.

The conference **to which** I was invited will be held next week.
내가 초대받은 회의는 다음 주에 열릴 것이다.

The project, **which** was completed ahead of schedule, received praise.
예정보다 일찍 완공된 프로젝트는 칭찬을 받았다.

The company **whose** profits increased is investing in new markets.
수익이 증가한 회사가 새로운 시장에 투자하고 있다.

토익 연습문제

1. This is the only solution __________ can effectively address the current issue.
   (A) who
   (B) whom
   (C) that
   (D) whose

2. The proposal, __________ was approved by the board, includes innovative strategies for growth.
   (A) that
   (B) which
   (C) whose
   (D) what

2. 관계부사(Relative Adverbs)

관계부사는 접속사와 부사 역할을 동시에 하고, 일반적으로 완전한 절이 뒤따른다.

✔ CheckPoint 5. 관계부사의 종류

선행사	관계부사
장소 (the place, the restaurant)	where
시간 (the year, the moment)	when
이유 (the reason)	why
방법 (the way)	how

☞ The way 뒤에는 how를 함께 쓸 수 없으므로 that 또는 접속사 없이 문장을 연결하는 것이 일반적이다.

This is **the place where** the meeting will be held.
여기가 회의가 열릴 장소이다.
He couldn't forget **the moment when** he received the award.
그는 상을 받았던 순간을 잊을 수 없었다.
The reason why the project was delayed was due to technical issues.
프로젝트가 지연된 이유는 기술적인 문제 때문이었다.
She explained **the way (that)** the company handles customer complaints.
그녀는 회사가 고객 불만을 처리하는 방법을 설명했다.

토익 연습문제

1. The city __________ the conference will be held has excellent transportation options.
   (A) where
   (B) when
   (C) that
   (D) why

2. The reason __________ the project was delayed was due to technical issues.
   (A) when
   (B) where
   (C) why
   (D) how

토익 종합 실전문제

1. The company implemented a strategy __________ was recommended by the consultant.
(A) that
(B) what
(C) when
(D) where

2. The scientist __________ theory changed the course of history was awarded the Nobel Prize.
(A) that
(B) which
(C) whose
(D) who

3. The employee __________ the manager assigned to lead the project demonstrated exceptional organizational skills.
(A) which
(B) whose
(C) who
(D) whom

4. The company, __________ the headquarters are located in New York, is expanding internationally.
(A) that
(B) of which
(C) which
(D) whose

5. The proposal __________ to the success of the project should be discussed first.
(A) important
(B) importantly
(C) importance
(D) most importantly

6. The building __________ in the center of the city is a historical landmark.
(A) locating
(B) located
(C) location
(D) was located

7. The documents __________ on the manager's desk must be reviewed by the end of the day.
(A) are
(B) placing
(C) placed
(D) place

8. The employee __________ responsible for overseeing the project will lead the meeting.
(A) will be
(B) is
(C) who is
(D) which is

9. The equipment __________ during the renovation has been moved to a secure location.
(A) is stored
(B) which stores
(C) storing
(D) stored

10. The policy __________ the company operates is strict but fair.
(A) in which
(B) with which
(C) under which
(D) for which

11. The project __________ they are collaborating is very ambitious.
(A) for which
(B) in which
(C) by which
(D) on which

12. The person __________ I sent the email has not replied yet.
(A) for whom
(B) of whom
(C) with whom
(D) to whom

13. The partnership __________ the company has been involved proved to be highly beneficial.
(A) for which
(B) with which
(C) in which
(D) by which

14. The regulations __________ all employees must adhere are quite strict.
(A) to which
(B) by which
(C) with which
(D) under which

15. The award, __________ was presented during the ceremony, recognized the team's outstanding achievements.
(A) that
(B) who
(C) which
(D) whose

16. The team developed the most efficient system __________ has ever been created in this industry.
(A) who
(B) that
(C) which
(D) whose

17. The report __________ findings were disputed by the committee needs to be revised.
(A) who
(B) that
(C) whose
(D) which

18. The employee, __________ was promoted last month, has taken on new responsibilities.
(A) that
(B) which
(C) who
(D) whom

19. The event, __________ was attended by hundreds of people, was a great success.
(A) where
(B) that
(C) who
(D) which

20. This is the very first project __________ has been completed ahead of schedule.
(A) who
(B) which
(C) that
(D) whose

21. The factory __________ the product was manufactured has received international certification.
(A) where
(B) which
(C) when
(D) that

22. The way __________ the experiment was conducted surprised the committee.
(A) how
(B) that
(C) which
(D) why

23. The day __________ the company was founded is celebrated annually.
(A) where
(B) that
(C) when
(D) how

24. The office __________ the CEO held the meeting has been newly renovated.
(A) that
(B) which
(C) where
(D) when

PART 6

Questions 1–4 refer to the following memo.

Dear Team,

In our continued effort to improve workplace productivity, we are implementing strategies that will create a more efficient work environment. These strategies include providing tools and resources which employees can use to enhance their daily tasks. The training sessions, 1________ were 2________ praised by last year's participants, will now be available online for greater accessibility. Employees who complete these sessions successfully will receive 3________ to acknowledge their achievements. Moreover, the management team, whose primary goal is to support all staff members, will host regular meetings to address concerns and gather feedback. 4________.

Thank you for your dedication and hard work. Together, we can achieve our company's goals.

Best regards,
HR Department

1. (A) which
   (B) that
   (C) when
   (D) who

2. (A) moderately
   (B) rarely
   (C) highly
   (D) barely

3. (A) recognition
   (B) certifications
   (C) awards
   (D) promotions

4. (A) Feedback from managers will help prioritize future training sessions.
   (B) Your input, which we value greatly, will be instrumental in making these initiatives successful.
   (C) The strategies will be assessed for further improvement next quarter.
   (D) Employees are encouraged to attend meetings to share their concerns.

PART 7

Questions 1–5 refer to the following article and notice.

Title: The Growth of Electric Vehicles and a Greener Future
Date: September 18, 2024
Source: Sustainable Transportation Journal

The automotive industry is rapidly shifting toward sustainability as electric vehicles (EVs) gain traction globally. Many governments support this shift through incentives for buyers and investment in charging station networks. According to the International Energy Association (IEA), the number of EVs on the road could surpass 145 million by 2030.

EVs provide significant environmental advantages and deliver a quieter, smoother driving experience compared to gasoline-powered cars. Manufacturers are focusing on enhancing battery technologies to improve driving ranges and minimize charging times.

Despite their benefits, EVs face challenges such as high initial costs, limited charging infrastructure, and shorter driving ranges. However, with continuous technological advancements, these obstacles are expected to lessen, solidifying EVs' role in future transportation.

Subject: Launch of New Electric Vehicle Charging Stations
From: Local City Council
Date: September 20, 2024

The City Council is pleased to announce the installation of 10 new EV charging stations in the central parking lot. This project aligns with our goal of advancing clean energy solutions and supporting sustainable transportation.

These stations, which will be available from October 1, 2024, are equipped with fast-charging technology, enabling most EVs to reach 80% battery capacity within 30 minutes. By adding these facilities, we aim to encourage more residents to transition to EVs, thereby reducing the city's overall carbon emissions.

For additional details on station locations and usage, visit our website or email us at contact@citycouncil.org.

1. According to the article, what is one benefit of electric vehicles?
   (A) They have unlimited driving range
   (B) They offer a smoother and quieter driving experience
   (C) They are cheaper than gasoline-powered cars
   (D) They can be charged in less than 10 minutes

2. What challenge is mentioned in the article regarding the adoption of electric vehicles?
   (A) High cost of charging stations
   (B) Difficulty in maintaining electric vehicles
   (C) Lack of government support
   (D) Limited availability of charging stations

3. When will the new charging stations in the city center become operational?
   (A) September 18, 2024
   (B) September 20, 2024
   (C) October 1, 2024
   (D) October 15, 2024

4. What is the purpose of the notice from the City Council?
   (A) To announce the ban on gasoline-powered cars in the city
   (B) To provide information about new EV charging stations
   (C) To promote discounts for electric vehicle buyers
   (D) To explain recent changes to city parking policies

5. What feature of the new charging stations is emphasized in the notice?
   (A) Free usage for residents
   (B) Ability to fully charge in under 15 minutes
   (C) Fast-charging technology capable of reaching 80% capacity in 30 minutes
   (D) Compatibility with both EVs and hybrid cars

Chapter

14

부사절

부사절은 문장에서 주로 동사, 형용사, 또는 다른 부사를 수식하며, 부사절 접속사 + 주어 + 동사 형태로 구성된다. 또한, 문장의 앞, 중간, 또는 끝 어디에나 위치할 수 있다.

1. 부사절 접속사의 종류

부사절 접속사에는 시간, 조건, 양보, 이유, 목적, 결과 등이 있다.

✔ CheckPoint 1. 시간의 부사절 접속사

when	~할 때	since	~한 이래로
while	~하는 동안	until	~할 때까지
as	~할 때, ~하면서	as soon as	~하자마자
before	~하기 전에	once	일단 ~하면
after	~한 후에		

When the manager arrives, we will begin the discussion.
매니저가 도착할 때, 우리는 논의를 시작할 것이다.
Since the company launched the new product, sales have doubled.
회사가 신제품을 출시한 이후로, 매출이 두 배로 증가했다.
The office will remain closed **until** the maintenance work is finished.
유지 보수 작업이 끝날 때까지 사무실은 계속 닫혀 있을 것이다.
Once you sign the contract, the project will officially begin.
일단 계약서에 서명하면, 프로젝트가 공식적으로 시작될 것이다.

토익 연습문제

1. The CEO will announce the new policy changes __________ the board meeting concludes.
   (A) while
   (B) after
   (C) before
   (D) since

2. You should save your work frequently __________ the system crashes unexpectedly.
   (A) until
   (B) when
   (C) before
   (D) as

✔ CheckPoint 2. 조건의 부사절 접속사

if	만약 ~하면	unless (= if ~ not)	만약 ~하지 않으면
as long as	~하는 한	provided (that)	~라는 조건에서
providing	~라는 조건에서	on condition that	~라는 조건에서
in case (that)	~할 경우에 대비하여	in the event (that)	~할 경우에 대비하여

You can access the file **as long as** you have the correct password.
올바른 비밀번호가 있는 한, 파일에 접근할 수 있다.

Providing you meet the qualifications, you will be considered for the position.
자격을 충족하는 조건에서, 그 직책에 고려될 것이다.

The contract will be valid **on condition that** both parties sign it.
양 당사자가 서명하는 조건에서 그 계약은 유효할 것이다.

In case that it rains tomorrow, the outdoor event will be moved indoors.
내일 비가 올 경우(에 대비하여), 야외 행사는 실내로 옮겨질 것이다.

토익 연습문제

1. The employees will receive their annual bonus __________ the company meets its sales target.
   (A) unless
   (B) if
   (C) because
   (D) as long as

2. You cannot enter the secured area __________ you have proper authorization.
   (A) unless
   (B) if
   (C) without
   (D) even if

3. The contract will only be valid __________ both parties agree to the terms.
   (A) in the event that
   (B) as
   (C) providing
   (D) until

✔ CheckPoint 3. 양보의 부사절 접속사: 주절과 역접 및 대조 관계

though	비록 ~일지라도	although	비록 ~일지라도
even if	비록 ~일지라도	even though	비록 ~일지라도
while	~인 반면에, ~이긴 하지만	whereas	~인 반면에

☞ 역접 관계: although, though, even though, even if, while

대조 관계: while, whereas

☞ Even though와 Even if의 차이점

Even though	Even if
실제 상황	가정적 상황
"비록 ~일지라도"	"비록 ~일지라도"
이미 일어난 사실이나 현재 상황	일어나지 않았거나 가정된 상황

Even if the weather is bad, the conference will be held as scheduled.
비록 날씨가 나쁘더라도, 회의는 예정대로 열릴 것이다.

The company increased its marketing budget **even though** sales remained steady.
비록 매출이 안정적이었지만 회사는 마케팅 예산을 늘렸다.

While the new system is more efficient, it requires extensive training for staff.
새 시스템이 더 효율적이긴 하지만, 직원들에게 광범위한 교육이 필요하다.

Whereas some employees prefer remote work, others find it less productive.
일부 직원들이 재택근무를 선호하는 반면에, 다른 직원들은 그것이 덜 생산적이라고 느낀다.

토익 연습문제

1. __________ the new policy improved efficiency, it also caused some confusion among employees.
   (A) Because
   (B) While
   (C) Even if
   (D) Unless

2. The product launch was successful __________ initial reviews were mixed.
   (A) whereas
   (B) while
   (C) when
   (D) even though

✔ CheckPoint 4. 이유의 부사절 접속사: 주절과 인과 관계

because	~때문에	as	~때문에
since	~때문에	now that	~이므로
in that	~이라는 점에서		

Because the client requested changes, the project deadline has been extended.
고객이 변경을 요청했기 때문에, 프로젝트 마감일이 연장되었다.

We decided to close the store early **since** most customers had already left.
대부분의 고객이 이미 떠났기 때문에 우리는 매장을 일찍 닫기로 결정했다.

Now that the training is complete, employees are ready to use the new system.
이제 교육이 완료되었으므로, 직원들은 새로운 시스템을 사용할 준비가 되었다.

The idea is brilliant **in that** it solves multiple problems at once.
그 아이디어는 여러 문제를 한 번에 해결한다는 점에서 훌륭하다.

토익 연습문제

1. The meeting was delayed __________ the manager was stuck in traffic.
   (A) as
   (B) even if
   (C) unless
   (D) in that

2. The team is more motivated __________ they received positive feedback from the manager.
   (A) now that
   (B) whereas
   (C) when
   (D) although

3. We need to revise the proposal __________ the client has requested additional changes.
   (A) even if
   (B) since
   (C) while
   (D) unless

✔ CheckPoint 5. 목적의 부사절 접속사

(so) that	~하기 위해서	in order that	~하기 위해서

The meeting was rescheduled **so that** all team members could attend.
모든 팀원들이 참석할 수 있도록 회의가 재조정되었다.
The company provided training **in order that** employees could improve their skills.
회사는 직원들이 기술을 향상시킬 수 있도록 교육을 제공했다.

토익 연습문제

1. The instructions were simplified __________ all users could understand them easily.
   (A) when
   (B) although
   (C) as long as
   (D) in order that

2. The company hired additional staff __________ it could meet the increased demand.
   (A) while
   (B) so that
   (C) because
   (D) unless

3. The company launched a marketing campaign __________ it could attract more customers.
   (A) although
   (B) while
   (C) in order that
   (D) unless

✔ CheckPoint 6. 결과의 부사절 접속사

so ~ that	너무 ~해서 ~하다	such ~ that	너무 ~해서 ~하다

The project was **so complex that it took several months to complete.**
그 프로젝트는 너무 복잡해서 완성하는 데 몇 달이 걸렸다.
The company faced **such a significant loss that it had to downsize its workforce.**
회사는 너무 큰 손실을 겪어서 직원을 감축해야 했다.

토익 연습문제

1. The product design was so innovative __________ it won several awards.
   (A) while
   (B) unless
   (C) that
   (D) because

2. It was such a successful campaign __________ the company decided to expand it to other markets.
   (A) if
   (B) that
   (C) because
   (D) when

3. The schedule was __________ a mess that the team had to reorganize the entire plan.
   (A) so
   (B) because
   (C) when
   (D) such

2. 부사절 접속사와 전치사

부사절 접속사 뒤에는 주어와 동사로 구성된 완전한 절이 오고, 전치사 뒤에는 명사나 동명사가 온다.

✔ CheckPoint 7. 부사절 접속사와 전치사의 유형

유형	부사절 접속사	의미	전치사	의미
시간	after	~한 후에	after	~한 후에
	while	~하는 동안	during, for	~하는 동안
	before	~하기 전에	before, prior to	~하기 전에
	since	~한 이래로	since	~한 이래로
	until	~할 때까지	until	~할 때까지
조건	in case that, in the event that	~할 경우에 대비하여	in case of, in the event of	~할 경우에 대비하여
	unless	만약 ~하지 않으면	without	~없다면
양보	although, even though	비록 ~일지라도	despite, in spite of	~에도 불구하고
이유	because, as, since	~때문에	because of, due to	~때문에
목적	(so) that, in order that	~하기 위해서	for the purpose of	~하기 위해서

Unless you complete the required training, you cannot start the project.
필수 교육을 이수하지 않으면 프로젝트를 시작할 수 없다.

The project cannot proceed **without proper approval.**
적절한 승인이 없으면 프로젝트를 진행할 수 없다.

Although the deadline was tight, the team completed the project on time.
기한이 촉박했음에도 불구하고 팀은 프로젝트를 제시간에 완료했다.

The team completed the project on time **despite the tight deadline.**
기한이 촉박했음에도 불구하고 팀은 프로젝트를 제시간에 완료했다.

토익 연습문제

1. __________ you complete the required training, you cannot start the project.
   (A) While
   (B) Unless
   (C) Because
   (D) During

2. The shipment was delayed __________ the severe weather conditions.
   (A) without
   (B) due to
   (C) before
   (D) in case of

3. The fire alarm will activate automatically __________ an emergency.
   (A) due to
   (B) in case of
   (C) until
   (D) prior to

3. 복합 관계부사

✔ CheckPoint 8. 복합 관계부사

▶ 관계부사 + ever 형태로, 뒤에 완전한 절이 온다.

▶ 부사절을 이끌고 시간, 장소, 방법을 나타낸다.

복합 관계부사	해석
Whenever	언제든지, ~할 때마다
Wherever	어디든지, 어디를 가든지
However	어떻게든지, 아무리 ~해도

You can submit your report **whenever it is ready.**
보고서가 준비되면 언제든지 제출하면 된다.

Wherever the company opens a branch, it quickly attracts local customers.
회사가 지점을 어디에 열든지, 빠르게 지역 고객을 유치한다.

However you approach the problem, ensure that you follow the guidelines.
문제에 어떻게 접근하든지, 지침을 따르도록 하세요.

However difficult the task may seem, it is important to stay focused.
그 작업이 아무리 어려워 보일지라도, 집중하는 것이 중요하다.

토익 연습문제

1. __________ the employees go on a business trip, they must submit a detailed report afterward.
   (A) Whenever
   (B) Wherever
   (C) However
   (D) Whatever

2. __________ the company expands its operations, it always adheres to local regulations.
   (A) Wherever
   (B) Whenever
   (C) However
   (D) Whatever

토익 종합 실전문제

1. The report will not be finalized __________ all team members have reviewed it thoroughly.
(A) until
(B) as
(C) once
(D) after

2. The team will finalize the budget proposal __________ all stakeholders have provided their feedback.
(A) while
(B) once
(C) before
(D) since

3. __________ the deadline approaches, the team is working overtime to complete the project.
(A) While
(B) After
(C) As
(D) Once

4. The employees left the office early __________ they finished all their tasks.
(A) while
(B) as soon as
(C) before
(D) since

5. __________ the manager was explaining the new procedures, some employees were taking notes.
(A) Before
(B) As soon as
(C) Since
(D) While

6. You can access the company database __________ you have the proper login credentials.
(A) unless
(B) as long as
(C) before
(D) since

7. __________ you have any questions, feel free to contact our customer support team.
(A) Unless
(B) Whenever
(C) As long as
(D) In case

8. The system will not process your payment __________ you provide all the required information.
(A) unless
(B) if
(C) as long as
(D) when

9. Employees are allowed to work flexible hours __________ their tasks are completed on time.
(A) unless
(B) provided that
(C) before
(D) while

10. The team managed to complete the project on time __________ they faced several unexpected obstacles.
(A) because
(B) unless
(C) though
(D) while

11. We will proceed with the launch __________ the market conditions remain uncertain.
(A) while
(B) unless
(C) even if
(D) because

12. The old system was faster, __________ the new system is more user-friendly.
(A) if
(B) even though
(C) unless
(D) whereas

13. The new policy improved customer satisfaction, __________ it increased operational costs.
(A) if
(B) unless
(C) while
(D) because

14. The company decided to proceed with the merger __________ some shareholders expressed concerns.
(A) because
(B) even though
(C) unless
(D) while

15. The new employees are adapting quickly __________ the training program was well-structured.
(A) though
(B) while
(C) because
(D) even if

16. The report is highly informative __________ it includes detailed data and thorough analysis.
(A) in the event that
(B) whereas
(C) as long as
(D) in that

17. The safety briefing will be conducted __________ the factory tour.

(A) because of
(B) in spite of
(C) prior to
(D) without

18. Employees are required to follow the safety procedures __________ a power outage.

(A) because of
(B) during
(C) for the purpose of
(D) in the event of

19. __________ the client requested several changes, the deadline was extended.

(A) Before
(B) In case
(C) Since
(D) Despite

20. The manager approved the proposal __________ several flaws in the report.

(A) due to
(B) in case of
(C) because of
(D) despite

21. The event will proceed __________ no major disruptions occur.

(A) unless
(B) without
(C) if
(D) in case of

22. The team should be ready to adapt __________ the market conditions change.

(A) however
(B) wherever
(C) whenever
(D) whatever

23. __________ challenging the project may be, we are confident in our ability to complete it.

(A) Wherever
(B) Whenever
(C) However
(D) Whatever

24. The company provides consistent service quality __________ its branches are located.

(A) whenever
(B) wherever
(C) however
(D) whatever

PART 6

Questions 1–4 refer to the following notice.

Dear Employees,

This is to inform you that the office will be undergoing renovations next month. Since the work will involve heavy machinery, there may be noise and disruptions during work hours. Although we aim to minimize the inconvenience, we ask for your understanding and 1________ throughout this process.

Additionally, 2________. 3________ you need a quieter environment, please feel free to use the meeting rooms, which will be open for personal use temporarily.

We will provide regular updates 4________ the renovation schedule so that you can plan your work accordingly. If you have any concerns or suggestions, do not hesitate to contact the HR department.

Thank you for your patience and understanding.

Sincerely,
John Smith
Office Manager

1. (A) cooperation
   (B) disruption
   (C) application
   (D) explanation

2. (A) we recommend that you use headphones if you need to focus on your tasks
   (B) the renovations will conclude in two months
   (C) temporary workstations will be set up in the cafeteria
   (D) all employees are encouraged to work remotely

3. (A) Whenever
   (B) Because
   (C) Despite
   (D) In case

4. (A) with
   (B) for
   (C) on
   (D) to

PART 7

Questions 1−5 refer to the following memo and survey results.

To: All Department Heads
From: Susan Carter, Operations Manager
Date: March 15
Subject: Office Space Reorganization

Dear Team,

Starting next month, we will begin the reorganization of office spaces to accommodate the growing number of staff and improve workflow efficiency. This will involve reallocating desks, updating shared work areas, and introducing a hot-desking policy for flexible seating.

Key Dates:

- March 20: Distribution of preliminary seating plans
- March 25: Submission deadline for feedback from team leaders
- April 1-5: Implementation of changes

Please ensure that your team members are informed and provide their input on the preliminary seating arrangements. We value your feedback to ensure the changes work effectively for everyone.
If you have any questions, feel free to contact me directly.

Best regards,
Susan Carter
Operations Manager

Office Reorganization Feedback:

The recent employee survey provided insights into the planned office reorganization. About 70% of employees supported the hot-desking policy, citing its flexibility and potential to enhance collaboration. Additionally, 55% of respondents preferred more shared meeting spaces over individual desks, emphasizing the importance of areas that foster teamwork and communication.

Key concerns included the loss of privacy in a shared workspace and the need for additional personal storage, such as lockers. While the feedback highlights overall support, addressing these concerns will be essential for a smooth transition.

1. What is the purpose of the memo?
   (A) To inform staff about upcoming office reorganization
   (B) To share survey results with department heads
   (C) To announce a new employee benefits program
   (D) To propose changes to the company's policies

2. When are team leaders expected to submit feedback?
   (A) March 20
   (B) March 25
   (C) April 1
   (D) April 5

3. According to the survey, what was a major concern regarding the reorganization?
   (A) Lack of collaboration opportunities
   (B) Limited availability of meeting spaces
   (C) High costs associated with the changes
   (D) Reduced privacy in shared workspaces

4. What percentage of employees supported the hot-desking policy?
   (A) 55%
   (B) 60%
   (C) 70%
   (D) 75%

5. What will happen between April 1 and April 5?
   (A) Final feedback will be collected from team leaders.
   (B) Preliminary seating plans will be distributed.
   (C) The reorganization will be implemented.
   (D) Team leaders will meet with the operations manager.

Chapter

15

명사절

1. 명사절의 역할과 자리

명사절(Noun Clauses)은 명사절 접속사 + 주어 + 동사로 구성되어 있고, 문장에서 명사처럼 주어, 보어, 목적어 자리에서 명사 역할을 한다.

That the new policy will benefit employees is widely accepted.
새 정책이 직원들에게 이익을 주리라는 것은 널리 받아들여지고 있다.
The issue is **whether we can trust the new software.**
문제는 우리가 그 새로운 소프트웨어를 신뢰할 수 있는가이다.
The supervisor emphasized **that teamwork is essential for success.**
관리자는 팀워크가 성공에 필수적이라고 강조했다.
We are talking about **how we can improve productivity**.
우리는 어떻게 생산성을 향상할 수 있는지 이야기하고 있다.

2. 명사절 접속사의 유형

명사절 접속사에는 that, 동격절 접속사 that, 관계대명사 what, if/whether, 의문사(who, whom, what, which, whose, when, where, why, how), 복합 관계대명사(whoever, whomever, whatever, whichever) 등이 있다.

✔ CheckPoint 1. that의 용례

▶ "~하는 것"으로 번역하고, 뒤에 완전한 절이 온다.
▶ 문장에서 주어, 보어, 목적어로 사용될 수 있고, 목적어로 사용될 때는 생략 가능하다.

That she was promoted to the manager surprised all of her colleagues.
그녀가 매니저로 승진했다는 것이 모든 동료를 놀라게 했다.
The reality is **that not all employees are satisfied with the new policy.**
현실은 모든 직원이 새로운 정책에 만족하는 것은 아니라는 것이다.
The CEO acknowledged **(that) the company faced several challenges.**
CEO는 회사가 여러 가지 도전에 직면해 있다는 것을 인정했다.

토익 연습문제

1. The manager emphasized __________ the project must be completed by the end of the month.
   (A) what
   (B) that
   (C) who
   (D) which

2. The main issue is __________ we need additional funding to continue the project.
   (A) that
   (B) what
   (C) whether
   (D) which

3. __________ the team met the deadline was a remarkable achievement.
   (A) What
   (B) Which
   (C) Whether
   (D) That

✔ CheckPoint 2. 동격절 접속사 that의 용례

▶ 앞의 명사를 구체적으로 설명하거나 보충하는 역할을 하고, 뒤에 완전한 절이 온다.

▶ 문장에서 주어, 보어, 목적어로 사용된다.

▶ 동격절 접속사 that과 자주 사용되는 명사: the assumption (~라는 가정), the belief (~라는 믿음), the claim (~라는 주장), the conclusion (~라는 결론), the decision (~라는 결정), the evidence (~라는 증거), the expectation (~라는 기대), the fact (~라는 사실), the hope (~라는 희망), the idea (~라는 생각, 개념), the impression (~라는 인상), the news (~라는 소식), the possibility (~라는 가능성), the rumor (~라는 소문), the statement (~라는 진술)

The belief that hard work leads to success is widely accepted.
노력이 성공으로 이어진다는 믿음은 널리 받아들여진다.

Our priority is **the decision that benefits the entire team.**
우리의 우선순위는 전체 팀에 이익이 되는 결정이다.

We must consider **the possibility that the deadline will be extended.**
우리는 마감일이 연장될 가능성을 고려해야 한다.

토익 연습문제

1. The news __________ the product launch was delayed disappointed shareholders.
(A) that
(B) what
(C) whether
(D) which

2. The team rejected the assumption __________ the project could be completed ahead of schedule.
(A) whether
(B) what
(C) which
(D) that

3. The most important factor is the evidence __________ the new system is more reliable.
(A) what
(B) that
(C) whether
(D) which

✔ CheckPoint 3. 관계대명사 what의 용례

▶ 선행사를 포함하는 관계대명사로, "~한 것"으로 번역하고, 뒤에 불완전한 절이 온다.
▶ the thing(s) that/which로 대체 가능하다.
▶ 문장에서 주어, 보어, 목적어로 사용된다.

What(= The thing(s) that/which) you decide + O will affect the entire project.
당신이 결정하는 것이 전체 프로젝트에 영향을 미칠 것이다.
The result was **what(= the thing(s) that/which) we had hoped for + O.**
결과는 우리가 희망했던 것이었다.
The company offered **what(= the thing(s) that/which) S seemed like a great opportunity.**
회사는 훌륭한 기회로 보이는 것을 제안했다.

토익 연습문제

1. __________ you need to focus on is improving customer satisfaction.
   (A) That
   (B) What
   (C) Which
   (D) How

2. The marketing team focused on __________ was most relevant to the target audience.
   (A) that
   (B) which
   (C) what
   (D) those

3. The result of the meeting was __________ the team had anticipated.
   (A) that
   (B) who
   (C) which
   (D) what

✔ CheckPoint 4. if/whether의 용례

▶ if와 whether는 "~인지 아닌지"로 번역하고, 뒤에 완전한 절이 온다.

▶ whether는 주어, 보어, 목적어 자리에 모두 사용 가능하지만, if는 주로 목적어 자리에서만 사용된다.

▶ whether ~ or not이나 whether + to부정사 구조로 사용될 수 있다.

Whether the new policy will be implemented is yet to be determined.
새로운 정책이 시행될지는 아직 결정되지 않았다.

The key question is **whether the company can sustain its growth.**
핵심 질문은 회사가 성장을 지속할 수 있는가이다.

The manager will check **whether the report is accurate or not.**
매니저는 보고서가 정확한지 아닌지 확인할 것이다.

I don't know **if the CEO will attend the meeting.**
나는 CEO가 회의에 참석할지 모르겠다.

토익 연습문제

1. __________ the company will expand into new markets remains unclear.
   (A) If
   (B) Whether
   (C) Which
   (D) What

2. I don't know __________ the manager will approve the proposal.
   (A) if
   (B) what
   (C) that
   (D) who

3. The key issue is __________ the team can deliver the project on time.
   (A) if
   (B) whether
   (C) that
   (D) whose

✔ CheckPoint 5. 의문사의 용례

▶ 의문대명사(who, whom, what, which)는 문장에서 주어, 보어, 목적어로 사용되고, 뒤에 불완전한 절이 온다.

▶ 의문형용사(which, what, whose)는 명사를 수식하고, 문장에서 주어, 보어, 목적어로 사용되며, 뒤에 완전한 절이 온다.

▶ 의문부사(where, when, why, how)는 문장에서 주어, 보어, 목적어로 사용되고, 뒤에 완전한 절이 온다.

☞ What과 Which의 차이점

What	Which
"무엇", "어떤 것"	"어떤 것"
선택지가 명확하지 않거나 제한되지 않은 경우 사용	선택지가 명확하거나 제한된 선택지가 주어진 경우 사용

☞ 의문사와 관계사의 차이점

의문사	관계사
명사절이나 부사절을 형성	선행사를 수식하여 형용사절을 형성
의문사를 해석	관계사는 해석하지 않고 선행사를 해석
선행사가 필요 없음	반드시 선행사가 필요
의문대명사: 불완전한 절 의문형용사/의문부사: 완전한 절	관계대명사: 불완전한 절 관계부사: 완전한 절

⇒ 의문형용사 뒤에 완전한 절이 온다는 주장도 있고, 불완전한 절이 온다는 주장도 있지만 이 책에서는 전자의 주장을 받아들인다.

Who S will lead the team has not been decided yet.
누가 팀을 이끌지는 아직 결정되지 않았다.

The important thing is **whom the manager trusts O to lead the project.**
중요한 것은 매니저가 프로젝트를 이끌도록 누구를 신뢰하는가이다.

I don't understand **what the client expects O from the new proposal.**
나는 고객이 새로운 제안에서 무엇을 기대하는지 이해하지 못하겠다.

Which option we should choose O depends on the budget.
어떤 옵션을 선택해야 할지는 예산에 달려 있다.

The team is trying to determine **how the error occurred.**
팀은 그 오류가 어떻게 발생했는지를 알아내려고 하고 있다.

토익 연습문제

1. The report highlights __________ should be addressed first to improve efficiency.
   (A) who
   (B) that
   (C) what
   (D) how

2. The manager is unsure __________ department should handle the issue.
   (A) which
   (B) what
   (C) when
   (D) who

3. The instructions explain __________ the system should be configured.
   (A) why
   (B) how
   (C) which
   (D) where

✔ CheckPoint 6. 복합 관계대명사의 용례

▶ 관계대명사 + ever 형태로 선행사를 포함하고 있고, 뒤에 불완전한 절이 온다.
▶ 문장에서 주어, 보어, 목적어로 사용된다.

whoever	anyone who	누구든지
whomever	anyone whom	누구든지
whatever	anything that	무엇이든지
whichever	anything that	어느 것이든지

☞ Whatever와 Whichever의 차이점

Whatever	Whichever
"무엇이든지"	"어느 것이든지"
제한되지 않은 포괄적인 상황에서 사용	제한된 특정 선택지가 있는 상황에서 사용
복합 관계대명사나 복합 관계형용사로 사용	복합 관계대명사나 복합 관계형용사로 사용

Whoever S finishes the task first will receive a bonus.
누구든지 그 일을 먼저 끝내는 사람이 보너스를 받을 것이다.

The best solution is **whatever S works best for the team.**
최선의 해결책은 팀에게 가장 잘 맞는 것이다.

The board will consider **whomever the CEO nominates O for the position.**
이사회는 CEO가 그 직책에 지명하는 누구든지 검토할 것이다.
The award will be given to **whoever S performs the best**.
상은 가장 뛰어난 성과를 내는 사람에게 주어질 것이다.

토익 연습문제

1. _________ submits the project first will receive additional funding.
   (A) Whoever
   (B) Whomever
   (C) Whatever
   (D) Whichever

2. _________ you recommend for the position will have to undergo an interview.
   (A) Whoever
   (B) Whomever
   (C) Whatever
   (D) Whichever

3. _________ you choose for the project will have to be approved by the team.
   (A) Whoever
   (B) Whomever
   (C) Whatever
   (D) Whichever

토익 종합 실전문제

1. __________ the company achieved record profits last year is commendable.
(A) That
(B) What
(C) If
(D) Which

2. The report confirmed __________ the new strategy had a positive impact on sales.
(A) what
(B) whose
(C) who
(D) that

3. It is important __________ all employees understand the new policy before it is implemented.
(A) which
(B) that
(C) what
(D) whether

4. The manager made it clear __________ the team needed to improve communication.
(A) that
(B) if
(C) who
(D) what

5. The manager emphasized the belief __________ teamwork is essential for success.
(A) what
(B) that
(C) whether
(D) whose

6. The fact __________ the team exceeded all expectations impressed the board.
(A) if
(B) which
(C) it
(D) that

7. The claim __________ the new product will revolutionize the market is yet to be proven.
(A) that
(B) if
(C) who
(D) which

8. The report failed to address __________ was considered the most urgent issue.
(A) what
(B) which
(C) that
(D) how

9. __________ the CEO proposed during the meeting was a complete restructuring of the company.

(A) That
(B) What
(C) Which
(D) How

10. What you decide to include in the presentation __________ critical to its success.

(A) are
(B) were
(C) is
(D) have been

11. What they suggested was __________ we had been considering all along.

(A) that
(B) this
(C) what
(D) which

12. The decision was influenced by __________ the manager had observed in previous projects.

(A) whom
(B) that
(C) which
(D) what

13. The manager will decide __________ to implement the new policy.

(A) whether
(B) if
(C) what
(D) that

14. The manager is unsure __________ the delay will affect the overall timeline.

(A) who
(B) which
(C) what
(D) whether

15. The decision will be based on __________ the contract terms are acceptable.

(A) whether
(B) if
(C) that
(D) whose

16. The team discussed __________ resources would be required for the new project.

(A) who
(B) what
(C) how
(D) which

17. The team analyzed __________ the error was not detected during the testing phase.

(A) that
(B) which
(C) when
(D) why

18. The CEO is reviewing __________ should take responsibility for the mistake.

(A) who
(B) which
(C) what
(D) when

19. The report details __________ the company should allocate additional resources.

(A) which
(B) what
(C) where
(D) whose

20. The question is __________ strategy will deliver the best results.

(A) who
(B) which
(C) when
(D) what

21. Submit your report to __________ is responsible for your department.

(A) whoever
(B) whomever
(C) whatever
(D) whichever

22. You can bring __________ you think will be useful for the presentation.

(A) whoever
(B) whomever
(C) whatever
(D) whichever

23. You may take __________ of the items suits your needs.

(A) whoever
(B) whomever
(C) whatever
(D) whichever

24. The position will be offered to __________ the hiring manager selects.

(A) whoever
(B) whomever
(C) whatever
(D) whichever

PART 6

Questions 1–4 refer to the following notice.

Dear Employees,

To maintain the integrity of our company's operations and safeguard sensitive information, we are introducing updated guidelines on how information should be managed and shared within and outside the organization.

First, employees must ensure that any data shared externally 1________ company policies and regulations. Always confirm 2________ the recipient has the proper authorization before transmitting sensitive details. By ensuring compliance, employees can help the company avoid legal and financial consequences.

Second, employees should know that internal communications must remain secure to protect the company from potential breaches. For this reason, only encrypted tools approved by the IT department should be used for sharing 3________ information. Sharing sensitive details through unauthorized platforms could expose the company to serious risks.

Finally, we encourage you to report any suspicious activity you notice regarding the misuse of company information. Immediate reporting helps us take swift action to minimize risks.

4________. If you have any questions, please contact your manager or the IT support team.

Thank you for your attention to this matter.

Best regards,
Corporate Security Team

1. (A) complies with
   (B) applies to
   (C) matches
   (D) supports

2. (A) that
   (B) whether
   (C) what
   (D) which

3. (A) confidential
(B) creative
(C) informal
(D) general

4. (A) Sharing information through encrypted platforms is essential.
(B) Immediate reporting ensures that risks are minimized effectively.
(C) Your compliance with these guidelines is essential to maintaining a secure and trustworthy work environment.
(D) Employees are encouraged to attend workshops on secure communication practices.

PART 7

Questions 1−5 refer to the following email and advertisement.

From: Brian Lee (b.lee@techsolutions.com)
To: Sarah Kim (s.kim@innovateworks.com)
Date: September 10
Subject: Sponsorship Inquiry for Annual Conference

Dear Ms. Kim,

I hope this message finds you well. I am writing on behalf of Tech Solutions to express our interest in sponsoring the upcoming Innovate Works Annual Conference. We believe this event provides an excellent platform to present our latest innovations to professionals across the industry.

Could you kindly share more information about the sponsorship options available? We are particularly interested in understanding the pricing, benefits, and how our company's branding and products would be highlighted during the event. Also, we would like to confirm if there are any early registration discounts for companies that commit to sponsorship before the end of this month.

Looking forward to your reply. Should you need further details, please don't hesitate to reach out to me directly at the number below.

Best regards,
Brian Lee
Marketing Manager, Tech Solutions
(555) 123-4567

Innovate Works Annual Conference 2024

Be part of the year's most prominent technology event! The Innovate Works Annual Conference connects industry experts and professionals, offering a unique opportunity to learn, network, and explore the latest advancements in technology.

Sponsorship Tiers:

- **Platinum Sponsor**: $10,000
  Prime placement of your logo on all event materials
  A dedicated booth to showcase your company
  A special mention during the opening keynote
- **Gold Sponsor**: $5,000
  Logo featured on event materials
  Company booth included
- **Silver Sponsor**: $2,000
  Logo featured on promotional materials

Special Promotion: Confirm your sponsorship by September 30 to receive a 10% early bird discount! Don't miss this chance to elevate your brand at one of the most impactful events in the tech world.
For additional details, contact us at sponsor@innovateworks.com.

1. What is the purpose of Brian Lee's email?
   (A) To request information about the conference sponsorship options
   (B) To invite Sarah Kim to attend Tech Solutions' annual event
   (C) To confirm Tech Solutions' sponsorship participation
   (D) To inquire about becoming a speaker at the conference

2. What is included in the Platinum sponsorship tier?
   (A) Exclusive use of conference materials
   (B) A featured mention during the opening keynote
   (C) Early access to conference sessions
   (D) Complimentary event tickets for employees

3. What is one benefit of confirming sponsorship by September 30?
   (A) Free promotional material inclusion
   (B) Priority booth placement
   (C) A 10% early bird discount
   (D) Complimentary tickets for attendees

4. What does Brian Lee want to know about the sponsorship packages?
   (A) The networking opportunities available
   (B) How Tech Solutions' products will be presented
   (C) The criteria for selecting keynote speakers
   (D) The list of other sponsors attending

5. What is mentioned as part of the Silver sponsorship package?
   (A) Company booth at the event
   (B) Sponsorship recognition during networking events
   (C) Prime logo placement during keynote sessions
   (D) Logo placement on promotional materials

Chapter

16

비교

비교(comparison)는 두 대상을 대조하거나 유사성을 평가하기 위해 형용사나 부사를 사용하고, 원급, 비교급, 최상급의 형태로 구분된다.

1. 규칙변화와 불규칙변화

① 규칙변화

종류	원급	비교급	최상급	변화 규칙
단음절 형용사/부사	tall	taller	tallest	어미에 -er, -est를 붙임
-y로 끝나는 형용사/부사	easy	easier	easiest	-y를 -ier, -iest로 바꿈
2음절 이상의 형용사/부사	beautiful	more expensive	most expensive	단어 앞에 more, most를 붙임

This task is as **short** as the one we completed yesterday.
이 업무는 우리가 어제 완료한 업무만큼 짧다.
The revised guidelines are **easier** to follow than the previous ones.
수정된 지침이 이전 지침보다 더 따르기 쉽다.
The new smartphone is **more expensive** than the previous model.
새 스마트폰은 이전 모델보다 더 비싸다.

② 불규칙변화

원급	비교급	최상급	의미
good	better	best	좋은
bad	worse	worst	나쁜
far	farther	farthest	먼(물리적 거리)
far	further	furthest	먼(추상적 거리, 추가적 개념, 심화된 의미)
little	less	least	적은
much	more	most	많은
many	more	most	많은

The new software performs **better** than the older version.
새로운 소프트웨어는 이전 버전보다 더 잘 작동한다.
That was the **worst** experience I've had with a delivery company.
그것은 내가 배송 회사와 겪은 최악의 경험이었다.

The new warehouse is **farther** from the city center than the old one.
새 창고는 이전 창고보다 도심에서 더 멀리 있다.
The CEO provided the **furthest** insights on the company's strategy.
CEO는 회사 전략에 대해 가장 심도 있는 통찰을 제공했다.

토익 연습문제

1. The updated manual is __________ to understand than the older version.
   (A) easiest
   (B) easier
   (C) easy
   (D) more easier

2. Before we proceed, we need to gather __________ information about the client's requirements.
   (A) farther
   (B) further
   (C) furthest
   (D) more

3. Among all the candidates, she has the __________ experience in marketing.
   (A) little
   (B) less
   (C) least
   (D) few

2. 원급(Positive Degree)

원급은 두 대상을 같은 수준에서 비교할 때 사용하고, 동등비교와 열등비교로 나뉜다.

✔ CheckPoint 1. 원급의 기본 구조

▶ 동등비교: as + 형용사/부사의 원급 + as (~만큼 ~하다)
▶ 열등비교: not as + 형용사/부사의 원급 + as (~만큼 ~하지 않다)

This product is **as effective as** the leading brand.
이 제품은 주요 브랜드만큼 효과적이다.
He didn't complete the task **as quickly as** his colleague.
그는 동료만큼 빠르게 업무를 완료하지 못했다.
The revised proposal is not **as detailed as** the original one.
수정된 제안서는 원래 제안서만큼 자세하지 않다.
The report was not delivered **as promptly as** expected.
보고서는 예상했던 만큼 신속하게 전달되지 않았다.

토익 연습문제

1. The new office is __________ spacious as the old one, providing enough room for all employees.
(A) as
(B) so
(C) very
(D) not

2. The project was not completed __________ efficiently as the management expected.
(A) most
(B) as
(C) more
(D) very

✔ CheckPoint 2. 원급으로 최상급을 나타내는 표현

▶ as + 형용사/부사의 원급 + as any 단수 명사 (어떤 ~와 비교해도 ~한)
▶ as + 형용사/부사의 원급 + as possible (가능한 한 ~하게)
▶ 부정주어 as + 형용사/부사의 원급 + as (~만큼 ~한 것은 없다)

He is **as hardworking as any employee** in the company.
그는 회사의 어떤 직원과 비교해도 열심히 일한다.

All team members must communicate **as clearly as possible.**
모든 팀원은 가능한 한 명확하게 의사소통해야 한다.

Nothing is **as critical as** understanding the client's needs.
고객의 요구를 이해하는 것만큼 중요한 것은 없다.

No one is **as creative as** Jane in designing advertisements.
광고를 디자인하는 데 있어 Jane만큼 창의적인 사람은 없다.

토익 연습문제

1. All employees are encouraged to complete their training as thoroughly __________ possible.
   (A) as
   (B) than
   (C) until
   (D) so

2. No one in the department is __________ efficient as Sarah in completing tasks on time.
   (A) very
   (B) as
   (C) too
   (D) more

3. This solution is as innovative as __________ developed in the industry.
   (A) each solution
   (B) every solution
   (C) another solution
   (D) any solution

✔ CheckPoint 3. 원급 관련 관용표현

▶ 배수사 + as + 형용사/부사의 원급 + as (~배 만큼 ~한)
▶ as many + 가산 복수 명사 + as (~만큼 많은)
▶ as much + 불가산 명사 + as (~만큼 많은)

The new system is **three times as efficient as** the previous one.
새 시스템은 이전 시스템보다 세 배 더 효율적이다.

We hired **as many new employees as** the HR department recommended.
우리는 인사팀이 추천한 만큼 많은 신입 사원을 고용했다.

She used **as much effort as** possible to complete the project on time.
그녀는 프로젝트를 제시간에 완료하기 위해 가능한 한 많은 노력을 기울였다.

토익 연습문제

1. The new system processes data three times __________ as the old one.
   (A) as much
   (B) more efficient
   (C) as efficiently
   (D) as efficient

2. The company hired __________ interns this year as last year to manage the increasing workload.
   (A) more
   (B) fewer
   (C) as many
   (D) as much

3. The team completed the task in half __________ time as originally expected.
   (A) as much
   (B) as many
   (C) as little
   (D) as

3. 비교급(Comparative Degree)

비교급은 두 대상을 비교할 때 사용하고, 주로 형용사/부사의 비교급 + than 구문을 사용한다.

✔ CheckPoint 4. 비교급의 기본 구조

▶ 우등비교: 형용사/부사의 비교급 + than (~보다 더 ~하다)
▶ 열등비교: less + 형용사/부사 + than (~보다 덜 ~하다)

The new smartphone is **faster than** the previous model.
새 스마트폰은 이전 모델보다 더 빠르다.
This hotel is **less expensive than** the one we stayed at last year.
이 호텔은 우리가 작년에 머물렀던 호텔보다 덜 비싸다.

토익 연습문제

1. The new manager is __________ than the previous one at resolving conflicts.
   (A) the most experienced
   (B) experienced
   (C) as experienced
   (D) more experienced

2. This product is __________ expensive than the previous model, making it more accessible to customers.
   (A) less
   (B) the most
   (C) very
   (D) as

3. Employees found the new policy more effective __________ they had initially expected.
   (A) as
   (B) than
   (C) of
   (D) so

✔ CheckPoint 5. 비교급으로 최상급을 나타내는 표현

▶ 형용사/부사의 비교급 + than any other + 단수 명사 (다른 어떤 ~보다 더 ~하다)
▶ 형용사/부사의 비교급 + than all the other + 복수 명사 (모든 다른 ~보다 더 ~하다)
▶ 형용사/부사의 비교급 + than anyone(anything) else (다른 누구(무엇)보다 더 ~하다)
▶ 부정주어 + 형용사/부사의 비교급 + than (어떤 것도 ~보다 더 ~하지 않다)

This smartphone is **faster than any other smartphone** on the market.
이 스마트폰은 시장의 다른 어떤 스마트폰보다 더 빠르다.
She is **more skilled than all the other designers** in the company.
그녀는 회사의 다른 모든 디자이너보다 더 능숙하다.
This product is **more reliable than anything else** we've tested.
이 제품은 우리가 테스트한 다른 모든 것보다 더 신뢰할 만하다.
No task is **more important than** meeting the deadline.
어떤 업무도 마감 기한을 맞추는 것보다 더 중요하지 않다.

토익 연습문제

1. She is more competent than __________ in managing complex projects.
(A) anyone else
(B) everyone
(C) any person
(D) the others

2. This project has achieved faster results than __________ attempted by our competitors.
(A) anyone else
(B) any project
(C) all other attempts
(D) anything else

3. The new restaurant is more popular than __________ in the area.
(A) all the other restaurants
(B) any restaurant
(C) all restaurants
(D) anyone else

✔ CheckPoint 6. 비교급 관련 관용표현

▶ the + 비교급 + of the two / of A and B (둘 중에서 더 ~한)
▶ the + 비교급 + 주어 + 동사, the + 비교급 + 주어 + 동사 (~할수록 더 ~하다)
▶ 비교급 + and + 비교급 (점점 더 ~하다)
▶ no sooner + 조동사/동사 + 주어 + 동사 + than + 절 (~하자마자 ~하다)
▶ 비교급 강조 부사(much, even, still, far, a lot) + 비교급 (훨씬 더 ~하다)
▶ no + 비교급 + than (~보다 더 ~하지 않다)
▶ 비교급 + than + expected/anticipated (예상/기대했던 것보다 더 ~하다)

This solution is **the better of the two** options we considered.
이 해결책은 우리가 고려한 두 옵션 중 더 나은 것이다.

The clearer the instructions are, **the fewer** mistakes employees will make.
지시가 더 명확할수록, 직원들이 실수를 덜 하게 된다.

This proposal is **no better than** the one we rejected last month.
이 제안은 우리가 지난달에 거절한 제안보다 더 나을 게 없다.

Customer feedback was **more positive than anticipated**.
고객 피드백이 예상했던 것보다 더 긍정적이었다.

☞ 라틴어 비교 표현: than 대신 전치사 to를 사용하는 형용사
superior(~보다 우수한), inferior(~보다 열등한), junior(~보다 하위의), senior(~보다 상위의), prior(~보다 앞선)

This product is **superior to** all other brands.
이 제품은 다른 모든 브랜드보다 우수하다.

This meeting was scheduled **prior to** the announcement.
이 회의는 발표 이전에 예정되었다.

토익 연습문제

1. The new policy is __________ of the two options under consideration.
   (A) the better
   (B) the best
   (C) the more well
   (D) the most

2. The instructions became __________ and __________ as the meeting progressed.
   (A) clear / clear
   (B) clearer / clearer
   (C) clearer / clearest
   (D) clearest / clearest

3. The results of the new strategy are __________ than we initially expected.
   (A) successful
   (B) more effective
   (C) the least effective
   (D) more positively

4. 최상급(Superlative Degree)

최상급은 세 개 이상의 대상을 비교할 때 사용하고, 주로 the + 형용사/부사의 최상급 구문을 사용한다.

✔ CheckPoint 7. 최상급의 기본 구조

▶ the + 형용사/부사의 최상급 + of all (the) + 복수명사 (모든 ~ 중에서 가장 ~하다)
▶ the + 형용사/부사의 최상급 + in + 장소/집합명사 (~에서 가장 ~하다)
▶ the + 형용사/부사의 최상급 + of + 시간 (특정 시간 범위 중 가장 ~한)
▶ the + 형용사/부사의 최상급 + (that) + 주어 + have ever + 과거분사(PP) (지금까지 ~한 것 중 가장 ~하다)

This is **the most efficient** solution **of all the options** we considered.
이것은 우리가 고려한 모든 옵션 중에서 가장 효율적인 해결책이다.

He is **the most experienced** engineer **in the company**.
그는 회사에서 가장 경험이 많은 엔지니어이다.

This quarter's performance was **the most impressive of the year**.
이번 분기의 실적은 올해 가장 인상적이었다.

This is **the best** customer service experience **that I have ever had.**
이것은 내가 겪었던 고객 서비스 경험 중 가장 좋았다.

토익 연습문제

1. This design has received __________ feedback of all the concepts submitted.
   (A) the most positive
   (B) the more positively
   (C) positive
   (D) the most positively

2. This achievement is __________ we have ever accomplished as a team.
   (A) as significant as
   (B) more significant
   (C) the most significant
   (D) the most significantly

✔ CheckPoint 8. 최상급 관련 관용표현

▶ one of the + 형용사/부사의 최상급 + 복수명사 (~중 하나)
▶ the + 형용사/부사의 최상급 + possible (가능한 한 가장 ~한)
▶ 최상급 강조 부사(by far, the very) + the + 형용사/부사의 최상급 (단연코 가장 ~한)

She is **one of the most talented designers** in the company.
그녀는 회사에서 가장 재능 있는 디자이너 중 한 명이다.

We aim to provide **the best** service **possible** to our customers.
우리는 고객들에게 가능한 한 최고의 서비스를 제공하는 것을 목표로 한다.

He is **by far the most experienced** engineer on the team.
그는 팀에서 단연 가장 경험 많은 엔지니어이다.

토익 연습문제

1. This is considered __________ solutions to the current crisis.
   (A) one of the best
   (B) the best possible
   (C) by far the better
   (D) as good as

2. The team delivered __________ performance possible under challenging circumstances.
   (A) the best
   (B) as good
   (C) one of the better
   (D) the best possible

3. She is regarded as __________ leader in the history of the organization.
   (A) one of the better
   (B) the more inspiring possible
   (C) by far the most inspiring
   (D) the very inspiring

토익 종합 실전문제

1. The CEO provided __________ details about the company's strategy than expected.
(A) least
(B) most
(C) many
(D) more

2. The new branch is located __________ from the headquarters than the old one.
(A) far
(B) farther
(C) farthest
(D) further

3. Of all the candidates, she has the __________ qualifications, making her the most suitable for the position.
(A) good
(B) better
(C) best
(D) well

4. Of all the competitors, her proposal went the __________ in addressing environmental issues.
(A) farther
(B) farthest
(C) further
(D) furthest

5. This year's sales are not __________ high as last year's, but the trend is improving.
(A) most
(B) as
(C) more
(D) much

6. She is as reliable __________ any team member we have ever worked with.
(A) so
(B) than
(C) as
(D) much

7. The company's latest model is twice __________ its predecessor in terms of energy efficiency.
(A) as efficient as
(B) more efficient than
(C) the most efficient
(D) efficient

8. We received as __________ complaints about the service as we expected.
(A) much
(B) many
(C) little
(D) few

9. No product is __________ than this one in terms of durability.
(A) as strong
(B) stronger
(C) most strong
(D) least strong

10. The customer service at this hotel is better than __________ provided by other luxury hotels.
(A) anyone else
(B) any other hotel
(C) anything else
(D) most services

11. This new model is more affordable than __________ we've launched before.
(A) all the products
(B) anything
(C) any other model
(D) the others

12. No one in the department is __________ than Sarah in resolving conflicts.
(A) better
(B) as good
(C) the best
(D) more well

13. The smartphone offers better performance than __________ available in its price range.
(A) anyone else
(B) any device
(C) all devices
(D) all the other devices

14. No sooner __________ the meeting start than the fire alarm went off.
(A) did
(B) does
(C) has
(D) had

15. This software performs __________ better than the previous version in handling large datasets.
(A) far
(B) less
(C) very
(D) most

16. The product launch was more successful than __________.
(A) anticipations
(B) anticipate
(C) anticipating
(D) anticipated

17. The new policy is no __________ than the previous one in addressing employee concerns.
(A) better
(B) more effectively
(C) less effectively
(D) as effective

18. The more carefully you review the contract, __________ you can avoid potential issues.
(A) the easier
(B) more easy
(C) the more easily
(D) the most easily

19. The candidate's qualifications are clearly inferior __________ those of the other applicants.
(A) than
(B) to
(C) with
(D) over

20. The seminar was __________ of all the training sessions conducted this year.
(A) more informative
(B) informative
(C) the most informative
(D) the most informatively

21. Of all the candidates, she demonstrated __________ understanding of the project requirements.
(A) as deep as
(B) the most deeply
(C) the deeper
(D) the deepest

22. This year's profits are __________ the company has ever recorded in its history.
(A) higher than
(B) the highest
(C) the most highly
(D) as high as

23. The sales team achieved __________ results of the year with their new campaign.
(A) the highest
(B) higher
(C) as high as
(D) most high

24. This store offers __________ discounts in the city during the holiday season.
(A) more generous
(B) the most generous
(C) as generous
(D) the most generously

PART 6

Questions 1–4 refer to the following information.

Customer Satisfaction Report

Date: March 12, 2024

Prepared by: Marketing Research Team

Summary of Findings:

The survey results show that the new product line has been received 1________ than the previous one. Customers have noted that the packaging is as eco-friendly as advertised, and the usability of the product is superior to 2________ brands. However, delivery times are not as fast as customers expected, which led to a slight decrease in overall satisfaction. 3________ this, the quality of the new product line is considered the best among all the products our company has launched.

Recommendations:

1. 4________.
2. Continue emphasizing the eco-friendly aspects of the product to maintain positive customer perceptions.
3. Implement feedback surveys earlier in the product life cycle to identify and address issues faster than anticipated.

1. (A) positive
   (B) more positive
   (C) positively
   (D) more positively

2. (A) compete
   (B) competing
   (C) competition
   (D) competitor

3. (A) Despite
   (B) Because
   (C) However
   (D) Although

4. (A) Improve the marketing strategy for better engagement
   (B) Increase production speed to address growing demand
   (C) Redesign the packaging to align with environmental standards
   (D) Collaborate with the logistics team to reduce delivery times to meet expectations

PART 7

Questions 1–5 refer to the following article and internal memo.

TechCorp to Launch New AI-Powered Tool

TechCorp, a leading innovator in artificial intelligence, has announced the launch of its new AI-powered analytics tool, InsightPro. Designed for businesses of all sizes, InsightPro promises to streamline data analysis and enhance decision-making processes.

According to TechCorp's CEO, InsightPro can analyze large datasets in real-time, providing actionable insights that can improve efficiency and boost profits. The tool will also feature customizable dashboards, allowing users to tailor the interface to their specific needs.

The product is set to be officially released on June 1, 2024, and will be available via subscription plans starting at $49.99 per month. Early adopters will receive a 10% discount if they sign up before May 15, 2024.

Industry experts predict that InsightPro could significantly impact the data analytics market, especially for small and medium-sized enterprises looking for affordable and scalable solutions.

To: Marketing and Sales Teams
Subject: Preparing for the InsightPro Launch

Dear Team,

As we approach the official release of InsightPro, we want to ensure that both marketing and sales are aligned in delivering a successful launch. Please note the following action items:

1. Marketing Materials

- Finalize the product brochures and promotional videos by April 20, 2024. These materials should highlight InsightPro's unique features, such as real-time analysis and customizable dashboards.

2. Training Sessions

- All sales representatives must complete the product training session scheduled for

April 25, 2024. This will equip the team to address potential customer questions effectively.

3. Early Adopter Campaign

- The marketing team should launch the 10% discount campaign by April 10, 2024, ensuring maximum visibility across all platforms.

If you have any questions or suggestions, please contact me directly at marketing@techcorp.com. Thank you for your dedication to making this launch a success.

Best regards,
Rachel Lin
Marketing Director

1. What is the primary purpose of the article?
   (A) To announce the launch of a new AI-powered tool
   (B) To explain the technical features of AI technologies
   (C) To introduce new training methods for employees
   (D) To compare InsightPro with competing products

2. According to the article, what is one prediction made by industry experts about InsightPro?
   (A) It will face strong competition from existing tools.
   (B) It may be too expensive for many businesses.
   (C) It will require frequent updates to remain relevant.
   (D) It could transform the data analytics market for small and medium-sized enterprises.

3. The word “customizable” in paragraph 2, line 3 of the article, is closest in meaning to
(A) personalized
(B) advanced
(C) detailed
(D) consistent

4. What can be inferred about the internal memo's intended audience?
(A) Employees who are not involved in marketing or sales
(B) Teams responsible for creating InsightPro
(C) Staff members preparing for the product launch
(D) Customers interested in AI analytics tools

5. According to the memo, what is one task the sales team must complete?
(A) Prepare a detailed report on InsightPro's performance
(B) Attend a training session scheduled for April 25, 2024
(C) Launch a promotional campaign by April 20, 2024
(D) Finalize the design of product brochures

체크 포인트 토익

정답 및 해설

Chapter 01 문장의 유형과 동사의 종류

1. 1형식 문형

CheckPoint 1. 1형식 동사

정답

1. (B) 2. (C)

1.

번역 그 종은 야생에 존재하지만, 인간에게는 거의 보이지 않는다.

해설 exists는 1형식 동사로, "존재하다"라는 의미를 가지며 보어나 목적어를 취하지 않으므로 (B) exists가 정답이다.

어휘 species 종, 생물의 종류

2.

번역 항공편은 악천후로 인해 30분 늦게 공항에 도착했다.

해설 arrived는 1형식 동사로, "도착하다"라는 의미를 가지며 보어나 목적어를 취하지 않으므로 (C) arrived가 정답이다.

어휘 flight 항공편, 비행 due to ~때문에

2. 2형식 문형

CheckPoint 2. 2형식 동사

정답

1. (A) 2. (B)

1.

번역 그 매니저는 예상치 못한 상황에서도 침착함을 유지했다.

해설 remained는 2형식 동사로, "~인 상태를 유지하다"라는 의미를 가지며 형용사(calm)를 보어로 취하므로 (A) remained가 정답이다.

어휘 calm 침착한 despite ~에도 불구하고 unexpected 예상치 못한 situation 상황

2.

번역 그 새 소프트웨어는 사용하기 쉽고 매우 효율적인 것처럼 보인다.

해설 seems는 2형식 동사로, "~처럼 보이다"라는 의미를 가지며 형용사(easy)를 보어로 취하므로 (B) seems가 정답이다.

어휘 efficient 효율적인, 능률적인

3. 3형식 문형

CheckPoint 3. 3형식 동사

정답

1. (A) 2. (A)

1.

번역 위원회는 회의 중에 그 제안을 승인했다.

해설 approved는 3형식 동사로, "승인하다"라는 의미를 가지며 목적어로 취하므로 (A) the proposal이 정답이다.

어휘 committee 위원회 during ~중에, ~동안

2.

번역 팀은 회의 후에 새로운 일정을 논의했다.

해설 discussed는 3형식 동사로, "논의하다"라는 의미를 가지며 목적어(the new schedule)를 취하므로 (A) discussed가 정답이다.

4. 4형식 문형

✔ CheckPoint 4. 4형식 동사

정답

1. (B) 2. (A)

1.

번역 회사는 마케팅 팀에게 다음 분기의 예산 제안을 제공했다.

해설 gave는 "주다"라는 의미의 4형식 동사로, 간접목적어(the marketing team)와 직접목적어(a budget proposal)를 취할 수 있으므로 (B) gave가 정답이다.

어휘 proposal 제안, 계획안 quarter 분기 remove 제거하다

2.

번역 매니저는 팀에게 프로젝트를 완료하기 위한 필요한 자원을 보냈다.

해설 sent는 "보내다"라는 의미의 4형식 동사로, 간접목적어(the team)와 직접목적어(the necessary resources)를 취할 수 있으므로 (A) sent가 정답이다. (D) trans- ferred는 "전달하다"는 의미는 있지만 전치사 to를 필요로 하므로 문법적으로 맞지 않다.

어휘 necessary 필요한

5. 5형식 문형

✔ CheckPoint 5. 5형식 동사

정답

1. (A) 2. (D) 3. (C)

1.

번역 우리는 인턴들이 발표 후에 회의실을 떠나는 것을 보았다.

해설 saw는 지각동사로, 목적보어 자리에 동사원형 또는 현재분사(-ing)를 취할 수 있으므로 (A) leave가 정답이다.

어휘 intern 인턴, 실습생 presentation 발표

2.

번역 교수는 학생들에게 마감일까지 보고서를 완성하게 했다.

해설 made는 사역동사로, 목적보어 자리에 동사원형을 취할 수 있으므로 (D) complete가 정답이다.

3.

번역 매니저는 팀에게 프로젝트를 위한 혁신적인 아이디어를 개발하라고 격려했다.

해설 encourage는 "격려하다"라는 의미의 5형식 동사로, to부정사를 목적보어로 취할 수 있으므로 (C) to develop가 정답이다.

어휘 innovative 혁신적인, 참신한

토익 종합 실전문제

정답

1. (B)	2. (A)	3. (B)	4. (C)	5. (A)
6. (D)	7. (B)	8. (B)	9. (C)	10. (B)
11. (C)	12. (D)	13. (C)	14. (C)	15. (B)
16. (D)	17. (C)	18. (C)	19. (A)	20. (C)
21. (D)	22. (C)	23. (A)	24. (B)	

1.

번역 공장은 제품에 대한 높은 수요를 충족하기 위해 24시간 내내 가동된다.

해설 works는 1형식 동사로, "일하다, 작동하다"라는 의미를 가지며 보어나 목적어를 취하지 않으므로 (B) works가 정답이다.

어휘 around the clock 하루 종일, 24시간 내내 demand 수요

2.

번역 사용자 수가 새로운 경쟁으로 인해 꾸준

히 감소했다.

해설 declined는 1형식 동사로, "감소하다"라는 의미를 가지며 보어나 목적어를 취하지 않으므로 (A) declined가 정답이다. 참고로 "줄이다"는 의미의 (C) reduced는 타동사를 목적어로 취하므로 적절하지 않다.

어휘 steadily 꾸준히, 점진적으로 due to ~ 때문에, ~으로 인해 competition 경쟁

3.

번역 그 건물은 개조되기 전에 몇 년 동안 비어 있었다.

해설 remained는 2형식 동사로, "~인 상태를 유지하다"라는 의미를 가지며 형용사(empty)를 보어로 취하므로 (B) remained가 정답이다.

어휘 empty 비어 있는 several 몇몇의, 여러 renovate 개조하다, 보수하다

4.

번역 새로운 정책은 직원들 사이에서 논란의 주제가 되었다.

해설 become은 2형식 동사로, "~하게 되다"라는 의미를 가지며 명사(a controversial topic)를 보어로 취하므로 (C) become이 정답이다.

어휘 policy 정책, 방침 controversial 논란이 되는 topic 주제 among ~사이에서

5.

번역 직원들은 비상 상황 동안 침착함을 유지하라는 지시를 받았다.

해설 stay는 2형식 동사로, "~인 상태를 유지하다"라는 의미를 가지며 형용사(calm)를 보어로 취하므로 (A) stay가 정답이다.

어휘 instruct 지시하다, 명령하다 calm 침착한, 차분한 emergency situation 비상 상황

6.

번역 몇 달 동안 방치된 후, 그 과일은 상해서 먹을 수 없게 되었다.

해설 gone은 2형식 동사로, "~하게 되다"라는 의미를 가지며 형용사(bad)를 보어로 취하므로 (D) gone이 정답이다.

어휘 neglect 방치, 소홀, 방치하다

7.

번역 그녀는 발표를 하기 전에 긴장하는 경향이 있다.

해설 get은 2형식 동사로, "~하게 되다"라는 의미를 가지며 형용사(nervous)를 보어로 취하므로 (B) get이 정답이다.

어휘 tend to ~하는 경향이 있다 nervous 긴장한, 초조한 presentation 발표

8.

번역 관리자는 그들에게 새로운 안전 절차를 따르라고 지시했다.

해설 instructed는 3형식 동사로, "지시하다"라는 의미를 가지며 목적어를 취하므로 (B) them이 정답이다.

어휘 supervisor 감독관, 관리자 safety procedure 안전 절차 effectively 효율적으로

9.

번역 팀은 프로젝트를 위해 추가 자원을 할당하기로 동의했다.

해설 agreed는 3형식 동사로, "동의하다"라는 의미를 가지며 to부정사를 목적어로 취하므로 (C) to allocate가 정답이다.

어휘 additional 추가적인 allocate 할당하다

10.

번역 직원들은 더 유연한 근무 일정을 도입할 것을 제안했다.

해설 suggested는 3형식 동사로, "제안하다"라는 의미를 가지며 동명사를 목적어로 취하므로 (B) implementing이 정답이다.

어휘 flexible 유연한, 융통성 있는 implement 도입하다, 시행하다, 실행하다

11.

번역 CEO는 회사가 내년에 해외로 확장할 것이라고 언급했다.

해설 mentioned는 3형식 동사로, "언급하다"라는 의미를 가지며 명사절 that절을 목적어로 취하므로 (C) that이 정답이다. (D) if는 명사절을 이끌 수 있으나, "확장 여부"를 묻는 문맥이 아니므로 적절하지 않다.

어휘 expand 확장하다 overseas 해외로, 해외에

12.

번역 CEO는 이벤트가 원활하게 진행되도록 보조에게 중요한 업무를 요청했다.

해설 asked는 "요청하다"라는 의미의 4형식 동사로, 간접목적어(the assistant)와 직접목적어(an important task)를 취하고, 또 간접목적어와 직접목적어의 어순이 바뀌면 전치사 of와 함께 사용되므로 (D) asked가 정답이다.

어휘 task 업무 assistant 보조 ensure 보장하다 smoothly 원활하게 analyze 분석하다

13.

번역 점원은 손상된 제품에 대해 고객에게 환불을 제공했다.

해설 gave는 "주다, 제공하다"라는 의미의 4형식 동사로, 간접목적어(the customer)와 직접목적어(a refund)를 취할 수 있으므로 (C) gave가 정답이다.

어휘 clerk 점원, 사무원 refund 환불 damaged 손상된, 파손된

14.

번역 회사는 직원들에게 후한 보상 패키지를 제공했다.

해설 offered는 "제공하다"라는 의미의 4형식 동사로, 간접목적어(its employees)와 직접목적어(a generous compensation package)를 취하고, 또 간접목적어와 직접목적어의 어순이 바뀌면 전치사 to와 함께 사용되므로 (C) offered가 정답이다.

어휘 generous 관대한, 후한 compensation 보상

15.

번역 그녀는 동료의 승진을 축하하기 위해 선물을 샀다.

해설 bought는 "구입하다"라는 의미의 4형식 동사로, 간접목적어(her colleague)와 직접목적어(a gift)를 취하고, 또 간접목적어와 직접목적어의 어순이 바뀌면 전치사 for와 함께 사용되므로 (B) for가 정답이다.

어휘 colleague 동료 celebrate 축하하다 promotion 승진, 진급

16.

번역 매니저는 늦은 회의 후 팀 전체를 위해 식사를 주문했다.

해설 ordered는 "주문하다"라는 의미의 4형식 동사로, 간접목적어(the entire team)와 직접목적어(a meal)를 취하고, 또 간접목적어와 직접목적어의 어순이 바뀌면 전치사 for와 함께 사용되므로 (D) ordered가 정답이다.

어휘 meal 식사 entire 전체의, 전부의

17.

번역 매니저는 회의 전에 비서가 문서를 검토하도록 했다.

해설 had는 사역동사로, 목적보어 자리에 동사원형과 과거분사를 취할 수 있는데, 문서가 비서에 의해 검토되는 수동적 상황을 나타내고 있으므로 (C) reviewed가 정답이다.

어휘 document 문서, 서류 assistant 보조, 비서 review 검토하다

18.

번역 강사는 학생들에게 실험실 세션 중 안전 수칙을 따르라고 상기시켰다.

해설 reminded는 "상기시키다"라는 의미의 5형식 동사로, to부정사를 목적보어로 취할 수 있으므로 (C) to follow가 정답이다.

어휘 instructor 강사, 지도자 safety rule 안전 수칙 lab 실험실

19.

번역 매니저는 팀이 프로젝트를 위해 추가 자원에 접근하는 것을 허락했다.

해설 allowed는 "허락하다"라는 의미의 5형식 동사로, to부정사를 목적보어로 취할 수 있으므로 (A) to access가 정답이다.

어휘 additional 추가적인

20.

번역 CEO는 직원들에게 주말까지 상세한 보고서를 준비하라고 요청했다.

해설 asked는 "요청하다"라는 의미의 5형식 동사로, to부정사를 목적보어로 취할 수 있으므로 (C) to prepare가 정답이다.

어휘 detailed 상세한, 자세한

21

번역 직원들은 교육 프로그램에 참여하도록 격려 받았다.

해설 encouraged는 "격려하다"라는 의미의 5형식 동사로, to부정사를 목적보어로 취할 수 있는데, 능동태 문장 They encouraged the employees to take part in the training program에서 직접목적어를 수동태의 주어로 변환하면 The employees were encouraged to take part in the training program이 되므로 (D) to take가 정답이다.

어휘 take part in ~에 참여하다 training program 교육 프로그램

22.

번역 학생들은 마감 기한 전에 과제를 제출하도록 요구받았다.

해설 required는 "요구하다"라는 의미의 5형식 동사로, to부정사를 목적보어로 취할 수 있는데, 능동태 문장 They required the students to submit the assignment before the deadline에서 직접목적어를 수동태의 주어로 변환하면 The students were required to submit the assignment be- fore the deadline이 되므로 (C) to submit가 정답이다.

어휘 assignment 과제, 숙제 deadline 마감 기한

23.

번역 프로젝트 팀은 분기 말까지 상당한 진전을 이루도록 기대되었다.

해설 expected는 "기대하다"라는 의미의 5형식 동사로, to부정사를 목적보어로 취할 수 있는데, 능동태 문장 They expected the project team to achieve significant progress by the end of the quarter에서 직접목적어를 수동태의 주어로 변환하면 The project team was expected to achieve significant progress by the end of the quarter가 되므로 (A) to achieve가 정답이다.

어휘 significant 중요한, 상당한 progress 진전, 발전 quarter 분기

24.

번역 참가자들은 발표 중에 질문할 수 있도록 허락받았다.

해설 allowed는 "허락하다"라는 의미의 5형식 동사로, to부정사를 목적보어로 취할 수 있는데, 능동태 문장 They allowed the participants to ask questions during the presentation에서 직접목적어를 수동태의 주어로 변환하면 The participants were allowed to ask questions during the presentation이 되므로 (B) allowed가 정답이다.

어휘 participant 참가자 presentation 발표

PART 6

다음 이메일과 관련된 질문 1-4번을 보세요.

> 팀 여러분께,
> 다음 주에 몇몇 신규 직원들을 맞이할 준비를 하며, 오리엔테이션 일정과 과업에 대한 업데이트를 드리고자 합니다. 우선, 오리엔테이션은 월요일 오전 9시에 메인 회의실에서 시작됩니다. 참고로, 모든 부서장들은 각 부서에 대해 간략히 발표

하도록 요청받았습니다. 발표 자료를 준비하시고, 제시간에 도착해 주시기 바랍니다. 둘째, HR팀이 일반 온보딩 세션을 진행할 예정입니다. 이 세션에서는 회사 정책, 복지 혜택 및 일과 삶의 균형에 대해 다룰 것입니다. 모든 신규 직원들이 이 세션에 참석하여 회사의 기대치와 지침을 충분히 이해하는 것이 중요합니다. 마지막으로, 각 신규 직원에게 멘토를 지정하는 것을 잊지 마세요. 멘토는 처음 몇 주 동안 이들을 안내하고, 질문에 답하며, 팀에 통합되도록 돕는 역할을 할 것입니다. 여러분의 협조에 감사드립니다. 원활한 온보딩 과정을 보장하고 신규 직원들이 환영받는다고 느낄 수 있도록 합시다. 추가 설명이 필요하면 알려주세요.

감사합니다,
HR 매니저, 마사 설리번

어휘 prepare 준비하다 orientation 오리엔테이션, 예비 교육 department head 부서장, 부서 책임자 brief 짧은, 간략한 respective 각각의, 각자의 general 일반적인 onboarding session 온보딩 세션, 신규 직원 교육 세션 benefit 복지, 혜택 essential 중요한, 필수적인 expectation 기대, 요구 사항 guideline 지침 assign 할당하다, 배정하다 integration 통합, 적응 cooperation 협력, 협조 smooth 원활한, 순조로운

정답

1. (C)　2. (A)　3. (C)　4. (D)

1.

해설 능동태 문장 They expect all department heads to give brief presentations about their respective teams에서 직접 목적어를 수동태의 주어로 변환하면 All depart- ment heads are expected to give brief presentations about their respective teams가 되므로 (C) are expected가 정답이다.

2.

(A) 일과 삶의 균형
(B) 고객 만족
(C) 연례 평가
(D) 회의 절차

해설 문맥상 HR팀이 다룰 주제는 회사 정책 및 혜택과 관련된 내용이므로, 이와 가장 자연스럽게 연결되는 (A)가 정답이다.

3.

해설 지문 These mentors will help guide them through the first few weeks, an- swer any questions, and 3________ with their integration into the team에서 "help", "answer"과 병렬 구조를 이루는 동사 원형을 찾아야 하므로 (C)가 정답이다.

4.

(A) 온보딩 일정을 유연하게 유지하세요.
(B) 함께 일하게 되기를 기대합니다.
(C) 오리엔테이션은 하루 종일 진행됩니다.
(D) 추가 설명이 필요하면 알려주세요.

해설 이메일은 새 직원의 원활한 적응을 돕기 위한 협조를 요청하고, 마지막 문장은 추가적인 질문이나 의문 사항이 있을 경우 소통할 것을 권장하는 문장이 적합하므로 (D)가 가장 적절하다.

PART 7

다음 공지와 관련된 질문 1-4번을 보세요.

수신: 모든 직원
발신: 시설 관리팀
날짜: 9월 12일
제목: 다가오는 사무실 개조

팀 여러분,
우리 사무실이 10월 1일부터 개조를 시작하여 이 달 말까지 진행될 예정임을 알려드립니다. 이번 개조는 업무 공간을 개선하고 모든 직원들에게 더 편안하고 효율적인 환경을 제공하기 위한 노력의 일환입니다.
이 기간 동안 건물의 일부 구역, 특히 3층과 4층은 임시로 폐쇄됩니다. 개조 작업이 진행되는 동안 낮 시간대에 소음이 발생할 수 있으니 양해 부탁드립니다. 이로 인해 불편을 끼쳐드리는 점 사과드리며, 여러분의 이해에 감사드립니다.

모든 분들을 수용하기 위해 1층과 2층에 임시 작업 공간을 마련하였습니다. 개조로 인해 영향을 받는 직원들에게는 사전에 공지되고, 임시 작업 공간에 대한 세부 사항이 제공될 예정입니다. 개조 기간 동안 작업 공간과 관련된 우려나 특별 요청이 있는 경우, 시설 관리팀에 직접 연락해 주시기 바랍니다.
여러분의 협조에 감사드리며, 곧 새롭게 단장된 공간을 공개하게 되기를 기대합니다.

감사합니다,
시설 관리팀

어휘 inform 알리다, 통지하다 undergo 겪다, 진행하다 renovation 보수 effort 노력 improve 개선하다, 향상시키다 comfortable 편안한 efficient 효율적인 temporarily 임시로, 일시적으로 ongoing 진행 중인 occasional 가끔의 noise disruption 소음 방해 apologize 사과하다 inconvenience 불편 appreciate 감사하다 accommodate 수용하다 notify 공지하다, 통보하다 regarding ~에 관하여 temporary 임시의, 일시적인 concerns 우려, 걱정 relate 관련시키다 directly 직접적으로 cooperation 협력, 협조 look forward to ~을 기대하다 unveil 공개하다, 발표하다 newly 새롭게

정답

1. (C) 2. (D) 3. (B) 4. (A)

1. 개조 작업은 언제 시작됩니까?
   (A) 9월 12일
   (B) 9월 30일
   (C) 10월 1일
   (D) 10월 말

정답 (C) On October 1

해설 본문에서 "our office will undergo renovations starting from October 1"라고 명시되어 있어, 개조 작업은 10월 1일에 시작된다는 것을 알 수 있으므로 (C)가 정답이다.

2.

해설 본문에서 "we have arranged for alternative workspaces on the first and second floors"라고 명시되어 있어, 영향을 받는 직원들은 1층과 2층의 임시 작업 공간에서 근무하게 되므로 (D)가 정답이다.

3. 개조 기간 동안 작업 공간에 대해 우려가 있는 직원들은 무엇을 해야 합니까?
   (A) 매니저와 상의한다.
   (B) 시설 관리팀에 연락한다.
   (C) 재택근무를 한다.
   (D) 추가 지시를 기다린다.

해설 본문에서 "If you have any concerns or special requests related to your workspace during the renovation period, please contact the Facilities Management team directly"라고 명시되어 있어, 작업 공간에 대해 우려가 있는 직원들은 시설 관리팀에 직접 연락하면 되므로 (B)가 정답이다.

4. 개조 기간 동안 3층과 4층에 대해 무엇을 추론할 수 있습니까?
   (A) 직원들이 이 구역에 접근할 수 없을 것이다.
   (B) 새로운 사무실 공간으로 전환될 것이다.
   (C) 공사 자재를 보관하는 용도로 사용될 것이다.
   (D) 변경 사항에 적응하기 위해 직원들이 초과근무를 해야 할 것이다.

해설 본문에서 "During this time, certain sections of the building, including the third and fourth floors, will be temporarily closed."라고 언급되어 있어, 3층과 4층이 임시로 폐쇄되어 직원들이 접근할 수 없다는 것을 알 수 있으므로 (A)가 정답이다.

Chapter 02 동사의 시제

2. 동사의 시제

✔ CheckPoint 1. 현재 시제

정답

1. (B) 2. (B) 3. (B)

1.

번역 매주 토요일, 그녀는 카페에서 친구들을 만난다.

해설 반복 되풀이되는 습관이나 동작을 표현할 때 현재 시제를 사용하므로 (B) meets가 정답이다.

2.

번역 버스는 매주 평일 오전 8시 15분에 터미널을 떠난다.

해설 일정표와 관련된 고정된 동작은 현재 시제를 사용하므로 (B) leaves가 정답이다.

3.

번역 회의가 시작되면, 우리는 새로운 정책에 대해 논의할 것이다.

해설 시간과 조건의 부사절에서는 미래시제 대신 현재시제를 사용하므로 (B) starts가 정답이다.

어휘 discuss 논의하다 policy 정책, 방침

✔ CheckPoint 2. 과거 시제

정답

1. (B) 2. (D) 3. (A)

1.

번역 그 회사는 2015년에 가장 성공적인 제품을 출시했다.

해설 In 2015는 과거의 동작이나 상태를 나타내는 시간 표현이므로 (B) launched가 정답이다.

어휘 successful 성공적인

2.

번역 우리는 어제 회의에서 새로운 정책에 대해 논의했다.

해설 yesterday는 과거의 동작이나 상태를 나타내는 시간 표현이므로 (D) discussed가 정답이다.

3.

번역 그들은 고객을 만나기 전에 계약서에 서명했다.

해설 계약서에 서명한 것과 고객을 만난 것 중 서명한 것이 먼저 일어났지만 두 사건의 순서가 명확한 경우 과거완료 대신 과거 시제를 사용할 수 있으므로 (A) signed가 정답이다.

어휘 contract 계약서

✔ CheckPoint 3. 미래 시제

정답

1. (B) 2. (D) 3. (C)

1.

번역 다음 주부터 회사는 생산성을 향상시키기 위해 새로운 소프트웨어 시스템을 도입할 것이다.

해설 Starting next week는 미래를 나타내는 부사/부사구이므로 (B) will implement가 정답이다.

어휘 improve 개선하다, 향상시키다 productivity 생산성

2.

번역 다가오는 금요일에 CEO는 연간 성과 검토 회의를 주재할 것이다.

해설 This coming Friday는 미래를 나타내는 부

사/부사구이므로 (D) will host가 정답이다.

어휘 annual 연례의, 매년의 performance 성과, 수행 review 검토, 평가

3.

번역 다음 달부터 마케팅 팀은 새로운 광고 캠페인을 시작할 것이다.

해설 As of next month는 미래를 나타내는 부사/부사구이므로 (C) will launch가 정답이다.

어휘 advertising campaign 광고 캠페인

✔ CheckPoint 4. 현재완료

정답

1. (B) 2. (B) 3. (D)

1.

번역 그는 이 프로젝트에서 3개월 동안 일해왔다.

해설 for three months는 현재완료의 계속 용법을 나타내고, 주절에 현재완료형이나 현재완료 진행형을 모두 사용 가능하므로 (B) has worked가 정답이다.

2.

번역 회사가 유연근무제를 도입한 이후로 직원 만족도가 향상되었다.

해설 since는 현재완료의 계속 용법을 나타내므로 주절에 현재완료형이나 현재완료 진행형을 모두 사용 가능하다. 하지만 since가 사용된 종속절은 과거 시제를 사용하여 사건의 시작 시점을 나타내므로 (B) introduced가 정답이다.

어휘 satisfaction 만족 improve 개선하다, 향상시키다 flexible 유연한, 융통성 있는

3.

번역 마케팅 팀은 지난 한 달 동안 캠페인을 성공적으로 시작했다.

해설 over the past month는 현재완료의 계속 용법을 나타내고, 주절에 현재완료형이나 현재완료 진행형을 모두 사용 가능하므로 (D) has launched가 정답이다.

어휘 successfully 성공적으로

✔ CheckPoint 5. 과거완료

정답

1. (B) 2. (C) 3. (C)

1.

번역 그들은 회의가 시작되기 전에 계약서에 서명했었다.

해설 회의를 시작한 것보다 계약서에 서명한 것이 먼저 일어난 사건이므로 (B) had signed가 정답이다.

2.

번역 CEO가 도착했을 때쯤, 팀은 발표를 준비했었다.

해설 CEO가 도착한 것보다 팀이 발표를 준비한 것이 먼저 일어난 사건이고, 또 과거 특정 시점을 나타내는 By the time + 과거 시제는 주절에 과거완료 시제를 사용하여 과거 특정 시점 이전에 완료된 동작을 나타내므로 (C) had prepared가 정답이다.

어휘 by the time ~할 때쯤 presentation 발표

3.

번역 팀은 고객이 승인하기 전에 3주 동안 디자인 변경을 검토하고 있었다.

해설 고객이 승인한 것보다 디자인 변경을 검토한 것이 먼저 일어난 사건이고, 또 for three weeks는 과거완료의 계속 용법으로 주절에 과거완료형이나 과거완료 진행형을 모두 사용 가능하므로 (C) had been reviewing이 정답이다.

어휘 change 변경, 수정 사항 approve 승인하다, 허가하다

✔ CheckPoint 6. 미래완료

정답

1. (A) 2. (D) 3. (C)

1.

번역 세미나가 끝날 때쯤이면 팀은 모든 필요한 데이터를 수집했을 것이다.

해설 By the time + 현재 시제(By the time the seminar ends)는 미래의 특정 시점을 나타내고, 주절에 미래완료 시제를 사용하여 그 시점 이전에 완료될 동작을 나타내므로 (A) will have gathered가 정답이다.

어휘 gather 수집하다, 모으다

2.

번역 회사는 다음 분기 말까지 확장 계획을 발표했을 것이다.

해설 By the end of the next quarter는 미래 특정 시점을 나타내고, 주절에는 미래완료 시제를 사용하여 미래 특정 시점 이전에 완료될 결과를 나타내므로 (D) will have announced가 정답이다.

어휘 expansion 확장, 확대 quarter 분기

3.

번역 그녀는 은퇴할 때쯤 회사에 대한 공로로 수많은 상을 받았을 것이다.

해설 By the time + 현재 시제(By the time she retires)는 미래 특정 시점을 나타내고, 주절에는 미래완료 시제를 사용하여 미래 특정 시점 이전에 완료될 경험을 나타내므로 (C) will have received가 정답이다.

어휘 retire 은퇴하다 numerous 수많은 award 상 contribution 공헌, 공로

토익 종합 실전문제

정답

1. (A)	2. (C)	3. (C)	4. (A)	5. (C)
6. (C)	7. (B)	8. (D)	9. (C)	10. (D)
11. (D)	12. (A)	13. (C)	14. (C)	15. (C)
16. (D)	17. (B)	18. (A)	19. (C)	20. (A)
21. (D)	22. (A)	23. (B)	24. (D)	

1.

번역 CEO는 다음 주에 비즈니스 정상 회의에 참석하기 위해 싱가포르로 떠난다.

해설 왕래 발착 동사(departs)는 가까운 미래를 표현할 때 현재 시제를 사용하므로 (A) departs가 정답이다.

어휘 attend 참석하다 business summit 비즈니스 정상회의

2.

번역 회의는 오전 9시에 정확히 시작하고, 오전 11시에 끝난다.

해설 일정표와 관련된 활동은 현재 시제를 사용하므로 (C) starts가 정답이다.

어휘 sharp 정확히, 정각에

3.

번역 CEO는 프로젝트가 제시간에 완료될지 묻고 싶어 한다.

해설 이 문장에서 if the project ________ completed on time은 wants to ask의 목적어 자리에 오는 명사절로, 미래를 표현할 때는 미래 시제를 그대로 사용하므로 (C) will be가 정답이다.

4.

번역 네가 참석해야 할 회의는 월요일로 예정되어 있다.

해설 이 문장에서 that you ______ to attend는 The meeting을 수식하는 형용사절로, 미래를 표현할 때는 미래 시제를 그대로 사용하므로 (A) will need가 정답이다.

어휘 schedule 일정, 일정을 잡다, 예정하다

5.

번역 그 팀은 지난달에 프로젝트를 제시간에 끝내기 위해 열심히 일했다.

해설 last month는 과거의 동작이나 상태를 나타내는 시간 표현이므로 (C) worked가 정답이다.

6.

번역 그녀는 회의가 시작되기 전에 발표를 마쳤다.

해설 발표를 마친 것이 회의를 시작한 것보다 먼저 일어난 사건이고, 전자가 과거완료(had finished)를 사용했으면 후자는 과거 시제를 사용해야 하므로 (C) started가 정답이다.

7.

번역 팀은 2주 전에 고객의 피드백을 검토했다.

해설 two weeks ago는 과거의 동작이나 상태를 나타내는 시간 표현이므로 (B) reviewed가 정답이다.

8.

번역 그는 작년에 런던으로 이사 가기 전에 3년 동안 파리에 살았다.

해설 파리에 거주한 것과 런던으로 이사한 것 중에서 파리에 거주한 것이 먼저 일어났지만 두 사건의 순서가 명확한 경우 과거완료 대신 과거 시제를 사용할 수 있으므로 (D) lived가 정답이다. 참고로 for three years는 기간을 나타내는 표현이지만, 현재와는 분리된 과거의 특정 시점에 완료된 기간을 나타내므로 과거 사건에 불과하다.

9.

번역 1월부터 HR팀은 직원 복지에 대한 새로운 정책을 도입할 것이다.

해설 Starting from January는 미래를 나타내는 부사/부사구이므로 (C) will introduce가 정답이다.

어휘 HR team 인사팀, 인사부 policy 정책, 방침 benefit 혜택, 복리후생, 복지

10.

번역 매니저는 다가오는 월요일에 고객들과 회의를 할 것이다.

해설 this coming Monday는 미래를 나타내는 부사/부사구이므로 (D) will have가 정답이다.

11.

번역 새로운 규정은 다음 달부터 발효될 것이다.

해설 "~부터"라는 의미를 가진 as of는 뒤에 미래 시제와 결합하여 미래를 나타내므로 (D) as of가 정답이다.

어휘 come into effect 발효되다

12.

번역 새 사무실 건물의 건설이 가까운 미래에 시작될 것이다.

해설 in the near future는 미래를 나타내는 부사/부사구이므로 (A) will begin이 정답이다.

어휘 construction 건설, 공사 near 가까운

13.

번역 그 직원은 회사에 입사한 이후로 여러 교육 세션에 참석했다.

해설 since joining the company는 현재완료의 계속 용법을 나타내고, 주절에 현재완료형이나 현재완료 진행형을 모두 사용 가능하므로 (C) has attended가 정답이다.

어휘 multiple 여러, 다수의

14.

번역 마케팅 팀이 새로운 전략을 실행한 이후로 매출이 크게 증가했다.

해설 since는 현재완료의 계속 용법을 나타내므로 주절에 현재완료형이나 현재완료 진행형을 모두 사용 가능하다. 하지만 since가 사용된 종속절은 과거 시제를 사용하여 사건의 시작 시점을 나타내므로 (C) implemented가 정답이다.

어휘 sales 매출, 판매량 increase 증가하다 significantly 상당히, 크게 strategy 전략

15.

번역 마케팅 팀은 지난 2주 동안 설문 조사를 실시하고 있다.

해설 the past two weeks는 숫자 기간을 가리키는 말이므로 (C) for가 정답이다. (C) for the past two weeks는 현재완료의 계속 용법을 나타내고, 주절에 현재완료형이나 현재완료 진행형을 모두 사용 가능하므로 has been conducting이 사용되었다.

어휘 conduct 수행하다, 실시하다 survey 조사, 설문 조사

16.

번역 그 팀은 마감일을 맞추기 위해 6개월 동안 소프트웨어를 개발해 왔다.

해설 for six months는 현재완료의 계속 용법을 나타내고, 주절에 현재완료형이나 현재완료 진행형을 모두 사용 가능하므로 (D) has been developing이 정답이다.

17.

번역 직원들은 어제부터 그 제안서 작업을 하고 있다.

해설 yesterday는 시점을 가리키는 말이므로 과거 시작 시점을 나타낼 때 사용하는 (B) since가 정답이다. since yesterday는 현재완료의 계속 용법을 나타내고, 주절에 현재완료형이나 현재완료 진행형을 모두 사용 가능하므로 have been working이 사용되었다. 참고로 (A) for는 숫자 기간과 함께 사용하므로 문맥에 맞지 않다.

어휘 proposal 제안서

18.

번역 우리가 더 많은 정보를 수집하면 곧 너에게 업데이트를 제공할 것이다.

해설 as soon as we ______ more information는 미래에 완료될 동작을 나타내는 시간의 부사절로, 현재완료가 미래완료를 대신하여 사용하므로 (A) have gathered가 정답이다.

19.

번역 매니저는 최근에 팀과 다가오는 변화에 대해 논의했다.

해설 recently는 과거와 현재완료 시제에 모두 사용 가능한데, 여기서는 과거부터 현재까지의 연속성 또는 현재와 연결된 사건을 나타내므로 (C) has discussed가 정답이다.

어휘 upcoming 다가오는 recently 최근에

20.

번역 그녀는 매니저에게 제출하기 전에 보고서를 철저히 검토했었다.

해설 매니저에게 보고서를 제출한 것보다 검토한 것이 먼저 일어난 사건이므로 (A) had reviewed가 정답이다.

어휘 thoroughly 철저히 submit 제출하다

21.

번역 팀이 중요한 세부 사항을 포함하는 것을 잊었기 때문에 보고서는 거부되었다.

해설 보고서가 거부된 것보다 중요한 세부 사항을 포함하지 않은 것이 먼저 일어난 사건이므로 (D) had forgotten이 정답이다.

어휘 reject 거부하다 include 포함하다 critical 중요한 detail 세부 사항

22.

번역 새로운 매니저가 인계받기 전에 그 프로젝트는 몇 달 동안 일정이 뒤처져 있었다.

해설 새로운 매니저가 인계받은 것보다 프로젝트 일정이 뒤처진 것이 먼저 일어난 사건이고, 또 for several months는 과거완료의 계속 용법으로 주절에 과거완료형이나 과거완료 진행형을 모두 사용 가능하므로 (A) had been이 정답이다.

[어휘] behind schedule 예정보다 늦은, 일정이 지연된 take over 인계받다, 맡다

23.

번역 시스템이 고장 났을 때쯤, IT 팀은 아침부터 그 문제를 해결하고 있었다.

[해설] 시스템이 고장 난 것보다 IT 팀이 문제 해결을 시도한 것이 먼저 일어난 사건이고, 또 since the morning은 과거완료의 계속 용법으로 주절에 과거완료형이나 과거완료 진행형을 모두 사용 가능하므로 (B) had been working이 정답이다.

[어휘] crash 고장 나다, 충돌하다

24.

번역 이 연구 프로젝트가 출판될 때쯤 우리는 2년 동안 이 프로젝트에서 일했을 것이다.

[해설] By the time + 현재 시제(by the time it is published)는 미래 특정 시점을 나타내므로 주절에는 미래완료 시제를 사용하여 그 시점 이전에 완료될 동작이나 상태를 나타낸다. 또 for two years가 있어 현재완료 계속을 나타내지만 by the time it is published로 인해 기준시점이 미래가 되므로 미래완료 계속이 되고, 미래완료형이나 미래완료 진행형이 모두 가능하므로 (D) will have worked on이 정답이다.

[어휘] research 연구, 연구하다 publish 출판하다, 게재하다

PART 6

다음 메모와 관련된 질문 1-4번을 보세요.

> 다가오는 팀 빌딩 워크숍
>
> 팀 여러분,
> 팀워크와 협업을 강화하기 위한 노력의 일환으로, 다음 달에 팀 빌딩 워크숍을 개최하게 되어 기쁘게 생각합니다. 이번 워크숍은 우리 팀의 역동성을 강화하고 전반적인 효율성을 향상시키는 것을 목표로 하고 있습니다.
> 원활한 진행을 위해, 우리는 더 나은 소통 및 문제 해결 능력을 배양하기 위해 설계된 다양한 상호작용 세션을 준비했습니다. 워크숍은 다음 달 15일에 우리 컨퍼런스 센터에서 열릴 예정입니다. 달력에 표시하시고, 팀으로서 성장할 수 있는 중요한 기회이니 꼭 참석해 주시기 바랍니다.
> 워크숍 동안, 우리는 재미있고 교육적인 다양한 팀 활동에 참여할 것입니다. 이러한 활동은 서로의 강점을 이해하고 집단성과를 개선하는 데 도움을 줄 것입니다.
> 식이 제한이나 특별한 요구 사항이 있는 경우, HR 부서에 미리 알려주시면 필요한 조치를 취하겠습니다. 모든 참가자가 편안하고 생산적인 경험을 할 수 있도록 노력하겠습니다.
> 마지막으로, 워크숍 일정 및 의제에 대한 자세한 정보는 날짜가 가까워지면 보내드리겠습니다. 그때까지, 즉각적인 질문이나 우려 사항이 있는 경우 언제든지 연락해 주시기 바랍니다.
> 관심과 협조에 감사드립니다.
>
> 감사합니다,
> 인사팀

[어휘] upcoming 다가오는 as part of ~의 일환으로 effort 노력 enhance 향상시키다, 강화하다 collaboration 협력, 협업 announce 발표하다, 알리다 aim 목표로 하다 strengthen 강화하다 team dynamics 팀의 역동성, 팀의 에너지 improve 개선하다, 향상시키다 overall 전반적인, 전체적인 efficiency 효율성 facilitate 촉진하다, 용이하게 하다 organize 조직하다 interactive 상호작용하는 foster 촉진하다 attend 참석하다 opportunity 기회 dietary 식이 요법의 restriction 제한, 제약 arrangement 준비, 마련 comfortable 편안한 productive 생산적인 experience 경험 send out 발송하다, 보내다 agenda 의제 immediate 즉각적인 concerns 우려, 걱정 attention 관심 cooperation 협력, 협조

정답

1. (B) 2. (C) 3. (D) 4. (B)

1.

[해설] 워크숍이 다음 달 15일(on the 15th of next month)에 개최된다고 했으므로 미래시제인 (B) will take place가 정답이다.

2.

해설 전후 문맥을 보면 이 워크숍의 목적은 팀워크를 강화하고 협업 능력을 키우는 데 초점이 맞춰져 있으므로 (C)가 가장 적절하다. (A)는 회사의 재무 보고서를 분석하는 것인데, 이는 워크숍의 취지와 관련이 없으므로 적절하지 않고, (B)는 연사가 동기 부여 연설을 한다는 내용이지만, 메모에서 연사에 대한 언급이 없으므로 문맥과 맞지 않으며, (D)는 팀 리더들이 분기별 실적 보고서를 발표한다는 것으로, 워크숍 활동으로 명시되지 않았기 때문에 문맥과 맞지 않다.

3.

해설 식이 제한이나 특별한 요구 사항은 워크숍 시작 전에 인사팀에 미리 알려야 한다는 문맥을 고려할 때, (D)가 정답이다.

4.

해설 워크숍 일정 및 의제에 대한 자세한 정보는 날짜가 가까워지면 보내드리겠다고 했으니 미래의 특정 시점까지 기다려야 한다는 의미의 (B)가 정답이다.

PART 7

다음 이메일과 관련된 질문 1-4번을 보세요.

> 수신: allstaff@sunnydayresorts.com
> 발신: Sarah Lee
> s.lee@sunnydayresorts.com
> 날짜: 9월 9일
> 제목: 연례 직원 리트릿 정보
>
> 팀 여러분께,
> 다가오는 연례 직원 리트릿(휴양 프로그램)이 10월 15일부터 16일까지 블루 라군 리조트에서 개최됨을 알려드리게 되어 기쁘게 생각합니다.
> 올해는 팀워크와 휴식을 증진하기 위해 다양한 활동을 준비했습니다. 이번 리트릿은 동료들과 교류하고 재충전할 수 있는 훌륭한 기회이므로 모든 직원들이 참여하시기를 권장합니다.
> 리트릿은 10월 15일 오전 9시, 전문 진행자가 이끄는 팀 빌딩 워크숍으로 시작됩니다. 점심이 제공되며, 오후에는 하이킹과 카누와 같은 야외 활동이 진행됩니다. 이러한 활동을 위해 편안한 옷과 신발을 준비해 오시기 바랍니다. 저녁에는 해변에서 바비큐가 제공되며, 이후 모닥불과 함께하는 자유 시간이 마련되어 있습니다.
> 10월 16일, 오전 8시에 요가 세션으로 하루를 시작하며, 이후 리더십 세미나가 진행됩니다. 리트릿은 오후 1시, CEO인 톰슨 씨의 폐회 연설과 점심 식사로 마무리됩니다.
> 9월 30일까지 이 이메일에 회신하여 참석 여부를 확인해 주시기 바랍니다.
> 특별한 식이 제한이 있거나 특별한 편의가 필요하신 경우, 가능한 한 빨리 알려주시면 필요한 준비를 하겠습니다.
> 그곳에서 여러분을 뵙기를 기대합니다!
>
> 감사합니다,
> Sarah Lee
> 이벤트 코디네이터, Sunny Day Resorts

어휘 announce 발표하다, 알리다 annual 연례의, 매년의 retreat 휴양, 리트릿 activity 활동 promote 촉진하다 relaxation 휴식 encourage 장려하다, 권장하다 opportunity 기회 connect 연결하다, 교류하다 colleague 동료 recharge 재충전하다 lead ~을 이끌다 professional 전문가의 facilitator 진행자, 조정자 outdoor 야외의 hiking 하이킹, 도보 여행 canoeing 카누 타기 comfortable 편안한 bonfire 모닥불 social time 사교 시간 conclude 끝나다, 마무리하다 confirm 확인하다 attendance 참석 reply 답장하다 dietary 식이 요법의 restriction 제한, 제약 accommodation 편의, 합의, 숙박 시설

정답

1. (C)   2. (A)   3. (D)   4. (B)

1.

해설 이메일에서 "Please confirm your attendance by replying to this email by September 30"라고 명확히 언급하고 있으므로 (C)가 정답이다.

2.

해설 이메일에서 "Lunch will be provided, followed by an afternoon of outdoor activities such as hiking and canoeing"라고 언급되어 있어,

점심 이후에는 야외 활동이 예정되어 있음을 알 수 있으므로 (A)가 정답이다.

3.

해설 이메일에서 “Please remember to bring comfortable clothing and shoes for these activities”라고 명시되어 있어, 활동에 적합한 편안한 옷과 신발을 가져와야 한다는 것을 알 수 있으므로 (D)가 정답이다.

4.

해설 이메일 본문에서 “This year, we have planned a series of activities to promote teamwork and relaxation”라고 명시되어 있어, 리트릿의 주요 목적이 팀워크와 휴식을 증진하는 것임을 암시하고 있으므로 (B)가 정답이다.

Chapter 03 능동태와 수동태

1. 태의 구조와 시제

✔ CheckPoint 1. 능동태와 수동태의 시제

정답

1. (A) 2. (B)

1.

번역 최종 결정은 회의가 끝나기 전에 이사회에 의해 내려졌다.

해설 능동태 문장 The board made the final decision before the end of the meeting에서 직접목적어를 수동태의 주어로 변환하면 The final decision was made by the board before the end of the meeting가 되고, 또 단수 주어에 과거 시제이므로 (A) was made가 정답이다.

어휘 decision 결정, 판단 board 위원회, 이사회

2.

번역 지진이 발생했을 때 건물은 수리 중이었다.

해설 능동태 문장 They were repairing the building when the earthquake struck에서 직접목적어를 수동태의 주어로 변환하면 The building was being repaired when the earthquake struck가 되고, 또 단수주어에 과거진행 시제이므로 (B) was being repaired가 정답이다.

어휘 repair 수리하다, 고치다 earthquake 지진

2. 타동사의 수동태

✔ CheckPoint 2. 4형식 동사의 수동태

정답

1. (B) 2. (C) 3. (A)

1.

번역 위원회는 연구자에게 연구를 위한 보조금을 수여했다.

해설 능동태 문장 The committee awarded the researcher a grant for her study에서 간접목적어를 수동태의 주어로 변환하면 The researcher was awarded a grant for her study by the committee가 되고, 또 주어가 단수이므로 (B) was awarded가 정답이다.

어휘 researcher 연구원, 연구자 award 수여하다, 상, 보상 grant 보조금, 연구비, 장학금 committee 위원회

2.

번역 팀 리더는 고객에게 새로운 디자인을 보여주었다.

해설 3형식 능동태 문장 The team leader showed the new design to the client (<= The team leader showed the client the new design (4형식))에서 직접목적어를 수동태의 주어로 변환하면 The new design was shown to the client by the team leader가 되고, 또 주어가 단수이므로 (C) was shown이 정답이다.

어휘 design 디자인, 설계, 디자인하다, 설계하다 client 고객, 의뢰인 team leader 팀장

3.

번역 팀은 다가오는 프로젝트와 관련하여 컨설턴트에게 여러 중요한 질문을 받았다.

해설 능동태 문장 The consultant asked the team several important questions regarding the upcoming project에서 간접목적어를 수동태의 주어로 변환하면 The team was asked several important questions by the consultant regarding the upcoming project가 되고, 또 주어가 단수이므로 (A) was asked가 정답이다.

어휘 consultant 컨설턴트, 상담가 regarding ~에 관하여 upcoming 다가오는

✔ CheckPoint 3. 5형식 동사의 수동태

정답

1. (B) 2. (A)

1.

번역 변호사는 문서가 클라이언트에 의해 서명되는 것을 보았다.

해설 지각동사 see의 능동태 문장 The lawyer saw the client sign the documents에서 목적어 이후는 the client(의미상의 주어), sign(의미상의 동사), the documents(의미상의 목적어)로 구성되어 있다. 이를 수동태로 변환하면, the documents가 수동태의 주어가 되고, sign은 과거분사(be signed에서 be가 생략됨)로 변환되므로 (B) signed가 정답이다.

어휘 lawyer 변호사 documents 문서, 서류

2.

번역 모든 직원들은 인사부에 의해 새로운 정책을 따르라는 조언을 받았다.

해설 원 문장 The HR department advised all employees to follow the new policy에서 직접목적어를 수동태의 주어로 변환하면 All employees were advised to follow the new policy by the HR department가 되므로 (A) to follow가 정답이다.

어휘 HR(Human Resources) department 인사부, 인사팀 advise 충고하다, 조언하다, 권고하다 employee 직원, 근로자 follow 따르다, 준수하다 policy 정책, 방침

✔ CheckPoint 4. 목적어가 명사절인 문장의 수동태

정답

1. (D) 2. (B) 3. (A)

1.

번역 그 보고서가 중요한 정보를 포함하고 있다고 생각된다.

해설 think는 명사절을 목적어로 취하고, 또 2가지 유형의 수동태로 변환될 수 있는 동사로서, 능동태 문장 They think that the report contains critical information에서 직접목적어인 that절을 수동태의 주어로 변환하면 주어가 너무 길어지므로 가주어 It을 수동태의 주어로 사용하면 It is thought that the report contains critical information가 되므로 (D) is thought가 정답이다.

어휘 report 보고서, 보고 critical 중요한, 비판적인 contain 포함하다

2.

번역 그 합병은 모든 이해관계자들에 의해 성공적인 것으로 여겨진다.

해설 consider는 명사절을 목적어로 취하고, 또 2

가지 유형의 수동태로 변환될 수 있는 동사로서, 능동태 문장 They consider the merger successful by all stakeholders에서 직접목적어를 수동태의 주어로 변환하면 The merger is considered successful by all stakeholders가 되므로 (B) is considered가 정답이다.

어휘 merger 합병 successful 성공적인 stakeholder 이해관계자 consider ~를 고려하다, 여기다, 간주하다

3.

번역 새로운 규정이 회사 운영에 상당한 영향을 미칠 것으로 믿어진다.

해설 believe는 명사절을 목적어로 취하고, 또 2가지 유형의 수동태로 변환될 수 있는 동사로서, 능동태 문장 They believe the new regulations to have a significant impact on the company's operations에서 직접목적어를 수동태의 주어로 변환하면 The new regulations are believed to have a significant impact on the company's operations가 되므로 (A) to have가 정답이다.

어휘 regulations 규정, 규제, 법규 significant 상당한, 중요한 impact 영향, 충격, 영향을 주다.

3. 수동태의 관용표현

✔ CheckPoint 5. 수동태를 포함하는 관용표현

정답

1. (C) 2. (A) 3. (C)

1.

번역 많은 전문가들이 인공지능 기술의 급속한 발전에 놀라고 있다.

해설 be amazed by는 "~에 놀라다"는 의미로, 전문가들이 인공지능 기술의 발전에 놀라는 상황을 나타내므로 (C) amazed가 정답이다.

어휘 expert 전문가 amaze 놀라게 하다 rapid 빠른, 신속한 advancement 발전, 진보, 향상 artificial intelligent 인공지능

2.

번역 그 회사의 새로운 프로젝트는 친환경 제품 개발에 집중하고 있다.

해설 be focused on은 "~에 집중하다"라는 의미로, 새로운 프로젝트가 eco-friendly products(친환경 제품)에 중점을 두고 있음을 나타내므로 (A) focused가 정답이다.

어휘 eco-friendly 친환경적인

3.

번역 공장에 의해 발생된 환경 피해는 유독성 화학 물질로 덮여 있었다.

해설 be covered with는 "~로 덮여 있다"는 의미로, 환경 피해가 유독성 화학 물질로 인해 덮여 있음을 나타내므로 (C) covered가 정답이다. (A) equipped 뒤에도 with가 오지만 "~이 갖춰져 있다"는 의미로 문맥에 맞지 않다.

어휘 environmental 환경의, 환경과 관련된 damage 손상, 피해, 손상을 입히다 cause 초래하다, 유발하다 toxic 유독한, 독성이 있는

토익 종합 실전문제

정답

1. (C)	2. (A)	3. (D)	4. (D)	5. (B)
6. (A)	7. (A)	8. (A)	9. (B)	10. (A)
11. (B)	12. (C)	13. (B)	14. (C)	15. (B)
16. (C)	17. (C)	18. (D)	19. (B)	20. (B)
21. (B)	22. (D)	23. (B)	24. (C)	

1.

번역 그 보고서는 팀 리더에 의해 마감 기한 전에 제출될 것이다.

해설 능동태 문장 The team leader will submit the report before the deadline에서 직접목적어를 수동태의 주어로 변환하면 The report will be submitted by the team leader before the deadline가 되고, 또 미래시제이므로 (C) will be submitted가 정답이다.

어휘 submit 제출하다

2.

번역 여러 문서가 현재 매니저에 의해 검토되고 있다.

해설 능동태 문장 The manager is reviewing several documents right now에서 직접목적어를 수동태의 주어로 변환하면 Several documents are being reviewed by the manager right now가 되고, 또 복수주어에 현재진행 시제이므로 (A) are being reviewed가 정답이다.

어휘 review 검토하다 right now 지금 바로, 현재 manager 관리자, 매니저

3.

번역 최종 발표는 프로젝트 마감일 전에 팀에 의해 완료되어 있을 것이다.

해설 능동태 문장 The team will have completed the final presentation before the project deadline에서 직접목적어를 수동태의 주어로 변환하면 The final presentation will have been completed by the team before the project deadline가 되고, 또 미래완료 시제이므로 (D) will have been completed가 정답이다.

어휘 final 최종적인 presentation 발표, 프레젠테이션 deadline 마감 기한, 최종 기한

4.

번역 CEO는 마케팅 팀에게 신제품 출시를 강화하기 위해 상당한 예산 증액을 해주었다.

해설 능동태 문장 The CEO made the marketing team a significant budget increase를 보면 4형식 동사 make가 간접목적어(the marketing team)와 직접목적어(a significant budget increase)를 모두 취하고 있는 4형식 문장이므로 (C) made가 정답이다.

어휘 marketing team 마케팅 팀 significant 중요한, 상당한 boost 강화하다, 신장시키다 budget increase 예산 증액

5.

번역 상세한 청구서가 회계 부서에 의해 고객에게 보내졌다.

해설 4형식 능동태 문장(The accounting department sent the client a detailed invoice)에서 파생된 3형식 능동태 문장(The accounting department sent a detailed invoice to the client)에서 직접목적어를 수동태의 주어로 변환하면 A detailed invoice was sent to the client by the accounting department가 되고, 또 주어가 단수이므로 (B) was sent가 정답이다.

어휘 detailed 상세한, 세부적인 invoice 송장, 거래 명세서 accounting department 회계 부서

6.

번역 매니저는 팀에게 상세한 지시 사항을 주었다.

해설 능동태 문장 The manager gave the team detailed instructions에서 직접목적어를 수동태의 주어로 변환하면 Detailed instructions were given to the team by the manager가 된다. 이 때 give는 뒤에 남은 간접목적어 앞에 전치사 to를 사용하고, 또 주어가 복수이므로 (A) were given to가 정답이다.

어휘 instructions 지시사항, 설명서

7.

번역 교수는 학생들에게 몇 가지 도전적인 질문을 했다.

해설 능동태 문장 The professor asked the students several challenging questions에서 직접목적어를 수동태의 주어가 되도록 변환하면 Several challenging questions were asked of the students by the professor가 된다. 이 때 ask는 뒤에 남은 간접목적어 앞에 전치사 of를 사용하고, 또 주어가 복수이므로 (A) were asked of가 정답이다.

어휘 challenging 도전적인, 어려운 professor 교수

8.

번역 맞춤형 책상이 매니저에 의해 직원을 위해 주문되었지만, 예상보다 늦게 도착했다.

해설 능동태 문장 The manager ordered a custom-built desk for the employee에서 직접목적어를 수동태의 주어로 변환하면 A custom-built desk was ordered for the employee by the manager가 되고, 또 주어가 단수이므로 (A) was ordered가 정답이다.

어휘 custom-built 주문 제작된, 맞춤형으로 제작된 order 주문하다 later than expected 예상보다 늦게

9.

번역 CEO는 새로운 마케팅 전략이 컨설턴트들에 의해 실행되게 했다.

해설 사역동사 have의 능동태 문장 The CEO had the consultants implement the new marketing strategy에서 목적어 이후는 the consultants(의미상의 주어), implement(의미상의 동사), the new marketing strategy(의미상의 목적어)로 구성되어 있다. 이를 수동태로 변환하면, the new marketing strategy가 수동태의 주어가 되고, implement는 과거분사(be implemented에서 be가 생략됨)로 변환되므로 (B) implemented가 정답이다.

어휘 marketing strategy 마케팅 전략 implement 실행하다, 이행하다

10.

번역 직원들은 어려움에도 불구하고 분기 목표를 달성하도록 기대 받고 있다.

해설 expect는 to부정사를 목적격 보어로 취하는 5형식 동사로서, 능동태 문장 The company expects the employees to meet the quarterly goals despite the challenges에서 직접목적어를 수동태의 주어로 변환하면 The employees are expected to meet the quarterly goals despite the challenges by the company가 되고, 또 복수주어이므로 (A) are expected가 정답이다.

어휘 meet 충족시키다, 달성하다 quarterly goal 분기별 목표 challenge 어려움, 도전 과제

11.

번역 팀은 매니저에 의해 마감 기한 전에 작업을 완료하라는 요청을 받았다.

해설 ask는 to부정사를 목적격 보어로 취하는 5형식 동사로서, 능동태 문장 The manager asked the team to complete the task before the deadline에서 직접목적어를 수동태의 주어로 변환하면 The team was asked to complete the task before the deadline by the manager가 되므로 (B) asked가 정답이다.

12.

번역 고객들은 회사에 의해 새로운 앱을 통해 주문을 추적할 수 있게 되었다.

해설 enable은 to부정사를 목적격 보어로 취하는 5형식 동사로서, 능동태 문장 The company enabled customers to track orders through the new app에서 직접목적어를 수동태의 주어로 변환하면 Customers were enabled to track orders through the new app by the company가 되고, 또 복수주어이므로 (C) were enabled가 정답이다.

어휘 enable 가능하게 하다 track 추적하다, 확인하다 through ~을 통해, ~을 통하여

13.

번역 참가자들은 강사에 의해 세미나 후에 피드백을 제출하라고 상기 받았다.

해설 remind는 to부정사를 목적격 보어로 취하는 5형식 동사로서, 능동태 문장 The instructor reminded the participants to submit their feedback after the seminar에서 직접목적어를 수동태의 주어로 변환하면 The participants were reminded to submit their feedback after the seminar by the instructor가 되므로 (B) were reminded가 정답이다.

어휘 participant 참가자 remind 상기시키다 submit 제출하다 feedback 피드백, 의견, 반응 instructor 강사, 지도자

14.

번역 직원들은 마감 기한을 맞추기 위해 회사에 의해 주말에 근무하도록 강요받았다.

해설 force는 to부정사를 목적격 보어로 취하는 5형식 동사로서, 능동태 문장 The company forced the employees to work on weekends to meet the deadline에서 직접목적어를 수동태의 주어로 변환하면 The employees were forced to work on weekends by the company to meet the deadline가 되므로 (C) to work가 정답이다.

어휘 force 강요하다

15.

번역 그 연구 결과는 신뢰할 만하다고 믿어진다.

해설 believe는 명사절을 목적어로 취하고, 또 2가지 유형의 수동태로 변환될 수 있는 동사로서, 능동태 문장 They believe the research results to be reliable에서 직접목적어를 수동태의 주어로 변환하면 The research results are believed to be reliable가 되므로 (B) are believed가 정답이다.

어휘 research 연구, 조사 result 결과, 성과 reliable 신뢰할 수 있는, 믿을 만한

16.

번역 예산이 다음 주에 승인될 것이라고 추정된다.

해설 suppose는 명사절을 목적어로 취하고, 또 2가지 유형의 수동태로 변환될 수 있는 동사로서, 능동태 문장 They suppose that the budget will be approved next week에서 직접목적어인 that절을 수동태의 주어로 변환하면 주어가 너무 길어지므로 가주어 It을 수동태의 주어로 사용하면 It is supposed that the budget will be approved next week가 되므로 (C) is supposed가 정답이다.

어휘 budget 예산 approve 승인하다, 인가하다 suppose 가정하다, 추정하다

17.

번역 후보가 선거 끝까지 충분한 표를 확보할 것이라고 기대된다.

해설 expect는 명사절을 목적어로 취하고, 또 2가지 유형의 수동태로 변환될 수 있는 동사로서, 능동태 문장 They expect that the candidate will have secured sufficient votes by the end of the election에서 직접목적어인 that절을 수동태의 주어로 변환하면 주어가 너무 길어지므로 가주어 It을 수동태의 주어로 사용하면 It is expected that the candidate will have secured sufficient votes by the end of the election가 되므로 (C) is expected가 정답이다.

어휘 candidate 후보자, 지원자 secure 확보하다, 획득하다 sufficient 충분한 expect 예상하다, 기대하다 election 선거

18.

번역 용의자는 조사가 시작되기 전에 출국했을 것이라고 믿어진다.

해설 believe는 명사절을 목적어로 취하고, 또 2가지 유형의 수동태로 변환될 수 있는 동사로서, 능동태 문장 They believe the suspect to have left the country before the investigation began에서 직접목적어를 수동태의 주어로 변환하면 The suspect is believed to have left the country before the investigation began가 되므로 (D) to have left가 정답이다.

어휘 suspect 용의자, 의심하다 investigation 조사, 수사

19.

번역 그 기술은 지난 몇 년 동안 재생 에너지 생산에서 획기적인 성과를 이뤘다고 한다.

해설 say는 명사절을 목적어로 취하고, 또 2가지 유형의 수동태로 변환될 수 있는 동사로서, 능동태 문장 They say that the technology has achieved a breakthrough in renewable energy production over the past few years에서 비록 존재하지는 않

지만 5형식 문장(They say the technology to have achieved a breakthrough in renewable energy production over the past few years)에서 직접목적어를 수동태의 주어로 변환하면 The technology is said to have achieved a breakthrough in renewable energy production over the past few years가 되므로 (B) to have achieved가 정답이다. 혹은 수동태 문장 It is said that the technology has achieved a breakthrough in renewable energy production over the past few years에서 that절 안에 있는 주어(the technology)를 수동태의 주어로 하고, 종속절의 동사를 to부정사 구조로 변환하면 The technology is said to have achieved a breakthrough in renewable energy production over the past few years가 된다.

어휘 technology 기술 breakthrough 획기적인 발전, 돌파구 renewable energy 재생 가능 에너지 achieve 성취하다, 달성하다

20.

번역 그 프로젝트는 지연에도 불구하고 회계 연도 말 이전에 완료될 것으로 기대된다.

해설 expect는 명사절을 목적어로 취하고, 또 2가지 유형의 수동태로 변환될 수 있는 동사로서, 능동태 문장 They expect the project to be completed before the end of the fiscal year, despite the delays에서 직접목적어를 수동태의 주어로 변환하면 The project is expected to be completed before the end of the fiscal year, despite the delays가 되므로 (B) to be completed가 정답이다.

어휘 project 프로젝트, 과제 fiscal year 회계 연도 delay 지연, 연기

21.

번역 그 조직은 환경 지속 가능성을 촉진하는 여러 활동에 참여하고 있다.

해설 be involved in은 "~에 참여하다"라는 의미로, 조직이 여러 환경 보호 활동에 적극적으로 참여하고 있음을 나타내므로 (B) involved가 정답이다.

어휘 organization 조직, 단체 multiple 다수의, 여럿의 initiative 계획, 활동 promote 촉진하다, 장려하다, 홍보하다 environmental sustainability 환경적 지속 가능성

22.

번역 그 팀은 프로젝트와 관련된 잠재적 위험에 대해 걱정하고 있다.

해설 be concerned about는 "~에 대해 걱정하다"는 의미로, 팀이 프로젝트의 잠재적 위험에 대해 우려하고 있음을 나타내므로 (D) concerned가 정답이다.

어휘 potential 잠재력, 잠재적인 risk 위험, 위험 요소 involve 포함하다, 수반하다

23.

번역 직원들은 회사 방향을 바꾸겠다는 갑작스러운 결정에 어리둥절해했다.

해설 be puzzled over는 "~에 대해 어리둥절해하다"라는 의미로, 갑작스러운 결정과 같은 예상치 못한 변화에 대한 혼란을 나타내므로 (B) puzzled가 정답이다.

어휘 direction 방향, 지시, 안내, 목적

24.

번역 새로운 마케팅 전략은 소셜 미디어를 통해 젊은 소비자들에게 도달하는 데 중점을 두고 있다.

해설 be centered on은 "~에 중심을 두다"라는 의미로, 마케팅 전략의 초점을 젊은 소비자들에 맞추고 있음을 나타내므로 (C) centered가 정답이다.

어휘 marketing strategy 마케팅 전략

PART 6

다음 공지와 관련된 질문 1-4번을 보세요.

> 직원 여러분께,
> 다음 달부터 시행될 사무실 근무 시간 변경에 대해 알려드리고자 합니다. 지난 회의에서 논의된 바와

같이, 새로운 근무 시간은 월요일부터 금요일까지 오전 8시부터 오후 5시까지입니다. 이번 조정은 고객의 요구를 더 잘 수용하고 전체적인 업무 흐름의 효율성을 높이기 위해 결정되었습니다.
추가적으로, 우리는 유연 근무제 옵션을 도입할 예정입니다. 근무 시간을 더 일찍 또는 늦게 시작하기를 원하는 직원들은 직접 상사와 일정을 논의할 수 있습니다. 다만, 모든 직원들이 사무실에 있어야 하는 핵심 근무 시간은 오전 10시부터 오후 3시까지 유지됩니다. 일상의 변화를 받아들이는 것이 쉽지 않음을 이해하고 있으나, 이러한 조정이 더 나은 일과 삶의 균형에 기여할 것이라 믿습니다. 게다가, 이러한 변화는 업무를 간소화하고 팀 간 협력을 개선하는 데 도움이 될 것입니다.
질문이나 새로운 근무 시간 및 유연 근무제에 대한 우려 사항이 있으시면 HR 부서에 연락 주시기 바랍니다. 다시 한 번, 새로운 근무 시간으로 전환하는 동안 협조해 주셔서 감사드립니다.
여러분의 이해와 지속적인 헌신에 감사드립니다.

감사합니다,
경영진

어휘 announcement 공지, 발표 effective 효력을 발생하는, 효과적인 office hours 근무 시간, 영업시간 adjustment 조정, 수정, 적응 take effect 효력을 발생하다 flexible work schedule 유연한 근무 일정 accommodate 수용하다, 맞추다 overall 전체적인, 전반적인 workflow efficiency 작업 흐름의 효율성 direct supervisor 직속 상사 core working hours 핵심 근무 시간 contribute 기여하다, 이바지하다 work-life balance 일과 삶의 균형 transition 전환, 변화 flexible 유연한 dedication 헌신, 전념 HR (Human Resources) 인사부 appreciate 감사하다, 고마워하다

정답

1. (C) 2. (A) 3. (D) 4. (A)

1.

해설 근무 시간 조정이 완료되었음을 나타내는 수동태 문장이므로 (C) has been made가 정답이다.

2.

(A) 핵심
(B) 공유된
(C) 연장된
(D) 제한된

해설 지문에서 “when all employees are expected to be in the office will remain from 10:00 AM to 3:00 PM”라고 언급되어 있어, 빈칸에 들어갈 단어는 모든 직원들이 사무실에 있어야 하는 특정 근무 시간을 강조하고 있으므로 (A) core가 정답이다.

3.

해설 ”모든 직원들이 사무실에 있을 것으로 기대된다”는 의미의 (D) are expected to가 정답이다. 즉, to부정사를 목적격 보어로 취하는 5형식 동사 expect의 능동태 문장 They expect all employees to be in the office에서 직접목적어(all employees)를 수동태의 주어로 변환하여 all employees are expected to be in the office가 되었다.

4.

(A) 이러한 변화는 업무를 간소화하고 팀 간 협력을 개선하는 데 도움이 될 것이다.
(B) 이러한 변화는 직원들이 더 많은 연차를 사용할 수 있게 할 것이다.
(C) 이러한 변화는 회사의 장기 목표와 일치하지 않는다.
(D) 이러한 변화는 팀 내 갈등을 심화시킬 수 있다.

해설 지문을 보면 새로운 사무실 근무 시간과 유연 근무제를 소개하면서 이 변화가 직원의 업무 효율성과 워크플로우를 개선하고, 일과 삶의 균형을 맞추는 데 기여할 것이라고 설명하고 있으므로 (A)가 가장 적절하다. 그리고 이런 변화는 (B)의 연차 사용과 관련이 없고, (C)의 회사의 장기 목표와 일치하지 않는다는 내용과 맞지 않으며, (D)의 변화로 인해 갈등이 생길 것이라는 내용은 문맥에 맞지 않다.

PART 7

다음 이메일과 관련된 질문 1-4번을 보세요.

팀 여러분께,
다가오는 연례 판매 회의가 3월 20일부터 3월 22일까지 시카고 도심에 위치한 그랜드 리버사이드 호텔에서 개최된다는 소식을 전하게 되어 기쁩니다. 올해의 주제는 "미래를 위한 혁신"이며, 우리는 고객 참여와 판매 전략의 최신 트렌드에 초점을 맞출 예정입니다. 항상 그렇듯이, 모든 팀원의 전원 참석을 기대합니다.
주요 세션에는 업계 리더들의 발표와 다음 분기에 도입될 새로운 판매 도구에 대한 워크숍이 포함될 것입니다. 또한, 각 지역 팀은 지난 한 해 동안의 성공 사례를 발표할 기회를 갖게 될 것이니, 여러분의 성과를 공유할 준비를 해주시기 바랍니다.
우리는 또한 새로운 고객 관계 관리(CRM) 소프트웨어를 도입할 예정이며, 이 소프트웨어는 고객과의 소통을 크게 간소화할 것으로 기대됩니다. 새로운 CRM에 대한 교육 세션은 모든 영업 직원들에게 필수적이며, 이 세션에 대한 자세한 내용은 회의에서 제공될 것입니다.
시카고 외부에서 오시는 분들을 위해 회사에서 호텔 숙박을 마련할 예정입니다. 숙소 예약을 보장받기 위해 2월 28일까지 여행 계획을 확정해 주시기 바랍니다. 만약 특별한 식이 요구 사항이 있거나 도움이 필요하신 경우, 3월 10일 이전에 HR 부서로 연락해 주십시오.
그곳에서 여러분 모두를 뵙기를 기대합니다!

감사합니다,
제시카 리
영업 부장

어휘 upcoming 다가오는 annual 연례의 conference 회의, 학회 theme 주제, 테마 customer engagement 고객 참여, 고객 유대감 industry leader 업계 리더, 선도 기업 sales strategies 판매 전략 implement 시행하다, 도입하다 regional team 지역 팀 CRM (Customer Relationship Management) 고객 관계 관리 streamline 간소화하다, 효율적으로 하다 hazardous materials 위험 물질 dietary requirements 식이 요구 사항 mandatory 의무적인 guarantee 보장하다 accommodation 숙박 시설 confirm 확인하다, 확정하다

정답

1. (C) 2. (D) 3. (B) 4. (B)

1. 이 이메일의 주요 목적은 무엇입니까?
   (A) 새로운 판매 캠페인을 발표하기 위해
   (B) 교육 세션에 대한 정보를 제공하기 위해
   (C) 다가오는 회의에 팀원들을 초대하기 위해
   (D) 지역성과에 대한 보고서를 요청하기 위해

해설 "As always, we expect full participation from all team members"라는 지문에서 알 수 있듯이, 팀원들이 참가할 것을 독려하는 내용이므로 (C)가 정답이다.

2. 회의 활동으로 언급되지 않은 것은 무엇입니까?
   (A) 지역 팀 발표
   (B) 새로운 판매 도구에 대한 워크숍
   (C) CRM 소프트웨어에 대한 교육
   (D) 고객의 발표

해설 "each regional team will have an opportunity to present its success stories from the past year", "workshops on new sales tools that will be implemented next quarter," "Training sessions on the new CRM will be mandatory for all sales personnel"라는 지문에서 알 수 있듯이, 지역 팀 발표, 워크숍, CRM 교육은 모두 언급되었지만, 고객의 발표에 대한 언급은 없으므로 (D)가 정답이다.

3. 직원들이 특별한 식이 요구 사항이 있을 경우 3월 10일까지 무엇을 해야 합니까?
   (A) 회의 참석을 취소하다
   (B) HR 부서에 연락하다
   (C) 상세한 비용 보고서를 제출하다
   (D) CRM 교육 세션에 등록하다

해설 지문에서 "If you have any special dietary requirements or need assistance, contact the HR department no later than March 10."라는 문장에서 알 수 있듯이, 식이 요구 사항이 있는 직원은 3월 10일까지 HR 부서에 연락해야 하므로 (B)가 정답이다.

4. CRM 소프트웨어에 대해 추론할 수 있는 것은 무엇입니까?
   (A) 대부분의 직원에게 선택 사항일 것이다.
   (B) 현재의 고객 커뮤니케이션 시스템을 대체할 것이다.
   (C) 현재 일부 팀에서 사용 중이다.
   (D) 회의 후 지역 사무소에 도입될 것이다.

해설 "We will also be introducing our new customer relationship management (CRM) software, which is expected to significantly streamline our communication with clients"라는 지문에서 알 수 있듯이, 새로운 CRM 소프트웨어가 현재 시스템을 대체할 가능성이 크다는 점을 암시하므로 (B)가 정답이다.

Chapter 04 가정법

1. 가정법 현재

✔ CheckPoint 1. 가정법 현재의 구조

정답

1. (D) 2. (C) 3. (B)

1.

번역 의사는 환자가 건강을 개선하기 위해 더 많은 운동을 해야 한다고 제안했다.

해설 suggest는 가정법 현재를 사용하는 동사로, that + 주어 + (should) + 동사원형 구조를 취하고, should는 생략될 수 있으므로 (D) do가 정답이다.

어휘 suggest 제안하다, 권하다 patient 환자 exercise 운동, 연습 improve 개선하다, 향상시키다 health 건강

2.

번역 위원회는 새로운 정책이 법률 전문가들에 의해 검토되어야 한다고 권고했다.

해설 recommend는 가정법 현재를 사용하는 동사로, that + 주어 + (should) + 동사원형 구조를 취하고, 수동태 구조이므로 (C) be reviewed가 정답이다.

어휘 committee 위원회, 위원들 recommend 권고하다, 추천하다 policy 정책, 방침 legal expert 법률 전문가 review 검토하다, 평가하다

3.

번역 활동을 시작하기 전에 모든 참가자가 안전 절차를 이해하는 것이 중요하다.

해설 이성적 판단을 나타내는 형용사 crucial은 가정법 현재를 사용하고, that + 주어 + (should) + 동사원형 구조를 취하며, should는 생략될 수 있으므로 (B) understand가 정답이다.

어휘 crucial 중요한, 필수적인 participant 참가자, 참여자 safety procedure 안전 절차

✔ CheckPoint 2. 조건절에서의 직설법 사용

정답

1. (A) 2. (B) 3. (C)

1.

번역 프로젝트가 제시간에 완료된다면, 우리는 마감일을 맞출 것이다.

해설 미래의 사건을 표현할 때 조건의 부사절에는 현재 시제를, 주절에는 미래 시제(will/shall + 동사 원형)를 사용하므로 (A) is completed가 정답이다.

어휘 complete 완료하다 on time 정시에, 제시간에 deadline 마감 기한

2.

번역 회의가 시작될 때까지 서류가 제출되지 않으면, 우리는 논의 일정을 다시 조정해야 할 것이다.

해설 미래의 사건을 표현할 때 조건의 부사절에는 현재 시제를, 주절에는 미래 시제(will/shall + 동사 원형)를 사용하고, 수동태 구조이므로 (B) aren't submitted가 정답이다.

어휘 document 문서, 서류 by the time ~할 때까지 reschedule 일정을 변경하다 discussion 논의, 토론

3.

번역 보고서가 준비되는 대로, 우리는 그것을 고객에게 제출할 것이다.

해설 미래의 사건을 표현할 때 조건의 부사절에는 현재 시제를, 주절에는 미래 시제(will/shall + 동사 원형)를 사용하므로 (C) will submit가 정답이다.

어휘 report 보고서, 보고 submit 제출하다, 건네다 client 고객, 의뢰인

2. 가정법 미래

✔ CheckPoint 3. 미래에 일어날 가능성이 거의 없는 상황

정답

1. (D) 2. (A) 3. (C)

1.

번역 만약 시장 상황이 변한다면, 우리는 투자 전략을 수정할 것이다.

해설 미래에 일어날 가능성이 거의 없는 상황을 나타내는 가정법 미래일 때, 조건절에는 If + 주어 + should + 동사원형 ~, 그리고 주절에는 주어 + will/can/may + 동사원형을 취하므로 (D) will revise가 정답이다.

어휘 market condition 시장 상황, 시장조건 revise 수정하다, 변경하다 investment strategy 투자 전략

2.

번역 만약 배송이 지연된다면, 생산 일정에 영향을 받을 것이다.

해설 미래에 일어날 가능성이 거의 없는 상황을 나타내는 가정법 미래일 때, 조건절에는 If + 주어 + should + 동사원형 ~, 그리고 주절에는 주어 + will/can/may + 동사원형을 취한다. 여기서 Should the shipment be delayed는 원 문장 If the shipment should be delayed의 도치 구조이고, 주절은 수동태 구조이므로 (A) will be affected가 정답이다.

어휘 shipment 배송, 선적 delay 지연, 연기, 지연시키다 production schedule 생산 일정 affect 영향을 미치다

3.

번역 만약 지연이 발생한다면, 우리는 회의 일정을 다시 잡아야 할 것이다.

해설 미래에 일어날 가능성이 거의 없는 상황을 나타내는 가정법 미래일 때, 조건절에는 If + 주어 + should + 동사원형 ~, 그리고 주절에는 주어 + will/can/may + 동사원형을 취하므로 (C) If가 정답이다.

어휘 occur 발생하다, 일어나다 reschedule 일정을 변경하다 meeting 회의, 모임

✔ CheckPoint 4. 실현 가능성이 희박한 순수한 가정

정답

1. (C) 2. (B) 3. (D)

1.

번역 만약 CEO가 예산 증액을 승인한다면, 프로젝트가 크게 확장될 것이다.

해설 실현 가능성이 희박한 순수한 가정을 나타내는 가정법 미래일 때, 조건절에는 If + 주어 + were to + 동사원형 ~, 그리고 주절에는 주어 + would/should/could/might + 동사원형을 취하므로 (C) If가 정답이다.

어휘 approve 승인하다, 찬성하다 budget 예산 increase 증가, 인상, 증가하다 expand 확장하다, 확대하다 significantly 상당히, 중요하게

2.

번역 만약 시장이 붕괴된다면, 많은 투자자들이 상당한 손실을 입을 것이다.

해설 실현 가능성이 희박한 순수한 가정을 나타내는 가정법 미래일 때, 조건절에는 If + 주어 + were to + 동사원형 ~, 그리고 주절에는 주어 + would/should/could/might + 동사원형을 취한다. 여기서 Were the market to crash는 원 문장 If the market were to crash의 도치 구조이므로 (B) Were가 정답이다.

어휘 market 시장 crash 붕괴하다, 급락하다, 붕괴, 폭락 investor 투자자 face 직면하다 significant 상당한, 중요한 loss 손실, 손해

3.

번역 만약 그들이 더 효율적인 방법을 발견한다면, 생산 비용이 많이 감소할 수 있을 것이다.

해설 실현 가능성이 희박한 순수한 가정을 나타내는 가정법 미래일 때, 조건절에는 If + 주어 + were to + 동사원형 ~, 그리고 주절에는 주어 + would/should/could/might + 동사원형을 취한다. 여기서 Were they to discover a more efficient method는 원 문장 If they were to discover a more efficient method의 도치 구조이므로 (D) to discover가 정답이다.

어휘 efficient 효율적인 method 방법, 방식 production 생산 cost 비용, 경비 decrease 감소하다, 줄다, 감소, 하락 significantly 상당히, 중요하게

3. 가정법 과거

✔ CheckPoint 5. 가정법 과거의 구조

정답

1. (D)　2. (C)

1.

번역 날씨가 더 따뜻하다면, 우리는 하루를 야외에서 보낼지도 모른다.

해설 현재 사실과 반대되는 상황을 나타내는 가정법 과거일 때, 조건절에는 If + 주어 + 과거동사/were ~, 그리고 주절에는 would/should/could/might + 동사원형을 취하므로 (D) were가 정답이다.

어휘 weather 날씨, 기상 spend (시간을) 보내다, 소비하다 outside 밖에서, 야외에서

2.

번역 제안서가 더 간단하다면, 더 많은 이해관계자들이 이를 승인할 가능성이 높다.

해설 현재 사실과 반대되는 상황을 나타내는 가정법 과거일 때, 조건절에는 If + 주어 + 과거동사/were ~, 그리고 주절에는 would/should/could/might + 동사원형을 취한다. 여기서 Were the proposal simpler는 원 문장 If the proposal were simpler의 도치 구조이므로 (C) Were가 정답이다.

어휘 proposal 제안, 제안서 simpler 더 간단한 stakeholder 이해관계자 approve 승인하다, 찬성하다

4. 가정법 과거완료

✔ CheckPoint 6. 가정법 과거완료의 구조

정답

1. (C)　2. (B)

1.

번역 만약 패키지가 제시간에 도착했더라면, 고객이 불평하지 않았을 것이다.

해설 과거 사실과 반대되는 상황을 나타내는 가정법 과거완료일 때, 조건절에는 If + 주어 + had P.P. ~, 그리고 주절에는 would/should/could/might + have P.P.을 취하므로 (C) had arrived가 정답이다.

어휘 package 소포 on time 정시에, 제시간에 customer 고객, 손님

2.

번역 만약 배송이 더 일찍 도착했더라면, 행사는 계획대로 진행될 수 있었을 것이다.

해설 과거 사실과 반대되는 상황을 나타내는 가정법 과거완료일 때, 조건절에는 If + 주어 + had P.P. ~, 그리고 주절에는 would/should/could/might + have P.P.을 취하므로 (B) could have proceeded가 정답이다.

어휘 shipment 배송, 선적, 화물 proceed 진행하다, 계속하다 event 행사, 사건 as planned 계획대로

5. 혼합 가정법

✔ CheckPoint 7. 혼합 가정법의 구조

정답

1. (D) 2. (B)

1.

번역 만약 그들이 더 많은 예방 조치를 취했더라면, 지금 이 위기에 직면하지 않았을 것이다.

해설 과거의 가정이 현재에 미치는 영향을 나타내는 혼합 가정법일 때, 조건절에는 If + 주어 + had P.P. ~, 그리고 주절에는 would/should/could/might + 동사원형을 취하므로 (D) had taken가 정답이다.

어휘 precaution 예방 조치, 사전 대비 face 직면하다 마주하다 crisis 위기

2.

번역 만약 날씨가 더 좋았더라면, 우리는 지금 야외에서 행사를 열고 있을 것이다.

해설 과거의 가정이 현재에 미치는 영향을 나타내는 혼합 가정법일 때, 조건절에는 If + 주어 + had P.P. ~, 그리고 주절에는 would/should/could/might + 동사원형을 취한다. 여기서 조건절 Had the weather been better는 원 문장 If the weather had been better의 도치 구조이므로 (B) Had가 정답이다.

어휘 weather 날씨, 기상 hold 개최하다, 열다 outdoors 야외에서, 밖에서

토익 종합 실전문제

정답

1. (A)	2. (B)	3. (A)	4. (C)	5. (C)
6. (D)	7. (A)	8. (D)	9. (A)	10. (B)
11. (D)	12. (B)	13. (B)	14. (C)	15. (D)
16. (B)	17. (A)	18. (D)	19. (B)	20. (C)
21. (D)	22. (A)	23. (C)	24. (B)	

1.

번역 강사는 학생들이 과제를 제시간에 제출해야 한다고 요구했다.

해설 require는 가정법 현재를 사용하는 동사로, that + 주어 + (should) + 동사원형 구조를 취하고, should는 생략될 수 있으므로 (A) submit가 정답이다.

어휘 instructor 강사, 지도자 require 요구하다 assignment 과제, 과업

2.

번역 CEO는 회의가 추후 공지가 있을 때까지 연기되어야 한다고 주장했다.

해설 insist는 가정법 현재를 사용하는 동사로, that + 주어 + (should) + 동사원형 구조를 취하고, 수동태 구조이므로 (B) be postponed가 정답이다.

어휘 insist 주장하다 postpone 연기하다, 미루다 until further notice 추후 공지가 있을 때까지

3.

번역 연례 보고서가 더 일찍 발표되어야 한다는 위원회의 제안이 고려되었다.

해설 suggestion은 가정법 현재를 사용하는 명사로, that + 주어 + (should) + 동사원형 구조를 취하고, 수동태 구조이므로 (A) be가 정답이다.

어휘 committee 위원회 suggestion 제안, 의견

annual report 연례 보고서 release 공개하다, 발표하다 earlier 더 일찍, 이전에

4.

번역 교육 프로그램이 연장되어야 한다는 권고가 이사회에서 받아들여졌다.

해설 recommendation은 가정법 현재를 사용하는 명사로, that + 주어 + (should) + 동사원형 구조를 취하고, 수동태 구조이므로 (C) be extended가 정답이다.

어휘 recommendation 추천, 권고 training program 훈련 프로그램, 교육 과정 accept 받아들이다, 인정하다 board 이사회, 위원회

5.

번역 모든 직원이 새로운 회사 정책에 대해 알고 있어야 한다는 것이 필수적이다.

해설 이성적 판단을 나타내는 형용사 essential은 가정법 현재를 사용하고, that + 주어 + (should) + 동사원형 구조를 취하며, should는 생략될 수 있으므로 (C) be가 정답이다.

어휘 essential 필수적인 aware 알고 있는, 인지하고 있는 company policy 회사 정책

6.

번역 팀이 다음 회의까지 상당한 진전을 이루지 못하면, 우리는 전략을 재평가해야 할 것이다.

해설 미래의 사건을 표현할 때 조건의 부사절에는 현재 시제를, 주절에는 미래 시제(will/shall + 동사 원형)를 사용하므로 (D) doesn't make가 정답이다.

어휘 significant 중요한, 상당한 progress 진전, 발전 reassess 재평가하다 strategy 전략

7.

번역 만약 프로젝트가 예산을 초과한다면, 추가 자금이 필요할 것이다.

해설 미래에 일어날 가능성이 거의 없는 상황을 나타내는 가정법 미래일 때, 조건절에는 If + 주어 + should + 동사원형 ~, 그리고 주절에는 주어 + will/can/may + 동사원형을 취한다. 여기서 Should the project exceed its budget는 원 문장 If the project should exceed its budget의 도치 구조이므로 (A) Should가 정답이다.

어휘 exceed 초과하다, 넘다 budget 예산 additional funding 추가 자금

8.

번역 만약 합병이 성사되지 않으면, 회사는 대체 전략을 마련해야 할 것이다.

해설 미래에 일어날 가능성이 거의 없는 상황을 나타내는 가정법 미래일 때, 조건절에는 If + 주어 + should + 동사원형 ~, 그리고 주절에는 주어 + will/can/may + 동사원형을 취한다. 여기서 Should the merger not go through는 원 문장 If the merger should not go through의 도치 구조이므로 (D) not go가 정답이다.

어휘 merger 합병 go through 성사되다, 진행되다 devise 고안하다, 계획하다 alternative strategies 대안 전략

9.

번역 만약 재무 보고서에서 어떤 차이점이 발견된다면, 감사원은 추가 조사를 시작할 것이다.

해설 미래에 일어날 가능성이 거의 없는 상황을 나타내는 가정법 미래일 때, 조건절에는 If + 주어 + should + 동사원형 ~, 그리고 주절에는 주어 + will/can/may + 동사원형을 취한다. 여기서 Should any discrepancies be found in the financial report는 원 문장 If any discrepancies should be found in the financial report의 도치 구조이고, 수동태 구조이므로 (A) be found가 정답이다.

어휘 discrepancy 불일치, 차이, 모순 financial report 재무 보고서 auditor 감사관, 회계감사인 initiate 시작하다, 착수하다 further investigation 추가 조사

10.

번역 만약 신제품 출시가 지연된다면, 마케팅 전략을 조정해야 할 것이다.

(해설) 실현 가능성이 희박한 순수한 가정을 나타내는 가정법 미래일 때, 조건절에는 If + 주어 + were to + 동사원형 ~, 그리고 주절에는 주어 + would/should/could/might + 동사원형을 취하고, 수동태 구조이므로 (B) were to be delayed가 정답이다.

(어휘) new product launch 신제품 출시 marketing strategy 마케팅 전략 adjust 조정하다, 수정하다

11.

번역 만약 그녀가 매주 몇 시간 더 일한다면, 그녀는 제때에 작업을 완료할 것이다.

(해설) 현재 사실과 반대되는 상황을 나타내는 가정법 과거일 때, 조건절에는 If + 주어 + 과거동사/were ~, 그리고 주절에는 would/should/could/might + 동사원형을 취하므로 (D) worked가 정답이다.

(어휘) complete 완료하다, 끝내다 on time 정시에, 기한 내에

12.

번역 만약 회사가 더 많은 자원을 가지고 있다면, 그것은 운영을 확장할 수 있을 것이다.

(해설) 현재 사실과 반대되는 상황을 나타내는 가정법 과거일 때, 조건절에는 If + 주어 + 과거동사/were ~, 그리고 주절에는 would/should/could/might + 동사원형을 취하므로 (B) would be가 정답이다.

(어휘) resources 자원, 재원 expand 확장하다, 넓히다 operation 운영, 활동

13.

번역 만약 고급 교육이 없다면, 직원들은 새로운 소프트웨어를 다룰 수 없을 것이다.

(해설) 현재 사실과 반대되는 상황을 나타내는 가정법 과거일 때, 조건절에 Without = But for = If it were not for = Were it not for = If not for가 오면 주절에는 would/should/could/might + 동사원형을 취하므로 (B) wouldn't be가 정답이다.

(어휘) advanced training 고급 훈련, 심화 교육 handle 다루다, 처리하다

14.

번역 만약 지원해주는 팀원들이 없다면, 프로젝트는 더 많은 어려움에 직면할 것이다.

(해설) 현재 사실과 반대되는 상황을 나타내는 가정법 과거일 때, 조건절에 Without = But for = If it were not for = Were it not for = If not for가 올 수 있으므로 (C) Were가 정답이다.

(어휘) supportive 지지하는, 협력적인 face 직면하다 challenge 도전, 어려움

15.

번역 만약 제품 출시가 지연되었더라면, 회사는 상당한 시장 점유율을 잃었을 수도 있다.

(해설) 과거 사실과 반대되는 상황을 나타내는 가정법 과거완료일 때, 조건절에는 If + 주어 + had P.P. ~, 그리고 주절에는 would/should/could/might + have P.P.을 취한다. 여기서 조건절은 수동태 구조이므로 (D) had been delayed가 정답이다.

(어휘) product launch 제품 출시 significant market share 상당한 시장 점유율

16.

번역 만약 그들이 위험에 대해 알았더라면, 그들은 프로젝트를 계속 진행하는 것을 거부했을지도 모른다.

(해설) 과거 사실과 반대되는 상황을 나타내는 가정법 과거완료일 때, 조건절에는 If + 주어 + had P.P. ~, 그리고 주절에는 would/should/could/might + have P.P.을 취한다. 여기서 Had they known about the risk는 원 문장 If they had known about the risk의 도치 구조이므로 (B)

might have refused가 정답이다.

어휘 risk 위험 refuse 거절하다 continue 계속하다, 지속하다

17.

번역 만약 그녀가 그 기회를 보았다면, 그녀는 즉시 그것을 잡았을 것이다.

해설 과거 사실과 반대되는 상황을 나타내는 가정법 과거완료일 때, 조건절에는 If + 주어 + had P.P. ~, 그리고 주절에는 would/should/could/might + have P.P.을 취한다. 여기서 Had she seen the opportunity는 원 문장 If she had seen the opportunity의 도치 구조이므로 (A) seen가 정답이다.

어휘 opportunity 기회 immediately 즉시, 즉각적으로

18.

번역 추가 자금이 없었다면, 프로젝트가 제시간에 완료되지 않았을지도 모른다.

해설 과거 사실과 반대되는 상황을 나타내는 가정법 과거완료일 때, 조건절에는 If + 주어 + had P.P. ~, 그리고 주절에는 would/should/could/might + have P.P.을 취한다. 여기서 Had it not been for the extra funding는 원 문장 If it had not been for the extra funding의 도치 구조이고, 주절은 수동태 구조이므로 (D) might not have been completed가 정답이다.

어휘 extra funding 추가 자금 on time 정시에, 기한 내에

19.

번역 만약 신속한 개입이 없었다면, 문제가 더 커졌을 것이다.

해설 과거 사실과 반대되는 상황을 나타내는 가정법 과거완료일 때, 조건절에는 If + 주어 + had P.P. ~, 그리고 주절에는 would/should/could/might + have P.P.을 취한다. 여기서 Had it not been for the prompt intervention는 원 문장 If it had not been for the prompt intervention의 도치 구조이므로 (B) Had가 정답이다.

어휘 prompt 신속한, 즉각적인 intervention 개입, 중재 issue 문제, 쟁점 escalate 악화시키다, 확대되다

20.

번역 만약 자금이 승인되지 않았다면, 프로젝트가 지연되었을 것이다.

해설 과거 사실과 반대되는 상황을 나타내는 가정법 과거완료일 때, 조건절에는 If + 주어 + had P.P. ~, 그리고 주절에는 would/should/could/might + have P.P.을 취한다. 여기서 Had the funding not been approved는 원 문장 If the funding had not been approved의 도치 구조이므로 (C) Had가 정답이다.

어휘 funding 자금, 재정 지원 approve 승인하다, 허가하다

21.

번역 만약 회사가 새로운 규정을 더 일찍 채택했더라면, 지금 법적 문제에 직면하지 않았을 것이다.

해설 과거의 가정이 현재에 미치는 영향을 나타내는 혼합 가정법일 때, 조건절에는 If + 주어 + had P.P. ~, 그리고 주절에는 would/should/could/might + 동사원형을 취한다. 여기서 조건절 Had the company adopted the new regulations earlier는 원 문장 If the company had adopted the new regulations earlier의 도치 구조이므로 (D) Had가 정답이다.

어휘 adopt 채택하다, 도입하다 regulation 규정 legal issue 법적 문제

22.

번역 만약 고객이 제안을 더 일찍 받아들였더라면, 지금 우리는 세부 사항을 마무리하고 있을 것이다.

해설 과거의 가정이 현재에 미치는 영향을 나타내는

내는 혼합 가정법일 때, 조건절에는 If + 주어 + had P.P. ~, 그리고 주절에는 would/should/could/might + 동사원형을 취한다. 여기서 조건절 Had the client accepted the proposal earlier는 원 문장 If the client had accepted the proposal earlier의 도치 구조이므로 (A) accepted가 정답이다.

[어휘] client 고객, 의뢰인 proposal 제안, 제안서 finalize 마무리하다, 최종 확정하다

23.

번역 만약 새로운 투자자들이 없었더라면, 지금 회사는 더 안정적인 재정 상태에 있지 못할 수도 있다.

[해설] 과거의 가정이 현재에 미치는 영향을 나타내는 혼합 가정법일 때, 조건절에는 If + 주어 + had P.P. ~, 그리고 주절에는 would/should/could/might + 동사원형을 취하므로 (C) might not be in가 정답이다.

[어휘] investor 투자자 stable financial position 안정적인 재정 상태

24.

번역 만약 초기 고객의 지원이 없었다면, 그 사업은 오늘날처럼 성공적이지 않을 것이다.

[해설] 과거의 가정이 현재에 미치는 영향을 나타내는 혼합 가정법일 때, 조건절에는 If + 주어 + had P.P. ~, 그리고 주절에는 would/should/could/might + 동사원형을 취한다. 여기서 Without = But for = If it had not been for = Had it not been for = If not for가 조건절에 대신 올 수 있으므로 (B) would not be가 정답이다.

[어휘] initial support 초기 지원

PART 6

다음 메일과 관련된 질문 1-4번을 보세요.

> To: 모든 부서 관리자
> From: Mark Thompson, 프로젝트 리더
> Subject: 프로젝트 일정 및 자원 배정
>
> 팀 여러분께,
>
> 현재 진행 중인 프로젝트를 계속해 나가면서, 마감일을 준수하는 것의 중요성에 대해 잠시 말씀드리고자 합니다. 만약 중요한 단계를 놓친다면 전체 일정에 영향을 미쳐, 최종 납기일이 지연될 가능성이 있습니다. 이러한 차질을 방지하기 위해, 각 팀이 필요한 자원을 확보하도록 해주시기 바랍니다.
> 당초 주요 고객의 지원이 없었더라면, 우리는 지금처럼 유리한 위치에 있지 않았을지도 모릅니다. 따라서 우리는 그들의 신뢰를 유지하고 기대를 충족하기 위해 최선을 다해야 합니다. 만약 추가 자원이 필요하거나 특정 문제에 대한 우려 사항이 있는 경우, 언제든지 저에게 직접 연락해 주십시오. 여러분의 노력과 헌신에 감사드립니다. 이 프로젝트를 성공적으로 완수합시다.
>
> 감사합니다,
> Mark Thompson

[어휘] project timeline 프로젝트 일정 resource allocation 자원 배분 milestone 이정표, 주요 목표 impact 영향, 충격 schedule 일정 setback 좌절, 방해 necessary 필요한, 필수적인 initial support 초기 지원 advantageous 유리한, 유익한 position 위치, 상태 hesitate 주저하다 specific 구체적인, 명확한 commitment 헌신, 전념 success 성공

정답

1. (C)　2. (A)　3. (B)　4. (B)

1.

[해설] "만약 중요한 단계를 놓친다면 전체 일정에 영향을 미쳐, 최종 납기일이 지연될 가능성이 있습니다"는 지문에서 어떤 일이 일어날 가능성을 표현하므로 (C) potentially가 정답이다. (A) especially는 "특히", (B) critically는 "중요하게, 비판적으로", (D) gradually는 "점진적으로"라는 의미로 문맥에 맞지 않다.

2.

[해설] To prevent는 부사적 용법의 목적을 나타내는 표현으로 "To prevent such setbacks (이러한 차질을 방지하기 위해)"에 가장 적절하므로 (A) To prevent가 정답이다. (D) To be prevented는

수동형으로 문법적으로 맞지 않다.

3.

해설 과거의 가정이 현재에 미치는 영향을 나타내는 혼합 가정법일 때, 조건절에는 If + 주어 + had P.P. ~, 그리고 주절에는 would/should/could/might + 동사원형을 취한다. 여기서 Without = But for = If it had not been for = Had it not been for = If not for가 조건절 대신 올 수 있으므로 주절에는 (B) would not be가 정답이다.

4. (A) 우리는 매달 말까지 진행 보고서를 제출해야 합니다.
(B) 우리는 그들의 신뢰를 유지하고 기대를 충족하기 위해 최선을 다해야 합니다.
(C) 이는 우리 팀이 고객의 기준을 충족하도록 보장할 것입니다.
(D) 마감일을 지키는 데는 일관된 소통과 명확한 계획이 필요합니다.

해설 앞 문장에서 주요 고객의 초기 지원 덕분에 지금처럼 유리한 위치에 있을 수 있음을 언급하고 있으므로, 이 문맥에서는 고객의 신뢰를 유지하고 기대를 충족시키기 위해 최선을 다해야 하는 이유를 강조해야 하므로 (B)가 가장 적절하다. (A)는 보고서 제출 일정에 대한 언급으로, 고객의 신뢰 유지와는 직접적으로 연결되지 않고, (C)는 기준 충족을 언급하지만, 고객의 신뢰 유지라는 문맥적 요소를 강조하지 않으며, (D)는 마감일 준수에 필요한 요소에 관한 언급으로 문맥에 맞지 않다.

PART 7

다음 이벤트 일정과 내부 이메일과 관련된 질문 1-5번을 보세요.

워크숍: 직무 능력 개발의 날
날짜: 2024년 10월 25일
장소: 그랜드 홀 컨퍼런스 센터

일정:
오전 9:00 - 오전 10:30: CEO 로버트 샌더스의 기조 연설
오전 10:45 - 오후 12:00: 워크숍 1: 리더십 기술 개발
오후 12:00 - 오후 1:30: 점심시간 (식사 제공)
오후 1:30 - 오후 3:00: 워크숍 2: 팀 협업 및 커뮤니케이션
오후 3:15 - 오후 4:45: 워크숍 3: 시간 관리 전략
오후 5:00 - 오후 6:00: 네트워킹 세션 (다과 제공)
모든 직원은 이 행사에 반드시 참석해야 하며, 10월 18일까지 등록을 완료해야 합니다. 등록은 회사 포털을 방문하거나 HR 부서(hr@company.com)로 문의해 주십시오.

제목: 알림: 직무 능력 개발의 날
수신: 전 직원
발신: 인사부
날짜: 2024년 10월 20일

팀 여러분,
다가오는 직무 능력 개발의 날 행사가 2024년 10월 25일 그랜드 홀 컨퍼런스 센터에서 열릴 예정임을 알려드립니다. 이전에 말씀드린 바와 같이, 이번 행사에는 리더십, 의사소통, 시간 관리에 관한 워크숍과 네트워킹 세션이 포함됩니다. 주요 직무 역량을 발전시키고 동료들과 교류할 수 있는 좋은 기회이니 많은 참여 바랍니다.
10월 18일까지 행사에 등록이 완료되었는지 확인해 주시기 바랍니다. 아직 등록하지 않으셨다면, 회사 포털을 방문하시거나 HR 부서(hr@company.com)로 직접 연락해 주시기 바랍니다. 또한, 행사 중 점심과 다과가 제공될 예정입니다.
여러분을 행사에서 뵙기를 기대하겠습니다!

감사합니다,
인사팀

어휘 workshop 워크숍, 세미나 upcoming 다가오는 professional development day 직업 개발의 날 location 장소, 위치 schedule 일정 keynote speech 기조연설 leadership skills development 리더십 기술 개발 mention 언급하다, 거론하다 previously 이전의 lunch break 점심시간 catering 음식 제공, 출장 연회 서비스 team collaboration & communication 팀 협업 및 커뮤니케이션 time management strategies 시간 관리 전략

networking session 네트워킹 세션 refreshments 다과, 가벼운 음식과 음료 require 요구하다 register 등록하다 contact 연락하다 HR (Human Resources) 인사부 company portal 회사 포털 reminder 알림, 상기 leadership 리더십 communication 의사소통, 커뮤니케이션 opportunity 기회 ensure 보장하다, 확실히 하다 register 등록하다 look forward to 기대하다

정답

1. (B) 2. (C) 3. (B) 4. (A) 5.(C)

1. 직무 능력 개발의 날의 등록 마감일은 언제입니까?
   (A) 10월 18일
   (B) 10월 20일
   (C) 10월 25일
   (D) 10월 30일

해설 "All employees are required to attend the event and must register by October 18."라는 일정표 문장에서 등록 마감일은 10월 18일이므로 (A)가 정답이다.

2. 직무 능력 개발의 날의 워크숍 주요 내용은 무엇입니까?
   (A) 마케팅 전략
   (B) 팀 빌딩 활동
   (C) 리더십, 커뮤니케이션, 시간 관리
   (D) 기술 능력 개발

해설 "This event will feature workshops on leadership, communication, and time management," 라는 이메일 문장에서 주요 워크숍 주제는 리더십, 커뮤니케이션, 그리고 시간 관리임을 명시하고 있으므로 (C)가 정답이다.

3. 행사에서 마지막으로 예정된 일정은 무엇입니까?
   (A) 시간 관리 전략 워크숍
   (B) 네트워킹 세션
   (C) 점심시간
   (D) 기조연설

해설 일정표에서 마지막 항목으로 "5:00 PM - 6:00 PM: Networking Session"이 명시되어 있으므로 (B)가 정답이다.

4. 네트워킹 세션에 할당된 시간은 얼마입니까?
   (A) 1시간
   (B) 1.5시간
   (C) 2시간
   (D) 45분

해설 일정표에 따르면 네트워킹 세션은 "5:00 PM-6:00 PM"으로 한 시간 동안 진행되므로 (A)가 정답이다.

5. 직무 능력 개발의 날에 예정된 워크숍의 중요성에 대해 추론할 수 있는 것은 무엇입니까?
   (A) 워크숍 참석이 직원 평가에 영향을 미칠 수 있다.
   (B) 워크숍의 주요 목적은 직원들 간의 관계 형성이다.
   (C) 회사는 이 워크숍을 기술 개발을 위한 중요한 학습 기회로 간주하고 있다.
   (D) 워크숍은 직원들이 다가오는 리더십 변화에 대비하도록 하기 위한 것이다.

해설 내부 이메일에서 "this event will feature workshops on leadership, communication, and time management... a great opportunity to develop key professional skills"라는 부분을 통해 이 워크숍이 주요 기술 개발과 전문 능력 향상을 목적으로 하고 있다는 것을 알 수 있으므로 (C)가 정답이다.

1. To부정사의 용법

✔ CheckPoint 1. To부정사를 목적어로 취하는 동사

정답

1. (B) 2. (D) 3. (B)

1.

번역 매니저는 매출을 증가시키기 위해 새로운 전략을 실행하기로 결정했다.

해설 decide는 To부정사를 목적어로 취하는 동사이므로 (B) to implement가 정답이다.

어휘 strategy 전략 increase 증가시키다, 늘리다 sales 판매, 매출

2.

번역 그녀는 현재 조건으로 계약서에 서명하기를 거부했다.

해설 refuse는 To부정사를 목적어로 취하는 동사이므로 (D) to sign이 정답이다.

어휘 refuse 거절하다, 거부하다 contract 계약 current 현재의 condition 조건, 상황

3.

번역 회사는 다음 분기에 추가 직원을 고용할 계획이다.

해설 plan은 To부정사를 목적어로 취하는 동사이므로 (B) to hire가 정답이다.

어휘 additional 추가적인 quarter 분기

✔ CheckPoint 2. To부정사를 목적어로 취하는 명사

정답

1. (C) 2. (A) 3. (C)

1.

번역 우리는 올해 말까지 현재의 서비스를 개선할 계획을 가지고 있다.

해설 plan은 To부정사를 목적어로 취하는 명사이므로 (C) to improve가 정답이다. 참고로 improve 뒤에 목적어(our current services)가 있으므로 수동형 (D) to be improved는 적절하지 않다.

2.

번역 리더십 역할을 맡고자 하는 욕구가 그녀가 추가 과정을 수강하게 만들었다.

해설 desire는 To부정사를 목적어로 취하는 명사이므로 (A) to assume이 정답이다.

어휘 desire 욕구 role 역할 motivate 동기를 부여하다 course 강좌, 과정

3.

번역 우리는 지난주에 계약 협상을 마무리하려고 시도했다.

해설 attempt는 To부정사를 목적어로 취하는 명사이므로 (C) to finalize가 정답이다. 참고로 finalize 뒤에 목적어(the contract negotiations)가 있으므로 수동형 (D) to be finalized는 적절하지 않다.

어휘 attempt 시도 contract 계약 negotiation 협상 finalize 마무리하다

✔ CheckPoint 3. 목적

정답

1. (B) 2. (D)

1.

번역 직원들은 마감일까지 프로젝트를 완료할 수 있도록 초과근무를 했다.

해설 in order that S + may/can/will (not) 구조는 목적을 나타내므로 (B) in order that이 정답이

다. (D) lest ~ (should)는 부정적인 결과를 피하기 위한 목적을 나타내므로 내용상 적절하지 않다.

어휘 work overtime 초과 근무를 하다

2.

번역 그녀는 발표를 놓치지 않기 위해 일찍 도착했다.

해설 (so as) (not) toV 구조는 목적을 나타내므로 (D) so as가 정답이다. (A) in order that, (B) lest, (C) so that은 모두 절을 필요로 하기 때문에 이 문장에서는 적절하지 않다.

✔ CheckPoint 4. 결과

정답

1. (B) 2. (A) 3. (B)

1.

번역 발표가 매우 명확해서 모두가 핵심 사항을 분명히 이해했다.

해설 so + 형용사/부사 + that S + V 구조는 결과를 나타내고, so 뒤에 형용사나 부사가 모두 올 수 있지만 특별한 경우를 제외하고 be동사(was) 뒤에 형용사만 주격보어로 사용되기 때문에 (B) so clear가 정답이다. (D) so clearly는 부사 형태로, 형용사 자리에 올 수 없으므로 문법적으로 적절하지 않다.

어휘 key point 핵심 사항 clearly 명확히, 분명히

2.

번역 그 과업은 너무 어려워서 팀의 추가 지원이 필요했다.

해설 so + 형용사/부사 + as toV 구조는 결과를 나타내므로 (A) so가 정답이다.

어휘 require 필요로 하다 additional support 추가 지원

3.

번역 그 새로운 정책은 너무 큰 변화여서 직원들이 적응할 시간이 필요하다.

해설 such + a(n) + 형용사 + 명사 + that S + V 구조는 결과를 나타내므로 (B) such가 정답이다.

어휘 significant 중요한, 중대한 change 변화 adjust 적응하다, 조정하다

✔ CheckPoint 5. 원인 및 이유나 판단의 근거

정답

1. (B) 2. (A)

1.

번역 그녀는 자신의 이름이 그 행사 중에 언급되었다는 것을 듣고 기뻤다.

해설 감정의 형용사 + To부정사 구조는 원인을 나타내므로 (B) to hear가 정답이다.

어휘 mention 언급하다 ceremony 행사, 의식

2.

번역 그는 이틀 만에 프로젝트를 끝내다니 정말 피곤할 것이다.

해설 must be + 형용사 + To부정사 구조는 이유나 판단의 근거를 나타내므로 (A) to finish가 정답이다. 참고로 finish 뒤에 목적어(the project)가 있으므로 수동형 (B) to be finished는 적절하지 않다.

2. To부정사의 의미상의 주어

✔ CheckPoint 6. To부정사의 의미상의 주어: For + 목적격

정답

1. (A) 2. (C) 3. (B)

1.

번역 그가 그렇게 짧은 시간 안에 발표를 준비하는 것은 어려웠다.

해설 형용사 difficult가 오면 의미상의 주어로 for + 목적격을 수반하는 It ~ for ~ toV 구문을 사용하므로 (A) to prepare가 정답이다.

2.

번역 학생들이 마감일 전에 과제를 제출하는 것이 필요하다.

[해설] 형용사 necessary가 오면 의미상의 주어로 for + 목적격을 수반하는 It ~ for ~ toV 구문을 사용하므로 (C) to submit가 정답이다.

[어휘] necessary 필요한 assignment 과제, 숙제 submit 제출하다

3.

번역 그들이 승인 없이 계약서에 서명하는 것은 불가능하다.

[해설] 형용사 impossible이 오면 의미상의 주어로 for + 목적격을 수반하는 It ~ for ~ toV 구문을 사용하므로 (B) for them이 정답이다.

[어휘] impossible 불가능한 contract 계약서 approval 승인, 허가

✔ CheckPoint 7. To부정사의 의미상의 주어: Of + 목적격

정답

1. (A) 2. (B) 3. (C)

1.

번역 그녀가 자선 단체에 그렇게 많은 돈을 기부한 것은 관대했다.

[해설] 사람의 성질이나 성격을 나타내는 형용사 generous가 오면 의미상의 주어로 of + 목적격을 수반하는 It ~ of ~ toV 구문을 사용하므로 (A) to donate가 정답이다.

[어휘] generous 관대한, 후한 charity 자선 단체, 자선

2.

번역 그가 경고 신호를 무시한 것은 어리석었다.

[해설] 사람의 성질이나 성격을 나타내는 형용사 foolish가 오면 의미상의 주어로 of + 목적격을 수반하는 It ~ of ~ toV 구문을 사용하므로 (B) to ignore가 정답이다.

[어휘] foolish 어리석은 warning 경고

3.

번역 그녀가 발표를 위해 추가 자료를 가져온 것은 사려 깊은 행동이었다.

[해설] 사람의 성질이나 성격을 나타내는 형용사 considerate가 오면 의미상의 주어로 of + 목적격을 수반하는 It ~ of ~ toV 구문을 사용하므로 (C) of her가 정답이다.

[어휘] considerate 사려 깊은, 배려하는 material 자료, 재료 presentation 발표

3. To부정사의 시제

✔ CheckPoint 8. 단순 부정사

정답

1. (D) 2. (B) 3. (C)

1.

번역 그들은 이번 주말까지 행사를 조직할 계획을 세웠다.

[해설] 원 문장 They planned that they would organize the event by the end of the week에서 주절과 종속절의 시제가 동일하면 복문을 단문으로 변경할 때 단순 부정사를 사용하고, 또 주절과 종속절의 주어가 동일하면 종속절의 주어는 생략하므로 (D) to organize가 정답이다.

2.

번역 매니저는 새로운 전략을 실행하기로 결정했다.

[해설] 원 문장 The manager decided that he would implement the new strategy에서 주절과 종속절의 시제가 동일하면 복문을 단문으로 변경할 때 단순 부정사를 사용하고, 또 주절과 종속절의 주어가 동일하면 종속절의 주어는 생략하므로 (B) to implement가 정답이다.

어휘 strategy 전략

3.

번역 직원들이 새로운 안전 지침을 따르는 것이 중요하다.

해설 원 문장 It is important that employees follow the new safety guidelines에서 주절과 종속절의 시제가 동일하면 복문을 단문으로 변경할 때 단순 부정사를 사용하고, 또 주절과 종속절의 주어가 다를 경우, 종속절의 주어를 for + 목적격으로 변경하여 사용하므로 (C) for employees가 정답이다.

어휘 safety guideline 안전 지침

✔ CheckPoint 9. 완료 부정사

정답

1. (B)	2. (D)	3. (B)

1.

번역 그녀는 보고서에서 실수를 했다고 인정했다.

해설 원 문장 She admitted that she had made a mistake in the report에서 주절보다 종속절의 시제가 한 시제 앞서면 복문을 단문으로 변경할 때 완료 부정사를 사용하고, 또 주절과 종속절의 주어가 동일하면 종속절의 주어는 생략하므로 (B) to have made가 정답이다.

어휘 admit 인정하다, 시인하다

2.

번역 그는 마감일 전에 프로젝트를 끝냈다고 주장했다.

해설 원 문장 He claimed that he had finished the project before the deadline에서 주절보다 종속절의 시제가 한 시제 앞서면 복문을 단문으로 변경할 때 완료 부정사를 사용하고, 또 주절과 종속절의 주어가 동일하면 종속절의 주어는 생략하므로 (D) to have finished가 정답이다.

어휘 claim 주장하다

3.

번역 그들은 회사가 지난 분기에 판매 목표를 초과 달성했다고 보고하였다.

해설 원 문장 They reported that the company had exceeded the sales target last quarter에서 주절보다 종속절의 시제가 한 시제 앞서면 복문을 단문으로 변경할 때 완료 부정사를 사용하므로 (B) to have exceeded가 정답이다.

어휘 sales target 판매 목표 quarter 분기 exceed 초과하다

토익 종합 실전문제

정답

1. (A)	2. (B)	3. (A)	4. (C)	5. (C)
6. (B)	7. (D)	8. (D)	9. (A)	10. (B)
11. (B)	12. (D)	13. (B)	14. (A)	15. (C)
16. (D)	17. (D)	18. (A)	19. (B)	20. (C)
21. (C)	22. (D)	23. (A)	24. (A)	

1.

번역 그 회사는 지역 기업들과 전략적 파트너십을 구축하려고 노력하고 있다.

해설 seek은 To부정사를 목적어로 취하는 동사이므로 (A) to form이 정답이다.

어휘 seek 찾다, 추구하다 strategic 전략적인 partnership 협력, 제휴 local 지역의

2.

번역 그들은 프로젝트에 추가 자원을 할당하기로 결정했다.

해설 decide는 To부정사를 목적어로 취하는 동사이므로 (B) to allocate가 정답이다.

어휘 additional 추가적인 resource 자원, 재원

3.

번역 직원은 승진을 대가로 추가적인 업무를 맡는 것에 동의했다.

해설 agree는 To부정사를 목적어로 취하는 동사이므로 (A) to take가 정답이다.

어휘 responsibility 책임, 업무 in exchange for ~의 대가로 promotion 승진

4.

번역 회사가 유럽에 새로운 지점을 개설하기로 한 결정은 주주들로부터 좋은 평가를 받았다.

해설 decision은 To부정사를 목적어로 취하는 명사이므로 (C) to open이 정답이다. 참고로 open 뒤에 목적어(a new branch)가 있으므로 수동형 (D) to be opened는 적절하지 않다.

어휘 branch 지점, 지부 well-received 좋은 반응을 얻은 shareholder 주주

5.

번역 고객은 제품에 결함이 있을 경우 환불을 요청할 권리가 있다.

해설 right는 To부정사를 목적어로 취하는 명사이므로 (C) to request가 정답이다. 참고로 request 뒤에 목적어(a refund)가 있으므로 수동형 (D) to be requested는 적절하지 않다.

어휘 right 권리 refund 환불 defective 결함이 있는, 하자가 있는

6.

번역 부서 간 더 나은 의사소통을 구축할 필요가 있다.

해설 need는 To부정사를 목적어로 취하는 명사이므로 (B) to establish가 정답이다.

어휘 department 부서

7.

번역 글로벌 팀을 이끌 기회는 어떤 직원에게도 귀중한 경험이다.

해설 opportunity는 To부정사를 목적어로 취하는 명사이므로 (D) to lead가 정답이다. 참고로 lead 뒤에 목적어(a global team)가 있으므로 수동형 (C) to be led는 적절하지 않다.

어휘 opportunity 기회 valuable 가치 있는, 귀중한 experience 경험

8.

번역 그녀는 문서가 분실되지 않도록 백업 사본을 보관했다.

해설 "~하지 않도록"이라는 의미의 lest ~ (should)는 부정적인 결과를 피하기 위한 목적을 나타내므로 (D) lest가 정답이다. (B)는 긍정적인 목적을 나타내며, (A)와 (C) 뒤에는 동사원형이 필요하기 때문에 이 문장에서는 적절하지 않다.

어휘 document 문서 get lost 분실하다, 없어지다

9.

번역 회사는 직원들이 기술을 향상시킬 수 있도록 추가 교육을 제공했다.

해설 so that S + may/can/will (not) 구조는 목적을 나타내므로 (A) so that이 정답이다.

어휘 additional 추가적인 enhance 향상시키다, 강화하다

10.

번역 고객 만족도를 향상시키기 위해, 회사는 새로운 피드백 시스템을 도입했다.

해설 (so as) (not) toV와 in order (not) toV 구조는 목적을 나타내므로 (B) To가 정답이다. (C) So that은 절을 필요로 하기 때문에 이 문장에서는 적절하지 않다.

어휘 improve 개선하다, 향상시키다 satisfaction 만족 implement 실행하다, 도입하다

11.

번역 사업을 글로벌하게 확장하기 위해, 회사는 새로운 파트너십을 찾고 있다.

해설 (so as) (not) toV와 in order (not) toV 구조는 목적을 나타내므로 (B) In order to가 정답이다. (C) In order that과 (D) Lest는 절을 필요로 하기 때문에 이 문장에서는 적절하지 않다.

어휘 expand 확장하다 globally 글로벌하게, 전세계적으로 look for 찾다, 모색하다 partnership 협력 관계, 제휴

12.

번역 시장 점유율을 높이기 위해, 회사는 새로운 제품을 출시할 계획이다.

해설 (so as) (not) toV와 in order (not) toV 구조는 목적을 나타내므로 (D) So as to가 정답이다. (A) So that과 (C) In order that은 절을 필요로 하기 때문에 이 문장에서는 적절하지 않다.

어휘 increase 증가시키다 market share 시장 점유율 launch 출시하다, 시작하다

13.

번역 그 결정은 너무 어려워서 이사회가 몇 시간 동안 논의해야 했다.

해설 so + 형용사 + a(n) + 명사 + that S + V 구조는 결과를 나타내므로 (B) so가 정답이다.

어휘 board 이사회, 위원회 discuss 논의하다, 토론하다

14.

번역 그 보고서는 매우 상세해서 고객의 모든 질문에 답을 제공했다.

해설 so + 형용사/부사 + that S + V 구조는 결과를 나타내므로 (A) so가 정답이다.

어휘 detailed 상세한, 구체적인 answer 답변하다, 해결하다

15.

번역 우리는 회의가 연기되었다는 것을 알려드리게 되어 유감이다.

해설 감정의 형용사 + To부정사 구조는 원인을 나타내므로 (C) to inform이 정답이다. 참고로 inform 뒤에 목적어(that the meeting has been postponed)가 있으므로 수동형 (D) to be informed는 적절하지 않다.

어휘 postpone 연기하다, 지연하다 inform 알리다, 통보하다

16

번역 그들이 이 프로젝트를 위해 매주말 일하다니 정말 헌신적인 것이 틀림없다.

해설 must be + 형용사 + To부정사 구조는 이유나 판단의 근거를 나타내므로 (D) to work가 정답이다. 참고로 work는 1형식 동사로서 수동태를 취할 수 없으므로 수동형 (C) to be worked는 적절하지 않다.

어휘 dedicate 헌신하다, 전념하다

17.

번역 직원들이 새로운 지침을 따르는 것이 가능하다.

해설 형용사 possible이 오면 의미상의 주어로 for + 목적격을 수반하는 It ~ for ~ toV 구문을 사용하므로 (D) for가 정답이다.

어휘 possible 가능한 guideline 지침

18.

번역 이번 달에 매출 목표를 달성하는 것은 우리에게 어려울 것이다.

해설 형용사 difficult가 오면 의미상의 주어로 for + 목적격을 수반하는 It ~ for ~ toV 구문을 사용하므로 (A) for us가 정답이다.

어휘 achieve 달성하다, 이루다 sales target 매출 목표

19.

번역 그 작업은 팀이 이틀 만에 완료하기에 쉬웠다.

해설 형용사 easy가 오면 의미상의 주어로 for + 목적격을 수반하는 It ~ for ~ toV 구문을 사용하고, 또 toV의 목적어(the task)는 주어 위치로 이동할 수 있다. 즉, 원 문장 It was easy for the team to complete the task in two days에서 The task was easy for the team to complete in two days가 도출되었으므로 (B) to complete가 정답이다.

20.

번역 신입 직원들이 모든 회사 정책을 한 번에 이해하는 것은 어렵다.

해설 형용사 hard가 오면 의미상의 주어로 for + 목적격을 수반하는 It ~ for ~ toV 구문을 사용하고, 또 toV의 목적어(all the company policies)는 주어 위치로 이동할 수 있다. 즉, 원 문장 It is hard for new employees to understand all the company policies at once에서 All the company policies are hard for new employees to understand at once가 도출되었으므로 (C) to understand가 정답이다.

어휘 policy 정책, 방침 at once 한 번에, 즉시

21.

번역 그녀가 미래의 투자를 위해 수입의 일부를 저축한 것은 현명했다.

해설 사람의 성질이나 성격을 나타내는 형용사 wise가 오면 의미상의 주어로 of + 목적격을 수반하는 It ~ of ~ toV 구문을 사용하므로 (C) of her가 정답이다.

어휘 wise 현명한, 지혜로운 portion 일부, 부분 income 수입, 소득 investment 투자

22.

번역 그녀가 회의 후에 꽃을 보낸 것은 사려 깊은 행동이었다.

해설 사람의 성질이나 성격을 나타내는 형용사 thoughtful이 오면 의미상의 주어로 of + 목적격을 수반하는 It ~ of ~ toV 구문을 사용하므로 (D) to send가 정답이다.

어휘 thoughtful 사려 깊은, 배려하는

23.

번역 그가 전문가의 도움 없이 컴퓨터 문제를 해결한 것은 현명한 행동이었다.

해설 사람의 성질이나 성격을 나타내는 형용사 clever가 오면 의미상의 주어로 of + 목적격을 수반하는 It ~ of ~ toV 구문을 사용하므로 (A) of him이 정답이다.

어휘 clever 영리한, 현명한 professional 전문가의, 직업의

24.

번역 그들이 다음 달에 프로젝트를 완료할 것으로 기대된다.

해설 원 문장 It is expected that they will complete the project next month에서 주절의 가주어 It과 종속절의 주어 they가 다르지만, 종속절의 주어를 주어로 한 수동태 문장 They are expected to complete the project next month로 변환할 수 있다. 또한 expect는 미래 지향적 의미를 내포하고 있으므로, 종속절에 미래시제(will complete)가 사용되더라도 동일한 시제로 간주되어 단순 부정사로 변경하므로 (A) to complete가 정답이다.

☞ 참고로 이 문장은 다음과 같은 파생과정으로 도출되었다고 보는 것이 더 타당하다.

We expect that they will complete the project next month. (3형식)

수동태 ⇒ It is expected that they will complete the project next month (by us).

We expect them to complete the project next month. (5형식)

수동태 ⇒ They are expected to complete the project next month (by us).

PART 6

다음 광고와 관련된 질문 1-4번을 보세요.

새로운 피트니스 앱 출시!

건강과 피트니스를 개선하고 싶으신가요? 저희는 목표를 효과적으로 달성할 수 있도록 도와줄 FitLife라는 새로운 피트니스 앱을 기쁜 마음으로 소개합니다. 이 앱은 개인 맞춤형 운동 계획, 영양 조언, 그리고 여러분을 동기부여할 피트니스 애호가 커뮤니티를 제공합니다.
추가적으로, 이 앱은 여러분이 목표를 꾸준히 달성할 수 있도록 매일 알림과 진행 상황 추적 기능을 제공합니다. 초보자와 고급 사용자 모두에게 완벽한 선택입니다.
앱은 무료로 다운로드 가능하며, 월간 멤버십에 가입하면 프리미엄 기능을 이용할 수 있습니다.

이 프리미엄 기능에는 개인 맞춤형 트레이닝 세션, 고급 식단 계획, 그리고 24시간 7일 내내 피트니스 코치에게 접근할 수 있는 기능이 포함되어 있습니다.
관심이 있으시면 지금 등록하여 프리미엄 기능의 14일 무료 체험을 받아보세요. 놓치지 마세요!
오늘 FitLife를 다운로드하여 즉시 피트니스 여정을 시작하세요!
궁금한 점이나 지원이 필요하면 support@fitlife.com으로 언제든지 연락해 주세요.
FitLife를 선택해 주셔서 감사합니다. 저희는 여러분이 피트니스 목표를 달성하는 데 있어 함께할 수 있기를 기대합니다!
건강과 피트니스를 개선하기 위해, FitLife가 여러분의 모든 단계에서 도와드릴 것입니다!

어휘 fitness 운동 launch 출시하다, 시작하다 improve 개선하다, 향상시키다 introduce 소개하다 brand-new 새로운 effectively 효과적으로 personalize 개인 맞춤형의 workout 운동, 운동하다 nutrition 영양 enthusiast 열정적인 사람들, 애호가 motivate 동기 부여하다 reminder 상기시키는 것, 알림 progress 진전, 진행 ensure 보장하다 feature 특징, 기능, 특색 subscribe 구독하다 achieve 달성하다

정답

1. (B) 2. (A) 3. (C) 4. (A)

1.

해설 빈칸에는 FitLife라는 새로운 피트니스 앱이 "목표를 효과적으로 달성할 수 있도록 돕기 위해 설계되었다"는 의미를 나타내는 수동형 구조가 필요하므로 (B) (which was) designed가 정답이다.

2.

해설 여기서는 앞 문장의 설명을 보충하여 추가 정보를 제공하고 있으므로 (A) Additionally가 정답이다. (B) As a result는 "결과적으로", (C) Otherwise는 "그렇지 않으면", (D) Nevertheless는 "그럼에도 불구하고"란 의미로 문맥에 맞지 않다.

3.

(A) 고급 기능을 위해 프리미엄 멤버십으로 업그레이드할 수 있습니다.
(B) 이 앱은 목표를 유지할 수 있도록 알림을 포함하고 있습니다.
(C) 지금 등록하여 프리미엄 기능의 14일 무료 체험을 받아보세요.
(D) 이 앱은 피트니스 진행 상황을 자동으로 추적하도록 설계되었습니다.

해설 지문에서 If you're interested(관심이 있으시면)라는 문구는 사용자가 앱에 관심이 있을 때 다음에 해야 할 행동을 안내하는 역할을 하고, 또 사용자가 앱의 프리미엄 기능을 체험하기 위해 무엇을 해야 하는지를 명확히 설명하는 문장이 있어야 하므로 (C)가 가장 적절하다. (A)는 앱의 업그레이드 정보를 제공하지만, 사용자가 즉시 해야 할 행동을 안내하지는 않으므로 문맥에 적절하지 않고, (B)는 앱의 기능 설명에 해당하며, 행동 지시와 관련이 없으므로 문맥과 맞지 않으며, (D)는 앱의 특징을 설명하지만, 구체적인 행동 지시를 제공하지 않으므로 문맥에 적절하지 않다.

4.

해설 "건강과 피트니스를 개선하기 위해서"라는 의미로 목적을 나타내므로 (A) In order to가 정답이다. (B) So as 뒤에는 to가 필요하고, (C) In order that과 (D) So that 뒤에는 절이 필요하므로 적절하지 않다.

PART 7

다음 편지와 관련된 질문 1-4번을 보세요.

수신자: Ms. Jessica Thompson
발신자: Emily Parker, 고객 서비스 매니저
날짜: 9월 10일
제목: 제품 환불 문의에 대한 응답

Jessica Thompson 님께,
귀하의 최근 구매에 대해 문의해 주셔서 감사합니다. 받은 제품이 기대에 미치지 못했다는 소식을 듣게 되어 유감입니다.
귀하의 환불 요청을 검토한 결과, 요청이 승인되었음을 알려드립니다. $120의 환불 금액은

5~7영업일 이내에 원래 결제 수단으로 환불 처리될 예정입니다. 은행에 따라 환불 처리에 추가 시간이 소요될 수 있습니다.
제품을 다른 항목으로 교환하고 싶으시다면, 기꺼이 도와드리겠습니다. 그럴 경우, 제품을 원래 포장 상태로 반환해 주시면 교환 절차를 진행해 드리겠습니다. 또는, 저희 매장을 방문하여 다른 제품들을 둘러보실 수도 있습니다.
추가 질문이나 궁금한 사항이 있으시면, 편하실 때 이메일이나 전화로 언제든지 저희에게 연락해 주십시오. 귀하의 이해에 감사드리며, 앞으로 다시 모실 수 있기를 기대합니다.

감사합니다,
Emily Parker
고객 서비스 매니저

어휘 inquiry 문의 refund 환불 contact 연락하다 regarding ~에 관하여 recent 최근의 purchase 구매, 구입 regret 유감스럽게 생각하다, 후회하다 expectation 기대 request 요청 approve 승인하다, 허가하다 credit 입금하다, 적립하다 payment 결제 method 수단, 방법 business day 영업일 transaction 처리, 거래 exchange 교환 assist 돕다, 지원하다 return 반환하다, 반송하다 arrange 준비하다, 조치하다 alternatively 그 대신에, 그렇지 않으면 explore 탐색하다, 살펴보다 further 더 이상의, 추가의 concerns 우려, 걱정 convenience 편의, 편리한 것 appreciate 감사하다 look forward to ~을 기대하다

정답

1. (B) 2. (D) 3. (A) 4. (B)

1. Ms. Thompson이 고객 서비스에 연락한 이유는 무엇입니까?
   (A) 배송 지연에 대해 문의하기 위해
   (B) 제품 환불을 요청하기 위해
   (C) 제품의 재고 여부를 문의하기 위해
   (D) 결제 수단을 변경하기 위해

해설 지문에서 "We have reviewed your request for a refund"라고 언급되어 있어, Ms. Thompson이 환불을 요청했음을 알 수 있으므로 (B)가 정답이다.

2. Ms. Thompson은 언제 환불을 받을 수 있습니까?
   (A) 제품 반송 직후
   (B) 제품이 교환된 후
   (C) 2-3영업일 이내에
   (D) 5-7영업일 이내에

해설 지문에서 "The refund amount of $120 will be credited to your original payment method within 5-7 business days"라고 언급되어 있으므로 (D)가 정답이다.

3. 환불 외에 Ms. Thompson에게 제시된 다른 옵션은 무엇입니까?
   (A) 제품 교환
   (B) 매장 크레딧
   (C) 할인 쿠폰과 함께 전액 환불
   (D) 제품 수리 서비스

해설 지문에서 "If you would like to exchange the product for another item, we would be happy to assist you"라고 언급되어 있어, 환불 외에도 Ms. Thompson은 제품 교환할 수 있기 때문에 (A)가 정답이다.

4. Ms. Thompson이 제품에 대해 어떤 경험을 했는지 추론할 수 있는 것은 무엇입니까?
   (A) 그녀는 품질에 만족했다.
   (B) 그녀는 제품이 결함이 있거나 적합하지 않다고 생각했다.
   (C) 그녀는 추가 제품을 구매하고 싶어 했다.
   (D) 그녀는 그 제품을 특별한 행사에 사용하려고 계획했다.

해설 지문에서 "We are sorry to hear that the product did not meet your expectations"라고 언급되어 있어, Ms. Thompson이 제품에 만족하지 않아 환불 요청을 했다는 사실을 통해, 제품이 결함이 있거나 사용 목적에 부적합했음을 추론할 수 있으므로 (B)가 정답이다.

Chapter 06 분사

1. 분사의 용법

✔ CheckPoint 1. 현재분사 + 명사

정답

1. (B) 2. (B) 3. (A)

1.

번역 식품의 상승하는 가격이 많은 가정에 어려움을 주고 있다.

해설 "상승하는 가격"을 의미하는 어휘는 rising prices이므로 (B) rising이 정답이다.

2.

번역 팀은 프로젝트의 다가오는 마감일을 맞추기 위해 늦게까지 작업하고 있다.

해설 "다가오는 마감일"을 의미하는 어휘는 approaching deadline이므로 (B) approaching이 정답이다.

3.

번역 사업을 확장할 흥미로운 기회를 놓쳐서는 안 됩니다.

해설 "흥미로운 기회"를 의미하는 어휘는 exciting opportunity이므로 (A) exciting이 정답이다.

어휘 opportunity 기회 expand 확장하다, 확대하다

✔ CheckPoint 2. 과거분사 + 명사

정답

1. (B) 2. (A) 3. (D)

1.

번역 선택된 후보자는 다음 달에 일을 시작할 것이다.

해설 "선택된 후보자"를 의미하는 어휘는 chosen candidate이므로 (B) chosen이 정답이다.

어휘 candidate 후보자, 지원자

2.

번역 기술자는 고장 난 장비를 신속히 수리했다.

해설 "고장 난 장비"를 의미하는 어휘는 broken equipment이므로 (A) broken이 정답이다.

어휘 technician 기술자 equipment 장비

3.

번역 첨부된 파일에는 프로젝트에 대한 최신 업데이트가 포함되어 있다.

해설 "첨부된 파일"을 의미하는 어휘는 attached file이므로 (D) attached가 정답이다.

어휘 contain 포함하다, 함유하다

✔ CheckPoint 3. 주어 + 동사 + 목적어 + 목적보어(형용사/현재분사/과거분사)

정답

1. (A) 2. (C) 3. (D)

1.

번역 CEO는 최종 세부 사항이 확인될 때까지 발표를 비밀로 유지했다.

해설 kept은 목적보어 자리에 형용사, 현재분사 및 과거분사를 취할 수 있으므로, "비밀의"라는 의미를 가진 (A) secret가 정답이다.

어휘 announcement 발표, 공지 detail 세부 사항, 상세 정보 confirm 확인하다

2.

번역 감독관은 프로젝트의 성공을 보장하기

위해 마감일을 엄격하게 설정했다.

해설 made는 목적보어 자리에 형용사, 현재분사 및 과거분사를 취할 수 있으므로, "엄격한"이라는 의미를 가진 (C) strict가 정답이다.

어휘 supervisor 감독관, 관리자 ensure 보장하다

3.

번역 선생님은 학생들이 집에서 완료할 수 있도록 과제를 미완성 상태로 두었다.

해설 left는 목적보어 자리에 형용사, 현재분사 및 과거분사를 취할 수 있으므로, "완성되지 않은" 이라는 의미를 가진 (D) unfinished가 정답이다. 참고로 (C) finishing은 현재분사로 뒤에 목적어를 취해야 하지만 없으므로 적절하지 않다.

어휘 assignment 과제, 숙제

2. 분사구문

✔ CheckPoint 4. 분사구문의 시제

정답

1. (A)　2. (A)

1.

번역 직원들은 새로운 소프트웨어를 사용하면서, 작업을 더 쉽게 관리할 수 있었다.

해설 원 문장 As the employees used the new software, they found it easier to manage their tasks을 보면 주절과 종속절의 시제가 동일한 단순 분사구문이고, 또 주절과 종속절의 주어가 동일하면 종속절의 주어를 생략하므로 (A) Using이 정답이다.

2.

번역 마감일이 다가오면서, 프로젝트는 서둘러 완료되었다.

해설 원 문장 As the deadline was approaching, the project was rushed to completion을 보면 주절과 종속절의 시제가 동일한 단순 분사구문이고, 또 주절과 종속절의 주어가 다르면 종속절의 주어(The deadline)를 생략하지 않으므로 (A) approaching이 정답이다.

어휘 rush 급히 움직이다, 서두르다 completion 완료, 완성

✔ CheckPoint 5. 분사구문의 태와 부정

정답

1. (B)　2. (D)　3. (C)

1.

번역 결과를 분석한 후, 매니저는 중대한 결정을 내렸다.

해설 원 문장 After the manager had analyzed the results, he made a significant decision을 보면 주절보다 종속절의 시제가 한 시제 앞서는 완료 분사구문이고, 또 주절과 종속절의 주어가 동일하므로 (B) Having analyzed가 정답이다.

어휘 significant 중요한, 중대한 decision 결정, 판단 analyze 분석하다

2.

번역 고객들에 의해 문제들이 보고된 후, 제품 디자인이 개선되었다.

해설 원 문장 After the issues had been reported by the customers, the product design was improved을 보면 주절보다 종속절의 시제가 한 시제 앞서는 완료 분사구문이고, 또 주절과 종속절의 주어가 다르므로 종속절의 주어(The issues)는 생략되지 않았다. 하지만 이 지문은 수동형 분사구문이므로 (D) having been reported가 정답이다.

어휘 improve 개선하다, 향상시키다

3.

번역 필요한 예방조치를 취하지 않았기 때문에 실험은 상당한 위험을 초래했다.

해설 원 문장 Since they did not take the

necessary precautions, the experiment posed significant risks을 보면 주절과 종속절의 시제가 동일한 단순 분사구문이고, 또 주절과 종속절의 주어는 다르지만 일반인 주어(they)이기 때문에 생략되었다. 하지만 이 지문은 부정문이므로 부정어를 분사 앞에 위치시킨 (C) Not taking이 정답이다.

어휘 necessary 필요한, 필수적인 precaution 예방조치, 주의 사항 experiment 실험 pose 초래하다, 제기하다, 야기하다

토익 종합 실전문제

정답

1. (A)	2. (B)	3. (D)	4. (D)	5. (C)
6. (A)	7. (D)	8. (B)	9. (C)	10. (D)
11. (B)	12. (C)	13. (A)	14. (D)	15. (C)
16. (C)	17. (A)	18. (D)	19. (A)	20. (C)
21. (D)	22. (B)	23. (A)	24. (C)	

1.

번역 제품에 대한 증가하는 수요 때문에 우리는 생산 라인을 확장하고 있다.

해설 "증가하는 수요"를 의미하는 어휘는 increasing demand이므로 (A) increasing이 정답이다.

어휘 due to ~ 때문에, ~로 인해 demand 수요, 요구 expand 확장하다, 확대하다 production line 생산 라인, 제조 라인

2.

번역 참여하는 회원들은 등록 데스크에서 서명해야 한다.

해설 "참여하는 회원들"을 의미하는 어휘는 participating members이므로 (B) participating이 정답이다.

어휘 sign in 서명하다 registration desk 등록 데스크, 접수처

3.

번역 팀은 진행 중인 프로젝트를 완료하기 위해 열심히 일하고 있다.

해설 "진행 중인 프로젝트"를 의미하는 어휘는 ongoing project이므로 (D) ongoing이 정답이다.

4.

번역 그 유망한 후보자는 마케팅과 판매 둘 다에서 경험이 있다.

해설 "유망한 후보자"를 의미하는 어휘는 promising candidate이므로 (D) promising이 정답이다.

어휘 candidate 후보자, 지원자 experience 경험, 경력 sales 판매, 영업

5.

번역 팀은 마감일 전에 도전적인 과제를 완료하는 데 집중하고 있다.

해설 "도전적인 과제"를 의미하는 어휘는 challenging task이므로 (C) challenging이 정답이다.

어휘 focus on 집중하다, 전념하다

6.

번역 마케팅 팀은 시장에서 변화하는 추세를 파악하기 위해 열심히 노력하고 있다.

해설 "변화하는 추세"를 의미하는 어휘는 changing trends이므로 (A) changing이 정답이다.

어휘 identify 확인하다, 알아내다 trend 경향, 추세

7.

번역 회사는 성장하는 시장에서 앞서 나가기 위해 새로운 기술에 투자하고 있다.

해설 "성장하는 시장"을 의미하는 어휘는 growing market이므로 (D) growing이 정답이다.

어휘 invest in ~에 투자하다 stay ahead 앞서다, 선두를 유지하다

8.

번역 만료된 계약은 이번 달 말 전에 갱신되어야 한다.

해설 "만료된 계약"을 의미하는 어휘는 expired contract이므로 (B) expired가 정답이다.

어휘 contract 계약, 계약서 renew 갱신하다, 연장하다

9.

번역 회사는 모든 재고 정리 품목에 대해 할인된 가격을 제공하기로 결정했다.

해설 "할인된 가격"을 의미하는 어휘는 reduced price이므로 (C) reduced가 정답이다.

어휘 offer 제공하다, 제안하다 clearance item 재고 정리 품목

10.

번역 모든 필요한 서류는 이번 주 말까지 제출해야 한다.

해설 "필요한 서류"를 의미하는 어휘는 required documents이므로 (D) required가 정답이다.

어휘 document 문서, 서류 submit 제출하다

11.

번역 정보에 근거한 결정을 내리려면 사용 가능한 모든 데이터를 신중히 분석해야 한다.

해설 "정보에 근거한 결정"을 의미하는 어휘는 informed decision이므로 (B) informed가 정답이다.

어휘 decision 결정 require 요구하다 careful 신중한, 세심한 analysis 분석 available 사용 가능한 extend 연장하다 cancel 취소하다

12.

번역 보고서에는 제품 사양에 대한 수정된 버전이 포함되어 있다.

해설 "수정된 버전"을 의미하는 어휘는 revised version이므로 (C) revised가 정답이다.

어휘 include 포함하다, 수반하다 specification 사양, 세부 설명

13.

번역 프리미엄 멤버십을 가진 직원들은 회사의 온라인 자원에 무제한으로 접근할 수 있다.

해설 "무제한 접근"을 의미하는 어휘는 unlimited access이므로 (A) unlimited가 정답이다.

어휘 resource 자료, 자원

14.

번역 고객은 손상된 상품을 받았기 때문에 환불을 요청했다.

해설 "손상된 상품"을 의미하는 어휘는 damaged goods이므로 (D) damaged가 정답이다.

어휘 request 요청하다, 요구하다 refund 환불 due to ~ 때문에 receive 받다, 수령하다 goods 상품, 물품

15.

번역 최근 정책 변경으로 많은 직원들이 혼란스러워하며 설명을 요구하고 있다.

해설 left는 목적보어 자리에 형용사, 현재분사 및 과거분사를 취할 수 있으므로, "혼란스러워하게 된"이라는 의미를 가진 (C) confused가 정답이다. (B) confusing은 현재분사로 뒤에 목적어를 취해야 하지만 없으므로 적절하지 않다.

어휘 recent 최근의 policy 정책, 방침 change 변화, 변경 seek 찾다, 구하다, 요구하다 clarification 설명, 명확화

16.

번역 발표 후, 고객은 제안이 만족스럽다고 느끼고 계약서에 서명했다.

해설 found는 목적보어 자리에 형용사, 현재분사 및 과거분사를 취할 수 있으므로, "만족을 주는, 만족스럽게 하는"이라는 의미를 가진 (C) satisfying이 정답이다. (B) satisfied는 과거분사로 "제안이 누군가에 의해 만족되었다"는 수동 의미를 갖는데, 제안 자체가 고객에게 어떤 감정을 불러일으킨다는 능동적 의미가 필요하므로 적절하지 않다.

어휘 presentation 발표 proposal 제안, 제안서 sign 서명하다, 계약하다 contract 계약, 계약서

17.

번역 위원회는 보고서가 명확하지 않다고 판단하고 추가적인 설명을 요청했다.

(해설) found는 목적보어 자리에 형용사, 현재분사 및 과거분사를 취할 수 있으므로, "명확하지 않은" 이라는 의미를 가진 (A) unclear가 정답이다. (C) clear는 의미상 적절하지 않다.

(어휘) committee 위원회 request 요청하다, 요구하다 further 추가적인

18.

번역 최근 업그레이드로 소프트웨어가 회사 전체 사용자에게 접근 가능해졌다.

(해설) made는 목적보어 자리에 형용사, 현재분사 및 과거분사를 취할 수 있으므로, "접근 가능한"이라는 의미를 가진 (D) accessible이 정답이다. (B) accessing은 현재분사로 뒤에 목적어를 취해야 하지만 없으므로 적절하지 않고, (D) accessed는 과거분사로 "소프트웨어가 접근된"이라는 의미로 사용될 수 있지만, 이는 사용자들이 소프트웨어에 접근할 수 있는 현재의 상태를 설명하는 데 적절하지 않다.

19.

번역 팀은 사무실을 깨끗한 상태로 두고 다음 날의 일을 준비했다.

(해설) left는 목적보어 자리에 형용사, 현재분사 및 과거분사를 취할 수 있으므로, "깨끗한"이라는 의미를 가진 (A) clean이 정답이다. 특히 (A) clean은 형용사로 사용되어 사무실이 깨끗한 상태로 남겨졌다는 것을 나타내며, 이는 사무실이 이미 청소되었거나 사용 후 깨끗이 정리된 상태를 의미하므로 문맥상 가장 적절하다. (B) cleaned는 과거분사로, 누군가에 의해 청소가 완료된 상태를 나타내는데, left의 경우 "상태"를 강조하므로 (A) clean이 더 적절하다. (C) cleaning은 현재분사로, 뒤에 목적어를 취해야하고, (D) cleaner는 비교급 형태로, 문맥에 맞지 않다.

20.

번역 새로운 시스템을 적용하면서, 그들은 업무를 더 효율적으로 완료할 수 있었다.

(해설) 원 문장 As they implemented the new system, they were able to complete their tasks more efficiently을 보면 주절과 종속절의 시제가 동일한 단순 분사구문이고, 또 주절과 종속절의 주어가 동일하면 종속절의 주어를 생략하므로 (C) Implementing이 정답이다.

(어휘) efficiently 효율적으로, 능률적으로 implement 시행하다, 적용하다

21.

번역 분석가는 모든 관련 정보를 수집한 후, 상세한 보고서를 제공했다.

(해설) 원 문장 After the analyst had collected all relevant information, he provided a detailed report을 보면 주절보다 종속절의 시제가 한 시제 앞서는 완료 분사구문이고, 또 주절과 종속절의 주어가 동일하면 종속절의 주어를 생략하므로 (D) Having collected가 정답이다.

(어휘) relevant 관련 있는, 적절한 analyst 분석가, 전문가 detailed 상세한, 구체적인

22.

번역 행사가 끝난 후, 장소는 신속하게 청소되고 다음 행사 준비가 완료되었다.

(해설) 원 문장 After the event had ended, the venue was quickly cleaned and prepared for the next occasion을 보면 주절보다 종속절의 시제가 한 시제 앞서는 완료 분사구문이고, 또 주절과 종속절의 주어가 다르면 종속절의 주어(The event)를 생략하지 않으므로 (B) having ended가 정답이다.

(어휘) venue 장소, 개최지 prepare 준비하다, 마련하다 occasion 경우, 행사

23.

번역 프로젝트를 완료한 후, 팀은 그들의 성공을 축하했다.

해설 원 문장 After the project had been completed, the team celebrated their success을 보면 주절보다 종속절의 시제가 한 시제 앞서는 완료 분사구문이고, 또 주절과 종속절의 주어가 다르므로 종속절의 주어(The project)는 생략되지 않았다. 하지만 이 지문은 수동형 분사구문이므로 (A) having been completed가 정답이다.

어휘 celebrate 축하하다

24.

번역 업데이트를 받지 못했기 때문에, 매니저는 문제를 인식하지 못했다.

해설 원 문장 Because the manager had not received the updates, he was unaware of the issues을 보면 주절보다 종속절의 시제가 한 시제 앞서는 완료 분사구문이고, 또 주절과 종속절의 주어가 동일하므로 종속절의 주어는 생략되었다. 하지만 이 지문은 부정문이므로 부정어를 분사 앞에 위치시킨 (C) Not having received가 정답이다.

어휘 unaware 알지 못하는, 인식하지 못하는

PART 6

다음 공지와 관련된 질문 1-4번을 보세요.

> 친애하는 직원 여러분,
> 우리는 다음 달에 회사가 새로운 사무실 건물로 이사할 것임을 알려드리게 되어 매우 기쁩니다. 이 이사는 더 나은 근무 환경을 제공하고 성장하는 팀을 수용하기 위한 우리의 지속적인 노력의 일환입니다. 새로운 사무실은 넓은 회의실, 협업 작업 공간, 그리고 최신식 카페테리아를 포함한 현대적인 시설로 갖춰져 있습니다.
> 추가적으로, 우리는 이번 이사가 직장 문화를 크게 향상시키고 생산성을 높일 것이라고 확신합니다. 공식적인 이사 날짜는 다음 달 15일로 설정되어 있습니다. 개인 소지품을 포장하고 이사를 위해 명확하게 라벨을 붙이는 것을 잊지 마세요. 우리는 전환을 돕기 위해 전문 이사 팀을 준비했습니다.
> 또한 각 부서는 혼란을 최소화하기 위해 이사할 특정 시간을 배정받게 됩니다. 상세한 지침은 이사 날짜가 가까워지면 제공될 것입니다. 질문이나 우려 사항이 있으시면 HR 부서에 언제든지 문의하시기 바랍니다.
> 우리는 이사가 스트레스를 줄 수 있음을 이해하지만, 이번 이사가 회사와 모든 직원에게 많은 이점을 가져올 것이라고 믿습니다. 마지막으로, 이 시간 동안 여러분의 협조와 인내에 감사드립니다.
> 새로운 사무실 위치는 대중교통으로 쉽게 접근할 수 있으며, 운전하는 분들을 위한 주차 공간도 마련될 것입니다.
> 우리는 여러분을 새로운 사무실로 환영할 날을 기대하며, 회사 여정의 새로운 장이 시작되는 것에 대해 기쁘게 생각합니다.
>
> 감사합니다,
> 경영팀

어휘 relocate 이전하다, 옮기다 provide 제공하다 accommodate 수용하다, 맞추다 modern facility 현대적인 시설 include 포함하다, 수반하다 spacious 넓은, 공간이 넉넉한 collaborative 공동의, 협업의 state-of-the-art 최신식의 enhance 향상시키다, 강화하다 culture 문화 boost 높이다 productivity 생산성 personal 개인의, 개인적인 belongings 재산, 소지품 arrange 마련하다, 처리하다 professional 전문적인 transition 이동, 전환 department 부서 minimize 최소화하다 disruption 혼란 concerns 우려, 걱정 stressful 스트레스가 많은 appreciate 감사하다 cooperation 협력, 협조 patience 인내 public transportation 대중교통 parking 주차 available 이용 가능한

정답

1. (A) 2. (B) 3. (A) 4. (D)

1.

해설 빈 칸에는 회사의 이사가 더 나은 근무 환경을 제공하고 성장하는 팀을 수용하기 위한 지속적인 노력의 일환임을 나타내는 어휘가 필요하므로 "지속적인 노력"이라는 의미를 가진 (A) ongoing efforts가 정답이다. (B) established procedures는 "수립된 절차", (C) increased efficiency는 "증가된 효율성", (D) temporary measures는 "일시적인 조치"란 의미로 문맥에 맞지 않다.

2.

(A) 우리는 이사하는 동안 원활한 전환이 이루어지기를 기대합니다.

(B) 이사 날짜가 가까워지면 상세한 지침이 제공될 것입니다.

(C) 포장 지침을 따르는 것이 중요합니다.

(D) 모든 직원이 이사 과정에 도움을 줄 것을 권장합니다.

해설 이전 문장에서 각 부서가 이사할 특정 시간을 배정받는다는 내용이 언급되었고, 그 후에는 이사 날짜가 다가오면서 직원들에게 상세한 지침이 제공될 것이라는 내용이 자연스럽게 이어져야 하므로 (B)가 가장 적절하다. (A)는 이사 과정이 순조로울 것이라는 기대를 나타내지만, 이는 구체적인 후속 조치를 설명하지 않으므로 문맥에 맞지 않고, (C)는 포장 지침을 따르라는 강조 내용이지만, 문맥에서 필요한 것은 정보 제공에 대한 설명이지 포장 방법에 대한 강조가 아니며, (D)는 직원들에게 이사 과정을 돕도록 권장하는 내용이지만, 앞뒤 문맥에서 강조되는 세부 지침 제공과는 거리가 있기 때문에 적절하지 않다.

3.

해설 문장에서 easily라는 부사는 형용사 accessible(접근 가능한)을 수식하고, 새로운 사무실 위치가 대중교통으로 접근 가능하다는 의미를 나타내므로 (A) accessible이 정답이다. (B) necessary는 "필수적인", (C) productive는 "생산적인", (D) expensive는 "비싼"이란 의미로 문맥에 맞지 않다.

4.

해설 지시대명사 those는 관계대명사 who 앞에 위치할 때, "~하는 사람들"이라는 의미로 자주 사용되므로 (D) those가 정답이다.

PART 7

다음 기사와 관련된 질문 1-4번을 보세요.

직원 복지를 위한 재택근무의 이점

최근 몇 년 동안 더 많은 회사들이 직원들에게 재택근무 옵션을 제공하기 시작했습니다. 재택근무는 직원들이 사무실이 아닌 다른 장소, 주로 집에서 업무를 수행할 수 있도록 합니다. 이 방식은 직원과 고용주 모두에게 여러 이점을 제공합니다. 재택근무의 가장 큰 장점 중 하나는 일과 삶의 균형이 개선된다는 것입니다. 출퇴근할 필요가 없어지면서, 직원들은 시간을 절약하고 그 시간을 가족과 함께 보내거나 개인적인 취미에 사용할 수 있습니다. 이러한 유연성은 직업 만족도를 높이고 스트레스 수준을 낮출 수 있습니다.

더구나, 재택근무는 생산성 향상으로 이어질 수 있습니다. 연구에 따르면, 재택근무를 하는 직원들은 사무실에서 일하는 직원들보다 병가를 덜 내며, 종종 더 긴 시간을 일하는 경향이 있습니다. 집의 조용한 환경은 더 집중할 수 있게 하고 방해 요소를 줄여, 더 높은 효율성을 가져옵니다.

그러나 재택근무에도 문제점이 없는 것은 아닙니다. 일부 직원들은 고립감을 느끼고, 사무실에서의 사회적 상호작용을 그리워할 수 있습니다. 또한, 일과 개인 생활의 명확한 구분이 없으면 시간 관리와 번아웃을 피하는 것이 어려울 수 있습니다.

결론적으로, 재택근무에는 단점이 있지만, 잠재적인 이점 때문에 많은 기업과 직원들에게 가치 있는 선택지가 될 수 있습니다.

어휘 remote work 원격 근무, 재택근무 perform 수행하다, 실행하다 job duty 직무, 업무 location 위치, 장소 arrangement 방식, 합의 significant 중요한, 상당한 advantage 장점, 이점 work-life balance 일과 삶의 균형 commute 통근하다, 출퇴근하다 engage in ~에 참여하다, ~에 종사하다 personal 개인적인, 개인의 flexibility 유연성, 융통성 satisfaction 만족도, 만족 reduce 낮추다, 줄이다 productivity 생산성, 효율성 take sick days 병가를 내다 counterpart 상대 distraction 방해, 산만함 contribute 기여하다 efficiency 효율성 focus 집중하다, 집중 isolate 고립시키다, 격리하다 interaction 상호작용 burnout 번아웃(소진, 탈진), 극도의 피로와 스트레스 separation 분리, 구분 drawback 단점, 결점 potential 잠재적인 valuable 가치 있는

정답

1. (B) 2. (C) 3. (A) 4. (A)

1. 기사에서 언급된 재택근무의 주요 이점 중 하나는 무엇입니까?
   (A) 직원들이 더 많은 휴가를 받을 수 있다.
   (B) 직원들이 가족과 더 많은 시간을 보낼 수 있다.
   (C) 고용주가 재택근무를 위해 더 나은 사무 장비를 제공한다.
   (D) 재택근무자들이 더 높은 급여를 받는다.

해설 지문에서 "employees can save time and use it to spend more time with their families or engage in personal hobbies"라고 명시되어 있어, 재택근무의 주요 이점 중 하나가 직원들이 가족과 더 많은 시간을 보낼 수 있으므로 (B)가 정답이다.

2. 기사에 따르면, 왜 재택근무가 생산성 향상으로 이어질 수 있습니까?
   (A) 직원들이 더 짧은 시간을 일할 수 있기 때문이다.
   (B) 직원들이 더 나은 기술을 이용할 수 있기 때문이다.
   (C) 직원들이 더 조용한 환경에서 더 잘 집중할 수 있기 때문이다.
   (D) 직원들이 추가 교육을 받기 때문이다.

해설 지문에서 "The quiet environment of home allows for more focus and fewer distractions"라고 명시되어 있어, 직원들이 더 조용한 환경에서 더 잘 집중할 수 있고, 이는 생산성 향상으로 이어질 수 있으므로 (C)가 정답이다.

3. 기사에서 언급된 재택근무의 잠재적인 문제점은 무엇입니까?
   (A) 재택근무자들이 사회적 상호작용이 부족하다.
   (B) 재택근무자들이 더 많은 스트레스를 느낀다.
   (C) 재택근무자들이 시간을 효과적으로 관리할 수 있다.
   (D) 재택근무자들이 기술에 대한 접근이 제한된다.

해설 지문에서 "Some employees may feel isolated and miss the social interaction that comes with working in an office"라고 명시되어 있어, 일부 직원들이 사무실에서의 사회적 상호작용을 그리워하며 고립감을 느낄 수 있으므로 (A)가 정답이다.

4. 고용주의 재택근무 운영 역할에 대해 무엇을 추론할 수 있습니까?
   (A) 직원들이 소통을 유지하도록 도와야 한다.
   (B) 재택근무자에게 적은 급여를 지급해야 한다.
   (C) 직원들의 인터넷 요금을 지불해야 한다.
   (D) 직원들에게 가끔 사무실에 방문하도록 요청해야 한다.

해설 지문에서 "Some employees may feel isolated and miss the social interaction that comes with working in an office"라고 명시되어 있어, 일부 직원들이 사무실에서의 사회적 상호작용을 그리워하며 고립감을 느낄 수 있으므로 (A)가 정답이다. 이 부분이 생략되었음

Chapter 07 동명사

1. 동명사의 용법

✔ CheckPoint 1. 동명사를 목적어로 취하는 동사

정답

1. (A) 2. (C) 3. (B)

1.

번역 매니저는 문제를 해결하기 위한 새로운 접근 방식을 도입할 것을 제안했다.

해설 동사 suggest는 동명사를 목적어로 취하는 동사이므로 (A) implementing이 정답이다.

어휘 suggest 제안하다, 추천하다 implement 실행하다, 이행하다 approach 접근, 방법, 접근하다

solve 풀다, 설명하다 issue 문제, 쟁점

2.

번역 그들은 고객의 사무실로 가는 도중 길을 물어보기 위해 멈췄다.

해설 stop 뒤에 to부정사가 오면 to부정사는 문장에서 부사적 용법의 목적(~하기 위해)을 나타내고, 주어가 다른 행동을 하기 위해 현재 하던 행위를 멈춘다는 의미를 전달한다. 따라서 여기서는 길을 물어보기 위해 현재 하던 행위를 멈췄다는 뜻이므로 (C) to ask가 정답이다.

어휘 ask 묻다, 요청하다, 부탁하다 direction 방향, 길안내, 지침 client 고객, 의뢰인

3.

번역 그 회사는 제품 출시를 내년으로 연기했다.

해설 동사 postpone은 동명사를 목적어로 취하는 동사이므로 (B) launching이 정답이다.

어휘 postpone 연기하다, 미루다 launch 출시, 출시하다, 시작하다 product 제품, 상품

✔ CheckPoint 3. To부정사와 동명사를 목적어로 취할 때 의미 차이가 있는 동사

정답

1. (C) 2. (B) 3. (B)

1.

번역 그는 작년에 회사를 떠나기로 한 결정을 후회한다.

해설 "regret + 동명사는 과거에 한 일을 후회하다"라는 의미로, 그가 작년에 이미 결정을 내렸고, 그것을 후회한다는 뜻이므로 (C) making이 정답이다. (B) to make는 "앞으로 할 일을 유감스럽게 여기다"라는 의미이므로 문맥에 맞지 않다.

어휘 regret 후회하다, 유감으로 생각하다 decision 결정, 판단

2.

번역 나는 집을 나서기 전에 열쇠를 챙긴 것을 기억했다.

해설 "remember + 동명사는 과거에 한 일을 기억하다"라는 의미로, 이 문맥에서는 열쇠를 챙긴 후 그 사실을 기억한다는 뜻이므로 (B) taking이 정답이다.

3.

번역 그들은 시스템을 더 효율적으로 개선하려고 노력하고 있다.

해설 "try + to부정사는 어떤 일을 하기 위해 노력하다"라는 의미로, 이 문맥에서는 시스템을 더 효율적으로 개선하려고 노력 중이라는 의미이므로 (B) to improve가 정답이다. (C) improving은 "시험 삼아 무언가를 해보다"라는 의미로 문맥에 맞지 않다.

어휘 improve 개선하다, 향상시키다 system 체계, 조직 efficient 효율적인, 능률적인

✔ CheckPoint 4. 동명사와 명사의 차이점

정답

1. (C) 2. (D) 3. (D)

1.

번역 위원회는 생산성을 향상시키기 위한 새로운 전략을 개발하는 데 집중하고 있다.

해설 전치사 on 뒤에는 명사와 동명사가 모두 올 수 있지만 빈 칸 뒤에 있는 명사 목적어(new strategies)를 취할 수 있는 것은 동사의 성질을 가지고 있는 동명사 (C) developing이 정답이다. (D) development는 명사이므로 뒤에 목적어를 취할 수 없다.

어휘 committee 위원회, 조직 focus 집중하다, 초점을 맞추다 develop 개발하다, 발전시키다 productivity 생산성 strategy 전략, 계획

2.

번역 그들의 새로운 시스템 적응은 운영 효율

성을 상당히 개선했다.

해설 소유격 Their 뒤에는 명사가 와야 하고, 전치사 of 앞에도 명사가 와야 하므로, 명사 (D) adaptation이 정답이다.

어휘 adapt 적응하다, 조정하다 adaption 적응, 조정 significantly 상당히, 두드러지게 improve 개선시키다 operational 운영상의, 사용 중인 efficiency 효율성, 능률

3.

번역 회사의 원격 근무 정책 도입은 직원 만족을 유지하는 데 매우 중요하다.

해설 소유격 The company's 뒤에는 명사가 와야 하고, 전치사 of 앞에도 명사가 와야 하므로, 명사 (D) adoption이 정답이다.

어휘 adopt 채택하다, 입양하다 adoption 채택, 입양 policy 정책, 방침 remote 원격의 crucial 결정적인, 중대한 satisfaction 만족, 만족감

2. 동명사의 시제

✔ CheckPoint 5. 단순 동명사와 완료 동명사

정답

1. (A) 2. (C) 3. (A)

1.

번역 직원들은 자신의 기술을 향상시키기 위해 더 많은 교육 세션을 열 것을 제안했다.

해설 원 문장 The employees suggested that they should hold more training sessions to improve their skills를 보면 주절과 종속절의 시제가 동일하고, 또 주절과 종속절의 주어가 동일하여 종속절의 주어를 생략하였기 때문에 단순 동명사 (A) holding이 정답이다.

어휘 hold 개최하다 training 훈련, 교육 session 회기, 세션, 교육 시간 skill 기술, 능력

2.

번역 그 컨설턴트는 재무 분석 중 실수를 한 것을 인정했다.

해설 원 문장 The consultant admitted that he had made a mistake during the financial analysis를 보면 주절보다 종속절의 시제가 한 시제 앞서 있고, 또 주절과 종속절의 주어가 동일하여 종속절의 주어를 생략하였기 때문에 완료 동명사 (C) having made가 정답이다.

어휘 admit 인정하다 mistake 실수, 오류 financial 재정의, 금융의 analysis 분석

3.

번역 회사는 고객 만족도를 향상시키기 위한 혁신적인 솔루션을 구현한 것을 인정했다.

해설 원 문장 The company acknowledged that it had implemented innovative solutions to improve customer satisfaction을 보면 주절보다 종속절의 시제가 한 시제 앞서 있고, 또 주절과 종속절의 주어가 동일하여 종속절의 주어를 생략하였기 때문에 완료 동명사 (A) having implemented가 정답이다.

어휘 acknowledge 인정하다, 승인하다 innovative 혁신적인, 창의적인 customer satisfaction 고객 만족

3. 동명사의 의미상의 주어

✔ CheckPoint 6. 동명사의 의미상의 주어

정답

1. (C) 2. (A)

1.

번역 감독은 그들이 실수에 대해 책임을 진 것에 감명을 받았다.

해설 문장의 주어와 동명사 taking의 의미상의 주어가 다르기 때문에 소유격 (C) their이 정답이다.

어휘 impress 감명을 주다, 인상을 남기다 responsibility 책임, 의무 error 실수, 오류

2.

번역 우리는 올해 회사의 성과를 향상시킬 것에 대해 자신이 있다.

해설 문장의 주어와 동명사 improving의 의미상의 주어가 동일하면 동명사의 의미상의 주어를 생략할 수 있으므로 (A) improving이 정답이다.

어휘 confident 자신 있는, 확신하는 performance 수행, 성과, 공연

4. 동명사의 관용표현

✔ CheckPoint 7. 동명사를 포함하는 관용표현

정답

1. (B) 2. (C)

1.

번역 그 회사는 시장 동향을 분석하는 데 상당한 시간을 보냈다.

해설 spend + 시간/돈 + 동명사는 "(돈/시간)을 ~하는 데 쓰다"는 뜻을 나타내는 관용표현이므로 동명사 (B) analyzing이 정답이다.

어휘 significant 상당한, 중요한 analyze 분석하다 market 시장 trend 경향, 추세

2.

번역 이 프로젝트에서 의사소통의 중요성을 부정할 수 없다.

해설 there is no + 동명사는 "~하는 것은 불가능하다"는 뜻을 나타내는 관용표현이므로 동명사 (C) denying이 정답이다.

어휘 deny 부인하다, 거부하다 importance 중요성 communication 의사소통

✔ CheckPoint 8. 전치사 to를 포함하는 동명사 관용표현

정답

1. (C) 2. (B) 3. (B)

1.

번역 그 회사는 새로운 에너지 효율 기술 개발에 헌신하고 있다.

해설 be dedicated to + 동명사는 "~에 헌신하다"는 뜻을 나타내는 관용표현이므로 동명사 (C) developing이 정답이다.

어휘 dedicate 헌신하다, 전념하다 energy-efficient 에너지 효율적인 technology 기술

2.

번역 팀은 새로운 마케팅 전략의 결과를 분석하는 것을 기대하고 있다.

해설 look forward to + 동명사는 "~을 기대하다"는 뜻을 나타내는 관용표현이므로 동명사 (B) analyzing이 정답이다.

어휘 analyze 분석하다 result 결과, 성과 strategy 전략, 계획

3.

번역 새 정책은 조직 내 더 효율적인 작업 흐름을 구축하는 데 기여했다.

해설 contribute to + 동명사는 "~에 기여하다"는 뜻을 나타내는 관용표현이므로 동명사 (B) establishing이 정답이다.

어휘 establish 설립하다, 확립하다 efficient 효율적인, 능률적인 workflow 작업 흐름, 업무 과정 organization 조직, 단체

토익 종합 실전문제

정답

1. (B)	2. (B)	3. (C)	4. (C)	5. (D)
6. (C)	7. (B)	8. (C)	9. (A)	10. (A)
11. (B)	12. (C)	13. (B)	14. (D)	15. (B)
16. (B)	17. (C)	18. (B)	19. (A)	20. (D)
21. (B)	22. (C)	23. (C)	24. (B)	

1.

번역 그들은 고객으로부터 피드백을 받은 후 프로젝트에 대한 논의를 멈췄다.

[해설] stop 뒤에 동명사가 오면 동명사는 문장에서 목적어 역할을 하고, 주어가 이미 하던 행위를 멈춘다는 의미를 전달한다. 따라서 여기서는 논의하는 것을 멈췄다는 의미를 나타내므로 (B) discussing이 정답이다. (C) to discuss는 "~하기 위해 멈추다"라는 다른 의미를 나타내므로 적절하지 않다.

[어휘] discuss 논의하다, 토론하다 receive 받다 feedback 의견 client 고객, 의뢰인

2.

번역 그 회사는 예산 삭감으로 인해 신제품 개발을 포기했다.

[해설] 동사 give up은 동명사를 목적어로 취하는 동사이므로 (B) developing이 정답이다.

[어휘] give up 포기하다 budget 예산, 비용 product 제품, 상품

3.

번역 그 팀은 회의 중에 민감한 주제를 논의하는 것을 피했다.

[해설] 동사 avoid은 동명사를 목적어로 취하는 동사이므로 (C) discussing이 정답이다.

[어휘] avoid 피하다, 회피하다 sensitive 민감한, 예민한 topic 주제, 화제

4.

번역 그는 오늘 아침 회의에 문서를 가져오는 것을 잊었다.

[해설] "forget + to부정사는 미래에 할 일을 잊다"라는 의미로, 그가 문서를 회의에 가져와야 했지만 잊었다는 의미이므로 (C) to bring이 정답이다. (B) bringing은 "과거에 한 일을 잊다"라는 의미로 문맥에 맞지 않다.

[어휘] bring 가져오다, 데려오다 document 문서, 서류 meeting 회의, 모임

5.

번역 그들은 문제를 해결할 수 있는지 확인하기 위해 새 소프트웨어를 설치해 보았다.

[해설] "try + 동명사는 시험 삼아 무언가를 해보다"라는 의미로, 여기서는 문제 해결을 위해 새 소프트웨어를 설치해 본 것이므로 (D) installing이 정답이다. (A) to install은 어떤 일을 하기 위해 노력하다"는 의미로 문맥에 맞지 않다.

[어휘] try 시도하다, 노력하다 solve 해결하다, 풀다 problem 문제, 어려움

6.

번역 그는 콘서트 티켓을 산 것을 기억했기 때문에, 우리는 입장할 수 있었다.

[해설] "remember + 동명사는 과거에 한 일을 기억하다"라는 의미로, 이 문맥에서는 티켓을 산 후 그 사실을 기억했다는 뜻이므로 (C) buying이 정답이다. (B) to buy는 "미래에 할 일을 기억하다"는 의미로 문맥에 맞지 않다.

[어휘] ticket 표, 입장권 concert 콘서트, 음악회

7.

번역 CEO의 사업 확장 결정은 이사회로부터 강력한 지지를 받았다.

[해설] 소유격 CEO's 뒤에 올 수 있는 것은 명사이므로 (B) decision이 정답이다.

[어휘] expand 확장하다, 확대하다 business 사업, 기업 board of directors 이사회

8.

번역 그 매니저는 모든 부서에 새로운 정책을 시행하는 데 책임이 있었다.

[해설] 전치사 for 뒤에는 명사와 동명사가 모두 올 수 있지만 빈 칸 뒤에 있는 명사 목적어(the new policy)를 취할 수 있는 것은 동사의 성질을 가지고 있는 동명사 (C) implementing이 정답이다. (D) implementation은 명사이므로 뒤에 목적어를 취할 수 없다.

어휘 responsible 책임이 있는 implement 시행하다, 이행하다 department 부서, 학과 implementation 시행, 이행

9.

번역 팀이 고객의 요구 사항을 이해한 것이 프로젝트 결과를 개선하는 데 도움이 되었다.

해설 소유격 The team's 뒤에는 명사가 와야 하고, 전치사 of 앞에도 명사가 와야 하므로, 명사 (A) understanding이 정답이다. 여기서 understanding은 '이해, 이해력, 지식, 합의' 등의 의미를 가진 명사로서의 기능을 수행한다.

어휘 outcome 결과, 성과

10.

번역 이사는 증가하는 수요를 충족시키기 위해 추가 자원을 할당하는 것을 승인했다.

해설 동사 approve 뒤에는 명사와 동명사가 모두 올 수 있지만 빈 칸 뒤에 있는 명사 목적어 (additional resources)를 취할 수 있는 것은 동사의 성질을 가지고 있는 동명사 (A) allocating이 정답이다. (D) allocation은 명사이므로 뒤에 목적어를 취할 수 없다.

어휘 approve 승인하다, 허가하다 allocate 할당하다, 배분하다 allocation 할당, 배분 demand 수요, 요구

11.

번역 그 팀은 부서 간 명확한 의사소통을 유지하는 것의 중요성을 강조했다.

해설 전치사 of 뒤에는 명사와 동명사가 모두 올 수 있지만 빈 칸 뒤에 있는 명사 목적어(clear communication)를 취할 수 있는 것은 동사의 성질을 가지고 있는 동명사 (B) maintaining이 정답이다. (D) maintenance은 명사이므로 뒤에 목적어를 취할 수 없다.

어휘 emphasize 강조하다, 중시하다 importance 중요성 maintain 유지하다, 보수하다 maintenance 유지, 보수

12.

번역 감독은 기밀 정보를 허가받지 않은 사람들과 공유한 것을 부인했다.

해설 원 문장 The director denied that he had shared the confidential information to unauthorized parties를 보면 주절보다 종속절의 시제가 한 시제 앞서 있고, 또 주절과 종속절의 주어가 동일하여 종속절의 주어를 생략하였기 때문에 완료 동명사 (C) having shared가 정답이다.

어휘 deny 부인하다, 거절하다 share 공유하다 confidential 비밀의, 기밀의 unauthorized 허가받지 않은, 승인받지 않은 information 정보, 자료

13.

번역 고객은 마감 기한 전에 자신이 모든 필요한 서류를 제출할 것을 고집했다.

해설 원 문장 The client insisted that he submit all the necessary documents before the deadline을 보면 주절과 종속절의 시제가 동일하고, 또 주절과 종속절의 주어가 동일하여 종속절의 주어를 생략하였기 때문에 단순 동명사 (B) submitting이 정답이다.

어휘 insist on ~을 주장하다, submit 제출하다 deadline 마감일, 기한 necessary 필요한, 필수적인

14.

번역 CEO는 파트너 회사와 협력할 기회를 놓친 것을 후회한다.

해설 원 문장 The CEO regrets that he missed the opportunity to collaborate with the partner company를 보면 주절보다 종속절의 시제가 한 시제 앞서 있고, 또 주절과 종속절의 주어가 동일하여 종속절의 주어를 생략하였기 때문에 완료 동명사 (D) having missed가 정답이다.

어휘 regret 후회하다, 유감스럽게 생각하다 miss 놓치다 opportunity 기회 collaborate 협력하다, 공동으로 일하다

15.

번역 우리는 그들이 그렇게 짧은 시간에 설문조사를 진행한 것에 감사한다.

해설 문장의 주어와 동명사 conducting의 의미상의 주어가 다르기 때문에 소유격 (B) their이 정답이다.

어휘 appreciate ~에 감사하다, 고마워하다 conduct a survey 설문조사를 하다

16.

번역 회의를 끝내자마자 그들은 즉시 프로젝트 작업을 시작했다.

해설 On(upon) + 동명사는 "~하자마자"라는 뜻을 나타내는 관용표현이므로 동명사 (B) finishing이 정답이다.

어휘 immediately 즉시, 즉각 finish 끝내다, 마치다

17.

번역 엔지니어들은 새 시스템의 오작동을 식별하는 데 어려움을 겪었다.

해설 have difficulty (trouble, problem, a hard time) (in) + 동명사는 "~하는 데 어려움을 겪다"는 뜻을 나타내는 관용표현이므로 동명사 (C) identifying이 정답이다.

어휘 malfunction 오작동, 기능 불량 identify 확인하다, 식별하다 system 시스템, 체계

18.

번역 CEO는 결정이 최종적으로 내려진 후에 예산 삭감에 대해 불평해 봤자 소용없다고 강조했다.

해설 it is no use + 동명사는 "~해봤자 소용없다"는 뜻을 나타내는 관용표현이므로 동명사 (B) complaining이 정답이다.

어휘 emphasize 강조하다 complain 불평하다 budget cuts 예산 삭감 finalize 마무리 짓다, 확정하다

19.

번역 매니저는 팀이 모든 기대를 초과 달성한 후 그들의 성과를 칭찬하지 않을 수 없었다.

해설 cannot help + 동명사는 "~하지 않을 수 없다"는 뜻을 나타내는 관용표현이므로 동명사 (A) praising이 정답이다.

어휘 praise 칭찬, 칭찬하다 performance 성과, 실적, 수행, 공연 exceed 초과하다, 능가하다 expectation 기대, 예상

20.

번역 그 회사가 경쟁업체로부터 더 나은 제안을 받았을 때, 이사는 합병 계약서에 서명하려던 참이었다.

해설 be on the point of + 동명사는 "막 ~하려고 하다"는 뜻을 나타내는 관용표현이므로 동명사 (D) signing이 정답이다.

어휘 sign 서명하다 merger 합병 offer 제의, 제안, 제안하다 competitor 경쟁자, 경쟁사

21.

번역 그 회사는 시장 변동과 같은 외부 요인으로 인해 실패하기 쉽다.

해설 be susceptible to + 동명사는 "~에 취약하다, 영향을 받기 쉽다"는 뜻을 나타내는 관용표현이므로 동명사 (B) failing이 정답이다.

어휘 external 외부의, 외적인 factor 요인, 요소 market fluctuations 시장 변동

22.

번역 그들은 프로젝트 계획에 더 이상의 변경을 가하는 것에 반대한다.

해설 be opposed to + 동명사는 "~에 반대하다"는 뜻을 나타내는 관용표현이므로 동명사 (C) making이 정답이다.

23.

번역 그들은 지역 사회에 고품질 의료 서비스를 제공하는 데 헌신하고 있다.

해설 be devoted to + 동명사는 "~에 헌신하다, 전념하다"는 뜻을 나타내는 관용표현이므로 동명사 (C) providing이 정답이다.

어휘 provide 제공하다, 공급하다

24.

번역 그 과학자는 암 연구에서 중요한 돌파구를 마련하는 데 가까워지고 있다.

해설 be close to + 동명사는 "~에 가까워지다"는 뜻을 나타내는 관용표현이므로 동명사 (B) making이 정답이다.

어휘 major breakthrough 중요한 돌파구, 획기적인 발견 cancer research 암 연구

PART 6

다음 정보와 관련된 질문 1-4번을 보세요.

> 직원 여러분께,
> 명확성과 일관성을 보장하기 위해 회사의 여행비 환급 절차에 대한 최신 정보를 제공합니다.
> 환급 요청을 제출할 때는 세부 영수증과 작성된 지출 보고서를 포함해야 합니다. 누락된 서류는 청구 처리 지연을 초래할 수 있습니다. 항공 여행이 포함된 출장의 경우, 환급 자격을 얻으려면 회사에서 승인한 여행사를 통해 항공편을 예약하는 것이 필수입니다. 또한, 직원들은 출장 중 비용을 결제할 때 회사법인 카드를 사용하는 것을 권장합니다. 이는 환급 과정을 간소화하고 불필요한 혼란을 방지하는 데 도움이 됩니다. 환급 청구는 출장 완료 후 30일 이내에 제출해야 합니다. 이 기간 이후에 제출된 청구는 처리되지 않으며, 예외적인 상황에서는 부서 관리자의 승인을 받아야 합니다. 자세한 내용이나 도움이 필요하시면 재무부로 문의하시기 바랍니다.
> 이 지침을 준수해 주셔서 감사합니다.
>
> 감사합니다,
> 재무팀

어휘 ensure 보장하다 clarity 명확성 consistency 일관성 provide 제공하다reimbursement 환급, 변제 process 절차, 과정 submit 제출하다 request 요청, 요청하다 include 포함하다 receipt 영수증 expense report 지출 보고서, 경비 보고서 involve 수반하다, 포함하다 booking 예약 mandatory 의무적인 encourage 권장하다 corporate credit card 회사법인 카드 streamline 간소화하다 avoid 피하다 unnecessary 불필요한 confusion 혼란 exceptional 예외적인 circumstance 상황, 환경 approve 승인하다, 허가하다 department 부서 assistance 도움, 지원 guideline 지침, 권장 사항

정답

1. (C) 2. (D) 3. (B) 4. (A)

1.

해설 regarding은 "~에 관하여"라는 의미로, 특정 주제(여기서는 회사의 여행비용 상환 절차)에 대해 언급할 때 자연스럽게 쓰이므로 (C) regarding이 정답이다.

2.

(A) 회사는 업무와 관련된 비용만 환급합니다.

(B) 직원들은 이메일을 통해 청구서를 제출해야 합니다.

(C) 모든 환급 요청에는 프로젝트 코드가 포함되어야 합니다.

(D) 누락된 서류는 청구 처리 지연을 초래할 수 있습니다.

해설 본문의 맥락을 보면, "청구서 제출 시 필요한 서류와 관련된 조건"에 대해 언급하고 있으며, 누락된 서류가 있을 경우 "청구 처리 지연"에 대한 경고가 적절하므로 (D)가 정답이다. (A)는 회사의 환급 범위에 관한 내용으로, 문맥상 "서류 누락" 문제와 맞지 않으므로 적절하지 않고, (B)는 제출 방식에 관한 내용이지만, 본문에서 다루는 주제는 서류 누락 문제에 대한 경고이므로 적절하지 않으며, (C)도 "프로젝트 코드"에 대한 내용으로는 문맥에 맞지 않으며, 서류 누락과 관련된 정보가 제공되지 않았기 때문에 문맥과 맞지 않다.

3.

해설 within 30 days는 "30일 이내에"라는 뜻으로, 특정 기한 내에 완료된 일을 표현할 때 사용되므로 (B) within이 정답이다. (A) by는 특정 시점 이전에 완료되는 일회성 행동이나 행위를 강조하므로 적절하지 않고, (C) after는 "30일 이후"라는 의미로 문맥과 맞지 않으며, (D) for는 "~동안"이라는 의미로 숫자 기간과 함께 사용되므로 문맥상 맞지 않다.

4.

해설 adhere to는 "지키다, 준수하다"라는 의미로, 지침을 따르는 것과 관련된 문맥에 가장 적절하므로 (A) adhering to가 정답이다. (B) consulting은 "상담하다", (C) respecting은 "존중하다", (D) considering은 "고려하다"라는 의미로 문맥상 맞지 않다.

PART 7

다음 공지와 관련된 질문 1-4번을 보세요.

> 교육 및 개발 기회 2024
>
> 경력 개발 개선을 위한 우리의 약속의 일환으로, 2024년 1월부터 시작되는 새로운 교육 프로그램을 발표하게 되어 기쁩니다. 이 프로그램은 최신 직원 참여 설문조사에서 받은 피드백을 바탕으로 설계되었습니다. 아래는 제공될 교육 세션의 일정입니다:
>
> • 리더십 개발 (2024년 1월 15-17일): 현재 관리자 및 리더십 역할을 맡고자 하는 직원을 위한 프로그램입니다.
> • 부서 간 커뮤니케이션 워크숍 (2024년 2월 5-6일): 팀 간의 의사소통 및 협업 향상에 중점을 둡니다.
> • 고급 기술 능력 교육 (2024년 3월 10-12일): 프로젝트 관리, 데이터 분석 및 소프트웨어 개발의 고급 기술을 다룹니다.
> • 워크-라이프 밸런스 전략 (2024년 4월 2일): 워크-라이프 밸런스를 보다 효과적으로 관리하기 위한 하루짜리 세션입니다.
>
> 모든 교육 세션은 본사 회의실에서 진행됩니다. 등록을 원하시는 분은 내부 포털을 방문하시거나 인사부에 문의해 주십시오.
> 이 기회를 꼭 활용하시기 바랍니다!

어휘 opportunity 기회 commitment 약속, 헌신 improve 개선하다, 향상시키다 announce 발표하다, 알리다 engagement 참여 survey 조사, 설문 조사 available 이용할 수 있는 aim at ~을 목표로 하다 aspire 바라다, 열망하다 inter-departmental 부서 간의 focus on ~에 집중하다, ~에 중점을 두다 collaboration 협업 analysis 분석 effectively 효과적으로 register 등록하다, 신청하다 internal 내부의 contact 연락하다

정답

1. (A)　2. (C)　3. (C)　4. (B)

1. 리더십 개발 교육은 언제 실시됩니까?
   (A) 2024년 1월 15-17일
   (B) 2024년 2월 5-6일
   (C) 2024년 3월 10-12일
   (D) 2024년 4월 2일

해설 지문에서 "Leadership Development (January 15-17, 2024)"라고 언급하고 있어, 교육 일정이 2024년 1월 15일부터 17일까지임을 알 수 있으므로 (A)가 정답이다.

2. 부서 간 커뮤니케이션 워크숍의 주요 초점은 무엇입니까?
   (A) 리더십 기술
   (B) 프로젝트 관리
   (C) 팀 간의 의사소통 및 협업
   (D) 워크-라이프 밸런스

해설 지문에서 "Focused on improving communication and collaboration between teams"라고 언급하고 있으므로 (C)가 정답이다.

3. 직원들은 교육 세션에 어떻게 등록할 수 있습니까?
   (A) 회의에 참석하여
   (B) 인사부에 이메일을 보내서
   (C) 내부 포털을 방문하거나 인사부에 문의하여
   (D) 종이 양식을 작성하여

해설 지문에서 "To register, please visit our internal portal or contact the HR Department"라고 언급하고 있으므로 (C)가 정답이다.

4. 다음 중 교육 프로그램에 대해 추론할 수 있는 내용은 무엇입니까?
   (A) 모든 직원에게 필수적이다.
   (B) 직원들의 피드백을 기반으로 만들어졌다.
   (C) 부서장의 사전 승인이 필요하다.
   (D) 기술 능력에만 초점을 맞추고 있다.

해설 지문에서 "These programs are designed based on employee feedback from the latest Employee Engagement Survey"라는 내용이 명확히 언급되어 있어, 교육 프로그램이 직원 피드백을 기반으로 설계되었음을 알 수 있으므로 (B)가 정답이다.

Chapter 08 명사

1. 명사의 역할 및 자리

✔ CheckPoint 1. 관사/소유격/형용사 + 명사

정답

1. (C) 2. (B) 3. (C)

1.

번역 매니저의 승인은 팀에 의해 매우 감사하게 받아들여졌다.

해설 소유격 manager's 뒤에 올 수 있는 것은 명사이므로 (C) approval이 정답이다. 동명사 (B) approving은 동사의 성질을 가지므로 뒤에 명사 목적어가 필요하지만, 이 문장에는 목적어가 없기 때문에 문법적으로 적절하지 않다.

어휘 approve 승인하다, 찬성하다 approval 승인, 찬성 appreciate 감사하다, 인정하다

2.

번역 그들의 성과는 기대를 초과했다.

해설 명사 performance 앞에 올 수 있는 것은 소유격이므로 (B) Their이 정답이다. (A) Theirs는 소유대명사로, 소유격 + 명사의 의미를 줄인 형태이므로 뒤에 명사를 수식할 수 없다.

어휘 performance 성과, 공연, 수행 exceed 초과하다, 능가하다 expectation 기대, 예상

3.

번역 정확한 보고서는 다가오는 회의에 필수적이다.

해설 명사 report 앞에 올 수 있는 것은 형용사이므로 (C) precise가 정답이다.

어휘 report 보고서, 보고 essential 필수적인 upcoming 다가오는 precisely 정확히, 정밀하게 precision 정확성, 정밀성 precise 정확한, 정밀한

2. 가산명사와 불가산명사

✔ CheckPoint 2. 토익 시험에 자주 나오는 가산명사와 불가산명사

정답

1. (B) 2. (B) 3. (D)

1.

번역 다가오는 프로젝트에 대한 더 많은 세부사항을 제공해 주세요.

해설 details는 가산 명사로, 복수형으로 사용할 수 있는 반면 information, advice, research는 불가산 명사이기 때문에 복수형으로 사용할 수 없으므로 (B) details가 정답이다.

어휘 provide 제공하다, 공급하다 regarding ~에 관하여 upcoming 다가오는, 곧 있을 information 정보 details 세부사항, 자세한 내용 advice 충고, 조언 research 연구, 조사

2.

번역 컨설턴트는 팀의 생산성을 높이는 데 도움이 될 귀중한 조언을 제공했다.

[해설] advice는 불가산 명사로, 복수형으로 사용될 수 없으므로 (B) advice가 정답이다. 동명사 (C) advising은 동사의 성질을 가지므로 뒤에 명사 목적어가 필요하지만, 이 문장에는 목적어가 없기 때문에 문법적으로 적절하지 않다.

[어휘] valuable 귀중한, 가치 있는 enhance 향상시키다, 강화하다 advisor 조언자

3.

번역 이 직무는 프로젝트 관리와 위험 평가에 대한 자격 인증을 요구한다.

[해설] certification은 불가산 명사로, 자격이나 인증 상태를 의미하므로 (D) certification이 정답이다. (A) certificate와 (B) certificates는 구체적인 증명서로, 단수와 복수형으로 사용할 수 있지만 문맥에 적합하지 않고, certified는 형용사로 적절하지 않다.

[어휘] require 필요로 하다, 요구하다 certificate 증명서 certify 증명하다, 자격을 인증하다, 보증하다 certification 자격 인증 assessment 평가

3. 복합명사(Compound Noun)

✔ CheckPoint 3. 토익 시험에 자주 나오는 복합명사

정답

1. (A) 2. (B) 3. (B)

1.

번역 재무팀은 다음 분기의 예산 계획을 이사회에 제출했다.

[해설] 특정 시기의 예산 계획을 의미하는 명사 + 명사 구조의 복합명사가 필요하므로 (A) budget plan이 정답이다.

[어휘] finance team 재무팀 board of directors 이사회

2.

번역 회사는 제품 기준을 개선하기 위해 품질 보증에 많은 투자를 했다.

[해설] 제품의 품질을 유지하고 개선하기 위한 절차를 의미하는 명사 + 명사 구조의 복합명사가 필요하므로 (B) quality assurance가 정답이다.

[어휘] product standards 제품 기준

3.

번역 팀은 프로젝트에서 발생할 수 있는 잠재적 위험을 해결하기 위한 위험 관리 방안을 준비했다.

[해설] 특정 프로젝트에서 발생할 수 있는 위험을 관리하고 완화하는 절차를 의미하는 명사 + 명사 구조의 복합명사가 필요하므로 (B) risk management가 정답이다.

[어휘] address 다루다, 해결하다, 처리하다 potential risks 잠재적 위험

✔ CheckPoint 4. 토익 시험에 자주 나오는 형용사 + 명사 구조

정답

1. (B) 2. (C) 3. (D)

1.

번역 재무부서는 다가오는 회계 연도의 연례 보고서를 준비하고 있다.

[해설] 한 해의 실적과 재정 상태 등을 요약한 보고서를 의미하는 형용사 + 명사 구조의 어휘가 필요하므로 (B) annual report가 정답이다.

[어휘] finance department 재무부서 work on ~에 대해 작업하다 upcoming fiscal year 다가오는 회계연도

2.

번역 비용을 최소화하기 위해 회사는 운영비용 절감에 집중하고 있다.

[해설] 운영에 필요한 비용을 의미하는 형용사 +

명사 구조의 어휘가 필요하므로 (C) operational costs가 정답이다.

어휘 minimize 최소화하다 expense 비용 focus on ~에 집중하다

3.

번역 회사는 제조 공정의 효율성을 높이기 위해 효과적인 해결책을 도입했다.

해설 문제를 해결하기 위한 효과적인 방법을 의미하는 형용사 + 명사 구조의 어휘가 필요하므로 (D) effective solution이 정답이다.

어휘 implement 실행하다, 도입하다 enhance 향상시키다, 강화하다 efficiency 효율성 manufacturing process 제조 공정, 생산 과정

CheckPoint 5. 사람명사와 사물/추상명사

정답

1. (D)	2. (A)	3. (D)

1.

번역 프로젝트의 성공은 모든 팀원의 참여에 크게 달려 있다.

해설 팀원들이 적극적으로 참여하는 행위를 의미하는 사물/추상명사가 필요하므로 (D) participation이 정답이다.

어휘 depend heavily on ~에 크게 의존하다 participate 참가하다 partnership 협력 participant 참가자

2.

번역 인사부는 모든 신규 직원에게 경력 개발 지원을 제공한다.

해설 도움이 필요한 사람들에게 제공되는 지원을 의미하는 사물/추상명사가 필요하므로 (A) assistance가 정답이다.

어휘 HR Department 인사부, 인사관리 부서 provide 제공하다 career development 경력 개발 assistant 보조자 applicant 지원자 attendance 출석

3.

번역 컨설턴트는 고객 참여를 개선하기 위한 몇 가지 전략을 제안했다.

해설 조언을 제공하는 전문가를 의미하는 사람명사가 필요하므로 (D) consultant가 정답이다.

어휘 suggest 제안하다 strategy 전략 customer engagement 고객 참여 consumer 고객, 소비자 consumption 소비 consultation 상담

토익 종합 실전문제

정답

1. (B)	2. (A)	3. (A)	4. (A)	5. (B)
6. (C)	7. (C)	8. (C)	9. (D)	10. (B)
11. (C)	12. (D)	13. (B)	14. (B)	15. (A)
16. (D)	17. (B)	18. (B)	19. (A)	20. (C)
21. (D)	22. (B)	23. (A)	24. (C)	

1.

번역 새로운 정책의 시행이 지연되었다.

해설 관사(The)와 전치사(of) 사이에 올 수 있는 것은 명사뿐이므로 (B) implementation이 정답이다. 동명사 (C) implementing은 동사의 성질을 가지므로 뒤에 명사 목적어가 필요하지만, 이 문장에는 목적어가 없기 때문에 문법적으로 적절하지 않다.

어휘 delay 지연, 연기, 지연시키다 implement 시행하다, 실행하다, 도입하다 implementation 시행, 실행, 도입

2.

번역 CEO의 새로운 기술에 투자하겠다는 결정은 이사회에서 호평을 받았다.

해설 소유격 CEO's 뒤에 올 수 있는 것은 명사이므로 (A) decision이 정답이다. 동명사 (D) deciding은 동사의 성질을 가지므로 뒤에 명사 목적어가 필요하지만, 이 문장에는 목적어가 없기 때문에 문법적으로 적절하지 않다.

어휘 invest 투자하다 board 이사회 decision 결정, 판단 decide 결정하다

3.

번역 마케팅 팀은 고객 참여를 늘리기 위한 효과적인 전략을 개발했다.

해설 명사 strategy 앞에 올 수 있는 것은 형용사이므로 (A) effective가 정답이다. (C) effect와 (D) effectiveness는 명사, (B) effectively는 부사로서 명사를 수식할 수 없기 때문에 적절하지 않다.
어휘 strategy 전략 effective 효과적인 effectively 효과적으로 effect 효과, 결과 effectiveness 유효성 customer engagement 고객 참여

4.

번역 회사는 고객의 요구를 이해하기 위해 광범위한 조사를 실시했다.

해설 research는 불가산 명사로, 복수형으로 사용될 수 없으므로 (A) research가 정답이다.

어휘 conduct 수행하다, 실시하다 extensive 광범위한, 대대적인 customer need 고객의 요구(사항)

5.

번역 CEO는 모든 미래 프로젝트에서 철저한 계획 수립의 중요성을 강조했다.

해설 planning은 불가산 명사로, 철저한 계획 수립을 의미하므로 (B) planning이 정답이다. (A) plan과 (C) plans는 가산 명사로 문맥에 맞지 않으며, (D) planned는 형용사로 적절하지 않다.

어휘 emphasize 강조하다 thorough 철저한

6.

번역 프로젝트 마감일을 맞추기 위해 팀은 이번 주말까지 모든 과제를 마무리해야 한다.

해설 assignment는 가산 명사로, 모든 과제라는 의미의 복수형으로 사용되었으므로 (C) assignments가 정답이다. (B) assign은 동사, (A) assignment는 단수형이므로 문맥에 맞지 않다.

어휘 in order to ~하기 위해 meet 맞추다 project deadline 프로젝트 기한 finalize 마무리하다, 최종 확정하다 by the end of this week 이번 주말까지 assignment 과제, 임무 assign 할당하다, 배정하다

7.

번역 프로그램을 성공적으로 완료하면 학생들은 그들의 성과에 대해 두 개의 증명서를 받게 된다.

해설 certificates는 가산 명사로, 성과에 대한 개별 증명서를 의미하므로 (C) certificates가 정답이다. (A) certifications은 불가산 명사로 복수형이 될 수 없고, 동명사 (D) certifying은 동사의 성질을 가지므로 뒤에 명사 목적어가 필요하지만, 이 문장에는 목적어가 없기 때문에 문법적으로 적절하지 않다.

어휘 successful 성공적인 completion 완료, 완성 receive 받다, 수취하다 achievement 성과, 업적

8.

번역 이 공원에서 행사를 열려면 지방 정부로부터 허가증을 받아야 한다.

해설 permit은 가산 명사로, 특정한 허가증을 의미하므로 (C) permit가 정답이다. (A) permission은 불가산 명사로 추상적인 허가나 승인을 의미하는데, 여기서는 구체적인 허가증이 필요하므로 문맥에 맞지 않다.

어휘 obtain 얻다, 획득하다 local government 지방 정부

9.

번역 마케팅 팀은 제품 출시 행사를 위한 여러 계획을 제시했다.

해설 plan은 가산 명사로, 여러 개의 구체적인 계획을 의미하므로 (D) plans가 정답이다. (C) planning은 불가산 명사로, 계획 수립의 과정을 의미하므로 문맥에 맞지 않다.

어휘 present 제시하다

10.

번역 직원들은 추가 휴가를 위해 매니저의 허락을 받아야 한다.

해설 permission은 불가산 명사로, 추상적인 허

가나 승인을 의미하므로 (B) permission이 정답이다. (A) permit와 (D) permits는 허가증이라는 구체적인 의미이므로 문맥에 맞지 않다.

어휘 additional 추가적인, 부가적인 leave days 휴가

11.

번역 모든 신규 직원은 고용 첫 달 안에 직원 교육을 완료해야 한다.

해설 직원에게 필요한 교육 과정을 의미하는 명사 + 명사 구조의 복합명사가 필요하므로 (C) employee training이 정답이다.

어휘 complete 완료하다 employment 고용

12.

번역 영업 부서는 향후 성과 향상을 위해 지난 분기의 비용 보고서를 분석했다.

해설 회사의 비용을 기록한 보고서를 의미하는 명사 + 명사 구조의 복합명사가 필요하므로 (D) expense report가 정답이다.

어휘 sales department 영업 부서 analyze 분석하다 last quarter 지난 분기 improve 개선하다 future performance 향후 성과

13.

번역 영업팀은 신제품 출시를 위한 상세한 마케팅 캠페인을 준비했다.

해설 제품을 홍보하기 위한 활동을 의미하는 명사 + 명사 구조의 복합명사가 필요하므로 (B) marketing campaign이 정답이다.

어휘 detailed 상세한 product release 제품 출시

14.

번역 팀은 다가오는 회계 연도의 추세를 예측하기 위해 상세한 데이터 분석을 수행했다.

해설 데이터를 분석하여 추세를 예측하는 활동을 의미하는 명사 + 명사 구조의 복합명사가 필요하므로 (B) data analysis가 정답이다.

어휘 conduct 수행하다, 실행하다 forecast 예측하다 trends 경향, 추세 upcoming fiscal year 다가오는 회계연도

15.

번역 회사는 제품 반품 및 환불에 대한 새로운 규정을 포함하도록 반품 정책을 업데이트했다.

해설 제품 반품과 관련된 규정을 의미하는 명사 + 명사 구조의 복합명사가 필요하므로 (A) return policy가 정답이다.

어휘 update 업데이트하다, 수정하다 include 포함하다 regulation 규정 regarding ~에 관하여, product 제품, 상품 return 반품 refund 환불

16.

번역 CEO는 시장의 최근 변화에 적응하기 위해 업데이트된 기업 전략을 승인했다.

해설 회사가 장기적으로 나아갈 방향을 나타내는 전략을 의미하는 명사 + 명사 구조의 복합명사가 필요하므로 (D) corporate strategy가 정답이다.

어휘 approve 승인하다 adapt 적응하다, 조정하다 recent 최근의

17.

번역 CEO는 프로젝트 지연을 방지하기 위해 주요 문제를 해결하는 것의 중요성을 강조했다.

해설 프로젝트 진행에 영향을 미칠 수 있는 중요한 문제를 의미하는 형용사 + 명사 구조의 어휘가 필요하므로 (B) major issues가 정답이다.

어휘 highlight 강조하다 importance 중요성 address 해결하다, 대처하다 prevent 방지하다 project delay 프로젝트 지연

18.

번역 재무팀은 불필요한 비용을 파악하고 비용을 줄이기 위해 내부 감사를 실시했다.

해설 회사 내부의 재정 및 운영 절차를 검토하기 위한 감사를 의미하는 형용사 + 명사 구조의 어휘

가 필요하므로 (B) internal audit이 정답이다.

어휘 finance team 재무팀 conduct 수행하다, 실행하다 identify 식별하다 unnecessary 불필요한 expense 비용 reduce 줄이다, 감소하다 cost 비용

19.

번역 회사는 시장 점유율을 높이기 위해 새로운 제품 라인 출시와 관련된 잠재적 위험을 분석하고 있다.

해설 미래에 발생할 수 있는 위험 요소를 의미하는 형용사 + 명사 구조의 어휘가 필요하므로 (A) potential risks가 정답이다.

어휘 analyze 분석하다 launch 출시하다 product line 제품 라인 market share 시장 점유율

20.

번역 팀은 국제 시장에서의 세계적 추세에 대한 철저한 분석을 수행했다.

해설 국제 시장에서 나타나는 변화나 추세를 의미하는 형용사 + 명사 구조의 어휘가 필요하므로 (C) global trends가 정답이다.

어휘 conduct 수행하다, 실행하다 thorough analysis 철저한 분석 international markets 국제 시장

21.

번역 최근 기술 발전 덕분에 회사는 업계에서 경쟁 우위를 얻게 되었다.

해설 시장에서 경쟁력을 높이는 요인을 의미하는 형용사 + 명사 구조의 어휘가 필요하므로 (D) competitive advantage가 정답이다.

어휘 technological advancement 최근의 기술 발전 gain 증가하다, 이익을 얻다

22.

번역 시설 검사는 안전 기준을 보장하기 위해 다음 달로 예정되어 있다.

해설 안전 기준 준수를 위해 수행하는 검사를 의미하는 사물/추상명사가 필요하므로 (B) inspection이 정답이다.

어휘 facilities 시설 ensure 보장하다 safety standards 안전 기준 inspector 검사자 investment 투자 execution 실행

23.

번역 계약자는 서명하기 전에 새 계약의 조건을 철저히 검토했다.

해설 계약을 맺고 작업을 수행하는 사람을 의미하는 사람명사가 필요하므로 (A) contractor가 정답이다.

어휘 review 검토하다, 살펴보다 terms of the contract 계약 조건 thoroughly 철저히 contract 계약서 competition 경쟁 presenter 발표자

24.

번역 우리 회사의 제품 품질에 대한 경쟁력이 회사의 명성에 기여했다.

해설 회사가 경쟁력을 유지하는 능력을 의미하는 사물/추상명사가 필요하므로 (C) competitiveness가 정답이다.

어휘 product quality 제품 품질 contribute to 기여하다 reputation 명성 foundation 설립 competitor 경쟁자 manufacturer 제조업자

PART 6

다음 광고와 관련된 질문 1-4번을 보세요.

GreenWave 태양광 패널

미래의 에너지로 집을 채울 준비가 되셨나요? GreenWave는 전기 요금을 절감하고 탄소 발자국을 줄이도록 설계된 새로운 태양광 패널을 소개하게 되어 기쁩니다. 최신 기술을 적용한 당사의 패널은 흐린 날씨에도 최고의 성능을 발휘합니다! GreenWave Solar를 선택하면 단순히 패널을 구매하는 것이 아니라 더 깨끗한 미래를 선택하는 것입니다. 당사의 패널은 30년 동안 최고의 효율성을 보장하며 유지보수가 거의 필요하지 않습니다. 주택 소유자든 사업체 소유자든, 태양광 에너지로 전환하는 것이 그 어느 때보다 쉬워졌습니다. 한정된 기간 동안 모든 신규 고객을 대상으로 설

치비 할인을 제공하고 있습니다. 또한 최대 절약과 효율성을 위해 최적의 설치 방안을 찾아드리는 무료 상담도 제공하고 있습니다.
왜 망설이세요? GreenWave 태양광 패널과 함께 더 밝고 지속 가능한 미래를 시작하세요. 지금 문의하셔서 친환경 에너지로의 여정을 시작하세요.

어휘 advertisement 광고 solar panels 태양광 패널 future energy 미래 에너지 save on ~을 절약하다 electricity bills 전기 사용 요금 lower 줄이다 latest technology 최신 기술 guarantee 보증 maintenance 유지, 보수 discount 할인 installation fees 설치비용 consultation 상담 sustainable 지속 가능한 eco-friendly 환경 친화적인, 친환경적인

정답

1. (C) 2. (D) 3. (A) 4. (B)

1.

해설 내용상 앞의 명사 solar panels를 수식하여 태양광 패널이 "절약을 위해 제작되었다"는 수동 의미를 전달해야 하므로 (C) (which are) made가 정답이다.

2.

(A) 설치되는 각 패널로 더 건강한 지구를 만드는 데 기여하고 있습니다.
(B) 각 패널은 혹독한 날씨 조건을 견디도록 설계되었습니다.
(C) 우리 제품에는 고객 만족 보증이 포함되어 있습니다.
(D) 단순히 패널을 구매하는 것이 아니라 더 깨끗한 미래를 선택하는 것입니다.

해설 이 문장은 단순히 제품을 구매하는 것이 아니라 환경을 위해 더 깨끗한 미래를 선택하는 것임을 강조하여 GreenWave의 브랜드 메시지와 일치하므로 (D)가 가장 적절하다. (A)는 패널 설치가 환경에 기여한다는 점을 언급하고 있지만, 제품의 가치를 전달하는 데는 부족하며, (B)와 (C)도 패널의 내구성이나 보증 조건에 대한 내용으로 문맥에 적절하지 않다.

3.

해설 GreenWave가 신규 고객을 대상으로 한정된 기간 동안 설치비 할인을 제공한다고 안내하고 있으므로 (A) limited time이 정답이다. (B) available choice는 "선택 가능 항목", (C) complete offer는 "완전한 제안", (D) select group은 "선별된 그룹"이라는 의미로 문맥에 맞지 않다.

4.

해설 최대 절약과 효율성을 위해 최적의 설치 방안을 찾아드리는 무료 상담을 제공한다는 의미이므로 (B) consultations가 정답이다. (A) assistance는 "도움", (C) guidelines는 "지침", (D) operations는 "운영"이라는 의미로 문맥에 맞지 않다.

PART 7

다음 채용 광고와 이메일 교환과 관련된 질문 1-5번을 보세요.

직책: 영업 사원
위치: 캘리포니아주 샌프란시스코
회사: 글로벌 테크 솔루션스

글로벌 테크 솔루션스는 확장 중인 팀에 합류할 경험 있는 영업 사원을 찾고 있습니다. 성공적인 지원자는 새로운 비즈니스 기회를 개발하고, 고객 관계를 관리하며, 영업 목표를 달성하는 역할을 담당하게 됩니다.
업무 내용:
- 잠재 고객 식별 및 접촉
- 영업 프레젠테이션 개발 및 제공
- 계약 협상 및 거래 성사
- 판매 후 지원 제공

자격 요건:
- 최소 3년 이상의 영업 경력, 기술 산업에서의 경력 선호
- 뛰어난 의사소통 및 협상 능력
- 강한 조직 및 시간 관리 능력

관심 있는 지원자는 10월 1일까지 이력서와 자기소개서를 recruitment@globaltechsolutions.com으로 보내주시기 바랍니다.

발신: David Chen (고객)

수신: Sarah Moore (영업 사원, 글로벌 테크 솔루션스)
날짜: 9월 10일
제목: 제품 시연 후속 질문

안녕하세요 Sarah,
지난주 제품 시연 감사드립니다. 귀사의 소프트웨어 기능에 깊은 인상을 받았고, 우리 회사에 귀중한 추가 요소가 될 수 있을 것 같습니다. 최종 결정을 내리기 전에 가격과 구매 후 지원에 대해 몇 가지 점을 명확히 하고자 합니다.
대량 구매 시 가능한 할인을 포함한 가격 구조에 대한 자세한 내역을 제공해 주실 수 있나요? 또한 구매 후 제공되는 지원 서비스의 종류도 설명해 주실 수 있을까요?
빠른 회신을 기대하겠습니다.

감사합니다,
David Chen

어휘 position 직위, 직책 sales representative 영업 대표, 영업 사원 location 위치, 장소 seek 찾다, 구하다 experienced 경험이 있는 expanding team 확장 중인 팀 candidate 후보자, 지원자 client relationships 고객 관계 achieve 달성하다 identify 식별하다, 찾아내다 contact 연락하다 potential 잠재적인 negotiate contracts 계약을 협상하다 close deals 거래를 성사시키다 sales experience 영업 경험 preferably 가급적이면, 되도록 technology industry 기술 산업 resume 이력서 cover letter 자기소개서 follow-up 후속 조치, 추가 논의 product demonstration 제품 시연 impress 감명을 주다, 깊은 인상을 주다 features 특징, 기능 valuable 가치 있는, 귀중한 clarify 명확히 하다, 설명하다 detailed breakdown 세부적인 내역 pricing structure 가격 구조 bulk purchases 대량 구매 support services 지원 서비스 look forward to ~을 기대하다

정답

1. (B) 2. (C) 3. (A) 4. (B) 5.(C)

1. Global Tech Solutions의 영업 사원의 책임 중 하나는 무엇입니까?
(A) 애프터서비스 지원 팀 관리
(B) 고객과의 거래 성사
(C) 새로운 소프트웨어 기능 개발
(D) 팀 빌딩 행사 조직

해설 직무 설명에 따르면, 영업 사원은 "Negotiating contracts and closing deals" 즉, 계약 협상과 거래 성사를 주요 업무로 하고 있으므로 (B)가 정답이다.

2. 영업 사원 직책에 지원할 수 있는 마감일은 언제입니까?
(A) 9월 10일
(B) 9월 30일
(C) 10월 1일
(D) 10월 15일

해설 채용 광고에 "Interested candidates should send their resume and cover letter to recruitment@globaltechsolutions.com by October 1"라고 명시되어 있어 지원 마감일이 10월 1일임을 알 수 있으므로 (C)가 정답이다.

3. David Chen이 Sarah Moore에게 추가로 요청한 정보는 무엇입니까?
(A) 가격 구조에 대한 세부 사항
(B) 새로운 제품 시연
(C) 다른 고객의 추천서
(D) 사용 가능한 제품 목록

해설 이메일에서 David Chen은 "Could you please provide me with a detailed breakdown of the pricing structure, including any potential discounts for bulk purchases?"라고 가격 구조를 요청하고 있으므로 (A)가 정답이다.

4. 채용 광고에 따르면, 영업직에는 얼마나 많은 경력이 요구됩니까?"
(A) 최소 1년
(B) 최소 3년
(C) 최소 5년
(D) 특별한 경력은 요구되지 않음

해설 채용 광고에서 "Minimum of 3 years of sales experience, preferably in the technology industry"라고 명시되어 있어 최소 3년의 경력이 필요함을 알 수 있으므로 (B)가 정답이다.

5. David Chen이 Sarah Moore에게 보낸 이메일의 주요 목적은 무엇입니까?
(A) 제품 시연에 대한 만족을 표현하기 위해
(B) 채용 지원 절차에 대해 묻기 위해
(C) 가격 및 지원 옵션에 대해 문의하기 위해
(D) 또 다른 제품 시연 일정을 잡기 위해

해설 이메일에서 David Chen은 "I would like to clarify a few points regarding pricing and post-purchase support"라고 하여 가격과 지원 서비스에 대한 정보를 요청하고 있으므로 (C)가 정답이다.

Chapter 09 대명사

1. 인칭 대명사

✔ CheckPoint 1. 소유격과 소유대명사

정답

1. (C) 2. (C) 3. (D)

1.

번역 이 노트북은 내 것이고, 저것은 네 것이다.

해설 yours는 소유대명사로 소유격 + 명사 구조인 your laptop의 축약형으로 사용되며, 뒤에 명사를 따로 붙이지 않고 소유를 나타내므로 (C) yours가 정답이다. (A) you는 주격과 목적격, (B) your는 소유격, (D) yourself는 재귀대명사이므로 문맥에 맞지 않다.

2.

번역 그녀는 과제를 완료했지만, 내 것은 시간이 더 필요하다.

해설 mine은 소유대명사로 소유격 + 명사 구조인 my assignment의 축약형으로 사용되며, 뒤에 명사를 따로 붙이지 않고 소유를 나타내므로 (C) mine이 정답이다. (A) hers는 소유대명사는 맞지만 문맥에 맞지 않고, (B) her와 (D) our는 소유격으로 뒤에 명사가 필요하여 문맥에 맞지 않다.

어휘 assignment 과제, 임무 need 필요하다, 필요로 하다

3.

번역 그들의 발표는 훌륭했으며, 그들의 것은 이사회로부터 높은 평가를 받았다.

해설 theirs는 소유대명사로 소유격 + 명사 구조인 their presentation의 축약형으로 사용되며, 뒤에 명사를 따로 붙이지 않고 소유를 나타내므로 (D) theirs가 정답이다. (A) hers와 (B) mine도 소유대명사는 맞지만 문맥에 맞지 않고, (C) my는 소유격으로 뒤에 명사가 필요하여 문맥에 맞지 않다.

어휘 presentation 발표, 프레젠테이션 praise 칭찬, 극찬 board 이사회, 위원회

2. 재귀 대명사

✔ CheckPoint 2. 재귀용법과 강조용법

정답

1. (A) 2. (B)

1.

번역 마케팅 부서가 전체 캠페인을 스스로 디자인했다.

해설 itself는 주어 The marketing department를 강조하는 재귀 대명사의 강조용법으로 사용되었고, The marketing department는 비인칭 단수 명사로 it을 사용하므로 (A) itself가 정답이다. (B) himself, (C) herself, (D) themselves는 각각 남성, 여성, 3인칭 복수를 가리키므로 문맥에 맞지 않다.

어휘 department 부서 design 설계하다, 디자인하다

2.

번역 그녀는 기한을 맞추기 위해 밤늦게까지 일하는 자신을 자주 발견한다.

해설 herself는 주어 She와 동일한 대상을 가리키는 재귀 대명사의 재귀용법으로, 여성 단수 주어(She)와 일치해야 하므로 (B) herself가 정답이다. (A) himself, (C) themselves, (D) itself는 각각 남성, 3인칭 복수, 비인칭 단수를 가리키므로 문맥에 맞지 않다.

어휘 meet 맞추다, 지키다

✔ CheckPoint 3. 재귀 대명사의 관용표현

정답

1. (C) 2. (D)

1.

번역 매니저는 다른 부서를 관여시키지 않고 혼자서 그 상황을 처리하기로 결정했다.

해설 매니저가 다른 부서의 도움 없이 혼자 상황을 처리하기로 결정했으므로 '혼자서'라는 의미를 가진 (C) by himself가 정답이다. (A) in itself는 '그 자체로', (B) for himself는 '혼자 힘으로, 자신을 위해', (D) of itself는 '저절로'라는 의미로 문맥에 맞지 않다.

어휘 handle 처리하다, 다루다 situation 상황 involve 포함하다, 관련시키다

2.

번역 디자이너의 아이디어는 그 자체로 혁신적이었지만, 실행을 위해 다듬어져야 했다.

해설 디자이너의 아이디어 그 자체가 혁신적임을 나타내므로 '그 자체로'라는 의미를 가진 (D) in itself가 정답이다.

어휘 innovative 혁신적인 refinement 개선, 세련됨 implement 실행하다, 이행하다

3. 지시 형용사/대명사

✔ CheckPoint 4. 비교구문에서의 지시 대명사

정답

1. (B) 2. (B) 3. (D)

1.

번역 이 회사가 제공하는 고객 서비스가 경쟁사들의 그것보다 더 낫다.

해설 지시 대명사는 that은 비교구문에서 반복을 피하고 문장의 간결함을 유지하기 위해 단수 명사 The customer service를 대신하는 대명사로 사용되었으므로 (B) that이 정답이다. (A) those는 복수 명사를 대신하므로 문맥에 맞지 않다.

어휘 competitor 경쟁자, 경쟁 회사

2.

번역 이 새로운 모델들의 생산 비용이 이전 버전들의 그것들보다 낮다.

해설 지시 대명사는 those는 비교구문에서 반복을 피하고 문장의 간결함을 유지하기 위해 복수 명사 The production costs를 대신하는 대명사로 사용되었으므로 (B) those가 정답이다. (D) that은 단수 명사를 대신하므로 문맥에 맞지 않다.

어휘 production cost 생산 비용 previous 이전의, 과거의

3.

번역 이 장치들에 사용된 기술이 이전 모델들에 사용된 그것보다 더 발전되었다.

해설 지시 대명사는 that은 비교구문에서 반복을 피하고 문장의 간결함을 유지하기 위해 단수 명사 The technology를 대신하는 대명사로 사용되었으므로 (D) that이 정답이다.

어휘 device 장치, 기기

4. 부정 형용사/대명사

✔ CheckPoint 5. 부정 형용사의 유형과 용례

정답

1. (B) 2. (D)

1.

번역 남은 문제들을 논의하기 위해 또 다른 회의 일정에 잡아야 한다.

해설 another는 '또 다른 하나'라는 의미로 단수 가산명사를 수식할 수 있으므로 (B) another가 정답이다. (A) some과 (C) other는 복수나 불가산 명사를 수식하고, (D) any는 단수, 복수 (가산) 명사나 불가산 명사를 수식하지만 의미상 적절하지 않다.

어휘 schedule 일정을 잡다, 예정하다 meeting 회의, 모임 remain 남다

2.

번역 매니저는 프로세스 효율성을 개선할 몇 가지 방법을 제안했다.

해설 some은 '몇몇의, 약간의'라는 의미로 긍정문에서 복수나 불가산 명사를 수식할 수 있으므로 (D) some이 정답이다. (A) another, (C) the other, (D) this는 단수 가산 명사를 수식하므로 문맥에 맞지 않다.

어휘 improve 개선하다, 향상시키다 efficiency 효율성

✔ CheckPoint 6. 부정 대명사의 유형과 용례

정답

1. (D) 2. (B)

1.

번역 두 명의 팀원 중 한 명은 원격으로 일하고 있지만, 나머지 한 명은 사무실에 있다.

해설 the other는 '(둘 중) 나머지 하나'를 의미하며, 두 명 중 한 명이 언급되었을 때 나머지 하나를 나타낼 때 사용하므로 (D) the other가 정답이다. (A) another는 단수 (가산) 명사를 대신하지만 '(불특정한) 또 다른 하나'를 의미하고, (B) others와 (C) the others는 복수 (가산) 명사를 대신하므로 문맥에 맞지 않다.

어휘 remotely 원격으로

2.

번역 몇몇 고객들이 피드백을 제출했지만, 다른 고객들은 아직 응답하지 않았다.

해설 others는 '(불특정한) 다른 사람들/사물들'라는 의미로 복수 (가산) 명사를 대신할 수 있는데, 여기서는 피드백을 제출하지 않은 불특정한 다른 고객들을 가리키므로 (B) others가 정답이다. (A) the other와 (C) another는 단수 (가산) 명사를 대신하고, (D) the others는 '(특정한) 나머지 사람들/사물들'을 의미하므로 문맥에 맞지 않다.

어휘 submit 제출하다 respond 응답하다

✔ CheckPoint 7. 특정 명사의 일부나 전체를 나타내는 부정 대명사의 유형과 용례

정답

1. (C) 2. (B) 3. (B)

1.

번역 각각의 전략이 시행 전에 신중하게 분석되었다.

해설 each of the/소유격 + 복수 (가산) 명사는 단수 취급하여 단수 동사를 사용하기 때문에 (C) is가 정답이다.

어휘 strategy 전략, 계획 analyze 분석하다 implementation 실행, 시행

2.

번역 문서 중 일부가 여전히 분실된 상태여서, 팀은 가능한 한 빨리 그것들을 찾아야 한다.

해설 some of the/소유격 + 복수 (가산) 명사는 복수 취급하여 복수 동사를 사용하기 때문에 (B) are가 정답이다.

어휘 locate 찾다, 위치하다

3.

번역 보고서에 제공된 정보의 대부분이 정확하지만, 몇 가지 세부 사항은 확인이 필요하다.

해설 most of the/소유격 + 불가산 명사는 단수 취급하여 단수 동사를 사용하기 때문에 (B) is가 정답이다.

어휘 accurate 정확한 require 필요로 하다, 요구하다 verification 검증, 확인

토익 종합 실전문제

정답

1. (C)	2. (B)	3. (B)	4. (C)	5. (D)
6. (B)	7. (D)	8. (C)	9. (C)	10. (C)
11. (A)	12. (C)	13. (D)	14. (C)	15. (C)
16. (D)	17. (B)	18. (A)	19. (A)	20. (D)
21. (C)	22. (B)	23. (D)	24. (D)	

1.

번역 매니저는 그의 예산안을 승인했고, 우리의 것은 다음에 제출될 것이다.

해설 ours는 소유대명사로 소유격 + 명사 구조인 our budget plan의 축약형으로 사용되며, 뒤에 명사를 따로 붙이지 않고 소유를 나타내므로 (C) ours가 정답이다. (A) me는 목적격으로 주어자리에 올 수 없고, (B) my와 (D) our는 각각 소유격으로 뒤에 명사가 필요하여 문맥에 맞지 않다.

어휘 approve 승인하다, 허가하다 budget plan 예산 계획 submit 제출하다

2.

번역 그들의 프로젝트는 잘 진행되고 있지만, 내 것은 몇 가지 지연이 발생했다.

해설 mine은 소유대명사로 소유격 + 명사 구조인 my project의 축약형으로 사용되며, 뒤에 명사를 따로 붙이지 않고 소유를 나타내므로 (B) mine이 정답이다. (A) my는 소유격으로 뒤에 명사가 필요하고, (C) theirs는 복수 소유대명사로 their project를 의미하지만 문맥상 적절하지 않으며, (D) our는 복수 소유격으로 뒤에 명사가 필요하여 문맥에 맞지 않다.

어휘 progress 진행되다, 진척되다 encounter 직면하다, 마주치다 delay 지연, 연기

3.

번역 우리 팀이 제출한 프로젝트 계획은 상세하고 철저했다. 그러나 그들의 계획이 고객으로부터 더 긍정적인 피드백을 받았다.

해설 theirs는 소유대명사로 소유격 + 명사 구조인 their project plan의 축약형으로 사용되며, 뒤에 명사를 따로 붙이지 않고 소유를 나타내므로 (B) theirs가 정답이다. (A) their과 (C) our는 소유격으로 뒤에 명사가 필요하고, (D) ours는 소유대명사로 our project plan을 의미하지만 문맥상 적절하지 않다.

어휘 submit 제출하다 detailed 상세한 thorough 철저한

4.

번역 회사 임원들이 직접 합병에 대한 최종 결정을 내렸다.

해설 themselves는 주어 The company executives를 강조하는 재귀 대명사의 강조용법으로 사용되었고, The company executives가 복수 주어이므로 (C) themselves가 정답이다. (A) itself, (B) himself, (D) ourselves는 각각 비인칭 단수, 남성, 1인칭 복수를 가리키므로 문맥에 맞지 않다.

어휘 executive 경영진, 회사 임원 merger 합병

5.

번역 팀원들은 기한을 맞추기 위해 스스로 업무를 나누었다.

해설 themselves는 주어 The team members와 동일한 대상을 가리키는 재귀 대명사의 재귀용법

으로, 복수 주어(The team members)와 일치해야 하므로 (D) themselves가 정답이다. (A) itself, (B) himself, (C) herself는 각각 비인칭 단수, 남성, 여성을 가리키므로 문맥에 맞지 않다.

어휘 divide 나누다, 분배하다 meet 맞추다, 지키다

6.

번역 그는 교육 세션이 시작되기 전에 새 소프트웨어에 익숙해져야 한다.

해설 himself는 주어 He와 동일한 대상을 가리키는 재귀 대명사의 재귀용법으로, 주어(He)와 일치해야 하므로 (B) himself가 정답이다. (A) themselves, (C) ourselves, (D) yourself는 각각 3인칭 복수, 1인칭 복수, 2인칭 단수를 가리키므로 문맥에 맞지 않다.

어휘 familiarize 익숙해지다, 숙지하다

7.

번역 그는 회사 행사 동안 혼자 있는 것을 선호하며 동료들과 거의 대화를 하지 않는다.

해설 keep to oneself는 '혼자 지내다, 다른 사람과 잘 어울리지 않다'는 뜻으로, 이 문맥에서 그가 혼자 있는 것을 선호하는 성향을 나타내므로 (D) to himself가 정답이다. (A) himself는 일반적인 재귀대명사로 쓰일 수 있으나 이 경우 의미가 완전하지 않고, (B) in itself와 (C) beside himself는 문맥에 맞지 않다.

어휘 rarely 거의 ~하지 않다 engage 관계를 맺다 colleague 동료

8.

번역 그 장치는 몇 시간 동안 계속 작동한 후 저절로 꺼졌다.

해설 장치가 외부의 도움 없이 스스로 멈췄으므로 '저절로'라는 의미를 가진 (C) of itself가 정답이다. (A), (B), (D)는 문맥에 맞지 않다.

어휘 device 장치, 기기 shut down 작동을 멈추다, 종료되다 continuously 계속해서

9.

번역 그는 목표를 달성하기 위해 누구에게도 의존하지 않고 혼자서 프로젝트를 진행하기로 결심했다.

해설 그가 외부의 도움 없이 독립적으로 어떤 일을 처리하기로 했으므로 '혼자서, 스스로'라는 의미를 가진 (C) by himself가 정답이다. (A) of itself는 '저절로', (B) in itself는 '그 자체로', (D) beside himself는 '제정신이 아닌'이라는 뜻으로 문맥에 맞지 않다.

어휘 achieve 이루다, 성취하다 resolve 결심하다, 다짐하다 rely on 의존하다

10.

번역 회사는 영업 부서에서 일하는 사람들에게 추가 교육을 제공했다.

해설 those가 관계절, 분사 및 전치사구에 의해 후치 수식을 받으면 '~한 사람들'이라는 의미로 사용되는데, 여기서는 현재분사 working에 의해 후치수식을 받고 있으므로 (C) those가 정답이다.

어휘 additional 추가의 department 부서

11.

번역 프로젝트를 책임지고 있는 사람들은 매니저에게 주간 보고서를 제출해야 한다.

해설 those가 관계절, 분사 및 전치사구에 의해 후치 수식을 받으면 '~한 사람들'이라는 의미로 사용되는데, 여기서는 전치사구 in charge of the project에 의해 후치수식을 받고 있으므로 (A) Those가 정답이다.

어휘 in charge of ~을 책임지고 있는, ~을 맡고 있는 submit 제출하다

12.

번역 우리의 최고 제품 라인이 창출한 수익은 다른 어떤 라인의 그것보다 두 배이다.

해설 지시 대명사는 that은 비교구문에서 반복을 피하고 문장의 간결함을 유지하기 위해 단수 명사 The revenue를 대신하는 대명사로 사용되었으므로

(C) that이 정답이다. (A) those는 복수 명사를 대신하므로 문맥에 맞지 않다.

어휘 revenue 수익, 매출 generate 생성하다, 발생시키다

13.

번역 그 연구의 결과가 이전 연구들의 그것보다 더 확실했다.

해설 지시 대명사는 those는 비교구문에서 반복을 피하고 문장의 간결함을 유지하기 위해 복수 명사 The results를 대신하는 대명사로 사용되었으므로 (D) those가 정답이다. (B) that은 단수 명사를 대신하므로 문맥에 맞지 않다.

어휘 conclusive 결정적인, 확실한

14.

번역 우리는 마감일 전에 보고서를 마무리하기 위해 시간이 조금 더 필요하다.

해설 some은 '몇몇의, 약간의'라는 의미로 긍정문에서 복수나 불가산 명사를 수식할 수 있으므로 (C) some이 정답이다. (A) other는 복수나 불가산 명사를 수식하지만 '다른'이라는 의미로 이 문맥에 적절하지 않고, (B) another는 단수 가산 명사를 수식하며, (D) any는 부정문, 의문문, 조건문외에 강조의 의미를 나타낼 때 긍정문에도 사용 가능하지만 의미상 적절하지 않다.

어휘 finalize 마무리하다, 확정하다

15.

번역 그 문서의 다른 사본 하나를 가져다줄래요? 제 것을 잃어버렸어요.

해설 another는 '또 다른 하나'라는 의미로 단수 가산명사를 수식할 수 있으므로 (C) another가 정답이다. (A) some과 (D) other는 복수나 불가산 명사를 수식하고, (B) the other는 단수 가산명사를 수식하지만 '(둘 중) 나머지 하나'라는 의미로 이 문맥에 적절하지 않다.

어휘 misplace 잃어버리다, 잘못 두다

16.

번역 그 직책에 세 명의 후보가 있다. 두 명은 이미 면접을 보았고, 나머지 한 명은 내일 면접을 볼 것이다.

해설 the other는 '(둘 중) 나머지 하나'라는 의미로 단수 (가산) 명사를 대신할 수 있는데, 여기서는 세 명의 후보 중 두 명이 면접을 본 후 남은 한 명을 가리키므로 (D) the other가 정답이다. (A) another는 단수 (가산) 명사를 대신하지만 '(불특정한) 또 다른 하나'를 의미하고, (B) the others는 복수 (가산) 명사를 대신하며, (C) one은 불특정한 하나를 의미하므로 문맥에 맞지 않다.

어휘 candidate 후보자 position 직위, 직책

17.

번역 첫 번째 회의는 매우 생산적이었고, 우리는 또 다른 회의도 그와 같기를 바란다.

해설 another는 '(불특정한) 또 다른 하나'라는 의미로 단수 (가산) 명사를 대신할 수 있는데, 여기서는 첫 번째 회의 외에 추가적으로 또 다른 회의가 있을 것을 언급하므로 (B) another가 정답이다. (A) the other는 단수 (가산) 명사를 대신하지만 '(둘 중) 나머지 하나'를 나타내며 특정 두 개 중 남은 하나를 의미하므로, 첫 번째 회의 외에 추가적인 회의를 언급하는 이 문맥에는 맞지 않고, (C) others와 (D) the others는 복수 (가산) 명사를 대신하므로 문맥에 맞지 않다.

어휘 productive 생산적인, 효율적인

18.

번역 두 부서는 효율성을 높이기 위해 서로 긴밀히 협력하고 있다.

해설 each other는 둘 사이의 상호 관계를 나타낼 때 사용되므로, 두 부서가 서로 협력하고 있음을 의미하는 (A) each other가 정답이다. (B) another는 단수 (가산) 명사를 대신하고, (C) others와 (D) the others는 복수 (가산) 명사를 대신하므로 문맥에 맞지 않다.

어휘 closely 긴밀히 improve 개선하다, 향상시키다 efficiency 효율성

19.

번역 회사는 일부 직원들에게 노트북을 제공하고, 다른 직원들에게는 태블릿을 제공했다.

해설 others는 '(불특정한) 다른 사람들/사물들'라는 의미로 복수 (가산) 명사를 대신할 수 있는데, 여기서는 불특정한 다른 직원들을 가리키므로 (A) others가 정답이다. (B) the other와 (C) another는 단수 가산 명사를 대신하고, (D) each other는 둘 사이의 상호 관계를 나타내므로 문맥에 맞지 않다.

20.

번역 일부 부서들은 예산 보고서를 제때 제출했지만, 나머지 부서들은 아직 보고서를 완료해야 한다.

해설 the others는 '(특정한) 나머지 사람들/사물들'라는 의미로 복수 (가산) 명사를 대신할 수 있는데, 여기서는 이미 언급된 특정 부서들 외에 남아 있는 부서들을 가리키므로 (D) the others가 정답이다. (A) another와 (B) the other는 단수 가산 명사를 대신하고, (C) other는 부정 형용사로 복수 (가산) 명사나 불가산 명사를 수식해야 하므로 문맥에 맞지 않다.

어휘 department 부서 submit 제출하다 finalize 마무리하다, 완료하다

21.

번역 후보자 중 한 명은 필요한 경험을 가지고 있는 반면, 나머지 후보들은 그렇지 않다.

해설 one of the/소유격 + 복수 (가산) 명사는 단수 취급하여 단수 동사를 사용하기 때문에 (C) has가 정답이다.

어휘 candidate 후보자 necessary 필요한 lack 부족하다

22.

번역 두 해결책 중 하나는 문제를 해결할 가능성이 있으니, 둘 중 하나를 선택할 수 있다.

해설 either of the/소유격 + 복수 (가산) 명사는 단수 취급하여 단수 동사를 사용하기 때문에 (B) is가 정답이다.

어휘 be likely to ~할 가능성이 있다 resolve 해결하다

23.

번역 연구 데이터의 많은 부분이 오래되었으며, 업데이트가 필요하다.

해설 much of the/소유격 + 불가산 명사는 단수 취급하여 단수 동사를 사용하기 때문에 (D) is가 정답이다.

어휘 outdated 구식의, 시대에 뒤떨어진

24.

번역 보고서에 제공된 모든 정보는 다가오는 발표에 필수적이다.

해설 some/all/most/any of the/소유격 + 불가산 명사는 단수 취급하여 단수 동사(is)를 사용한다. 하지만 이 지문에서는 전치사 of가 생략된 구조(all the/소유격 + 불가산 명사)로, 이런 구조에 적합한 것은 all 밖에 없기 때문에 (D) All이 정답이다.

어휘 essential 필수적인 upcoming 다가오는

PART 6

다음 메모와 관련된 질문 1-4번을 보세요.

> 팀 여러분께,
> 우리 운영을 지원하기 위해 새로운 프로젝트 관리 도구를 곧 도입하게 되었음을 기쁘게 알려드립니다. 이 소프트웨어는 업무 과정을 간소화하고 팀의 효율성을 높이도록 설계되었습니다. 원활한 전환을 돕기 위해 향후 2주 동안 일련의 교육 세션을 준비했습니다. 첫 번째 세션은 이번 금요일 오전 10시에 메인 회의실에서 열립니다. 이 세션에서는 일상 업무에 필수적인 소프트웨어의 주요 기능을 다룰 예정이므로, 모두의 참석을 적극 권장합니다. 노트북을 지참해 주십시오. 실습 세션을 통해 소프트웨어를 직접 체험할 기회가 주어질 것입니다. 추가로, 소프트웨어의 기본 기능을 익히는 데 도움을 줄 사용자 매뉴얼이 제공될 것입니다. 어느 세션에든 참석이 어려운 경우, 부서장에게 미리 알려주시기 바랍니다. 추가 세션을 마련하거나 참석할 수 없는 분들을 위해 온라인 자료를 제공할 수 있도록 노력하겠습니다. 이 새로운

도구를 채택하는 데 있어 여러분의 협조에 감사드리며, 이를 통해 우리의 생산성이 향상되고 프로젝트 관리가 더 원활해질 것이라 확신합니다.

감사합니다.
관리팀 드림

어휘 implement 실행하다, 도입하다 project management tool 프로젝트 관리 도구 streamline 간소화하다, 효율적으로 만들다 initial 초기의, 첫 번째의 hands-on 실습 중심의, 직접 체험하는 essential 필수적인, 중요한 unable ~할 수 없는 arrange 준비하다, 마련하다 enhance 향상시키다, 강화하다 productivity 생산성 transition 전환, 변화 cooperation 협력, 협조

정답

1. (C) 2. (A) 3. (A) 4. (D)

1.

해설 이 문장에서 To assist는 To부정사의 부사적 용법의 목적을 나타내고, '원활한 전환을 돕기 위해서'라는 의미로 문맥에 가장 적절하므로 (C) To assist가 정답이다. (A) Assisting와 (D) Assisted는 각각 현재분사와 과거분사로 내용상 문맥에 맞지 않고, (B) To be assisted는 목적어가 필요 없는 수동형으로 문법적으로 맞지 않다.

2.

(A) 소프트웨어의 기본 기능을 익히는 데 도움을 줄 사용자 매뉴얼이 제공될 것입니다.
(B) 주요 기능을 배우는 데 도움이 될 간편 참고 자료가 제공될 것입니다.
(C) 필수 작업 및 문제 해결 팁을 다룬 교육 자료가 준비될 것입니다.
(D) 고급 기능에 대한 비디오 튜토리얼을 제공할 예정입니다.

해설 문맥상 새로운 도구를 사용자가 쉽게 익힐 수 있도록 기본 기능에 대한 안내가 필요한 상황에서, 사용자 매뉴얼은 소프트웨어의 기본 기능 사용법을 안내하므로 (A)가 가장 적절하다. (B)와 (C)는 교육 자료를 언급하고 있으나, 간편 참고 자료나 필수 작업 및 문제 해결 팁이 구체적으로 언급된 것은 아니므로 기본 기능을 안내하는 사용자 매뉴얼이라는 문맥과 일치하지 않고, (D)는 고급 기능을 위한 비디오 튜토리얼을 제공한다는 내용으로, 기본 기능 교육에 집중하는 문맥에 적절하지 않다.

3.

해설 이 문장에서 in advance는 참석 불가능한 경우 부서 책임자에게 사전 통보가 필요함을 나타내므로 (A) in advance가 정답이다. (B) on time은 "정시에", (C) at the latest는 "늦어도", (D) as expected는 "예상대로"라는 의미로 문맥에 맞지 않다.

4.

해설 those (who are) unable to join에서 those는 부정 대명사로 "세션에 참석할 수 없는 사람들"이라는 의미로 사용되었으므로 (D) those가 정답이다. (A) this, (B) that, (C) these는 사람을 지칭하지 않기 때문에 문맥에 맞지 않다.

PART 7

다음 공지와 이메일과 관련된 질문 1-5번을 보세요.

제목: 회사 회의 일정 변경
날짜: 9월 10일
대상: 모든 직원
발신: 인사부

팀 여러분,
다음과 같이 주간 회의 일정이 변경되었음을 알려드립니다.
팀 리더 회의
매주 월요일 오전 9시 (이전에는 오전 10시)
장소: B 회의실
전 직원 회의
매주 수요일 오전 11시
장소: 대강당
프로젝트 검토 회의
매주 금요일 오후 3시
장소: 프로젝트 회의실 1
모든 직원은 매주 수요일에 진행되는 전 직원 회의에 참석해야 합니다. 다른 회의 중 어느 회의에라도 참석할 수 없는 경우, 미리 관리자에게 알려

주시기 바랍니다.

감사합니다.
인사부

발신자: Sarah Kim (프로젝트 매니저)
수신자: Paul Johnson (팀 리더)
날짜: 9월 11일
제목: 프로젝트 검토 회의

안녕하세요 Paul,
이번 금요일 오후 3시에 예정된 프로젝트 검토 회의가 업데이트된 회사 회의 일정에 따라 프로젝트 회의실 1에서 열릴 것임을 확인하고자 합니다. 또한 최신 프로젝트 보고서를 가져오시길 바랍니다. 우리는 현재 상태를 검토하고 다음 단계에 대해 계획을 세울 필요가 있습니다.
회의 전에 추가로 필요한 정보가 있으면 알려주세요.

감사합니다,
Sarah Kim
프로젝트 매니저

어휘 announcement 공지, 알림 updated 업데이트된, 수정된 location 위치, 장소 main auditorium 대강당 notify 알리다, 통지하다 in advance 사전에, 미리 HR department 인사부 attend 참석하다 confirm 확인하다 remind 상기시키다, 다시 알려주다 review 검토하다, 점검하다 current 현재의 status 상태 additional 추가의

정답

1. (C) 2. (C) 3. (B) 4. (D) 5. (A)

1. 팀 리더 회의에 어떤 변경 사항이 있습니까?
   (A) 팀 리더 회의가 취소되었습니다.
   (B) 이제 회의실 A에서 열립니다.
   (C) 시간이 오전 9시로 변경되었습니다.
   (D) 이제 매주 수요일에 열립니다.

해설 첫 번째 문서에서 "Team Leaders Meeting: Every Monday at 9:00 AM (previously 10:00 AM)"이라고 명시되어 있어 시간이 9:00 AM으로 변경되었음을 알 수 있으므로 (C)가 정답이다.

2. All Staff Meeting은 어디에서 열립니까?
   (A) 회의실 B
   (B) 프로젝트 룸 1
   (C) 메인 강당
   (D) 프로젝트 룸 2

해설 첫 번째 문서에서 "All Staff Meeting: Every Wednesday at 11:00 AM, Location: Main Auditorium"이라고 명시되어 있어 All Staff Meeting이 대강당(Main Auditorium)에서 열릴 것임을 알 수 있으므로 (C)가 정답이다.

3. Sarah Kim은 Paul Johnson에게 Project Review Meeting에 무엇을 가져오라고 요청합니까?
   (A) 새로운 프로젝트 제안서
   (B) 최신 프로젝트 보고서
   (C) 재무 보고서
   (D) 고객 프레젠테이션

해설 두 번째 문서에서 "remind you to bring the latest project report"라고 명시되어 있어 Sarah Kim은 Paul에게 최신 프로젝트 보고서를 가져오라고 요청한 것을 알 수 있으므로 (B)가 정답이다.

4. Project Review Meeting은 언제 열립니까?
   (A) 매주 수요일 오전 11시
   (B) 매주 월요일 오전 9시
   (C) 매주 목요일 오후 4시
   (D) 매주 금요일 오후 3시

해설 첫 번째 문서에서 "Project Review Meeting: Every Friday at 3:00 PM"이라고 명시되어 있어 프로젝트 리뷰 미팅은 매주 금요일 오후 3시에 열린다는 것을 알 수 있으므로 (D)가 정답이다.

5. 이메일은 공지 사항의 정보를 어떻게 보완하는가?
   (A) 공지 사항에 나와 있는 회의 장소를 확인한다.
   (B) 회의 일정에 대한 피드백을 요청한다.
   (C) 휴일 회의에 대한 추가 정보를 제공한다.
   (D) 회사 메인 회의실에 대한 변경 사항을 설명한다.

해설 이메일에서 Sarah Kim이 "Project Review Meeting scheduled for this Friday at 3:00 PM will be held in Project Room 1"이라고 명확히 확인해주고 있어, 공지 사항에 명시된 회의 장소를 재확인하고 있음을 알 수 있으므로 (A)가 정답이다. (B)는 회의 일정에 대한 피드백 요청이 아니며, (C)와 (D) 또한 회의 장소나 휴일 일정에 관련된 정보가 포함되지 않으므로 문맥에 맞지 않다.

Chapter 10 형용사

1. 형용사의 역할 및 자리

✔ CheckPoint 1. 형용사의 한정 용법

정답

1. (B) 2. (A)

1.

번역 워크숍은 참가자들에게 생산성을 높이기 위한 유용한 팁을 제공했다.

해설 useful은 형용사로 명사 tips를 전치 수식하여 '유용한 팁'이라는 의미를 전달하므로 (B) useful이 정답이다. (A) usefulness는 명사, (C) use는 동사 또는 명사, (D) usage는 사용법이라는 의미의 명사로 문맥에 맞지 않다.

어휘 workshop 워크숍 participant 참가자 tip 조언, 유용한 정보 usefulness 유용성

2.

번역 매니저는 최근 프로젝트에서의 인상적인 성과에 대해 팀을 칭찬했다.

해설 impressive는 형용사로 명사 performance를 전치 수식하여 '인상적인 성과'라는 의미를 전달하므로 (A) impressive가 정답이다. (C) impressing은 현재분사로 사람이나 대상이 인상 깊은 행동을 하고 있는 중이라는 진행 중인 상황을 나타낼 때 사용한다. She is impressing her new colleagues with her dedication to the project. (그녀는 프로젝트에 대한 헌신으로 새로운 동료들에게 깊은 인상을 주고 있다.)

어휘 manager 관리자, 책임자 praise 칭찬하다 performance 성과, 실적, 수행

✔ CheckPoint 2. 형용사의 서술 용법

정답

1. (B) 2. (A)

1.

번역 매니저는 새로운 마케팅 전략이 현재 시장 동향에 적합하다고 여겼다.

해설 5형식 동사(make, find, keep, leave, consider)는 형용사/현재분사/과거분사를 목적격 보어로 취하므로 (B) suitable이 정답이다. (A) suitability는 명사, (C) suitably는 부사, (D) suit는 동사로 문법적으로 적절하지 않다.

어휘 manager 관리자, 책임자 consider 여기다, 간주하다 current market trends 현재 시장 동향 suitability 적합성

2.

번역 CEO는 그 발표가 흥미롭고 유익하다고 생각했다.

해설 5형식 동사(make, find, keep, leave, consider)는 형용사/현재분사/과거분사를 목적격 보어로 취하므로 (A) interesting이 정답이다. ☛ 현재분사 interesting은 "흥미를 주는"이라는 능동적 의미를 가지며, 발표처럼 다른 대상에 흥미를 제공하는 경우에 사용되므로 문맥에 맞다. 반면, 과거분사 interested는 "흥미를 느끼는"이라는 수동적 의미를 가지며, 사람이 특정 대상에 흥미를 느끼는

상황에 사용되므로 문맥에 맞지 않다.

어휘 CEO 최고경영자 presentation 발표, 프레젠테이션 informative 유익한

2. 형용사의 종류

✔ CheckPoint 3. 수량형용사의 종류

정답

1. (A) 2. (D)

1.

번역 설문조사에 따르면 많은 직원들이 사무실 근무보다 원격 근무를 선호했다.

해설 many는 복수 가산명사(employees)와 함께 사용되며, "많은"이라는 의미를 전달하므로 (A) many가 정답이다. (B) much, (C) a little, (D) little은 모두 불가산명사와 함께 사용되므로 문법적으로 적절하지 않다.

어휘 survey 조사, 설문 reveal 밝히다, 드러내다 remote work 원격 근무 prefer 선호하다, 더 좋아하다

2.

번역 팀은 프로젝트에 대해 현명한 결정을 내리기 위해 충분한 정보를 수집했다.

해설 plenty of는 가산명사와 불가산명사(information)에 모두 사용되며, "충분한"이라는 의미를 전달하므로 (D) plenty of가 정답이다. (A) several, (B) few, (C) a few는 모두 가산명사와 함께 사용되므로 문법적으로 적절하지 않다.

어휘 collect 수집하다, 모으다 information 정보, 자료

3. 형용사의 관용표현

✔ CheckPoint 4. 토익에 자주 출제되는 관용표현

정답

1. (B) 2. (C) 3. (C)

1.

번역 매니저는 회의 중 제기된 우려 사항들에 무관심한 것 같았다.

해설 be indifferent to는 "~에 무관심하다"는 의미의 관용 표현으로, concerns(우려)에 대해 무관심하다는 의미를 전달하므로 (B) indifferent가 정답이다.

어휘 manager 관리자, 책임자

2.

번역 회사는 국제 고객들에게 시장을 확장할 수 있는 능력이 있다.

해설 be capable of는 "~할 수 있다"는 의미의 관용 표현으로, 회사가 시장을 확장할 능력이 있다는 의미를 전달하므로 (C) capable이 정답이다.

어휘 expand 확장하다 market 시장 international client 국제 고객, 해외 고객

3.

번역 직원들은 고객 불만을 효율적으로 처리하는 데 책임이 있다.

해설 be responsible for는 "~에 책임이 있다"는 의미의 관용 표현으로, 직원들이 고객 불만을 처리하는 책임을 지고 있다는 의미를 전달하므로 (C) responsible이 정답이다.

어휘 handle 다루다, 처리하다 customer complaint 고객 불만 efficiently 효율적으로, 능률적으로

4. 혼동하기 쉬운 형용사

✔ CheckPoint 5. 토익에 자주 출제되는 혼동하기 쉬운 형용사

정답

1. (C) 2. (B) 3. (D)

1.

번역 새로운 정책은 직원들의 다양한 요구에 반응하도록 설계되었다.

해설 responsive는 "반응하는"이라는 의미로, 정책이 직원들의 요구에 반응한다는 의미를 전달하므로 (C) responsive가 정답이다.

어휘 policy 정책 designed 설계된, 계획된 diverse needs 다양한 요구

2.

번역 그 보고서는 산업에 영향을 미치는 경제 동향에 대한 포괄적인 분석을 제공했다.

해설 comprehensive는 "포괄적인, 종합적인"이라는 의미로, 분석(analysis)의 성격을 잘 전달하므로 (B) comprehensive가 정답이다.

어휘 report 보고서 provide 제공하다, 주다 analysis 분석, 해석 economic trends 경제 동향, 경기 흐름 affect 영향을 미치다

3.

번역 실험 결과는 놀랍고 인상적이었다.

해설 impressive는 "인상적인"이라는 의미로, 실험 결과의 특성을 잘 설명하므로 (D) impressive가 정답이다.

어휘 result 결과 experiment 실험 surprising 놀라운, 예상치 못한

토익 종합 실전문제

정답

1. (D)	2. (B)	3. (D)	4. (C)	5. (B)
6. (B)	7. (A)	8. (B)	9. (D)	10. (B)
11. (D)	12. (A)	13. (A)	14. (C)	15. (A)
16. (D)	17. (A)	18. (A)	19. (D)	20. (B)
21. (C)	22. (A)	23. (B)	24. (C)	

1.

번역 팀은 프로젝트의 성공적 완료를 위해 관련된 문제를 논의했다.

해설 선행사(명사) + (주격 관계대명사 + Be동사) + 형용사/현재분사/과거분사 + 전치사구 구조에 따라 형용사 relevant가 명사 issues를 후치 수식하고 있으므로 (D) relevant가 정답이다.

어휘 discuss 논의하다, 토론하다 issue 문제 successful completion 성공적인 완료

2.

번역 위원회는 회사의 미래 계획과 관련된 여러 주제를 논의했다.

해설 선행사(명사) + (주격 관계대명사 + Be동사) + 형용사/현재분사/과거분사 + 전치사구 구조에 따라 (B) related와 (C) relating이 모두 가능하지만, 타동사 relate의 목적어가 없는 수동 구조이므로 (B) related가 정답이다.

어휘 committee 위원회 topic 주제

3.

번역 새로운 디자인을 개발 중인 엔지니어들은 성공을 확신하고 있다.

해설 선행사(명사) + (주격 관계대명사 + Be동사) + 형용사/현재분사/과거분사 + 전치사구 구조에 따라 (C) developed와 (D) developing이 모두 가능하지만, 타동사 develop의 목적어(the new design)가 있는 능동 구조이므로 (D) developing이 정답이다.

어휘 confident 자신 있는, 확신하는

4.

번역 설문조사 결과를 분석 중인 팀이 회의에서 그들의 결과를 발표할 것이다.

해설 선행사(명사) + (주격 관계대명사 + Be동사) + 형용사/현재분사/과거분사 + 전치사구 구조에 따라 (C) analyzing과 (D) analyzed 모두 가능하지만, 타동사 analyze의 목적어(the results of the survey)가 있는 능동 구조이므로 (C) analyzing이 정답이다.

어휘 survey 설문조사 present 발표하다 finding 결과, 발견 conference 회의

5.

번역 창고에 보관된 장비는 배송 준비가 되었다.

해설 선행사(명사) + (주격 관계대명사 + Be동사) + 형용사/현재분사/과거분사 + 전치사구 구조에 따라 (A) storing과 (B) stored 모두 가능하지만, 타동사 store의 목적어가 없는 수동 구조이므로 (B) stored가 정답이다.

어휘 equipment 장비, 기기 warehouse 창고, 저장소 shipment 배송

6.

번역 새로운 디자인은 팀이 그 잠재적인 성공에 대해 흥분되게 만들었다.

해설 5형식 동사(make, find, keep, leave, consider)는 형용사/현재분사/과거분사를 목적격 보어로 취하므로 (B) excited가 정답이다.

☞ 현재분사 exciting은 "흥분을 유발하는"이라는 능동적 의미를 가지며, 대상이 능동적으로 감정을 유발할 때 사용되므로 문맥에 맞지 않다. 반면, 과거분사 excited는 "흥분을 느끼는"이라는 수동적 의미를 가지며, the team이 잠재적인 성공에 대해 흥분을 느끼므로 문맥에 맞다.

어휘 potential success 잠재적인 성공

7.

번역 고객들의 피드백은 개발 팀이 새로운 기능에 대해 자신감을 가지게 만들었다.

해설 5형식 동사(make, find, keep, leave, consider)는 형용사/현재분사/과거분사를 목적격 보어로 취하므로 (A) confident가 정답이다. (B) confidence는 명사, (C) confidently는 부사, (D) confide는 동사로 문법적으로 적절하지 않다.

어휘 feedback 피드백, 의견 customer 고객 development team 개발팀 feature 기능

8.

번역 그 보고서는 재무 예측에 대해 경영진을 걱정하게 했다.

해설 5형식 동사(make, find, keep, leave, consider)는 형용사/현재분사/과거분사를 목적격 보어로 취하므로 (B) concerned가 정답이다.

☞ 현재분사 concerning은 "걱정을 일으키는"이라는 능동적 의미로 문맥에 맞지 않다. 반면, 과거분사 concerned는 "걱정을 느끼는"이라는 수동적 의미를 가지며, 경영진이 걱정을 느끼므로 문맥에 맞다.

어휘 management team 경영진, 관리팀 financial forecast 재무 예측

9.

번역 직원들은 바쁜 시즌 동안 사무실 환경을 정리된 상태로 유지했다.

해설 5형식 동사(make, find, keep, leave, consider)는 형용사/현재분사/과거분사를 목적격 보어로 취하므로 (D) organized가 정답이다.

☞ 현재분사 organizing은 "정리하는 중인"이라는 능동적 의미로 문맥에 맞지 않다. 반면, 과거분사 organized는 "정리된 상태"라는 수동적 의미를 가지며, 사무실 환경이 정리된 상태를 유지해야 하므로 문맥에 맞다.

어휘 employee 직원 office environment 사무실 환경 during ~하는 동안

10.

번역 새로운 매니저는 팀 생산성을 향상시키기 위해 많은 변화를 도입했다.

해설 many는 복수 가산명사(changes)와 함께 사용되며, "많은"이라는 의미를 전달하므로 (B) many가 정답이다. (A) much와 (C) little은 불가산명사와 함께 사용되므로 적절하지 않고, (D) few는 복수 가산명사와 함께 사용되지만, "거의 없는"이라는 부정적 의미를 전달하므로 적절하지 않다.

어휘 implement 실행하다, 도입하다 change 변화, 변경 사항 improve 향상시키다, 개선하다 productivity 생산성

11.

번역 회의에 참석한 직원들이 거의 없어서 매

니저는 회의 일정을 변경하기로 결정했다.

해설 few는 복수 가산명사(employees)와 함께 사용되며, “거의 없는”이라는 부정적인 의미를 전달하므로 (D) few가 정답이다. (A) little와 (B) a little은 불가산명사와 함께 사용되므로 적절하지 않고, (C) many는 복수 가산명사와 함께 사용되지만, “많은”이라는 의미를 전달하므로 적절하지 않다.

어휘 attend 참석하다, 출석하다 reschedule 일정을 변경하다

12.

번역 이 문제를 해결하기 위해 이용 가능한 여러 가지 옵션이 있지만, 우리는 그것들을 신중히 평가해야 한다.

해설 several은 복수 가산명사(options)와 함께 사용되며, “몇 가지의”라는 의미를 전달하므로 (A) several이 정답이다. (B) much와 (C) a little은 불가산명사와 함께 사용되므로 적절하지 않고, (D) few는 복수 가산명사와 함께 사용되지만, “거의 없는”이라는 부정적인 의미를 전달하므로 적절하지 않다.

어휘 option 옵션, 선택지 available 이용 가능한, 사용 가능한 address 해결하다 evaluate 평가하다 carefully 신중하게

13.

번역 작업을 완료할 시간이 거의 남지 않아, 팀은 더 빠르게 작업해야 했다.

해설 little은 불가산명사(time)와 함께 사용되며, “거의 없는”이라는 부정적인 의미를 전달하므로 (A) little이 정답이다. (B) a little은 “약간의”라는 긍정적인 의미를 전달하므로 적절하지 않고, (C) few는 복수 가산명사와 함께 사용되므로 적절하지 않으며, (D) some도 불가산명사(time)와 함께 사용될 수는 있지만 긍정적인 의미를 전달하므로 적절하지 않다.

14.

번역 이 치료법의 장기적인 효과를 이해하기 위해 약간의 연구가 진행되었다.

해설 Some은 가산명사와 불가산명사(research)에 모두 사용되며, “약간의”라는 의미를 전달하므로 (C) Some이 정답이다. (A) Few, (B) A few, (D) Many는 복수 가산명사와 함께 사용되므로 적절하지 않다.

어휘 research 연구, 조사 long-term effect 장기적인 영향 treatment 치료(법)

15.

번역 직원들은 새로운 정책과 관련된 잠재적 위험을 알고 있다.

해설 be aware of는 “~을 알고 있다”는 의미의 관용 표현으로, 직원들이 정책과 관련된 위험을 알고 있다는 의미를 전달하므로 (A) aware가 정답이다.

어휘 potential risk 잠재적 위험 associate 관련하다 policy 정책

16.

번역 CEO는 회사가 올해 재무 목표를 달성할 수 있을 것이라고 자신하고 있다.

해설 be confident about는 “~에 대해 자신이 있다”는 의미의 관용 표현으로, 회사의 목표 달성에 대한 자신감이 있다는 의미를 전달하므로 (D) confident가 정답이다. be satisfied with는 “~에 만족하다”, be impressed with “~에 감명 받다”, be hesitant to는 ~을 망설이다”는 의미로 문맥상 적절하지 않다.

어휘 ability 능력 financial target 재무 목표

17.

번역 직원들은 회사 정책 변경에 익숙해졌다.

해설 be accustomed to는 “~에 익숙하다”는 의미의 관용 표현으로, 직원들이 회사 정책 변경에 익숙해졌다는 의미를 전달하므로 (A) accustomed가 정답이다.

18.

번역 일정이 고객의 요청과 일치하므로 변경이 필요 없다.

해설 be consistent with는 "~와 일치하다"라는 의미의 관용 표현으로, 일정(schedule)이 요청(request)과 일치한다는 의미를 전달하므로 (A) consistent가 정답이다.

어휘 schedule 일정 consist 구성되다, 이루어지다

19.

번역 새로운 제품 디자인은 최신 시장 동향과 관련이 있어 매우 경쟁력이 있다.

해설 be relevant to는 "~와 관련이 있다"는 의미의 관용 표현으로, 제품 디자인이 시장 동향과 관련 있다는 의미를 전달하므로 (D) relevant가 정답이다.

어휘 highly 매우 competitive 경쟁력 있는

20.

번역 팀은 어려움에도 불구하고 주어진 일정 내에 프로젝트를 완료하는 데 전념하고 있다.

해설 be committed to는 "~에 헌신하다, 전념하다"는 의미의 관용 표현으로, 프로젝트 완료에 헌신했다는 의미를 전달하므로 (B) committed가 정답이다.

어휘 within the given timeline 주어진 일정 내에 despite ~에도 불구하고

21.

번역 팀은 효율성과 비용 문제를 모두 해결하는 현명한 해결책을 제시했다.

해설 sensible는 "분별 있는, 현명한"이라는 의미로, 해결책(solution)의 특성을 잘 설명하므로 (C) sensible이 정답이다.

어휘 present 제시하다, 발표하다 solution 해결책 address 해결하다 efficiency 효율성

22.

번역 매뉴얼은 장비 조립에 대해 이해할 수 있는 지침을 제공한다.

해설 comprehensible는 "이해할 수 있는"이라는 의미로, 매뉴얼(manual)의 성격을 잘 설명하므로 (A) comprehensible이 정답이다.

어휘 provide 제공하다, 제시하다 instruction 지침 assemble 조립하다 equipment 장비

23.

번역 매니저는 계약서에 서명하기 전에 철저히 검토하는 것이 바람직하다고 말했다.

해설 advisable는 "바람직한, 권장할 만한"이라는 의미로, 계약서를 검토하는 것이 바람직하다는 의미를 전달하므로 (B) advisable이 정답이다.

어휘 review 검토하다 contract 계약 thoroughly 철저히

24.

번역 정책 변화는 직원 만족에 유익한 영향을 미칠 것으로 예상된다.

해설 beneficial은 "유익한"이라는 의미로, 변화가 유익한 영향을 미친다는 의미를 잘 전달하므로 (C) beneficial이 정답이다.

어휘 expect 예상하다, 기대하다 impact 영향 satisfaction 만족

PART 6

다음 메모와 관련된 질문 1-4번을 보세요.

팀 여러분께,
신입 직원들이 회사에 빠르게 적응하고 효과적으로 기여할 수 있도록 돕기 위해 교육 프로그램 업데이트를 발표하게 되어 기쁩니다.
이 프로그램에는 온라인 세션과 대면 세션이 포함됩니다. 이러한 세션에서는 회사의 업무 흐름과 목표를 이해하기 위한 명확한 지침과 실용적인 팁을 제공합니다.
또한, 매니저들은 이 전환 기간 동안 팀원들의 특정한 요구에 민감하게 대응할 것을 권장합니다.

직원들은 회사의 현재 시스템 및 정책과 호환되는 자료에도 접근할 수 있습니다.
마지막으로, 참가자들의 피드백은 프로그램을 지속적으로 개선하는 데 사용될 것입니다. 여러분의 통찰은 소중하며, 이 교육을 가능한 한 효과적으로 만드는 데 도움이 될 것입니다.
전문성 향상을 위한 여러분의 협력과 헌신에 감사드립니다.

감사합니다.
인사팀 드림

어휘 adapt 적응하다, 맞추다 contribute 기여하다, 공헌하다 program 프로그램, 계획 online and in-person sessions 온라인 및 대면 세션 clear guidance 명확한 지침 practical 실용적인 workflow 업무 흐름, 작업 절차 goal 목표, 목적 responsive 반응하는, 대응하는 transition 전환, 변화 resource 자원, 자료 insight 통찰력, 의견 as ~ as possible 가능한 한 ~하게 commitment 헌신, 전념 professional growth 직업적 성장, 전문성 개발

정답

1. (B) 2. (D) 3. (A) 4. (B)

1.

해설 both는 등위상관접속사로 both A and B 구조에 사용되어 A와 B 둘 다 포함한다는 의미를 전달한다. 지문에서는 온라인 세션과 대면 세션 두 가지 모두를 포함한다는 의미를 전달하므로 (B) both가 정답이다. (C) either ~ or, (D) neither ~ nor이므로 문맥과 맞지 않다.

2.

해설 are compatible with는 "~와 호환되다"는 의미의 관용 표현으로, 자원이 회사의 시스템 및 정책과 호환된다는 뜻을 전달하므로 (D) are compatible with가 정답이다. (A) be in alignment with는 "~와 일치하다"는 의미로 사용 가능하나, "호환"의 의미를 직접적으로 전달하지는 못하고, (B) be dependent on는 "~에 의존하다", (C) be in contrast to는 "~와 대조되다"는 의미로 문맥상 적절하지 않다.

3.

(A) 참가자들의 피드백은 프로그램을 지속적으로 개선하는 데 사용될 것입니다.
(B) 이 프로그램은 모든 직원을 대상으로 한 인증 과정으로 마무리될 것입니다.
(C) 팀원들은 어떤 평가도 완료할 필요가 없을 것입니다.
(D) 교육 구조에 대한 추가 변경 사항은 없을 것입니다.

해설 문맥상 새로운 직원 교육 프로그램이 소개되고, 마지막 부분에서는 프로그램의 향후 발전 가능성을 언급하고 있다. 특히 Finally로 시작하는 문장은 프로그램 개선 방향에 대한 추가 정보를 제공해야 하며, 참가자들의 피드백을 활용하여 프로그램을 개선한다는 내용이 자연스러운 흐름을 형성하므로 (A)가 가장 적절하다. (B)의 인증 과정으로 끝난다는 내용은 프로그램 개선과는 관련이 없고, (C)의 평가 과정을 요구하지 않는다는 내용은 교육 프로그램의 효과성과 발전을 언급하는 문맥과 동떨어져 있으며, (D)의 교육 프로그램의 발전을 위해 지속적인 개선을 논의하는 맥락에서 "변경이 없을 것"이라는 내용은 문맥상 부적합하다.

4.

해설 교육의 "효과적인 성과"를 언급하는 문맥과 가장 잘 어울리는 어휘가 필요하므로 (B) effective가 정답이다. (A) colorful은 "화려한", (C) optional은 "선택적인", (D) adaptable은 "적응할 수 있는, 융통성 있는"이라는 의미로 문맥에 맞지 않다.

PART 7

다음 공지와 직원 리뷰와 관련된 질문 1-5번을 보세요.

제목: 사무실 개조 공지
날짜: 2024년 9월 1일
수신: 모든 직원
발신: 시설 관리팀

팀 여러분께,
2024년 9월 15일부터 본사 건물의 3층과 4층

에서 개조 작업이 시작된다는 소식을 전하게 되어 기쁩니다. 이번 개조 작업은 작업 공간의 배치를 개선하고 사무실 장비를 업그레이드하기 위해 진행됩니다. 개조 작업은 약 6주간 진행될 예정이며, 완료 예정일은 2024년 10월 27일입니다. 이 기간 동안 3층과 4층에서 근무하는 직원들은 임시로 2층으로 이동하게 됩니다. 원활한 이전을 위해 2024년 9월 12일까지 개인 물품을 정리해 주시기 바랍니다. 좌석 배치와 관련된 자세한 내용은 별도의 이메일로 안내드릴 예정입니다.
이로 인해 발생할 불편함에 대해 사과드리며, 협조해 주셔서 감사드립니다. 질문이나 우려 사항이 있으시면 시설 관리팀(facilities@company.com)으로 언제든지 연락해 주시기 바랍니다.

감사합니다.
시설 관리팀 드림

제목: 최근 사무실 개조에 대한 제 경험
날짜: 2024년 11월 5일
발신: 마케팅 부서, 사라 김

최근 진행된 3층과 4층의 사무실 개조 작업은 성공적이었으며, 이에 대한 제 경험을 공유하고 싶습니다. 공사 기간은 예상대로 6주간 진행되었고, 초기에는 2층으로 임시 이동하면서 약간의 불편함이 있었습니다. 그러나 시설 관리팀은 전 과정에서 매우 도움을 주었고, 모든 직원들이 적절한 좌석과 필요한 자원을 제공받을 수 있도록 신경 써 주었습니다.
4층의 새로운 레이아웃은 정말 훌륭합니다. 열린 작업 공간과 업그레이드된 장비 덕분에 생산성이 향상되었으며, 팀원들은 특히 새로운 협업 공간에 매우 만족하고 있습니다. 전체적으로 보았을 때, 개조 작업은 일시적인 불편함 이상의 가치를 제공했습니다.
저는 이번 개조 작업이 훨씬 더 효율적이고 쾌적한 작업 환경을 조성했다고 믿으며, 앞으로의 개조 작업도 이번과 같은 접근 방식을 따르기를 권장합니다.

어휘 renovation 수리, 개조 layout 배치, 구성 upgrade 개선하다 expect 예상하다, 기대하다 projected 예상된, 추정된 temporarily 일시적으로, 임시로 relocate 이전하다, 재배치하다 facilitate 용이하게 하다, 촉진하다 transition 변화, 전환 seating arrangements 좌석 배치 inconvenience 불편, 번거로움 cooperation 협력, 협조 concerns 우려, 걱정 facilities management team 시설 관리팀 success 성공 construction period 공사 기간 temporary 임시적인, 임시의 relocation 이전 adequate 충분한, 적절한 open workspace 개방형 작업 공간 collaborative area 협업 공간 productivity 생산성 disruption 혼란, 중단 efficient 효율적인 pleasant 쾌적한, 기분 좋은 recommend 추천하다, 권장하다

정답

1. (C) 2. (B) 3. (D) 4. (B) 5.(A)

1. 3층과 4층 개조 작업은 언제 시작되었습니까?
   (A) 9월 1일
   (B) 9월 12일
   (C) 9월 15일
   (D) 10월 27일

해설 첫 번째 문서에서 “starting September 15, we will begin renovations on the 3rd and 4th floors”라고 명시되어 있어, 개조 작업이 9월 15일에 시작되었음을 알 수 있으므로 (C)가 정답이다. (A) September 1은 공지 발송일, (B) September 12는 개인 물품 포장 마감일, (D) October 27은 개조 완료 예상일로, 모두 문맥에 맞지 않다.

2. 개조 작업은 얼마나 걸렸습니까?
   (A) 4주
   (B) 6주
   (C) 8주
   (D) 2개월

해설 첫 번째 문서에서 “The renovation work is expected to last six weeks”라고 명시되어 있고, 두 번째 문서에서도 “The construction period lasted six weeks as expected”라고 언급되어 있어, 개조 작업이 6주 동안 진행되었음을 알 수 있으므로 (B)가 정답이다.

3. Sarah Kim이 개조 작업의 혜택으로 강조한 것은 무엇입니까?
   (A) 새로운 카페테리아

(B) 새로운 개인 사무실
(C) 개선된 조명 시스템
(D) 열린 작업 공간

해설 두 번째 문서에서 Sarah Kim은 "The new layout of the 4th floor is fantastic. The open workspaces and updated equipment have improved our productivity"라고 언급하며, 열린 작업 공간과 업데이트된 장비가 생산성을 높였다고 말했으므로 (D)가 정답이다.

4. 개조 작업 동안 직원들은 어디로 임시 이전하였습니까?
(A) 1층으로
(B) 2층으로
(C) 5층으로
(D) 인근 건물로

해설 첫 번째 문서에서 "employees working on the 3rd and 4th floors will be temporarily relocated to the 2nd floor"라고 명시되어 있어, 직원들이 임시로 2층으로 이전했음을 알 수 있으므로 (B)가 정답이다.

5. 문서에 따르면, 개조된 사무실의 주요 특징은 무엇입니까?
(A) 4층의 새로운 협업 공간
(B) 직원을 위한 업그레이드된 카페테리아
(C) 관리 직원을 위한 확장된 개인 사무실
(D) 방문객을 위한 개선된 주차 시설

해설 두 번째 문서에서 Sarah Kim은 "The team is particularly happy with the new collaborative areas"라고 언급하며, 새로운 협업 공간을 개조 작업의 주요 혜택으로 강조했으므로 (A)가 정답이다.

Chapter 11 부사

1. 부사의 위치

✔ CheckPoint 1. 동사 수식

정답

1. (A)　2. (A)　3. (D)

1.

번역 연구원들은 새 소프트웨어를 대중에게 공개하기 전에 광범위하게 테스트했다.

해설 동사 (+ 목적어) 뒤에 위치하여 동사 tested를 수식하는 부사를 찾는 문제이므로 (A) extensively가 정답이다.

어휘 release 출시하다, 공개하다 extensive 광범위한, 대규모의 extension 연장, 확장 extend 연장하다, 확장하다

2.

번역 프로젝트는 규정을 준수하기 위해 반드시 법률 팀에 의해 신중히 검토되어야 한다.

해설 조동사(must) 뒤에 위치하는 부사를 찾는 문제이므로 (A) carefully가 정답이다. 특히 이 지문처럼 조동사 2개(must, be)와 본동사(reviewed)가 있으면 제1 조동사 뒤에 부사가 위치한다.

어휘 review 검토하다 legal team 법률 팀 compliance 준수 regulation 규제, 규정

3.

번역 직원의 성과 평가는 공정성을 보장하기 위해 철저히 진행되었다.

해설 Be 동사(was) 뒤에 위치하는 부사를 찾는 문제이므로 (D) thoroughly가 정답이다.

어휘 performance evaluation 업무 평가, 성과 평가 conduct 수행하다, 진행하다 ensure 보장하다, 확실하게 하다 fairness 공정성, 공평함 thorough 철저한, 빈틈없는

2. 부사의 종류

✔ CheckPoint 2. 시간 부사

정답

1. (C) 2. (B) 3. (A)

1.

번역 그 팀은 이미 보고서를 완성하고 고객에게 보냈다.

해설 already는 "이미"라는 의미로, 긍정문의 현재완료 시제에 자주 사용되고, 특히 조동사 has와 본동사 finalized 사이에 위치하므로 (C) already가 정답이다. (A) yet은 부정문과 의문문에 주로 사용되지만 긍정문에는 사용되지 않고, (B) still은 "여전히"라는 의미로, 문맥에 맞지 않으며, (D) ago는 과거 시제에는 사용되지만 현재완료 시제에는 사용되지 않는다.

어휘 finalize 마무리하다, 완결하다 report 보고서, 리포트 client 고객, 의뢰인

2.

번역 회사는 새로운 정책에 대해 아직 어떤 결정도 내리지 않았다.

해설 yet은 부정문에서 "아직"이라는 의미로 사용되고, 문장의 뒤에 위치하므로 (B) yet이 정답이다. (A) already는 긍정문과 의문문에 주로 사용되지만 부정문에는 사용되지 않고, (C) soon은 "곧"이라는 의미로 미래 시제에 주로 사용되며, (D) once는 "한때"라는 의미로, 과거나 조건절에서 미래 시제에 사용되므로 문맥에 맞지 않다.

어휘 make a decision 결정을 내리다 policy 정책, 방침

3.

번역 새로운 CEO는 곧 회사의 장기 전략을 발표할 것이다.

해설 soon은 "곧"이라는 의미로 미래 시제에 주로 사용되고, 문장의 앞 또는 뒤에 위치하므로 (A) soon이 정답이다. (B) ago는 과거 시제에만 사용되므로 적절하지 않고, (C) still은 "여전히"라는 의미로, 미래 시제에 사용되지 않으며, (D) once는 "한때"라는 의미로, 과거나 조건절에서 미래 시제에 사용될 수 있지만 문맥에 맞지 않다.

어휘 announce 발표하다, 알리다 long-term strategy 장기 전략

✔ CheckPoint 3. 빈도나 정도 부사

정답

1. (A) 2. (B) 3. (D)

1.

번역 회사는 규정을 준수하기 위해 항상 안전점검을 시행한다.

해설 빈도 부사 always는 "항상"이라는 의미로 본동사(conducts) 앞에 위치하므로 (A) always가 정답이다. (B) slightly는 정도 부사로 "약간", (C) almost는 정도 부사로 "거의", (D) completely는 정도 부사로 "완전히"라는 의미를 가지며, 문맥에 적합하지 않다.

어휘 conduct 수행하다, 실시하다 safety inspection 안전 점검 compliance 준수 regulation 규정, 규제

2.

번역 마케팅 계획은 회사의 새로운 목표에 맞게 완전히 수정되었다.

해설 정도 부사 completely는 "완전히"라는 의미로, Be동사(was) 뒤에 위치하므로 (B) completely가 정답이다. (A) rarely는 빈도 부사로 "거의 ~않다", (C) sometimes는 빈도 부사로 "때때로", (D) very는 정도 부사로 "매우"라는 의미를 가지며, 문맥에 적합하지 않다. 특히 이 문장은 "수정이 얼마나 자주 이루어졌는지"가 아니라, "수정된 정도"를 묻고 있으므로 빈도 부사 sometimes는 문맥에 맞지 않다.

어휘 revise 수정하다, 개정하다 align with ~와 맞추다, ~와 일치하다

3.

번역 팀은 압박을 받을 때 때때로 긴급 작업을 완료할 수 있다.

해설 빈도 부사 sometimes는 "때때로"라는 의미로 조동사 can 뒤에 위치하므로 (D) sometimes가 정답이다. (A) slightly는 정도 부사로 "약간", (C) very는 정도 부사로 "매우", (D) completely는 정도 부사로 "완전히"라는 의미를 가지며, 문맥에 적합하지 않다.

어휘 complete 완료하다, 끝내다 urgent 긴급한 under pressure 압박을 받는

✔ CheckPoint 4. 접속 부사

정답

1. (D) 2. (A) 3. (B)

1.

번역 연구 데이터는 철저히 분석되었다; 그 결과, 팀은 주요 트렌드를 식별할 수 있었다.

해설 consequently는 "그 결과"라는 의미로 인과관계를 표현하며, 앞 문장의 원인(철저한 분석)과 뒤 문장의 결과(트렌드 식별)를 논리적으로 연결하므로 (D) consequently가 정답이다.

어휘 analyze 분석하다 thoroughly 철저히, 완전히 identify 확인하다

2.

번역 기한이 촉박했다; 그러나 팀은 프로젝트를 일정에 맞춰 완료할 수 있었다.

해설 however는 "그러나"라는 의미로 대조관계를 표현하며, 앞 문장의 부정적 상황(기한이 촉박함)과 뒤 문장의 긍정적 결과(일정 완료)를 논리적으로 연결하므로 (A) however가 정답이다.

어휘 deadline 마감 기한 tight 빠듯한, 엄격한 on schedule 예정대로, 일정에 맞춰

3.

번역 회사 행사에서 복장 규정을 따라야 한다; 그렇지 않으면 퇴장을 요청받을 수도 있다.

해설 otherwise는 "그렇지 않으면"이라는 의미로 조건적 상황을 표현하며, 앞 문장의 조건(복장 규정 준수)과 뒤 문장의 결과(퇴장 요청)를 논리적으로 연결하므로 (B) otherwise가 정답이다.

어휘 follow 따르다, 준수하다 dress code 복장 규정

3. 혼동하기 쉬운 부사

✔ CheckPoint 5. 혼동하기 쉬운 부사와 그 의미

정답

1. (B) 2. (C) 3. (C)

1.

번역 새 사무실 건물은 도심 근처에 있어 사업에 이상적인 위치이다.

해설 near는 "가까이"라는 의미로, 물리적 거리와 위치를 나타내는 문맥에 적합하므로 (B) near가 정답이다. (A) nearly는 "거의", (C) closely는 "면밀히", (D) high는 "높이"라는 의미로 문맥상 맞지 않다.

어휘 city center 도심, 시내 중심부 ideal location 이상적인 위치

2.

번역 작업자들은 수리를 완료하기 위해 지붕 위로 높이 올라갔다.

해설 high는 "높이"라는 의미로, 작업자들이 지붕 위로 높이 올라갔다는 내용과 부합하므로 (C) high가 정답이다. (A) closely는 "면밀히, 철저히", (B) mostly는 "대부분, 주로", (D) highly는 "매우"라는 의미로 문맥상 맞지 않다.

어휘 worker 노동자, 작업자 repair 수리, 보수 작업

3.

번역 새로운 매니저는 뛰어난 리더십 능력으로 팀원들로부터 매우 높이 평가받는다.

해설 highly는 "매우, 대단히"라는 의미로, 긍정적 평가나 감탄을 표현할 때 사용되며, 문맥에서 뛰어난 리더십 능력으로 팀원들로부터 매우 높이 평가받는다는 내용과 부합하므로 (C) highly가 정답이다. (A) close는 "가깝게", (B) lately는 "최근에", (C) high는 "높이"라는 의미로 문맥상 맞지 않다.

어휘 regard 간주하다, 평가하다 leadership skill 리더십 능력

✔ CheckPoint 6. 형용사와 부사의 형태가 같은 단어

정답

1. (A) 2. (C)

1.

번역 회사는 제품에 대한 증가하는 수요를 충족하는 데 어려운 도전에 직면하고 있다.

해설 hard는 "어려운"이라는 의미의 형용사로, 명사 challenge를 수식하여 '어려운 도전에 직면하고 있다'는 내용을 전달하므로 (A) hard가 정답이다. (B) most는 "대부분의", (C) close는 "가까운", (D) late는 "늦은"이라는 의미로 문맥상 맞지 않다.

어휘 face 직면하다 challenge 도전, 어려움 growing demand 증가하는 수요

2.

번역 고객 서비스 담당자는 고객의 문제를 해결하기 위해 신속히 응답했다.

해설 fast는 "신속히, 빨리"라는 의미의 부사로, 고객의 문제 해결을 위해 신속히 응답했다는 내용을 전달하므로 (C) fast가 정답이다. (A) late는 "늦게", (B) most는 "가장", (D) high는 "높이"라는 의미로 문맥상 맞지 않다.

어휘 customer service representative 고객 서비스 담당자 respond 응답하다, 대응하다 resolve 해결하다

토익 종합 실전문제

정답

1. (A)	2. (B)	3. (A)	4. (A)	5. (D)
6. (C)	7. (C)	8. (A)	9. (C)	10. (A)
11. (B)	12. (C)	13. (C)	14. (D)	15. (A)
16. (D)	17. (B)	18. (B)	19. (A)	20. (A)
21. (D)	22. (A)	23. (C)	24. (D)	

1.

번역 CEO는 직원들이 제기한 우려를 해결하기 위해 변경 사항을 공개적으로 발표했다.

해설 동사 (+ 목적어) 뒤에 위치하여 동사 announced를 수식하는 부사를 찾는 문제이므로 (A) publicly가 정답이다. (B) public은 형용사, (C) publicity는 명사, (D) publicize는 동사로, 문맥상 적절하지 않다.

어휘 announce 발표하다, 알리다 change 변화, 변경 사항 concerns 우려, 걱정

2.

번역 팀은 예정된 마감 기한보다 일찍 프로젝트를 완료했다.

해설 early는 "일찍"이라는 의미로, "예정보다 일찍(ahead of the deadline)"과 문맥상 가장 잘 부합할 수 있는 부사이므로 (B) early가 정답이다. (A) effectively는 "효과적으로", (C) easily는 "쉽게", (D) barely는 "간신히"라는 의미로, 문맥상 적절하지 않다.

어휘 complete 완료하다

3.

번역 이번 분기의 매출 수치는 이전 분기보다 상당히 높았다.

해설 significantly는 "상당히"라는 의미로, 비교급 higher를 수식하여 큰 차이를 나타내는 부사이므로 (A) significantly가 정답이다. (B) shortly는 "간단히, 곧", (C) rarely는 "드물게", (D) hastily는 "서둘러"라는 의미로, 문맥상 적절하지 않다.

어휘 sales figures 매출 수치, 매출액 quarter 분기 higher than ~보다 높은

4.

번역 그녀는 막 출장에서 돌아왔으며, 다음 프로젝트를 시작할 준비가 되어 있다.

해설 just는 긍정문의 현재완료 시제에서 조동사와 본동사 사이에 위치하여 "막"이라는 의미를 전달하므로 (A) just가 정답이다. (B) soon은 미래 시제에 주로 사용되고, (C) still은 "여전히"라는 의미로, 문맥상 적절하지 않으며, (D) yet은 부정문과 의문문에는 사용되지만 긍정문에는 사용되지 않는다.

어휘 business trip 출장

5.

번역 팀이 여전히 데이터를 수집하고 있기 때문에 그 보고서는 아직 제출되지 않았다.

해설 yet은 부정문에서 "아직"이라는 의미로 사용되고, 문장의 뒤에 위치하므로 (D) yet이 정답이다. (A) still은 "여전히"라는 의미로, 부정문에서 부정어 앞에 위치하므로 적절하지 않고, (B) just는 "막"이라는 의미로 긍정문, 부정문, 의문문에서 사용가능하지만 조동사와 본동사 사이에 위치해야 하므로 적절하지 않으며, (C) already는 긍정문과 의문문에서 "이미"라는 의미로 사용되지만 부정문에는 사용되지 않는다.

어휘 submit 제출하다 collet 수집하다, 모으다

6.

번역 3년 전에 그 회사는 심각한 어려움에 직면했지만, 그 이후로 놀라운 회복을 보여주었다.

해설 ago는 과거 시제와 결합하여 시간 표현 뒤에 사용되므로 (C) ago가 정답이다. (B) soon은 미래 시제에 주로 사용되고, (C) just는 현재완료나 과거 시제에서 "막"이라는 의미로 사용되지만, 문맥에 맞지 않으며, (D) already는 "이미"라는 의미로, 주로 현재완료나 과거 시제에서 사용되지만, ago처럼 시간 표현 뒤에 사용되지 않으므로 문맥에 맞지 않다.

어휘 face 직면하다, 마주하다 significant 심각한 recover 회복하다 remarkable 놀라운, 놀랄 만한

7.

번역 배송이 여전히 창고에 도착하지 않아 생산에 지연이 발생하고 있다.

해설 still은 부정문에서 "여전히"라는 의미로 사용되고, 부정어 앞에 위치하므로 (C) still이 정답이다. (A) yet은 부정문에서 "아직"이라는 의미로 사용되지만 문장의 뒤에 위치하므로 적절하지 않다.

어휘 shipment 배송, 선적 warehouse 창고 cause ~을 야기하다 production 생산

8.

번역 감독관은 바쁜 시기에는 결코 휴가 요청을 승인하지 않는다.

해설 빈도 부사 never는 "결코 ~않다"라는 의미로 본동사(approves) 앞에 위치하므로 (A) never가 정답이다. (B) almost는 정도 부사로 "거의", (C) completely는 정도 부사로 "완전히", (D) slightly는 정도 부사로 "약간"이라는 의미를 가지며, 문맥에 적합하지 않다.

어휘 supervisor 감독관, 관리자 approve 승인하다 vacation request 휴가 요청

9.

번역 고객의 피드백은 제안을 개선하는 데 매우 유용했다.

해설 정도 부사 very는 "매우, 아주"라는 의미로 Be동사(was) 뒤에 위치하여 형용사 helpful을 수식하므로 (C) very가 정답이다. (B) rarely는 빈도 부사로 "거의 ~않다", (C) sometimes는 빈도 부사로 "때때로", (D) seldom 빈도 부사로 "거의 ~않다"라는 의미를 가지며, 문맥에 적합하지 않다.

어휘 feedback 피드백, 의견 client 고객, 의뢰인 helpful 유용한 proposal 제안

10.

번역 그녀는 계속된 방해 때문에 마감 기한 전에 보고서를 거의 완료할 수 없었다.

해설 정도 부사 hardly는 "거의 ~않다"라는 의미로 조동사(could) 뒤에 위치하므로 (A) hardly가 정답이다. (B) occasionally는 빈도 부사로 "가끔", (C) usually는 빈도 부사로 "보통"이라는 의미를 가지며, 문맥에 적합하지 않고, (D) totally는 정도 부사로 "완전히"라는 의미를 가지지만 긍정적인 뉘앙스가 포함되어 부정적인 맥락에 적절하지 않다.

어휘 report 보고서 deadline 마감 기한 constant 끊임없는, 계속되는 interruption 방해

11.

번역 팀 리더는 업무량이 증가할 때 후배 직원들에게 거의 지침을 제공하지 않는다.

해설 빈도 부사 seldom은 "거의 ~않다"라는 의미로 조동사(can) 뒤에 위치하므로 (B) seldom이 정답이다. (A) almost는 정도 부사로 "거의", (C) slightly는 정도 부사로 "약간", (D) completely는 정도 부사로 "완전히"라는 의미를 가지며, 문맥에 적합하지 않다.

어휘 team leader 팀장 provide 제공하다 guidance 지침 workload 업무량, 작업량 increase 증가하다

12.

번역 마케팅 캠페인은 매우 성공적이었다; 그러므로, 회사는 다음 분기의 예산을 늘리기로 결정했다.

해설 accordingly는 "그러므로"라는 의미로 인과관계를 표현하며, 앞 문장의 원인(캠페인의 성공)과 뒤 문장의 결과(예산 증가)를 논리적으로 연결하므로 (C) accordingly가 정답이다.

어휘 budget 예산 next quarter 다음 분기

13.

번역 공장은 생산 능력을 확장했다; 그럼에도 불구하고, 공급망은 증가하는 수요를 충족할 수 없었다.

해설 nonetheless는 "그럼에도 불구하고"라는 의미로 대조관계를 표현하며, 앞 문장의 긍정적 상황(생산 능력 확장)과 뒤 문장의 부정적 결과(공급망 부족)를 논리적으로 연결하므로 (C) nonetheless가 정답이다.

어휘 production capacity 생산 능력 supply chain 공급망

14.

번역 프로젝트를 시작하기 전에 반드시 안전 교육을 완료해야 한다; 그렇지 않으면 참여가 허용되지 않을 것이다.

해설 otherwise는 "그렇지 않으면"이라는 의미로 조건적 상황을 표현하며, 앞 문장의 조건(교육 완료)과 뒤 문장의 결과(참여 불가)를 논리적으로 연결하므로 (D) otherwise가 정답이다.

어휘 allow 허용하다 participate 참여하다, 참가하다

15.

번역 팀은 오늘 프레젠테이션을 최종 확정해야 한다; 그렇지 않으면 제출 기한을 놓치게 될 것이다.

해설 or else는 "그렇지 않으면"이라는 의미로 조건적 상황을 표현하며, 앞 문장의 조건(프레젠테이션 확정)과 뒤 문장의 결과(기한 초과)를 논리적으로 연결하므로 (A) or else가 정답이다.

어휘 finalize 마무리 짓다 presentation 프레젠테이션 submission deadline 제출 기한

16.

번역 새로운 전략은 효과가 입증되었으며, 비용을 줄이고 효율성도 또한 증가시킨다.

해설 as well은 "또한, 게다가"라는 의미로, 문장의 뒤에서 추가적인 정보를 덧붙일 때 사용되므로 (D) as well이 정답이다. (C) also는 "또한, 역시"라는 의미로, 문장 중간에 사용되므로 여기서는 적합하지 않다.

어휘 prove 입증하다, 드러나다 effective 효과적

인 reduce 줄이다, 감소하다 increase 높이다, 증가하다 efficiency 효율성

17.

번역 지침이 너무 불명확해서 나는 무엇을 해야 할지 거의 이해할 수 없었다.

해설 hardly는 "거의 ~않다"라는 의미로, 설명이 불명확해 이해하지 못한다는 내용과 부합하므로 (B) hardly가 정답이다. (A) hard는 "열심히", (C) nearly는 "거의", (D) carefully는 "신중히"라는 의미로 문맥상 맞지 않다.

어휘 instruction 지침, 설명서 unclear 불명확한

18.

번역 회사 정책은 조직에 대한 직원들의 기여를 공정하게 보상하도록 설계되었다.

해설 justly는 "공정하게"라는 의미로, 회사 정책이 직원의 기여를 공정하게 평가하고 보상하는 상황에 적합하므로 (B) justly가 정답이다. (A) highly는 "매우", (C) hardly는 "거의 ~않다", (D) slightly는 "약간"이라는 의미로 문맥상 맞지 않다.

어휘 policy 정책, 방침 contribution 기여, 공헌

19.

번역 감독관은 모든 안전 수칙이 준수되었는지 직원들을 면밀히 감시했다.

해설 closely는 "면밀히, 철저히"라는 의미로, 감독이나 관찰과 같은 상황에서 사용되며, 안전 수칙이 준수되었는지 면밀히 감시했다는 내용과 부합하므로 (A) closely가 정답이다. (B) close는 "가깝게", (C) nearly는 "거의", (D) most는 "가장"이라는 의미로 문맥상 맞지 않다.

어휘 supervisor 감독관, 관리자 monitor 관찰하다, 감시하다 ensure 확인하다, 보장하다 safety protocol 안전 수칙

20.

번역 팀은 촉박한 기한을 맞추기 위해 열심히 일하며 큰 결단력을 보여주었다.

해설 hard는 "열심히"라는 의미로, 팀이 촉박한 기한을 맞추기 위해 열심히 일했다는 내용과 부합하므로 (A) hard가 정답이다. (B) hardly는 "거의 ~않다", (C) rarely는 "거의 ~않다", (D) nearly는 "거의"라는 의미로 문맥상 맞지 않다.

어휘 tight deadline 촉박한 기한 determination 결단력, 투지

21.

번역 그녀는 프로젝트에 대한 혁신적인 기여로 매우 칭송받고 있다.

해설 highly는 "매우, 대단히"라는 의미로, 긍정적 평가나 감탄을 표현할 때 사용되며, 문맥에서 혁신적 기여로 높은 칭찬을 받았다는 내용과 부합하므로 (D) highly가 정답이다. (A) slightly는 "약간", (B) hardly는 "거의 ~않다", (C) high는 "높이"라는 의미로 문맥상 맞지 않다.

어휘 praise 칭찬하다 innovative 혁신적인 contribution 기여, 공헌

22.

번역 매니저는 모든 사람이 지침을 이해할 수 있도록 충분히 명확하게 말했다.

해설 enough는 "충분히"라는 의미의 부사로, 부사 clearly를 후치 수식하여 "충분히 명확하게 말했다"는 내용을 전달하므로 (A) enough가 정답이다. (B) hard는 "열심히", (C) near는 "가까이", (D) well는 "잘"이라는 의미로 문맥상 맞지 않다.

23.

번역 자재의 높은 품질이 고객들에게 깊은 인상을 주었고 프로젝트의 성공을 보장했다.

해설 high는 "높은"이라는 의미의 형용사로, 명사 quality를 수식하여 "높은 품질"이라는 내용을 전달하므로 (C) high가 정답이다. (A) late는 "늦은", (B) highly는 "매우", (D) early는 "이른, 초기의"이라는 의미로 문맥상 맞지 않다.

어휘 quality 품질 material 자재 impress 깊은 인상을 주다

24.

번역 기술자는 안전 지침에 따라 장비가 정확히 설치되었는지 확인했다.

해설 right는 "바로, 정확히"라는 의미의 부사로, 장비가 안전 지침에 따라 정확히 설치되었음을 강조하므로 (D) right가 정답이다. (A) closely는 "면밀히", (B) high는 "높이", (C) late는 "늦게"라는 의미로 문맥상 맞지 않다.

어휘 technician 기술자 equipment 장비 install 설치하다 according to ~에 따라 safety guideline 안전 지침

PART 6

다음 기사와 관련된 질문 1-4번을 보세요.

> 직장 내 의사소통 개선
>
> 효과적인 직장 내 의사소통은 협업과 생산성을 촉진하는 데 매우 중요합니다. 명확하고 간결한 의사소통은 직원들이 자신의 역할과 책임을 이해하도록 도와주며, 오해의 위험을 줄입니다. 또한, 직원들에게 회사 목표와 변화에 대한 정기적인 업데이트를 제공하면 모두가 집중하고 동기를 유지할 수 있도록 도와줍니다. 매니저는 직원들의 피드백에 신속히 응답하여 그들의 우려가 존중받고 있음을 보여주어야 합니다. 또한, 조직은 팀 회의와 피드백 세션을 통해 개방적인 의사소통을 장려해야 합니다. 이러한 실천은 투명성을 보장하고 팀원 간 신뢰를 구축합니다. 직원들이 자신의 목소리가 반영된다고 느낄 때, 아이디어를 제안하거나 우려를 표현할 가능성이 더 높아지며, 이는 보다 포용적인 업무 환경으로 이어집니다. 의사소통 개선 활동의 성공을 보장하기 위해, 회사는 고유한 직장 문화에 실용적이고 효과적인 전략을 채택해야 합니다.

어휘 workplace 직장, 작업장 communication 의사소통, 소통 effective 효과적인 collaboration 협업, 협력 concise 간결한 responsibility 책임, 의무 misunderstanding 오해 regular 정기적인 update 최신 정보, 최신 정보를 제공하다 goal 목표 motivated 동기 부여된, 의욕이 있는 feedback 피드백, 반응 respond 응답하다, 반응하다 concerns 우려, 걱정 contribute 기여하다, 공헌하다 express 표현하다 work environment 근무 환경 initiative 주도권, 계획 unique 독특한, 고유한

정답

1. (C) 2. (A) 3. (C) 4. (A)

1.

해설 직장 내 의사소통이 협업(collaboration)을 촉진한다는 내용에서 협업이 원활히 이루어지면 업무 진행이 효과적이고 생산성이 높아지므로, 협업과 생산성(productivity)이라는 조합이 가장 적절하므로 (C) productivity가 정답이다. (A) relaxation은 "휴식", (B) confusion은 "혼란", (D) retention은 "유지"라는 의미로 문맥에 맞지 않다.

2.

해설 문맥에서 매니저가 직원들의 피드백에 빠르게 응답하는 것이 중요하다는 내용을 정확히 전달할 어휘가 필요하므로 (A) promptly가 정답이다. (B) nearly는 "거의", (C) highly는 "매우", (D) lately는 "최근에"라는 의미로 문맥에 맞지 않다.

3.

(A) 정기적인 업데이트는 직장 내 사기를 높이는 데 매우 중요합니다.

(B) 명확한 의사소통은 직원들이 업무에 집중하도록 돕습니다.

(C) 이러한 실천은 투명성을 보장하고 팀원 간 신뢰를 구축합니다.

(D) 직원들은 정기적으로 피드백을 제공하도록 권장됩니다.

해설 앞 문장에서 팀 회의와 피드백 세션에 대해 언급된 후, 이러한 실천의 결과와 효과를 설명하는 문장이 필요하므로 (C)가 가장 적절하다. (A)는 앞 문장에서 "정기적인 업데이트"에 대해 이미 다루었으므로 문맥상 중복되고, (B)는 의사소통의 일반적인 중요성을 언급하지만, 팀 회의와 피드백 세션의 효과를 구체적으로 설명하지 않으므로 적절하지 않으며, (D)는 앞 문장에서 피드백 제공과 관련된 내용이 이미 다뤄졌으므로 문맥상 적절하지 않다.

4.

해설 직원들이 자신의 목소리가 반영된다고 느낄 때, 아이디어를 제안하거나 우려를 표현할 가능성이 더 높아지며, 이는 더 포용적인 업무 환경으로 이어지므로 (A) inclusive가 정답이다. (B) demanding은 "요구가 많은, 힘든", (C) chaotic은 "혼란스러운", (D) exclusive는 "배타적인"이라는 의미로 문맥에 맞지 않다.

PART 7

다음 채용 공고와 내부 이메일과 관련된 질문 1-5번을 보세요.

> 직책: 마케팅 매니저
> 근무지: 뉴욕, NY
> 회사: 에이펙스 이노베이션즈
>
> Apex Innovations는 선도적인 기술 회사로, 당사의 팀에 합류할 고도로 숙련된 마케팅 매니저를 찾고 있습니다. 이상적인 지원자는 신제품을 홍보하고 시장 점유율을 확대하기 위한 마케팅 전략을 개발하고 실행하는 역할을 맡게 됩니다. 채용된 지원자는 영업팀, 제품 개발자, 외부 파트너와 긴밀히 협력하게 될 것입니다.
> 주요 업무:
> •마케팅 캠페인 기획 및 관리
> •시장 동향 및 경쟁사 분석
> •마케팅 예산 관리 및 높은 ROI(투자 대비 수익률) 보장
> •제품 출시와 마케팅 전략을 일치시키기 위한 제품팀과의 협업
> •캠페인 결과를 경영진에게 보고
> 자격 요건:
> •마케팅 또는 관련 분야 학사 학위
> •마케팅 경력 5년 이상
> •성공적인 마케팅 캠페인에 대한 입증된 실적
> •뛰어난 의사소통 및 리더십 능력
> 지원하려면 9월 15일까지 이력서와 자기소개서를 careers@apexinnovations.com으로 보내주세요.

> 보낸 사람: 제임스 리 (마케팅 디렉터)
> 받는 사람: 마케팅 부서
> 날짜: 8월 5일
> 제목: 팀 회의 - OmegaX 제품 출시
>
> 팀 여러분,
> 여러분이 아시는 바와 같이, 많은 기대를 받고 있는 OmegaX 스마트워치가 8월 20일에 출시될 예정입니다. 성공적인 출시를 위해 철저히 준비하고자 합니다. 8월 10일 오전 10시에 회의를 열어 마케팅 캠페인의 세부 사항을 마무리할 예정입니다.
> 회의 안건:
> •현재 시장 동향 및 경쟁사 분석 검토
> •OmegaX 마케팅 전략 논의
> •예산 및 자원 배분 확정
> •캠페인 실행을 위한 업무 분담
> 최대한의 효과를 낼 수 있는 아이디어를 준비해 오시기 바랍니다. 이번 제품 출시를 성공적으로 이루기 위해 우리가 효과적으로 협력하는 것이 중요합니다.
>
> 감사합니다.
> 제임스 리
> 에이펙스 이노베이션즈 마케팅 디렉터

어휘 position 직위, 직책 marketing manager 마케팅 매니저 location 위치, 장소 leading 선도적인, 주요한 skilled 숙련된, 능숙한 develop 개발하다, 발전시키다 execute 실행하다, 수행하다 marketing strategy 마케팅 전략 market share 시장 점유율 collaborate 협력하다 external partner 외부 파트너 campaign 캠페인, 홍보 활동 analyze 분석하다 competitor 경쟁자, 경쟁사 ROI (Return On Investment) 투자 대비 수익률 align 맞추다, 정렬하다 product launch 제품 출시 track record 실적, 경력 resume 이력서 cover letter 자기소개서 subject 제목 anticipate 기대하다 ensure 보장하다, 확실히 하다 fully 완전히 prepare 준비하다 finalize 마무리하다, 확정하다 details 세부 사항 agenda 의제, 안건 strategy 전략 budget 예산 resource 자원 allocation 할당 execution 실행 maximize 극대화하다

정답

1. (C) 2. (A) 3. (D) 4. (B) 5.(C)

1. Apex Innovations의 마케팅 매니저 직책 지원 마감일은 언제입니까?
   (A) 8월 10일

(B) 8월 20일
(C) 9월 15일
(D) 8월 5일

해설 첫 번째 문서(Job Posting)에서 "To apply, send your resume and cover letter to careers@apexinnovations.com by September 15."라고 명시되어 있어 지원 마감일이 9월 15일임을 알 수 있으므로 (C)가 정답이다.

2. 채용 공고에 나열된 마케팅 매니저의 책임 중 하나는 무엇입니까?
(A) 마케팅 캠페인 기획 및 관리
(B) 고객 서비스 팀 관리
(C) 제품 개발 감독
(D) OmegaX 스마트워치 설계

해설 첫 번째 문서(Job Posting)의 "Responsibilities include" 섹션에 "Creating and managing marketing campaigns"이라고 명시되어 있으므로 (A)가 정답이다.

3. 내부 이메일에 따르면 8월 10일 회의에서 논의될 내용은 무엇입니까?
(A) 신입 사원 채용 절차
(B) 새로운 스마트워치 출시
(C) 내년 제품 개발 전략
(D) OmegaX 마케팅 캠페인 계획

해설 두 번째 문서(Internal Email)에서 "We will hold a meeting on August 10 at 10:00 AM to finalize the details of the marketing campaign."이라고 명시되어 있어 8월 10일 회의의 주요 논의 주제가 OmegaX 마케팅 캠페인 계획임을 알 수 있으므로 (D)가 정답이다.

4. 채용 공고에 따르면 마케팅 매니저 직책에 필요한 자격 요건은 무엇입니까?
(A) 경영학 석사 학위
(B) 마케팅 경력 5년 이상
(C) 기술 회사 근무 경험
(D) 뛰어난 그래픽 디자인 기술

해설 첫 번째 문서(Job Posting)의 "Qualifications" 섹션에서 "5+ years of marketing experience"라고 명시되어 있어 마케팅 경력 5년 이상이 필수 자격 요건임을 알 수 있으므로 (B)가 정답이다.

5. 내부 이메일은 채용 공고와 어떻게 관련이 있습니까?
(A) OmegaX 스마트워치 출시가 지연될 것임을 확인합니다.
(B) 미래 마케팅 매니저의 책임을 강조합니다.
(C) Apex Innovations의 현재 마케팅 팀의 업무를 설명합니다.
(D) 마케팅 매니저 역할이 더 이상 필요하지 않음을 보여줍니다.

해설 두 번째 문서(Internal Email)는 현재 마케팅 팀이 OmegaX 출시를 준비하기 위해 수행하는 업무와 계획에 대해 설명하고 있으므로 (C)가 정답이다.

Chapter 12 전치사

1. 시간(Time) 전치사

CheckPoint 1. 시간 전치사의 종류

정답

1. (C) 2. (C) 3. (B)

1.

번역 도서관은 주중에 오후 9시까지 운영된다.

해설 이 문장은 "주중에 오후 9시까지"라는 특정 시점까지 지속되는 상태나 행동, 특히 지속성 강조하므로 (C) until이 정답이다. (A) by는 특정 시점 이전에 완료되는 일회성 행동이나 행위, 특히 기한을 강조하므로 도서관 운영처럼 지속성 행위와는 맞지 않다.

2.

번역 직원들은 3시간 동안 쉬지 않고 보고서를 작성해 왔다.

해설 이 문장은 "3시간 동안"이라는 숫자 기간과 함께 사용되었으므로 (C) for가 정답이다. (A) during은 특정 기간 동안 발생한 일을 나타내고, (B) since는 특정 시점부터 현재까지의 기간을 나타낼 때 사용하며, (C) within은 "5년 이내에"라는 의미로 특정 기한 내에 완료된 일을 표현할 때 사용되며, (D) until은 특정 시점까지 지속되는 상태나 행동을 나타내므로 문맥과 맞지 않다.

3.

번역 새로운 정책은 1월 1일부터 시행되었다.

해설 이 문장은 "1월 1일부터"라는 특정 시점부터 현재까지의 기간을 나타내므로 (B) since가 정답이다.

어휘 policy 정책, 방침 effective 효과적인

2. 장소(Place) 전치사

✔ CheckPoint 2. 장소 전치사의 종류

정답

1. (A) 2. (B) 3. (D)

1.

번역 홍보 포스터는 쇼핑센터의 벽에 부착되었다.

해설 홍보 포스터가 벽 표면에 붙어 있으므로 (A) on이 정답이다.

어휘 promotional 홍보의, 판촉의

2.

번역 사무실 건물은 강 근처에 위치하여 직원들에게 아름다운 경관을 제공한다.

해설 강 근처에 있는 사무실의 위치를 설명하고 있으므로 (B) near가 정답이다.

어휘 locate 위치하다 offer 제공하다, 제시하다

3.

번역 기념 명판은 박물관 출입구 위에 설치되어 있다.

해설 접촉 없이 출입구보다 더 높은 위치에 고정된 기념 명판의 위치를 설명하고 있으므로 (D) above가 정답이다.

어휘 memorial 기념의 plaque 명판, 표지판 doorway 출입구

기타 주요 전치사

✔ CheckPoint 3. 기타 주요 전치사의 종류

정답

1. (C) 2. (A) 3. (C)

1.

번역 회의는 예상치 못한 날씨 조건 때문에 연기되었다.

해설 "예상치 못한 날씨 때문에"는 이유를 나타내므로 (C) because of가 정답이다.

어휘 conference 회의 postpone 연기하다 unexpected 예상치 못한 condition 조건

2.

번역 교육 프로그램에는 고객 불만을 처리하는 것과 관련된 섹션이 포함되어 있다.

해설 "고객 불만을 처리하는 것과 관련된"은 주제를 나타내므로 (A) regarding이 정답이다.

어휘 include 포함하다 handle 다루다, 처리하다 complaint 불만, 불평

3.

번역 예상치 못한 일정 변경에도 불구하고, 팀은 제시간에 프로젝트를 완료했다.

해설 "일정 변경에도 불구하고"는 양보를 나타내므로 (C) Despite가 정답이다.

4. 전치사의 관용표현

✔ CheckPoint 4. 전치사의 관용표현

정답

1. (A)	2. (D)	3. (B)

1.

번역 공장의 생산 공정이 현재 고장 나 있으며 다음 주에 재개될 것이다.

해설 "out of order"는 "고장 난"이라는 의미로, 생산 공정이 현재 작동하지 않음을 나타내는 문맥에 적합하므로 (A) out of order가 정답이다.

어휘 currently 현재, 지금 resume 재개하다

2.

번역 팀 리더는 다가오는 행사의 물류를 조정하는 것을 담당하고 있다.

해설 "in charge of"는 "~을 담당하여"라는 의미로, 팀 리더가 물류 조정을 맡고 있음을 설명하는 문맥에 적합하므로 (D) in charge of가 정답이다.

어휘 coordinate 조정하다 logistics 물류 upcoming 다가오는

3.

번역 기술자는 적절한 도구와 장비의 도움으로 기계를 수리할 수 있었다.

해설 "with the help of"는 "~의 도움으로"라는 의미로, 기술자가 도구와 장비를 사용하여 기계를 수리했다는 문맥에 적합하므로 (B) with the help of가 정답이다.

어휘 technician 기술자 repair 수리하다 proper 적절한 equipment 장비

토익 종합 실전문제

정답

1. (A)	2. (A)	3. (C)	4. (B)	5. (D)
6. (C)	7. (B)	8. (C)	9. (C)	10. (B)
11. (D)	12. (A)	13. (A)	14. (B)	15. (B)
16. (D)	17. (B)	18. (A)	19. (B)	20. (C)
21. (C)	22. (D)	23. (A)	24. (A)	

1.

번역 직원들은 금요일 정오까지 보고서를 제출해야 한다.

해설 이 문장은 "금요일 정오"라는 특정 시점까지 보고서를 제출해야 하는 마감일을 나타내므로 특정 시점 이전에 완료되는 일회성 행동이나 행위, 특히 기한을 강조하므로 (A) by가 정답이다. (B) until은 특정 시점까지 지속되는 상태나 행동, 특히 지속성 강조하므로 제출이라는 단발성 행위와는 맞지 않다.

어휘 submit 제출하다

2.

번역 그 회사는 지난 5년 동안 괄목할 만한 성장을 경험했다.

해설 이 문장은 "지난 5년 동안"이라는 특정 기간 동안 발생한 일을 나타내므로 (A) during이 정답이다. (B) since는 특정 시점부터 현재까지의 기간을 나타낼 때 사용하고, (C) within은 "5년 이내에"라는 의미로 특정 기한 내에 완료된 일을 표현할 때 사용되며, (D) for는 숫자 기간과 함께 사용되므로 문맥상 맞지 않다.

어휘 remarkable 놀라운, 괄목할 만한 growth 성장

3.

번역 모든 고객 불만은 제출 후 36시간 이내에 처리될 것이다.

해설 이 문장은 "36시간 이내에"라는 특정 기한 내에 완료된 일을 나타내므로 (C) within이 정답이다.

어휘 address 처리하다, 다루다 submission 제출

4.

번역 이 제품은 2년 동안 개발 중이었으며 이번 분기에 출시될 예정이다.

해설 이 문장은 "2년 동안"이라는 숫자 기간과 함께 사용되었으므로 (B) for가 정답이다.

어휘 development 개발 launch 출시하다, 시작하다 quarter 분기

5.

번역 발표는 추가 공지가 있을 때까지 연기되었다.

해설 이 문장은 "추가 공지가 있을 때까지"라는 특정 시점까지 지속되는 상태나 행동을 나타내므로 (D) until이 정답이다.

어휘 announcement 발표 further notice 추가 공지

6.

번역 직원들은 지난주 회의가 연기된 이후로 업데이트를 받지 못했다.

해설 이 문장은 "회의가 연기된 이후로"라는 특정 시점부터 현재까지의 기간을 나타내므로 (C) since가 정답이다.

어휘 receive 받다 postpone 연기하다, 지연하다

7.

번역 새로운 쇼핑몰은 도시 스카이라인 위에 건설 중이며, 멀리서도 볼 수 있다.

해설 쇼핑몰이 스카이라인보다 접촉 없이 더 높은 위치에 건설 중이라는 의미이므로 (B) above가 정답이다.

어휘 construct 건설하다 skyline 스카이라인, 하늘과 맞닿은 윤곽선 visible 보이는, 알아볼 수 있는

8.

번역 팀은 새 프로젝트 제안을 논의하기 위해 회의 테이블에 앉아 있다.

해설 회의 테이블이라는 특정 지점을 가리키므로 (C) at이 정답이다.

어휘 discuss 논의하다, 토의하다 proposal 제안

9.

번역 회의실은 CEO 사무실과 대회의실 사이에 위치해 있다.

해설 CEO 사무실과 대회의실이라는 두 장소 사이의 위치를 나타내므로 (C) between이 정답이다.

어휘 locate 위치하다

10.

번역 주차장은 직원들의 편의를 위해 사무실 건물 아래에 위치해 있다.

해설 물리적 접촉 여부와 상관없이 사무실보다 더 낮은 위치를 나타내므로 (B) below가 정답이다.

어휘 convenience 편의

11.

번역 보안 카메라는 주차장 구석구석에 설치되어 있다.

해설 보안 카메라가 주차장의 모든 구석에 설치되었다는 의미이므로 (D) throughout이 정답이다.

어휘 security camera 보안 카메라 install 설치하다

12.

번역 매니저는 프로젝트 동안의 뛰어난 성과 때문에 팀을 칭찬했다.

해설 "뛰어난 성과 때문에"는 이유를 나타내므로 (A) on account of가 정답이다.

어휘 praise 칭찬하다 outstanding 뛰어난, 훌륭한 performance 성과, 실적

13.

번역 새로운 정책은 직원 생산성을 향상시키기 위해 도입되었다.

해설 "직원 생산성을 향상시키기 위해"는 목적을 나타내므로 (A) for가 정답이다.

어휘 implement 실행하다, 도입하다 improve 개선하다, 향상시키다 productivity 생산성

14.

번역 팀은 이용 가능한 제한된 자원에도 불구하고 프로젝트를 성공적으로 완료했다.

해설 "제한된 자원에도 불구하고"는 양보를 나타내므로 (B) in spite of가 정답이다.

어휘 limited 제한된 available 이용 가능한

15.

번역 모든 직원은 새롭게 발표된 지침에 관한 회의에 참석해야 한다.

해설 "새롭게 발표된 지침에 관한"은 주제를 나타내므로 (B) concerning이 정답이다.

어휘 require 요구하다 attend 참석하다 guideline 지침

16.

번역 최종 보고서는 매니저의 구체적인 지시를 통해 준비되었다.

해설 "구체적인 지시를 통해"는 수단을 나타내므로 (D) via가 정답이다.

어휘 prepare 준비하다 specific 구체적인, 특정한 instruction 지시, 지침

17.

번역 기조 연설자를 제외하고 모든 참석자는 30분 일찍 도착해야 한다.

해설 "기조 연설자를 제외하고"는 제외를 나타내므로 (B) except for가 정답이다.

어휘 keynote speaker 기조 연설자 attendee 참석자, 참가자

18.

번역 뛰어난 학업 성적 외에도 그 후보자는 광범위한 업무 경험을 가지고 있다.

해설 "뛰어난 학업 성적 외에도"는 부가를 나타내므로 (A) In addition to가 정답이다.

어휘 excellent 뛰어난 academic performance 학업 성적 candidate 지원자, 후보자 extensive 광범위한

19.

번역 장비는 고객에게 추가 비용 없이 교체될 것이다.

해설 "at no extra charge"는 "추가 비용 없이"라는 의미로, 고객이 추가 요금을 지불하지 않고 장비를 교체 받을 수 있음을 나타내는 문맥에 적합하므로 (B) at no extra charge가 정답이다.

어휘 equipment 장비 replace 교체하다

20.

번역 회사는 직원들의 지속적인 성장을 보장하기 위해 정기적으로 성과 평가를 실시한다.

해설 "on a regular basis"는 "정기적으로"라는 의미로, 회사가 직원들의 성장을 위해 정기적으로 평가를 실시한다는 문맥에 적합하므로 (C) on a regular basis가 정답이다.

어휘 conduct 수행하다, 실시하다 performance evaluation 성과 평가 ensure 보장하다 consistent 일관된, 지속적인 development 성장, 개발

21.

번역 모든 참가자를 수용하기 위해 회의실이 미리 예약되었다.

해설 "in advance"는 "미리, 사전에"라는 의미로, 참가자 수를 고려하여 사전에 예약되었다는 문맥에 적합하므로 (C) in advance가 정답이다.

어휘 reserve 예약하다 accommodate 수용하다 participant 참가자

22.

번역 회사는 프로젝트에 대한 혁신적인 접근 방식을 통해 계약을 확보할 수 있었다.

해설 "by means of"는 "~을 통해, ~을 수단으로"라는 의미로, 혁신적인 접근 방식을 통해 계약을 확보했다는 문맥에 적합하므로 (D) by means of가 정답이다.

어휘 contract 계약, 계약서 innovative 혁신적인 approach 접근 방식, 접근법

23.

번역 고객 문의는 만족도를 유지하기 위해 시기적절하게 처리되어야 한다.

해설 "in a timely manner"는 "시기적절하게"라는 의미로, 고객 만족을 위해 고객 문의가 적절한 시간에 처리되어야 한다는 문맥에 적합하므로 (A) in a timely manner가 정답이다.

어휘 inquiry 문의, 질문 address 처리하다, 다루다 maintain 유지하다 satisfaction 만족

24.

번역 안전 규정은 정부 규정의 최근 변경 사항과 관련하여 개정되었다.

해설 "with respect to"는 "~에 관하여"라는 의미로, 정부 규정의 변경 사항과 관련하여 안전 규정을 개정했다는 문맥에 적합하므로 (A) with respect to가 정답이다.

어휘 safety protocol 안전 규정 revise 수정하다 recent 최근의 government 정부 regulation 규제, 규정

PART 6

다음 편지와 관련된 질문 1-4번을 보세요.

> 팀원 여러분께,
> 다음 달부터 시행될 직원 핸드북의 최근 업데이트 내용을 알려드리고자 이 편지를 작성합니다. 이번 변경 사항은 우리의 직장 정책을 개선하고 모든 직원에게 보다 지원적인 환경을 제공하는 것을 목표로 하고 있습니다.
> 먼저, 휴가 정책이 조정되었습니다. 직원들은 관리자들이 일정 계획을 더 효과적으로 수립할 수 있도록, 최소 2주 전에 휴가 요청서를 제출할 것을 권장합니다.
> 둘째, 재택근무 지침을 다루는 새로운 섹션이 추가되었습니다. 핸드북에는 재택근무를 하는 직원들을 위한 명확한 기대 사항이 포함되어 있으며, 여기에는 근무 가능 시간과 관리자와의 정기 체크인이 포함됩니다.
> 마지막으로, 직장 안전 규정에 대한 업데이트된 섹션을 주목해 주시기 바랍니다. 모든 직원은 이 업데이트를 검토하고 첨부된 양식에 서명함으로써 이를 확인해야 합니다.
> 변경 사항에 대해 궁금한 점이 있으시면 부서장이나 HR팀에 언제든 문의하시기 바랍니다. 긍정적이고 생산적인 근무 환경을 위해 협조해 주셔서 감사합니다.
>
> 감사합니다,
> Alex Johnson
> HR 매니저

어휘 take effect 효력이 발생하다 aim at ~을 노리다, ~을 목표로 하다 improve 개선하다, 향상시키다 supportive 지원하는, 도와주는 adjustment 조정, 수정 encourage 권장하다 submit 제출하다 request 요청 time off 휴식 시간 at least 적어도, 최소한 effectively 효과적으로 expectation 기대 include 포함하다 availability hour 근무 가능 시간 regular 정기적인 acknowledge 인정하다 cooperation 협력 strive 추구하다, 갈망하다 productive 생산적인

정답

1. (C) 2. (B) 3. (A) 4. (C)

1.

해설 "일정 계획을 더 효과적으로 수립할 수 있도록, 최소 2주 전에 휴가 요청서를 제출할 것을 권장"하는 문장에서 "최소 2주 전에"라는 표현은 "사전에"라는 의미를 나타내므로 (C) in advance가 정답이다. (A) on time는 "제시간에", (B) in detail은 "자세히", (D) by tomorrow는 "내일까지"라는 의미로 문맥과 맞지 않다.

2.

(A) 현재 휴가 정책에 대한 조정이 필요합니다.
(B) 재택근무 지침을 다루는 새로운 섹션이 추가되었습니다.
(C) 재택근무자를 위한 추가 혜택이 발표되었습니다.
(D) 재택근무 정책은 변경되지 않았습니다.

해설 전후 문맥을 보면 "다음 달부터 시행될 업데이트된 정책"과 "직장 정책을 개선하고 모든 직원에게 보다 지원적인 환경을 제공하는 새로운 추가 사항"을 강조하고 있으므로 재택근무 지침을 다루는 새로운 섹션이 추가되었다는 내용의 (B)가 가장 적절하다. (A)의 "휴가 정책"에 대한 내용이 본문에 언급되지 않았고, (C)의 "추가 혜택"에 대한 내용도 본문에 언급되지 않았으며, (D)는 본문과 상반된 내용이므로 적절하지 않다.

3.

해설 on은 특정 주제나 내용을 언급할 때 사용하는 가장 적합한 전치사이므로 (A) on이 정답이다.

4.

해설 문맥상 직원들이 "첨부된 양식(attached form)"에 서명해야 한다는 의미를 나타내므로 (C) attached가 정답이다. (A) accompanying은 "수반하는, 동반하는"이라는 의미로, 첨부 파일이 아닌 함께 제공되거나 동반된 내용을 나타낼 때 사용되고, (B) affixed는 "부착된"이라는 의미로, 보통 물리적으로 붙어 있는 상태를 지칭하고 디지털 문서나 첨부 파일을 나타내는 데는 적절하지 않으며, (D) limited는 "제한된"이라는 의미로 첨부 파일이나 문서의 상태를 나타낼 수 없으므로 문맥과 맞지 않다.

PART 7

다음 이메일, 공지, 그리고 일정표와 관련된 질문 1-5번을 보세요.

수신자: 모든 직원
발신자: 인사부
제목: 다가오는 교육 세션
날짜: 5월 15일

팀원 여러분,
"직장 내 의사소통 및 갈등 해결"을 주제로 한 필수 교육 세션이 다음 주 금요일 메인 컨퍼런스룸에서 열릴 예정임을 알려드립니다. 이 교육은 부서 간 팀워크와 생산성을 향상시키기 위한 지속적인 노력의 일환입니다.

세부사항:
날짜: 다음 주 금요일
시간: 오전 10시 ~ 오후 1시
장소: 메인 컨퍼런스룸
이 교육은 우리의 전문성 개발 프로그램의 핵심 요소이므로 반드시 참석해 주시기 바랍니다. 일정에 차질이 있는 경우 이번 주 말까지 직속 상사와 인사부에 알려주시기 바랍니다.
협조해 주셔서 감사합니다.

감사합니다,
인사부

회의실 시설에 대해 다음과 같은 유지보수 작업이 예정되어 있음을 알려드립니다:
- 메인 회의실: 기술 점검으로 인해 목요일 오후 6시부터 금요일 오전 8시까지 폐쇄됩니다.
- 소형 회의실(A & B): 재도색 작업으로 인해 수요일부터 금요일 오후까지 폐쇄됩니다.

이로 인해 발생하는 불편에 대해 사과드리며 양해를 부탁드립니다.
긴급 문의 사항이 있으시면 내선 1023으로 시설 관리부에 연락 주시기 바랍니다.

시설 관리부

주간 컨퍼런스룸 일정표

요일	시간	룸	이벤트	비고
목요일	오후 3:00	소형 컨퍼런스룸 A	마케팅 팀 회의	오후 5:30 종료
금요일	오전 10:00	메인 컨퍼런스룸	직장 내 의사소통 교육	인사부에서 일정 조율
금요일	오후 2:00	소형 컨퍼런스룸 B	프로젝트 킥오프 미팅	유지보수로 사용 가능 여부 확인 필요

어휘 department 부서 announce 알리다 mandatory

의무적인 resolution 해결, 결의안 continuous 지속적인 effort 노력 enhance 향상시키다, 증강시키다 productivity 생산성 professional 직업의, 전문적인 conflict 충돌 supervisor 관리자, 감독관, 상사 cooperation 협력 maintenance 유지 advise 알리다, 공지하다 facility 시설 technical 기술의 repaint 재도장하다 apologize 사과하다 inconvenience 불편 appreciate 감사하다 urgent 긴급한 inquiry 문의, 질문 contact 연락하다, 접촉하다 extension(number) 내선 번호

정답

1. (B)　2. (A)　3. (D)　4. (A)　5. (C)

1. 인사부에서 보낸 이메일의 주요 목적은 무엇입니까?
   (A) 직장 내 새로운 정책에 대한 세부 사항을 제공하기 위해
   (B) 직원들에게 필수 교육 세션에 대해 알리기 위해
   (C) 최근 이벤트에 대한 피드백을 요청하기 위해
   (D) 회의실 일정 변경을 발표하기 위해

해설 이메일 본문에서 "We are pleased to announce that a mandatory training session on 'Workplace Communication and Conflict Resolution' will be held next Friday"라고 언급하며, 다가오는 필수 교육 세션에 대해 알리는 데 목적이 있음을 명확히 알 수 있으므로 (B)가 정답이다.

2. 공지에 따르면, 회의실 유지 보수 후 메인 회의실은 언제 다시 이용 가능합니까?
   (A) 금요일 오전 8시
   (B) 금요일 오전 10시
   (C) 목요일 오후 6시
   (D) 수요일 오후 6시

해설 공지에 따르면, "Main Conference Room: Closed for technical checks from 6:00 PM on Thursday to 8:00 AM on Friday"라고 명시되어 있어 금요일 오전 8시부터 사용할 수 있음을 의미하므로 (A)가 정답이다.

3. 어떤 이벤트가 유지 보수 일정에 직접적으로 영향을 받습니까?
   (A) 마케팅 팀 회의
   (B) HR 부서 브리핑
   (C) 직장 내 커뮤니케이션 교육
   (D) 프로젝트 킥오프 미팅

해설 공지에 따르면, Small Conference Rooms (A & B)는 "Closed for repainting from Wednesday to Friday afternoon"이라고 명시되어 있고, 또 주간 일정표에 따르면, "Project Kickoff Meeting"은 금요일 오후 2시에 Small Conference Room B에서 예정되어 있다. 따라서 Project Kickoff Meeting은 유지 보수 작업이 완료되기 전에 예정된 이벤트로 직접적으로 영향을 받을 가능성이 높으므로 (D)가 정답이다.

4. 직원들이 이번 주말까지 상사에게 알리도록 요청받은 이유는 무엇입니까?
   (A) 교육 세션 참석 여부를 확인하기 위해
   (B) 회의실 일정 문제를 보고하기 위해
   (C) 유지 보수로 인해 취소된 이벤트를 다시 예약하기 위해
   (D) 직장 내 커뮤니케이션 정책을 논의하기 위해

해설 이메일에서 "If you have any scheduling conflicts, kindly inform your supervisor and the HR Department by the end of this week"라고 언급하며, 직원들이 교육 세션과 관련하여 일정 충돌이 있는 경우 직속 상사와 인사부에 알리도록 요청하고 있는 것은 교육 세션 참석 여부를 확인하고 필요한 조치를 취하기 위한 것이므로 (A)가 정답이다.

5. 시설 관리부에 대해 무엇을 추론할 수 있습니까?
   (A) 교육 세션을 조직하는 책임이 있다.
   (B) 다른 작업보다 기술 점검을 우선시한다.
   (C) 회의실 유지 보수 관련 문의를 처리한다.
   (D) 매주 메인 회의실에서 회의를 예약한다.

해설 공지문에서 "For urgent inquiries, please contact the Facilities Department at extension

1023."라고 명시되어 있어 시설 관리부가 회의실 유지 보수와 관련된 긴급 문의를 처리한다는 것을 알 수 있으므로 (C)가 정답이다.

Chapter 13 형용사절

1. 관계대명사(Relative Pronouns)

✔ CheckPoint 1. 관계대명사의 종류

정답

1. (A) 2. (B)

1.

번역 실행된 전략은 생산성 향상에 도움이 되었다.

해설 선행사(The strategy)가 사물이고, 선행사를 수식하는 형용사절(S was implemented) 안에 동사(was)의 주어가 없어, 주격 관계대명사 that이나 which가 필요하므로 (A) which가 정답이다.

어휘 strategy 전략 implement 실행하다, 시행하다 increase 증가하다 productivity 생산성

2.

번역 가장 높은 매출을 달성한 팀의 직원이 보너스를 받을 것이다.

해설 선행사(The employee)가 사람이고, 선행사와 형용사절(team achieved the highest sales) 사이에 소유관계가 있으므로 소유격 관계대명사 (B) whose가 정답이다.

어휘 employee 직원 achieve 성취하다, 달성하다 sales 판매, 매출 receive 받다

✔ CheckPoint 2. 관계대명사의 생략

정답

1. (A) 2. (D) 3. (C)

1.

번역 밖에 주차된 차는 CEO의 것이다.

해설 원 문장은 The car that/which is parked outside belongs to the CEO이고, 선행사 + (주격 관계대명사 + be동사) + 형용사/ 현재분사/ 과거분사/ 전치사구 구조에서 주격 관계대명사와 be동사를 생략할 수 있으므로 (A) that is가 정답이다.

어휘 belong to ~에 속하다, ~의 소유이다 CEO 최고경영자

2.

번역 새로운 소프트웨어를 설계하는 엔지니어는 매우 재능이 있다.

해설 원 문장은 The engineer who/that is designing the new software is very talented이고, 선행사 + (주격 관계대명사 + be동사) + 형용사/ 현재분사/ 과거분사/ 전치사구 구조에서 주격 관계대명사와 be동사를 생략할 수 있으므로 (D) designing이 정답이다. (B) designed가 정답이 될 수 없는 것은 동사 design의 목적어(the new software)가 있으므로 능동 의미의 현재분사가 정답이 된다. 만약 목적어가 없으면 (B) designed가 정답이 된다.

어휘 engineer 엔지니어, 기술자 talented 재능 있는, 뛰어난 design 설계하다

3.

번역 작년에 출시된 제품은 큰 성공을 거두었다.

해설 원 문장은 The product that/which was launched last year has been a great success이고, 선행사 + (주격 관계대명사 + be동사) + 형용사/ 현재분사/ 과거분사/ 전치사구 구조에서 주격 관계대명사

명사와 be동사를 생략할 수 있으므로 (C) launched 가 정답이다. (B) launching이 정답이 될 수 없는 것은 동사 launch의 목적어가 없기 때문이다.

[어휘] launch 출시하다, 시작하다

✔ CheckPoint 3. 전치사 + 관계대명사

정답

1. (B) 2. (A) 3. (D)

1.

번역 내가 근무하는 회사는 글로벌 리더이다.

[해설] 이 문장은 다음과 같은 파생과정을 거쳐 도출되므로 (B) for which가 정답이다.
The company is a global leader. + I work for the company.
⇒ The company which/that I work for O is a global leader.
⇒ The company for which I work is a global leader.
여기서 work for는 "~에서 일하다"는 의미로 사용되는 관용표현이다.

2.

번역 자금을 받은 재단은 자선 활동으로 유명하다.

[해설] 이 문장은 다음과 같은 파생과정을 거쳐 도출되므로 (A) from which가 정답이다.
The foundation is renowned for its charitable work. + The funds were received from the foundation.
⇒ The foundation which the funds were received from O is renowned for its charitable work.
⇒ The foundation from which the funds were received is renowned for its charitable work.

[어휘] foundation 재단, 기초 fund 자금, 기금 renowned 유명한, 명성이 높은 charitable work 자선 활동

3.

번역 신제품이 출시된 그 회의는 많은 미디어의 주목을 받았다.

[해설] 이 문장은 다음과 같은 파생과정을 거쳐 도출되므로 (D) at which가 정답이다.
The conference attracted a lot of media attention. + The new product was launched at the conference.
⇒ The conference which/that the new product was launched at O attracted a lot of media attention.
⇒ The conference at which the new product was launched attracted a lot of media attention.

[어휘] conference 회의 launch 출시하다, 시작하다 attract 끌다, 유인하다 media attention 언론의 주목

✔ CheckPoint 4. 관계대명사 that의 용례

정답

1. (C) 2. (B)

1.

번역 이것이 현재 문제를 효과적으로 해결할 수 있는 유일한 해결책이다.

[해설] 선행사(The only solution)에 the only라는 강조 표현을 포함하고 있으므로 (C) that이 정답이다.
[어휘] solution 해결책, 해법 effectively 효과적으로 address 다루다, 해결하다 current 현재의

2.

번역 이사회에서 승인된 그 제안에는 혁신적인 성장 전략이 포함되어 있다.

[해설] 선행사(The proposal)가 사물이고, 선행사를 수식하는 형용사절(S was approved by the board) 안에 동사(was)의 주어가 없어, 주격 관계대명사 that이나 which가 모두 가능하지만 that은 쉼표(,)가 있는 계속적 용법에 사용할 수 없으므로 (B) which가 정답이다.

[어휘] proposal 제안, 제안서 approve 승인하다,

찬성하다 board 이사회 innovative 혁신적인, 창의적인 strategy 전략, 방책

2. 관계부사(Relative Adverbs)

✔ CheckPoint 5. 관계부사의 종류

정답

1. (A) 2. (C)

1.

번역 회의가 열릴 그 도시는 뛰어난 교통 옵션을 제공한다.

해설 선행사(The city)가 장소를 나타내고, 선행사를 수식하는 형용사절(the conference will be held)이 완전한 절이므로 (A) where이 정답이다.

어휘 conference 회의 transportation option 교통 옵션

2.

번역 프로젝트가 지연된 이유는 기술적인 문제 때문이었다.

해설 선행사(The reason)가 이유를 나타내고, 선행사를 수식하는 형용사절(the project was delayed)이 완전한 절이므로 (C) why가 정답이다.

어휘 delay 지연시키다, 연기하다 technical issue 기술적 문제

토익 종합 실전문제

정답

1. (A)	2. (C)	3. (D)	4. (B)	5. (A)
6. (B)	7. (C)	8. (C)	9. (D)	10. (C)
11. (D)	12. (D)	13. (C)	14. (A)	15. (C)
16. (B)	17. (C)	18. (C)	19. (D)	20. (C)
21. (A)	22. (B)	23. (C)	24. (C)	

1.

번역 회사는 컨설턴트가 추천한 전략을 실행했다.

해설 선행사(a strategy)가 사물이고, 선행사를 수식하는 형용사절(S was recommended by the consultant) 안에 동사(was)의 주어가 없어, 주격 관계대명사 that이나 which가 필요하므로 (A) that이 정답이다.

어휘 implement 실행하다, 시행하다 strategy 전략 recommend 추천하다, 권장하다 consultant 컨설턴트

2.

번역 역사의 흐름을 바꾼 이론을 제시한 과학자가 노벨상을 받았다.

해설 선행사(The scientist)가 사람이고, 선행사와 형용사절(theory changed the course of history) 사이에 소유관계가 있으므로 소유격 관계대명사 (C) whose가 정답이다.

어휘 theory 이론 award 수여하다, 상을 주다

3.

번역 매니저가 프로젝트를 이끄는 역할을 맡긴 그 직원은 뛰어난 조직력을 보여주었다.

해설 선행사(The employee)가 사람이고, 선행사를 수식하는 형용사절(the manager assigned O to lead the project) 안에 동사(assigned)의 목적어가 없어, 목적격 관계대명사 that이나 whom이 필요하므로 (D) whom이 정답이다.

어휘 assign 할당하다, 배정하다 demonstrate 보여주다, 증명하다 exceptional 뛰어난, 예외적인 organizational skill 조직력

4.

번역 본사가 뉴욕에 위치한 그 회사는 국제적으로 확장하고 있다.

해설 원 문장 the headquarters of the company are located in New York에서 of the company가 선행사(the company)와 소유관계를 나타내므로 of the company를 선행사(the company)와 연결하기 위해 of which로 변경한다. 따라서 (B) of which가 정답이다.

어휘 headquarters 본사 locate 위치하다 expand 확장하다 internationally 국제적으로

5.

번역 프로젝트의 성공에 중요한 제안이 먼저 논의되어야 한다.

해설 원 문장은 The proposal that/which is important to the success of the project should be discussed first이고, 선행사 + (주격 관계대명사 + be동사) + 형용사/ 현재분사/ 과거분사/ 전치사구 구조에서 주격 관계대명사와 be동사를 생략할 수 있으므로 (A) important가 정답이다.

어휘 proposal 제안, 제안서 discuss 논의하다

6.

번역 도심에 있는 건물은 역사적인 랜드마크이다.

해설 원 문장은 The building that/which is located in the center of the city is a historical landmark이고, 선행사 + (주격 관계대명사 + be동사) + 형용사/ 현재분사/ 과거분사/ 전치사구 구조에서 주격 관계대명사와 be동사를 생략할 수 있으므로 (B) located가 정답이다.

어휘 historical 역사적인, 역사와 관련된

7.

번역 매니저 책상 위에 놓인 문서들은 오늘까지 검토되어야 한다.

해설 원 문장은 The documents that/which are placed on the manager's desk must be reviewed by the end of the day이고, 선행사 + (주격 관계대명사 + be동사) + 형용사/ 현재분사/ 과거분사/ 전치사구 구조에서 주격 관계대명사와 be동사를 생략할 수 있으므로 (C) placed가 정답이다.

어휘 review 검토하다

8.

번역 프로젝트를 감독할 책임이 있는 직원이 회의를 주도할 것이다.

해설 원 문장은 The employee who is responsible for overseeing the project will lead the meeting이고, 선행사 + (주격 관계대명사 + be동사) + 형용사/ 현재분사/ 과거분사/ 전치사구 구조에서 주격 관계대명사와 be동사를 생략할 수 있으므로 (C) who is가 정답이다.

어휘 responsible 책임이 있는 oversee 감독하다

9.

번역 개조 기간 동안 보관된 장비는 안전한 장소로 옮겨졌다.

해설 원 문장은 The equipment that/which was stored during the renovation has been moved to a secure location이고, 선행사 + (주격 관계대명사 + be동사) + 형용사/ 현재분사/ 과거분사/ 전치사구 구조에서 주격 관계대명사와 be동사를 생략할 수 있으므로 (D) stored가 정답이다.

어휘 store 저장하다 renovation 개조 secure location 안전한 장소

10.

번역 회사가 운영되는 정책은 엄격하지만 공정하다.

해설 이 문장은 다음과 같은 파생과정을 거쳐 도출되므로 (C) under which가 정답이다.

The policy is strict but fair. + The company operates under the policy.

⇒ The policy which/that the company operates under O is strict but fair.

⇒ The policy under which the company operates is strict but fair.

어휘 strict 엄격한 fair 공정한

11.

번역 그들이 협력하고 있는 프로젝트는 매우 야심찬 것이다.

해설 이 문장은 다음과 같은 파생과정을 거쳐 도출되므로 (D) on which가 정답이다.

The project is very ambitious. + They are collaborating on the project.

⇒ The project which they are collaborating on O is very ambitious.

⇒ The project on which they are collaborating is very ambitious.

여기서 collaborate on은 "(특정 주제나 프로젝트)에 대해 협력하다, 공동으로 작업하다", collaborate with는 "(사람이나 조직)과 협력하다"는 의미로 사용되는 관용표현이다.

어휘 ambitious 야심찬, 포부가 큰

12.

번역 내가 이메일을 보낸 사람은 아직 답장을 하지 않았다.

해설 이 문장은 다음과 같은 파생과정을 거쳐 도출되므로 (D) to whom이 정답이다.

The person has not replied yet. + I sent the email to the person.

⇒ The person whom/that I sent the email to O has not replied yet.

⇒ The person to whom I sent the email has not replied yet.

13.

번역 회사가 참여한 그 파트너십은 매우 유익한 것으로 판명되었다.

해설 이 문장은 다음과 같은 파생과정을 거쳐 도출되므로 (C) in which가 정답이다.

The partnership proved to be highly beneficial. + The company has been involved in the partnership.

⇒ The partnership which the company has been involved in O proved to be highly beneficial.

⇒ The partnership in which the company has been involved proved to be highly beneficial.

여기서 be involved in은 "~에 관여하다, 참여하다"는 의미로 사용되는 관용표현이다.

어휘 partnership 협력, 동업 prove 판명되다 beneficial 유익한, 이로운

14.

번역 모든 직원이 준수해야 할 규정은 매우 엄격하다.

해설 이 문장은 다음과 같은 파생과정을 거쳐 도출되므로 (A) to which가 정답이다.

The regulations are quite strict. + All employees must adhere to the regulations.

⇒ The regulations which all employees must adhere to O are quite strict.

⇒ The regulations to which all employees must adhere are quite strict.

여기서 adhere to는 "~을 지키다, 준수하다"라는 의미로 사용되는 관용표현이다.

어휘 regulation 규정, 규칙

15.

번역 시상식 중에 수여된 그 상은 팀의 뛰어난 업적을 인정했다.

해설 선행사(The award)가 사물이고, 선행사를 수식하는 형용사절(S was presented during the ceremony) 안에 동사(was)의 주어가 없어, 주격 관계대명사 that이나 which가 모두 가능하지만 that은 쉼표(,)가 있는 계속적 용법에 사용할 수 없으므로 (C) which가 정답이다.

어휘 award 상, 상장 present 수여하다, 발표하다 ceremony 시상식 recognize 인정하다, 표창하다 outstanding 뛰어난 achievement 업적

16.

번역 팀은 이 업계에서 지금까지 만들어진 가장 효율적인 시스템을 개발했다.

해설 선행사(The most efficient system)에 the most라는 최상급 표현을 포함하고 있으므로 (B) that이 정답이다.

어휘 develop 개발하다, 발전시키다 efficient 효율적인

17.

번역 결과가 위원회에 의해 논란이 된 보고서는 수정되어야 한다.

해설 선행사(The report)가 사물이고, 선행사와 형용사절(findings were disputed by the committee) 사이에 소유관계가 있으므로 소유격 관계대명사 (C) whose가 정답이다.

어휘 report 보고서, 보고 finding 발견, 결과 dispute 논쟁하다, 이의를 제기하다 committee 위원회 revise 수정하다, 개정하다

18.

번역 지난달 승진한 직원이 새로운 책임을 맡았다.

해설 선행사(The employee)가 사람이고, 선행사를 수식하는 형용사절(S was promoted last month) 안에 동사(was)의 주어가 없어, 주격 관계대명사 who나 that이 모두 가능하지만 that은 쉼표(,)가 있는 계속적 용법에 사용할 수 없으므로 (C) who가 정답이다.

어휘 promote 승진시키다, 촉진하다 responsibility 책임, 업무 take on 맡다, 떠맡다

19.

번역 수백 명이 참석한 그 행사는 큰 성공을 거두었다.

해설 선행사(The event)가 사물이고, 선행사를 수식하는 형용사절(S was attended by hundreds of people) 안에 동사(was)의 주어가 없어, 주격 관계대명사 that이나 which가 모두 가능하지만 that은 쉼표(,)가 있는 계속적 용법에 사용할 수 없으므로 (D) which가 정답이다.

어휘 attend 참석하다, 출석하다 hundreds of 수백의

20.

번역 이것이 예정보다 일찍 완료된 바로 첫 번째 프로젝트이다.

해설 선행사(The very first project)에 the very first라는 강조 표현을 포함하고 있으므로 (C) that이 정답이다.

어휘 ahead of schedule 예정보다 일찍

21.

번역 제품이 제조된 공장은 국제 인증을 받았다.

해설 선행사(The factory)가 장소를 나타내고, 선행사를 수식하는 형용사절(the product was manufactured)이 완전한 절이므로 (A) where이 정답이다.

어휘 manufacture 제조하다, 생산하다 receive 받다, 수령하다 international certification 국제 인증

22.

번역 실험이 진행된 방식은 위원회를 놀라게 했다.

해설 선행사(The way)가 방법을 나타내고, 선행사를 수식하는 형용사절(the experiment was conducted)이 완전한 절이므로 관계부사가 필요한데, The way 뒤에는 how를 함께 쓸 수 없으므로 (B) that이 정답이다.

어휘 experiment 실험 conduct 실행하다 surprise 놀라게 하다 committee 위원회

23.

번역 회사가 설립된 날은 매년 기념된다.

해설 선행사(The day)가 시간을 나타내고, 선행사를 수식하는 형용사절(the company was founded)이 완전한 절이므로 (C) when이 정답이다.

어휘 found 설립하다 celebrate 축하하다 annually 매년

24.

번역 CEO가 회의를 연 사무실은 새로 리모델링되었다.

해설 선행사(The office)가 장소를 나타내고, 선행사를 수식하는 형용사절(the CEO held the meeting)이 완전한 절이므로 (C) where이 정답이다.

어휘 CEO 최고경영자 newly 새롭게 renovate 개조하다, 리모델링하다

PART 6

다음 메모와 관련된 질문 1-4번을 보세요.

> 팀 여러분께,
> 직장 생산성을 향상시키기 위한 지속적인 노력의 일환으로, 우리는 더 효율적인 작업 환경을 조성할 전략을 실행하고 있습니다. 이 전략에는 직원들이 일상 업무를 향상시키는 데 사용할 수 있는 도구와 자료를 제공하는 것이 포함됩니다.
> 작년에 참여자들로부터 큰 호평을 받은 교육 세션이 이제 더 많은 사람들이 접근할 수 있도록 온라인으로 제공됩니다. 이 세션을 성공적으로 완료한 직원들은 그들의 성과를 인정받아 인증서를 받게 될 것입니다.
> 더불어, 직원들을 지원하는 것을 주요 목표로 하는 경영팀이 정기적인 회의를 주최하여 문제를 논의하고 피드백을 수집할 것입니다. 여러분의 의견은 저희가 매우 중요하게 생각하며, 이러한 계획들을 성공적으로 이끄는 데 중요한 역할을 할 것입니다.
> 헌신과 노력에 감사드립니다. 함께라면 회사의 목표를 달성할 수 있을 것입니다.
>
> 감사합니다,
> 인사부

어휘 strategy 전략, 방책 boost 증진시키다, 향상시키다 workplace 직장 productivity 생산성 continued effort 지속적인 노력 improve 개선하다, 향상시키다 implement 실행하다, 도입하다 efficient 효율적인 work environment 작업 환경 enhance 강화하다, 향상시키다 daily tasks 일상적인 업무 training sessions 훈련 세션 praise 칭찬하다 participant 참가자 accessible 접근 가능한 accessibility 접근성 acknowledge 인정하다 achievement 성과, 업적 management team 관리팀 primary 주된, 주요한 regular 정기적인 address 다루다, 처리하다, 해결하다 concerns 걱정, 우려 gather 모으다, 수집하다 dedication 헌신, 전념

정답

1. (A)　2. (C)　3. (B)　4. (B)

1.

해설 선행사(The training sessions)가 사물이고, 선행사를 수식하는 형용사절(S were highly praised by last year's participants) 안에 동사 were의 주어가 없으므로 주격 관계대명사 that이나 which가 필요하지만 that은 계속적 용법에 사용할 수 없으므로 (A) which가 정답이다.

2.

해설 highly는 "매우, 대단히"라는 의미로, 긍정적 평가나 감탄을 표현할 때 사용되며, 문맥에서 작년에 참여자들로부터 큰 호평을 받았다는 내용과 부합하므로 (C) highly가 정답이다. (A) moderately는 "적당히", (B) rarely와 (D) barely는 "거의 ~않다"라는 의미로 문맥에 맞지 않다.

3.

해설 Employees will receive certifications는 직원들이 교육 세션의 성공적인 완료에 대해 공식적으로 인정받는 것을 의미하므로 "인증서"라는 의미를 가진 (B) certifications가 정답이다. (A) recognition은 "인증"이라는 포괄적인 의미를 가지므로, 인증서와는 거리가 멀고, (C) awards와 (D) promotions는 문맥에 맞지 않다.

4.

(A) 관리자들의 피드백은 향후 교육 세션의 우선순위를 정하는 데 도움이 될 것입니다.
(B) 여러분의 의견은 저희가 매우 중요하게 생각하며, 이러한 계획들을 성공적으로 이끄는 데 중요한 역할을 할 것입니다.
(C) 이 전략들은 다음 분기에 추가 개선을 위해 평가될 것입니다.
(D) 직원들이 문제를 공유하기 위해 회의에 참석할 것을 권장합니다.

해설 이전 문장에서 새로운 생산성 향상 전략으로 경영팀이 정기적인 회의를 주최하여 문제를 논의하고, 피드백을 수집할 것이라고 하였고, 팀의 의견이 중요하다는 점을 다시 강조하는 것이 자연스러운 흐름을 형성하므로 (B)가 가장 적절하다. (A)는 관리자들의 피드백을 언급하고 있으나, 이

문장은 직원들의 피드백을 다루고 있어 문맥에 적합하지 않고, (C)는 다음 분기의 개선 가능성을 다루지만, 여기서 강조하고 있는 "현재의 피드백"이라는 맥락과 맞지 않으며, (D)는 직원들의 참여를 장려하지만, 이는 피드백을 강조하는 문맥과 약간 동떨어져 있으므로 문맥상 적절하지 않다.

PART 7

다음 기사와 공지와 관련된 질문 1-5번을 보세요.

> 제목: 전기차의 성장과 친환경적인 미래
> 날짜: 2024년 9월 18일
> 출처: 지속 가능한 교통 저널
>
> 자동차 산업은 전 세계적으로 전기차(EV)의 인기가 높아짐에 따라 빠르게 지속 가능성을 향해 변화하고 있습니다. 많은 정부가 구매자에게 인센티브를 제공하고 충전소 네트워크에 투자함으로써 이러한 변화를 지원하고 있습니다. 국제에너지기구(IEA)에 따르면, 도로 위의 전기차 수는 2030년까지 1억 4천 5백만 대를 초과할 것으로 예상됩니다.
> 전기차는 환경적 이점 외에도 기존 휘발유 차량에 비해 더 조용하고 부드러운 주행 경험을 제공합니다. 제조업체들은 주행 거리를 늘리고 충전 시간을 줄이기 위해 배터리 기술을 개선하는 데 주력하고 있습니다.
> EV는 여러 장점에도 불구하고 초기 비용이 높고 충전 인프라가 부족하며 주행 거리가 짧다는 문제에 직면해 있습니다. 그러나 지속적인 기술 발전으로 이러한 문제는 점차 해결될 것이며, 전기차는 미래 교통수단에서 중요한 역할을 하게 될 것입니다.

> 제목: 새로운 전기차 충전소 개소
> 발신: 지역 시의회
> 날짜: 2024년 9월 20일
>
> 시의회는 중심가 주차장에 10개의 새로운 전기차 충전소 설치를 발표하게 되어 기쁩니다. 이 프로젝트는 깨끗한 에너지 솔루션을 촉진하고 지속 가능한 교통수단을 지원하려는 우리의 목표와 일치합니다.
> 이 충전소는 2024년 10월 1일부터 이용 가능하며, 대부분의 전기차가 30분 안에 80% 충전할 수 있는 고속 충전 기술을 갖추고 있습니다. 이 시설의 추가로 더 많은 주민들이 전기차로 전환하도록 독려하여 도시의 전체 탄소 배출량을 줄일 것으로 기대됩니다.
> 충전소 위치와 이용 방법에 대한 추가 정보는 웹사이트를 방문하거나 contact@citycouncil.org로 이메일을 보내주시기 바랍니다.

어휘 growth 성장, 발전 electric vehicles (EVs) 전기차 greener 더 친환경적인 sustainable 지속 가능한 transportation 운송, 교통수단 automotive industry 자동차 산업 rapidly 빠르게, 신속히 shift 변화하다, 전환하다 sustainability 지속 가능성 gain traction 인기를 얻다, 주목받다 globally 전 세계적으로 government 정부 incentive 인센티브, 장려책 investment 투자 charging station networks 충전소 네트워크 according to ~에 따르면 international energy association (IEA) 국제 에너지기구 surpass 초과하다, 능가하다 significant 중요한, 중대한 environmental advantage 환경적 이점 gasoline-powered car 가솔린 차량 manufacturer 제조업체, 생산업체 enhance 향상시키다 minimize 최소화하다 despite ~에도 불구하고 challenge 도전, 문제 initial cost 초기 비용 limited charging infrastructure 제한된 충전 인프라 continuous 지속적인 local city council 지역 시의회 announce 발표하다 installation 설치 align with ~와 일치하다, 조화를 이루다 advance 진전시키다, 발전시키다 transportation 교통 equipped with ~이 갖춰진 enable 가능하게 하다 reach 도달하다 capacity 용량 aim to ~을 목표로 하다 encourage 장려하다 thereby 그로 인해, 따라서 reduce 줄이다, 감소하다 emission 배출 additional 추가적인 detail 세부사항 usage 사용, 이용

정답

1. (B) 2. (D) 3. (C) 4. (B) 5. (C)

1. 기사에 따르면, 전기차의 한 가지 이점은 무엇입니까?
   (A) 그들은 무제한 주행 거리를 가지고 있다.
   (B) 그들은 더 부드럽고 조용한 주행 경험을 제공한다.

(C) 그들은 가솔린 차량보다 저렴하다.
(D) 그들은 10분 이내에 충전될 수 있다.

해설 첫 번째 문서에서 "EVs provide significant environmental advantages and deliver a quieter, smoother driving experience compared to gasoline-powered cars"라고 언급하며, 전기차의 이점 중 하나로 더 부드럽고 조용한 주행 경험을 제시하고 있으므로 (B)가 정답이다.

2. 기사에서 전기차 보급과 관련된 도전 과제는 무엇입니까?
(A) 충전소의 높은 비용
(B) 전기차 유지의 어려움
(C) 정부 지원 부족
(D) 충전소의 제한된 가용성

해설 첫 번째 문서에서 "EVs face challenges such as high initial costs, limited charging infrastructure, and shorter driving ranges"라고 언급하며, 전기차 보급의 장애물로 충전소의 제한된 가용성을 제시하고 있으므로 (D)가 정답이다.

3. 새로운 도심 전기차 충전소는 언제 운영을 시작합니까?
(A) 2024년 9월 18일
(B) 2024년 9월 20일
(C) 2024년 10월 1일
(D) 2024년 10월 15일

해설 두 번째 문서에서 "These stations, which will be available from October 1, 2024"라고 언급하며, 충전소가 2024년 10월 1일부터 이용 가능하다고 제시하고 있으므로 (C)가 정답이다.

4. 시의회의 공지의 목적은 무엇입니까?
(A) 도시에서 가솔린 차량 금지를 발표하기 위해
(B) 새로운 전기차 충전소에 대한 정보를 제공하기 위해
(C) 전기차 구매자 할인을 홍보하기 위해
(D) 도시 주차 정책의 최근 변경 사항을 설명하기 위해

해설 두 번째 문서에서 "The City Council is pleased to announce the installation of 10 new EV charging stations in the central parking lot"라고 언급하며, 새로운 전기차 충전소 설치에 대한 정보를 제공하고 있으므로 (B)가 정답이다.

5. 공지에서 새로운 충전소의 어떤 특징이 강조됩니까?
(A) 주민들을 위한 무료 이용
(B) 15분 이내에 완전 충전 가능
(C) 30분 안에 80% 충전이 가능한 급속 충전 기술
(D) EV와 하이브리드 차량 모두 지원

해설 두 번째 문서에서 "These stations, which will be available from October 1, 2024, are equipped with fast-charging technology, enabling most EVs to reach 80% battery capacity within 30 minutes"라고 언급하며, 급속 충전 기술을 지원하며, 대부분의 전기차를 30분 안에 80% 충전 가능하다고 설명하고 있으므로 (C)가 정답이다.

Chapter 14 부사절

1. 부사절 접속사의 종류

✔ CheckPoint 1. 시간의 부사절 접속사

정답

1. (B) 2. (C)

1.

번역 CEO는 이사회가 끝난 후 새로운 정책 변경 사항을 발표할 것이다.

해설 이 문장은 "이사회가 끝난 후에"라는 시간의 순서를 나타내므로 (B) after가 정답이다. (A) while은 "~하는 동안"으로 시간의 동시성을 강조하므로 시간의 순서와 맞지 않고, (C) before는 "~

하기 전에"로 시간 순서와 맞지 않으며, (D) since는 "~한 이래로"라는 의미로 시간의 시작점을 나타내므로 문맥과 맞지 않다.

어휘 CEO 최고경영자 announce 발표하다, 알리다 policy 정책, 방침 board meeting 이사회 회의 conclude 끝나다, 종료하다

2.

번역 시스템이 예상치 못하게 고장 나기 전에 작업을 자주 저장해야 한다.

해설 이 문장은 "시스템이 고장 나기 전에" 작업을 저장해야 한다는 경고를 하고 있으므로 (C) before가 정답이다. (A) until은 "~할 때까지"로 지속성을 나타내므로 문맥과 맞지 않고, (B) when은 "~할 때"로 특정 시간을 나타내지만, 예방의 의미를 전달하지 못하며, (D) as는 "~할 때" 또는 "~하면서"로 동시성을 나타내므로 문맥과 맞지 않다.

어휘 frequently 자주 crash 고장 나다, 멈추다 unexpectedly 뜻밖에, 예기치 않게

✔ CheckPoint 2. 조건의 부사절 접속사

정답

1. (B) 2. (A) 3. (C)

1.

번역 회사가 판매 목표를 달성하면 직원들은 연간 보너스를 받을 것이다.

해설 이 문장은 "회사가 판매 목표를 달성하면" 이라는 조건을 나타내므로 (B) if가 정답이다. (A) unless는 "만약 ~하지 않으면"이라는 부정적인 조건을 나타내므로 문맥과 맞지 않고, (C) because는 "~때문에"로 이유를 나타내지만 이 문장은 조건을 설명하고 있으므로 문맥에 맞지 않으며, (D) as long as는 "~하는 한"으로 반복적이거나 지속적인 조건에 적합하며, 단발성 조건을 나타내는 문장에는 맞지 않다.

어휘 receive 받다 annual 연간의, 매년의 meet 충족하다, 달성하다

2.

번역 적절한 권한이 없으면 보안 구역에 들어갈 수 없다.

해설 이 문장은 부정적인 조건을 강조하며, "적절한 권한이 없으면" 보안 구역에 접근할 수 없다는 의미를 전달하므로 (A) unless가 정답이다. (B) if는 "만약 ~하면"으로 긍정적인 조건을 나타내므로 문맥과 맞지 않고, (C) without은 "~없이"라는 의미의 전치사로 조건절을 구성할 수 없으므로 문법적으로 적절하지 않으며, (D) even if는 "비록 ~하더라도"로 양보를 나타내어 문맥과 맞지 않다.

어휘 secured area 보안 구역 proper 적절한 authorization 허가, 승인

3.

번역 양측이 조건에 동의한다는 조건에서만 계약은 유효할 것이다.

해설 이 문장은 "양측이 조건에 동의한다는 조건에서"라는 의미를 전달하며, 조건적인 의미를 명확히 나타내는 접속사가 필요하므로 (C) providing이 정답이다. (A) in the event that는 "~할 경우에 대비하여"로 특정 조건이 발생할 가능성을 염두에 두고 대비책을 언급할 때 사용되므로 문맥과는 맞지 않고, (B) as는 "~하면서" 또는 "~할 때"로 시간의 동시성을 나타내므로 문맥에 맞지 않으며, (D) until은 "~할 때까지"라는 지속성을 나타내므로 문맥과 맞지 않다.

어휘 contract 계약 valid 유효한 both parties 양측 agree to ~에 동의하다 terms 조건, 계약 세부사항

✔ CheckPoint 3. 양보의 부사절 접속사: 주절과 역접 및 대조 관계

정답

1. (B) 2. (D)

1.

번역 새로운 정책이 효율성을 높인 반면, 직원들 사이에서 혼란을 일으키기도 했다.

해설 이 문장은 "효율성을 개선했지만 혼란을 초

래했다"라는 두 가지 상반된 사실을 비교하며 대조 관계를 나타내므로 (B) While이 정답이다. (A) Because는 "~때문에"로 이유를 나타내므로 문맥과 맞지 않고, (C) Even if는 "비록 ~일지라도"로 가정적인 상황에 대한 양보를 나타내므로 문맥과 맞지 않으며, (D) Unless는 "만약 ~하지 않으면"이라는 부정적인 조건을 나타내므로 문맥과 맞지 않다.

어휘 policy 정책 improve 개선하다, 향상시키다 efficiency 효율성 cause 야기하다, 일으키다 confusion 혼란 among ~의 사이에서

2.

번역 초기 평가가 엇갈렸음에도 불구하고, 제품 출시는 성공적이었다.

해설 이 문장은 "초기 평가가 엇갈렸음에도 불구하고 성공했다"라는 역접 관계의 양보를 나타내므로 (D) even though가 정답이다. (A) whereas와 (B) while은 "~인 반면에"로 대조 관계를 나타내므로 문맥과 맞지 않고, (C) when은 "~할 때"로 특정 시간을 나타내므로 문맥과 맞지 않다.

어휘 launch 출시하다, 시작하다 successful 성공적인 initial 초기의, 처음의 mixed 엇갈린, 다양한, 혼합된

✔ CheckPoint 4. 이유의 부사절 접속사: 주절과 인과 관계

정답

1. (A)　2. (A)　3. (B)

1.

번역 매니저가 교통 체증에 갇혔기 때문에 회의가 지연되었다.

해설 이 문장은 "교통 체증 때문에 회의가 지연되었다"는 인과 관계를 나타내므로 (A) as가 정답이다. (D) in that은 특정 관점에서 이유를 강조하거나 근거를 설명할 때 사용되므로 문맥과 맞지 않다.

어휘 delay 지연하다 stuck in traffic 교통 체증에 갇히다

2.

번역 팀은 매니저로부터 긍정적인 피드백을 받았으므로 더 동기부여를 받고 있다.

해설 이 문장은 "긍정적인 피드백을 받은 현재 상황"이 팀의 동기부여 증가의 이유로 연결되므로 (A) now that이 정답이다. (B) whereas는 대조 관계를 나타내므로 문맥과 맞지 않다.

어휘 motivate 동기부여하다 receive 받다 positive feedback 긍정적인 피드백

3.

번역 고객이 추가 변경을 요청했기 때문에 우리는 제안서를 수정해야 한다.

해설 이 문장은 "고객의 요청 때문에 제안서를 수정해야 한다"는 이유를 나타내므로 (B) since가 정답이다.

어휘 revise 수정하다, 개정하다 proposal 제안서 client 고객, 의뢰인 request 요청하다, 요구하다 additional 추가적인 change 변경, 수정 사항

✔ CheckPoint 5. 목적의 부사절 접속사

정답

1. (D)　2. (B)　3. (C)

1.

번역 모든 사용자가 쉽게 이해할 수 있도록 지침이 간소화되었다.

해설 이 문장은 "지침을 간소화한 이유가 사용자의 이해를 돕기 위해서"라는 목적을 나타내므로 (D) in order that이 정답이다.

어휘 instruction 지침, 설명서 simplify 단순화하다

2.

번역 회사는 증가된 수요를 충족하기 위해 추가 직원을 고용했다.

해설 이 문장은 "추가 직원을 고용한 이유가 수요를 충족하기 위해서"라는 목적을 나타내므로 (B) so that이 정답이다.

어휘 hire 고용하다, 채용하다 additional 추가적인 meet 충족하다 increase 증가하다 demand 수요

3.

번역 더 많은 고객을 유치하기 위해 회사는 마케팅 캠페인을 시작했다.

해설 이 문장은 "마케팅 캠페인을 시작한 이유가 더 많은 고객을 유치하기 위해서"라는 목적을 나타내므로 (C) in order that이 정답이다.

어휘 launch 시작하다, 출시하다 attract 끌어들이다, 유치하다, 유도하다

✔ CheckPoint 6. 결과의 부사절 접속사

정답

1. (C) 2. (B) 3. (D)

1.

번역 제품 디자인이 너무 혁신적이어서 여러 상을 수상했다.

해설 이 문장은 "제품 디자인의 혁신성이 여러 상을 수상한 결과"로 이어졌으므로 결과를 나타내는 "so ~ that" 구조에서 (C) that이 정답이다.

어휘 innovative 혁신적인 win 이기다, 수상하다

2.

번역 그것은 너무 성공적인 캠페인이어서 회사는 이를 다른 시장으로 확장하기로 결정했다.

해설 이 문장은 "성공적인 캠페인이 다른 시장으로의 확장"이라는 결과를 초래했으므로 결과를 나타내는 "such ~ that" 구조에서 (B) that이 정답이다.

어휘 successful 성공적인 decide 결정하다 expand 확장하다

3.

번역 일정이 너무 엉망이어서 팀은 전체 계획을 다시 정리해야 했다.

해설 이 문장은 "엉망인 일정이 계획의 재정리"라는 결과를 초래했으므로 결과를 나타내는 "such ~ that" 구조에서 (D) such가 정답이다. (A) so는 결과를 나타내는 "so ~ that" 구조에서 사용되지만 "so ~ that" 구조는 형용사나 부사를 수식할 때 사용되며, 명사인 "a mess"를 수식할 수 없으므로 문맥과 맞지 않다.

어휘 schedule 일정, 스케줄 reorganize 재조직하다, 개편하다 entire 전체의, 전부의

2. 부사절 접속사와 전치사

✔ CheckPoint 7. 부사절 접속사와 전치사의 유형

정답

1. (B) 2. (B) 3. (B)

1.

번역 필수 교육을 이수하지 않으면 프로젝트를 시작할 수 없다.

해설 이 문장은 "교육을 이수하지 않는다면"이라는 부정적인 조건을 나타내므로 (B) Unless가 정답이다. (D) During은 "~하는 동안"으로 특정 시간의 범위를 나타내는 전치사로 접속사가 필요한 자리에 사용할 수 없다.

어휘 complete 완료하다 required 필수의, 요구되는

2.

번역 심각한 날씨 조건 때문에 배송이 지연되었다.

해설 이 문장은 "날씨 조건이 배송 지연의 이유"임을 설명하므로 이유를 나타내는 전치사 (B) due to가 정답이다. (A) without은 "~없이"로 부정적인 조건을 나타내므로 문맥과 맞지 않고,
(D) in case of 는 "~할 경우에 대비하여"로 특정 조건에 대한 대비를 나타내므로 문맥과 맞지 않다.

어휘 shipment 배송, 선적 delay 지연하다 severe 심각한, 극심한

3.

번역 비상사태가 발생할 경우 화재 경보가 자동으로 작동한다.

해설 이 문장은 "비상사태가 발생할 경우"라는 특정 조건에 대한 대비를 나타내는 전치사가 필요하므로 (B) in case of가 정답이다. (A) due to는 "~때문에"로 이유를 나타내므로 문맥과 맞지 않고, (D) prior to 는 "~하기 전에"로 시간적 순서를 나타내므로 문맥과 맞지 않다.

어휘 activate 작동하다, 활성화하다 automatically 자동으로 emergency 비상사태

3. 복합 관부사

✔ CheckPoint 8. 복합 관계부사

정답

1. (A) 2. (A)

1.

번역 직원들이 출장 갈 때마다, 그들은 이후에 상세한 보고서를 제출해야 한다.

해설 이 문장은 "출장 갈 때마다"라는 반복적인 시간적 조건을 나타내는 부사절 접속사가 필요하므로 "언제든지, ~할 때마다"라는 의미를 가진 복합 관계부사 (A) Whenever가 정답이다. (B) Wherever는 "어디든지, 어디를 가든지"라는 의미를 가진 복합 관계부사로 장소를 나타내므로 문맥과 맞지 않고, (C) However는 "어떻게든지, 아무리 ~해도"라는 의미를 가진 복합 관계부사로 방법이나 조건을 나타내므로 문맥과 맞지 않으며, (D) Whatever는 복합 관계대명사로 명사절을 이끌 때 사용되므로 문맥과 맞지 않다.

어휘 business trip 출장 submit 제출하다 detailed 자세한, 세부적인 afterward 이후에

2.

번역 회사가 어디로 사업을 확장하든지, 항상 지역 규정을 준수한다.

해설 이 문장은 "어디로 사업을 확장하든지"라는 장소를 나타내는 복합 관계부사가 필요하므로 "어디든지, 어디를 가든지"라는 의미를 가진 복합 관계부사 (A) Wherever가 정답이다.

어휘 expand 확장하다 operation 운영, 사업 adhere to ~을 준수하다 local 지역의 regulation 규정, 규칙

토익 종합 실전문제

정답

1. (A)	2. (B)	3. (C)	4. (B)	5. (D)
6. (B)	7. (D)	8. (A)	9. (B)	10. (C)
11. (C)	12. (D)	13. (C)	14. (B)	15. (C)
16. (D)	17. (C)	18. (D)	19. (C)	20. (D)
21. (B)	22. (C)	23. (C)	24. (B)	

1.

번역 모든 팀원이 철저히 검토할 때까지 보고서는 최종 확정되지 않을 것이다.

해설 until은 부정문에서 특정 조건이 충족되지 않을 때까지 어떤 일이 이루어지지 않음을 나타낼 때 자주 사용되므로 (A) until이 정답이다. (B) as는 "~할 때" 또는 "~하면서"로 시간의 동시성을 나타내지만, 이 문장에서 필요한 "특정 조건이 충족될 때까지"라는 의미와는 맞지 않고, (C) once는 "일단 ~하면"으로 조건적 의미를 나타내지만, 긍정적인 상황에서 주로 사용되며, 부정적인 조건과는 잘 맞지 않으며, (D) after는 "~한 후에"로 시간 순서를 나타내지만, 부정적인 조건을 전달하지 못하므로 적절하지 않다.

어휘 finalize 마무리하다, 확정하다 thoroughly 철저히

2.

번역 모든 이해관계자가 피드백을 제공하면 팀은 예산 제안서를 확정할 것이다.

해설 이 문장은 "모든 이해관계자가 피드백을 제

공한 후"라는 완료 조건을 나타내는 (B) once가 정답이다. (A) while은 "~하는 동안"으로 시간의 동시성을 나타내지만, 문맥상 맞지 않고, (C) before는 "~하기 전에"로 시간 순서와 맞지 않으며, (D) since는 "~한 이래로"라는 의미로 시간의 시작점을 나타내므로 문맥과 맞지 않다.

어휘 budget proposal 예산 제안서 stakeholder 이해관계자 provide 제공하다

3.

번역 마감일이 다가오면서, 팀은 프로젝트를 완성하기 위해 초과 근무를 하고 있다.

해설 이 문장은 "마감일이 다가오면서"라는 동시성을 나타내므로 (C) As가 정답이다.

어휘 approach 다가오다, 접근하다 work overtime 초과 근무하다 complete 완료하다

4.

번역 직원들은 모든 작업을 완료하자마자 사무실을 일찍 떠났다.

해설 이 문장은 "작업을 완료하자마자"라는 즉시성을 나타내므로 (B) as soon as가 정답이다.

5.

번역 매니저가 새로운 절차를 설명하는 동안, 일부 직원들은 필기하고 있었다.

해설 이 문장은 "매니저가 새로운 절차를 설명하는 동안"과 "직원들이 필기하고 있었다"라는 두 동작이 동시에 진행되는 상황이므로 (D) While이 정답이다.

어휘 explain 설명하다, 알리다 procedure 절차, 과정, 방법

6.

번역 적절한 로그인 자격이 있는 한, 회사 데이터베이스에 접근할 수 있다.

해설 이 문장은 조건을 나타내며, "올바른 로그인 자격이 있는 한"이라는 상황을 명확히 전달하므로 (B) as long as가 정답이다.

어휘 access 접근하다, 이용하다 database 데이터베이스 proper 적절한, 올바른 credential 자격, 증명서

7.

번역 질문이 있을 경우, 언제든 고객 지원팀에 연락 주시기 바랍니다.

해설 이 문장은 "질문이 있을 경우에 대비하여"라는 의미로, 특정 상황이 발생할 가능성을 염두에 두고 대비책을 언급할 때 사용되는 (D) In case가 정답이다. (B) Whenever는 "~할 때마다"로 반복적인 상황을 나타내어 문맥과 맞지 않다.

어휘 contact 연락하다

8.

번역 필요한 모든 정보를 제공하지 않으면 시스템이 결제를 처리하지 않을 것이다.

해설 이 문장은 부정적인 조건을 나타내며, "필요한 정보를 제공하지 않는다면" 결제가 이루어지지 않는다는 의미를 전달하므로 (A) unless가 정답이다.

어휘 process 처리하다, 실행하다 payment 결제, 구매 provide 제공하다 required 필요한, 필수적인

9.

번역 직원들은 작업을 제시간에 완료한다는 조건에서 유연한 근무 시간을 사용할 수 있다.

해설 이 문장은 "작업을 제시간에 완료한다는 조건에서"라는 의미를 전달하며, 조건을 나타내는 표현이 필요하므로 (B) provided that가 정답이다.

어휘 allow 허용하다, 승인하다 flexible 유연한 complete 완료하다, 끝내다

10.

번역 비록 여러 예상치 못한 장애물에 직면했지만, 팀은 프로젝트를 제시간에 완료할 수 있었다.

해설 이 문장은 "예상치 못한 장애물에도 불구하고 프로젝트를 완료했다"라는 역접 관계의 양보를 나타내므로 (C) though가 정답이다.

어휘 manage to 간신히 ~하다 on time 제 시간에 face 직면하다, 맞서다 unexpected 예상치 못한 obstacle 장애물, 문제

11.

번역 시장 상황이 불확실하더라도, 우리는 출시를 진행할 것이다.

해설 이 문장은 "시장 상황이 불확실하더라도 출시를 진행한다"라는 가정적 상황에 대한 양보를 나타내므로 (C) even if가 정답이다.

어휘 proceed 진행하다, 실행하다 launch 출시, 출시하다 market condition 시장 상황 remain 계속하다, 유지하다 uncertain 불확실한, 명확하지 않은

12.

번역 이전 시스템은 더 빨랐던 반면, 새 시스템은 더 사용하기 쉽다.

해설 이 문장은 "이전 시스템은 빠르지만 새 시스템은 사용하기 쉽다"라는 두 가지 상반된 사실을 비교하며 대조 관계를 나타내므로 (D) whereas가 정답이다.

어휘 user-friendly 사용자 친화적인

13.

번역 새로운 정책은 고객 만족도를 높인 반면, 운영비용을 증가시켰다.

해설 이 문장은 "고객 만족도를 높인 반면 운영비용도 증가했다"라는 두 가지 상반된 사실을 비교하며 대조 관계를 나타내므로 (C) while이 정답이다.

어휘 policy 정책 improve 향상시키다, 개선하다 satisfaction 만족 increase 증가하다 operational cost 운영비용

14.

번역 일부 주주들이 우려를 표명했음에도 불구하고, 회사는 합병을 진행하기로 결정했다.

해설 이 문장은 "주주들이 우려를 표명했음에도 불구하고 합병을 진행했다"라는 역접 관계의 양보를 나타내므로 (B) even though가 정답이다.

어휘 decide 결정하다 proceed 진행하다, 실행하다 merger 합병 shareholder 주주 express 표현하다, 나타나다 concern 우려, 걱정

15.

번역 교육 프로그램이 잘 짜여 있었기 때문에 신입 직원들이 빠르게 적응하고 있다.

해설 이 문장은 "교육 프로그램이 잘 짜인 것이 신입 직원들의 적응에 영향을 미쳤다"는 인과 관계를 나타내므로 (C) because가 정답이다.

어휘 adapt 적응하다, 조정하다 quickly 빠르게 well-structured 잘 구성된, 체계적인

16.

번역 이 보고서는 세부 데이터와 철저한 분석을 포함했다는 점에서 매우 유익하다.

해설 이 문장은 "세부 데이터와 철저한 분석"이 보고서의 유익함을 뒷받침하는 이유로 제시되므로 (D) in that이 정답이다. (A) in the event that은 "~할 경우에 대비하여"로 특정 조건이 발생할 가능성을 염두에 두고 대비책을 언급할 때 사용되므로 문맥과는 맞지 않다.

어휘 highly 매우, 대단히 informative 유익한 include 포함하다 detailed 상세한, 세부적인 thorough 철저한 analysis 분석

17.

번역 공장 견학 전에 안전 교육이 실시될 것이다.

해설 이 문장은 "공장 견학 전에 안전 교육이 진행된다"는 시간적 순서를 설명하는 전치사가 필요하므로 (C) prior to가 정답이다. (A) because of는 "~때문에"로 이유를 나타내므로 문맥과 맞지 않고, (B) in spite of는 "~에도 불구하고"로 양보를 나타내므로 문맥과 맞지 않으며, (D) without은 "~없이"로 부정적인 조건을 나타내므로 문맥과 맞지 않다.

어휘 safety briefing 안전 교육 conduct 진행하다, 수행하다

18.

번역 정전이 발생할 경우 직원들은 안전 절차를 따라야 한다.

해설 이 문장은 "정전이 발생할 경우"라는 특정 조건에 대한 대비를 나타내는 전치사가 필요하므로 (D) in the event of가 정답이다. (C) for the purpose of는 "~하기 위해서"로 목적을 나타내므로 문맥과는 맞지 않으며, (D) during은 "~하는 동안"으로 특정 시간의 범위를 나타내므로 문맥과는 맞지 않다.

어휘 safety procedure 안전 절차 power outage 정전

19.

번역 고객이 여러 가지 변경을 요청했기 때문에 마감일이 연장되었다.

해설 이 문장은 "변경 요청이 마감일 연장의 이유"를 설명하므로 이유를 나타내는 접속사 (C) Since가 정답이다. (B) In case는 "~할 경우에 대비하여"로 특정 조건에 대한 대비를 나타내므로 문맥과 맞지 않으며, (D) Despite는 "~에도 불구하고"로 양보를 나타내는 전치사로 접속사가 필요한 자리에 사용할 수 없다.

어휘 request 요청하다, 요구하다 several 여러, 몇 가지의 extend 연장하다

20.

번역 매니저는 보고서에 몇 가지 결함이 있음에도 불구하고 제안을 승인했다.

해설 이 문장은 "결함이 있음에도 불구하고 승인했다"라는 양보 관계를 나타내는 전치사가 필요하므로 (D) despite가 정답이다. (A) due to는 "~때문에"로 이유를 나타내므로 문맥과 맞지 않다.

어휘 approve 승인하다, 허가하다 proposal 제안, 제안서 flaw 결함

21.

번역 큰 혼란이 없다면 행사는 진행될 것이다.

해설 이 문장은 "큰 혼란이 없을 경우"라는 조건을 설명하는 전치사가 필요하므로 (B) without이 정답이다.

어휘 proceed 진행하다, 계속하다 major 주요한, 중요한 disruption 혼란, 방해

22.

번역 시장 상황이 변할 때마다 팀은 적응할 준비가 되어 있어야 한다.

해설 이 문장은 "시장이 변할 때마다"라는 반복적인 시간적 조건을 나타내는 부사절 접속사가 필요하므로 "언제든지, ~할 때마다"라는 의미를 가진 복합 관계부사 (C) whenever가 정답이다.

어휘 adapt 적응하다, 조정하다 market condition 시장 상황 change 변화, 변화하다

23.

번역 프로젝트가 아무리 도전적일지라도, 우리는 이를 완료할 능력이 있다고 확신한다.

해설 이 문장은 "프로젝트가 아무리 도전적일지라도"라는 양보를 나타내는 부사절 접속사가 필요하므로 "어떻게든지, 아무리 ~해도"라는 의미를 가진 복합 관계부사 (C) However가 정답이다.

어휘 challenging 도전적인, 힘든 confident 자신감 있는, 확신하는 ability 능력, 역량 complete 완료하다, 끝내다

24.

번역 회사는 지점이 어디에 있든지 일관된 서비스 품질을 제공한다.

해설 이 문장은 "지점이 어디에 있든지"라는 장소를 나타내는 복합 관계부사가 필요하므로 "어디든지, 어디를 가든지"라는 의미를 가진 복합 관계부사 (B) wherever가 정답이다.

어휘 provide 제공하다, 공급하다 consistent 일관된, 변함없는 quality 품질, 수준 branch 지점, 지사 locate 위치하다

PART 6

다음 공지와 관련된 질문 1-4번을 보세요.

> 친애하는 직원 여러분,
> 다음 달 사무실 리모델링 공사가 진행될 예정임을 알려드립니다. 이번 공사는 중장비가 사용되기 때문에 근무 시간 동안 소음과 업무 방해가 발생할 수 있습니다. 불편을 최소화하려고 노력하겠지만, 이 과정에서 여러분의 이해와 협조를 부탁드립니다.
> 또한, 업무에 집중이 필요하신 경우 헤드폰 사용을 권장합니다. 더 조용한 환경이 필요하신 경우, 개인 용도로 임시 개방된 회의실을 이용하시기 바랍니다.
> 업무 계획을 세우실 수 있도록 공사 일정에 대한 정기적인 업데이트를 제공할 예정입니다. 궁금한 점이나 제안 사항이 있으시면 인사부에 주저하지 말고 문의해 주십시오.
> 여러분의 인내와 이해에 감사드립니다.
>
> 감사합니다,
> 존 스미스
> 사무실 관리자

어휘 renovation 개조, 보수 notice 공지, 알림 inform 알리다, 공지하다 undergo 겪다, 진행하다 involve 포함하다, 수반하다 machinery 기계, 장비 noise 소음 disruption 방해, 혼란 aim to ~하려고 노력하다 minimize 최소화하다 inconvenience 불편 understanding 이해, 양해 throughout ~동안 내내 additionally 추가로, 또한 environment 환경 personal 개인적인 temporarily 임시로, 일시적으로 provide 제공하다 regular 정기적인 schedule 일정 accordingly 그에 맞게, 적절히 concern 우려, 걱정 suggestion 제안 hesitate 망설이다 contact 연락하다 HR department 인사부 patience 인내

정답

1. (A) 2. (A) 3. (D) 4. (C)

1.

해설 이 문장은 "우리는 직원들의 이해와 협조를 요청한다"가 맥락상 가장 적절하므로 (A) cooperation이 정답이다. (B) disruption은 "혼란", (C) application은 "신청", (D) explanation은 "설명"이라는 의미로 문맥에 맞지 않다.

2.

(A) 업무에 집중이 필요하신 경우 헤드폰 사용을 권장합니다.
(B) 공사는 두 달 안에 마무리될 예정입니다.
(C) 임시 작업 공간이 구내식당에 마련될 것입니다.
(D) 모든 직원들은 재택근무를 하도록 권장됩니다.

해설 전후 문맥을 보면 "공사 기간 동안 방해를 최소화하기 위해"라는 내용이 강조되었고, (A)가 "업무에 집중이 필요할 경우 헤드폰을 사용하는 것이 좋다"는 실질적이고 구체적인 권장 사항을 제시하고 있으므로 (A)가 가장 적절하다. (B)는 공사 종료 시점을 안내하는 정보일 뿐, 방해를 줄이기 위한 조치가 아니므로 문맥과 맞지 않고, (C)는 방해를 줄이기 위한 대안일 수는 있지만, 본문에서 이와 관련된 정보가 제공되지 않았으므로 문맥과 어울리지 않으며, (D)는 방해를 줄이는 방법이 될 수는 있지만, 본문에서 이를 구체적으로 권장하거나 언급하지 않으므로 문맥과 맞지 않다.

3.

해설 "더 조용한 환경이 필요하신 경우"라는 특정 조건에 대한 대비를 나타내므로 "~할 경우에 대비하여"라는 의미를 가진 부사절 접속사 (D) In case가 정답이다.

4.

해설 문맥상 "공사 일정에 대한 정기 업데이트를 제공한다"는 내용으로, "~에 대해" 또는 "~에 관한"이라는 의미로 특정 주제에 대한 정보를 제공하거나 논의할 때 적합한 전치사 (C) on이 정답이다. (A) with는 "~와 함께" 또는 "특정 도구를 사용하여"라는 의미를 주로 가지며, 주제나 특정 사항에 대한 업데이트를 언급하는 문맥에 적합하지 않고, (B) for는 "~을 위해" 또는 "~의 목적을 위해"라는 의미로 사용되며, "업데이트 주제"를 나타내는 문맥과는 맞지 않으며, (D) to는 주로 방향이나 대상(사람, 사물)으로 사용되며, "주제"와 관련된 정보

를 표현하기에는 적절하지 않다.

PART 7

다음 메모와 설문조사 결과와 관련된 질문 1-5번을 보세요.

> 수신자: 모든 부서장
> 발신자: Operations Manager 수잔 카터
> 날짜: 3월 15일
> 제목: 사무실 공간 재구성
>
> 팀원 여러분,
> 다음 달부터 늘어나는 직원 수를 수용하고 작업 흐름의 효율성을 개선하기 위해 사무실 공간 재구성을 시작할 예정입니다. 이번 재구성에는 책상 재배치, 공유 작업 공간 업데이트, 유연한 좌석 배정을 위한 공유 좌석제 정책 도입이 포함됩니다.
>
> 주요 일정:
> 3월 20일: 예비 좌석 배치 계획 배포
> 3월 25일: 팀 리더 피드백 제출 마감
> 4월 1-5일: 변경 사항 실행
> 팀원들이 예비 좌석 배치 계획에 대해 통보받고 의견을 제시할 수 있도록 해주시기 바랍니다. 모든 사람에게 변경 사항이 효과적으로 작용할 수 있도록 여러분의 의견을 소중히 여기겠습니다. 궁금한 점이 있으시면 언제든 저에게 직접 연락 주세요.
>
> 감사합니다,
> Operations Manager
> 수잔 카터

> 사무실 재구성 피드백:
>
> 최근 직원 설문 조사는 계획된 사무실 재구성에 대한 통찰을 제공했습니다. 약 70%의 직원들이 유연성과 협업 증진 가능성을 이유로 공유 좌석제 정책을 지지했습니다. 또한, 응답자의 55%는 개별 책상보다 더 많은 공유 회의 공간을 선호하며, 팀워크와 의사소통을 촉진하는 공간의 중요성을 강조했습니다.
> 주요 우려 사항으로는 공유 업무 공간에서의 사생활 침해와 사물함과 같은 추가 개인 수납공간의 필요성이 포함되었습니다. 피드백에서 전반적인 지지를 보여주지만, 이러한 우려를 해결하는 것이 원활한 전환을 위해 반드시 필요할 것입니다.

어휘 department head 부서장, 관리자 operation manager 운영 관리자 subject 주제 reorganization 재구성, 재조정 accommodate 수용하다, 충족하다 improve 개선하다, 향상시키다 workflow 작업 흐름 efficiency 효율성 reallocate 재배치하다 distribution 배포, 분배 preliminary 초기의, 예비의 submission 제출 implementation 실행, 도입 ensure 보장하다 input 의견, 제안 arrangement 배치 value 소중히 여기다 effectively 효과적으로 directly 직접 recent 최근의 survey 설문조사 insight 통찰, 이해 planned 계획된, 예정된 support 지지하다, 찬성하다 hot-desking 공유 좌석제 cite 인용하다 flexibility 유연성, 융통성 potential 잠재력, 가능성 enhance 강화하다, 증진하다 collaboration 협업, 공동 작업 respondent 응답자 prefer 선호하다 individual 개인적인 emphasize 강조하다 importance 중요성 foster 촉진하다, 육성하다 concern 우려, 걱정 loss 손실, 상실 privacy 사생활 additional 추가적인 personal 개인의 storage 저장, 보관 highlight 강조하다 overall 전반적인 address 해결하다 essential 필수적인 smooth 순조로운 transition 전환, 변화

정답

1. (A) 2. (B) 3. (D) 4. (C) 5 (C)

1. 메모의 목적은 무엇입니까?
   (A) 다가오는 사무실 재구성에 대해 직원들에게 알리기 위해
   (B) 부서장들과 설문조사 결과를 공유하기 위해
   (C) 새로운 직원 복지 프로그램을 발표하기 위해
   (D) 회사 정책 변경을 제안하기 위해

해설 첫 번째 문서에서 "Starting next month, we will begin the reorganization of office spaces to accommodate the growing number of staff and improve workflow efficiency."라고 언급하며, 다음 달에 시작될 사무실 재구성과 관련된 세부 사항을 알리는 데 목적이 있음을 명확히 알 수 있으므로 (A)가 정답이다.

2. 팀 리더들이 피드백을 제출해야 하는 날짜

는 언제입니까?

(A) 3월 20일

(B) 3월 25일

(C) 4월 1일

(D) 4월 5일

해설 첫 번째 문서의 주요 일정 부분에서 “March 25: Submission deadline for feedback from team leaders”라는 문장이 명시되어 있으므로 팀 리더가 피드백을 제출해야 하는 기한은 (B)가 정답이다.

3. 설문조사에 따르면, 사무실 재구성과 관련된 주요 우려 사항은 무엇입니까?

(A) 협업 기회의 부족

(B) 회의 공간의 제한된 이용 가능성

(C) 변경과 관련된 높은 비용

(D) 공유 작업 공간에서의 사생활 감소

해설 두 번째 문서에서 “Key concerns included the loss of privacy in a shared workspace”라고 명시되어 있고, 이는 공유 작업 공간에서의 사생활 감소가 주요 우려 사항임을 알 수 있으므로 (D)가 정답이다.

4. 공유 좌석제 정책에 찬성한 직원들의 비율은 얼마입니까?

(A) 55%

(B) 60%

(C) 70%

(D) 75%

해설 두 번째 문서에서 “About 70% of employees supported the hot-desking policy”라고 명시되어 있어 공유 좌석제 정책을 지지한 직원의 비율이 70%임을 알 수 있으므로 (C)가 정답이다.

5. 4월 1일부터 5일까지 무슨 일이 예정되어 있습니까?

(A) 팀 리더들로부터 최종 피드백이 수집될 것입니다.

(B) 예비 좌석 배치 계획이 배포될 것입니다.

(C) 재구성이 실행될 것입니다.

(D) 팀 리더들이 운영 관리자와 만날 것입니다.

해설 첫 번째 문서의 주요 일정에서 “April 1-5: Implementation of changes”라는 문구가 명시되어 있으므로, 4월 1일부터 5일까지 사무실 재구성이 실행될 예정임을 알 수 있으므로 (C)가 정답이다.

Chapter 15 명사절

2. 명사절 접속사의 유형

✔ CheckPoint 1. that의 용례

정답

1. (B) 2. (A) 3. (D)

1.

번역 매니저는 프로젝트가 이번 달 말까지 완료되어야 한다고 강조했다.

해설 the project must be completed by the end of the month는 완전한 절이고, 또 동사 emphasized의 목적어 역할을 하므로 (B) that이 정답이다. (A) what, (C) who, (D) which는 불완전한 절을 이끄는 관계대명사이므로 적절하지 않다.

어휘 emphasize 강조하다 complete 완료하다

2.

번역 주요 문제는 우리가 프로젝트를 계속하기 위해 추가 자금이 필요하다는 것이다.

해설 we need additional funding to continue the project는 완전한 절이고, 또 동사 is의 보어 역할을 하므로 (A) that이 정답이다. (B) what과 (D) which는 불완전한 절을 이끄는 관계대명사이므로 적절하지 않고, (C) whether는 “~인지 아닌지”라는 두 가지 선택지를 나타내는 접속사이지만 이 문장

에서는 선택지가 언급되지 않았으므로 적절하지 않다.

어휘 additional funding 추가 자금 continue 계속하다, 지속하다

3.

번역 팀이 마감일을 맞췄다는 것은 놀라운 성과였다.

해설 the team met the deadline은 완전한 절이고, 또 동사 was의 주어 역할을 하므로 (D) That이 정답이다.

어휘 meet (마감 시한을) 맞추다 remarkable 주목할 만한, 놀라운 achievement 업적, 성과

✔ CheckPoint 2. 동격절 접속사 that의 용례

정답

1. (A) 2. (D) 3. (B)

1.

번역 제품 출시가 지연되었다는 소식이 주주들을 실망시켰다.

해설 the news는 완전한 절(the product launch was delayed)을 이끄는 접속사 that과 동격 관계를 이루므로 (A) that이 정답이다.

어휘 launch 출시, 출시하다 delay 지연시키다 disappoint 실망시키다 shareholder 주주

2.

번역 팀은 프로젝트가 일정보다 앞서 완료될 수 있다는 가정을 거부했다.

해설 the assumption은 완전한 절(the project could be completed ahead of schedule)을 이끄는 접속사 that과 동격 관계를 이루므로 (D) that이 정답이다.

어휘 reject 거절하다, 부인하다 assumption 가정 complete 완료하다 ahead of schedule 예정보다 앞서

3.

번역 가장 중요한 요소는 새로운 시스템이 더 신뢰할 만하다는 증거이다.

해설 the evidence는 완전한 절(the new system is more reliable)을 이끄는 접속사 that과 동격 관계를 이루므로 (B) that이 정답이다.

어휘 important 중요한 factor 요소, 요인 evidence 증거 reliable 신뢰할 수 있는

✔ CheckPoint 3. 관계대명사 what의 용례

정답

1. (B) 2. (C) 3. (D)

1.

번역 당신이 집중해야 하는 것은 고객 만족도를 개선하는 것이다.

해설 ________ you need to focus on은 동사 is의 주어 역할을 하는 명사절이고, 또 전치사 on의 목적어가 없는 불완전한 절이면서 선행사가 없으므로 선행사를 포함하고 있는 (B) What이 정답이다.

어휘 focus on ~에 집중하다 improve 개선하다, 향상시키다 satisfaction 만족

2.

번역 마케팅 팀은 대상 고객에게 가장 관련성이 높은 것에 집중했다.

해설 ________ was most relevant to the target audience는 전치사 on의 목적어 역할을 하는 명사절이고, 또 동사 was의 주어가 없는 불완전한 절이면서 선행사가 없으므로 선행사를 포함하고 있는 (C) what이 정답이다.

어휘 relevant 관련 있는, 적절한 target audience 대상 고객

3.

번역 회의 결과는 팀이 예상했던 것이었다.

해설 ________ the team had anticipated는

동사 was의 보어 역할을 하는 명사절이고, 또 동사 anticipated의 목적어가 없는 불완전한 절이면서 선행사가 없으므로 선행사를 포함하고 있는 (D) what이 정답이다.

어휘 anticipate 예상하다, 기대하다

✔ CheckPoint 4. if/whether의 용례

정답

1. (B) 2. (A) 3. (B)

1.

번역 회사가 새로운 시장으로 확장할지는 여전히 불확실하다.

해설 _________ the company will expand into new markets는 동사 remains의 주어 역할을 하는 명사절이고, 또 완전한 절이므로 (B) Whether가 정답이다. (A) If는 명사절 접속사로 사용되지만, 주어 자리에는 사용할 수 없으므로 부적절하고, (C) Which와 (D) What은 불완전한 절을 이끄는 관계대명사이므로 적절하지 않다.

어휘 expand 확장하다 remain 남다, 남아 있다 unclear 불확실한

2.

번역 나는 매니저가 그 제안을 승인할지 모르겠다.

해설 _________ the manager will approve the proposal은 동사 know의 목적어 역할을 하는 명사절이고, 또 완전한 절이므로 (A) if가 정답이다. (C) that은 명사절 접속사로 사용될 수 있지만, 문맥상 "매니저가 승인할지 여부"를 전달하는 선택 여부의 의미를 전달하지 못하므로 부적절하다.

어휘 approve 승인하다 proposal 제안, 제안서

3.

번역 핵심 문제는 팀이 프로젝트를 제시간에 전달할 수 있는가이다.

해설 _________ the team can deliver the project on time은 동사 is의 보어 역할을 하는 명사절이고, 또 완전한 절이므로 (B) whether가 정답이다. (A) if는 명사절 접속사로, 보어 자리에는 사용할 수 없으므로 부적절하다.

어휘 deliver 전달하다

✔ CheckPoint 5. 의문사의 용례

정답

1. (C) 2. (A) 3. (B)

1.

번역 그 보고서는 효율성을 높이기 위해 무엇이 먼저 다루어져야 하는지를 강조한다.

해설 _________ should be addressed first to improve efficiency는 동사 highlights의 목적어 역할을 하는 명사절이고, 또 주어가 생략된 불완전한 절이므로 의문대명사 (C) what이 정답이다. (A) who는 사람을 지칭하는 의문대명사로, 문맥상 적절하지 않고, (B) that은 완전한 절을 이끄는 명사절 접속사 혹은 불완전한 절을 이끄는 관계대명사는 맞지만, 선행사가 없어서 적합하지 않으며, (D) how는 의문부사로, 뒤에 완전한 절이 와야 하며 "방법"을 나타내므로 문맥상 적절하지 않다.

어휘 highlight 강조하다, 부각시키다 address 다루다, 해결하다 improve 개선하다, 향상시키다 efficiency 효율성

2.

번역 매니저는 어떤 부서가 그 문제를 처리해야 할지 확신하지 못하고 있다.

해설 _________ department should handle the issue는 동사 is unsure의 목적어 역할을 하는 명사절이고, 또 완전한 절로 명사 department를 수식하므로 의문형용사 (A) which가 정답이다. (B) what은 선택지가 명확하지 않거나 제한되지 않은 경우에 사용하므로 여기서는 적절하지 않다.

어휘 department 부서 handle 처리하다, 다루다

3.

번역 설명서는 시스템을 어떻게 구성해야 하는지를 설명한다.

해설 _________ the system should be configured는 동사 explain의 목적어 역할을 하는 명사절이고, 또 완전한 절이므로 "방법"을 나타내는 의문부사 (B) how가 정답이다. (A) why는 의문부사로, "이유"를 나타내고, (D) where은 의문부사로, "장소"를 나타내므로 문맥상 적절하지 않다.

어휘 instruction 지시사항, 설명서 explain 설명하다 configure 구성하다, 설정하다

✔ CheckPoint 6. 복합 관계대명사의 용례

정답

1. (A) 2. (B) 3. (D)

1.

번역 먼저 프로젝트를 제출하는 사람이 추가 자금을 받을 것이다.

해설 _________ submits the project first는 동사 receive의 주어 역할을 하는 명사절이고, 또 주어가 생략된 불완전한 절이면서 선행사를 포함하고 있는 복합 관계대명사 (A) Whoever가 정답이다. (B) Whomever는 목적어가 생략된 불완전한 절을 가지므로 문맥상 적절하지 않고, (C) Whatever와 (D) Whichever는 사물을 지칭하는 데 사용하므로 문맥상 적절하지 않다.

어휘 submit 제출하다 receive 받다, 수여하다 additional funding 추가 자금

2.

번역 당신이 그 직책에 추천하는 사람은 누구든지 면접을 봐야 할 것이다.

해설 _________ you recommend for the position은 동사 undergo의 주어 역할을 하는 명사절이고, 또 목적어가 생략된 불완전한 절이면서 선행사를 포함하고 있는 복합 관계대명사 (B) Whomever가 정답이다. (A) Whoever는 주어가 생략된 불완전한 절을 가지므로 문맥상 적절하지 않다.

어휘 recommend 추천하다 position 직위, 위치 undergo 경험하다, 겪다

3.

번역 당신이 프로젝트를 위해 선택하는 것은 어느 것이든 팀의 승인을 받아야 한다.

해설 _________ you choose for the project는 동사 approved의 주어 역할을 하는 명사절이고, 또 목적어가 생략된 불완전한 절이면서 선행사를 포함하고 있는 복합 관계대명사 (D) Whichever가 정답이다. 문맥상 "프로젝트를 위해 선택할 수 있는 여러 가지 옵션 중 하나"를 가리키기 때문에, 선택지가 명확하지 않거나 제한되지 않은 경우에 사용되는 (C) Whatever는 적절하지 않다.

어휘 choose 선택하다, 고르다 approve 승인하다

토익 종합 실전문제

정답

1. (A)	2. (D)	3. (B)	4. (A)	5. (B)
6. (D)	7. (A)	8. (A)	9. (B)	10. (C)
11. (C)	12. (D)	13. (A)	14. (D)	15. (A)
16. (B)	17. (D)	18. (A)	19. (C)	20. (B)
21. (A)	22. (C)	23. (D)	24. (B)	

1.

번역 회사가 작년에 기록적인 수익을 냈다는 것은 칭찬할 만하다.

해설 the company achieved record profits last year는 완전한 절이고, 또 동사 is의 주어 역할을 하므로 (A) That이 정답이다.

어휘 achieve 달성하다 record profit 기록적인 수익 commendable 칭찬할 만한, 훌륭한

2.

번역 보고서는 새로운 전략이 매출에 긍정적인 영향을 미쳤다는 것을 확인했다.

해설 the new strategy had a positive impact on sales는 완전한 절이고, 또 동사 confirmed의 목적어 역할을 하므로 (D) that이 정답이다.

어휘 confirm 확인하다, 입증하다 strategy 전략

3.

번역 모든 직원이 새로운 정책을 시행하기 전에 이를 이해하는 것이 중요하다.

해설 all employees understand the new policy before it is implemented는 완전한 절이고, 또 동사 is의 진주어 역할을 하므로 (B) that이 정답이다. 이 문장에서 It은 가주어 역할을 하고, that all employees understand the new policy before it is implemented는 동사 is의 진주어 역할을 한다.

어휘 policy 정책 implement 시행하다, 실시하다

4.

번역 매니저는 팀이 의사소통을 개선할 필요가 있음을 분명히 했다.

해설 the team needed to improve communication은 완전한 절이고, 또 동사 made의 진목적어 역할을 하므로 (A) that이 정답이다. 이 문장에서 it은 가목적어 역할을 하고, that the team needed to improve communication은 동사 made의 진목적어 역할을 한다.

어휘 clear 분명한 improve 개선하다, 향상시키다 communication 의사소통

5.

번역 매니저는 팀워크가 성공에 필수적이라는 믿음을 강조했다.

해설 the belief는 완전한 절(teamwork is essential for success)을 이끄는 접속사 that과 동격 관계를 이루므로 (B) that이 정답이다.

어휘 emphasize 강조하다 essential 필수적인

6.

번역 팀이 모든 기대를 초과 달성했다는 사실이 이사회를 감명하게 했다.

해설 the fact는 완전한 절(the team exceeded all expectations)을 이끄는 접속사 that과 동격 관계를 이루므로 (D) that이 정답이다.

어휘 impress 감명을 주다, 깊은 인상을 주다 board 이사회

7.

번역 새로운 제품이 시장을 혁신할 것이라는 주장은 아직 증명되지 않았다.

해설 the claim은 완전한 절(the new product will revolutionize the market)을 이끄는 접속사 that과 동격 관계를 이루므로 (A) that이 정답이다.

어휘 revolutionize 혁신을 일으키다 prove 입증하다, 증명하다

8.

번역 그 보고서는 가장 긴급한 문제로 여겨졌던 것을 다루지 못했다.

해설 __________ was considered the most urgent issue는 동사 address의 목적어 역할을 하는 명사절이고, 동사 was의 주어가 없는 불완전한 절이면서 선행사가 없으므로 선행사를 포함하고 있는 (A) what이 정답이다.

어휘 fail to ~하지 못하다 address 다루다, 해결하다 consider 여기다, 간주하다 urgent 긴급한, 시급한

9.

번역 CEO가 회의 중에 제안한 것은 회사의 전면적인 구조 조정이었다.

해설 __________ the CEO proposed during the meeting은 동사 was의 주어 역할을 하는 명사절이고, 동사 proposed의 목적어가 없는 불완전한 절이면서 선행사가 없으므로 선행사를 포함하고 있는 (B) What이 정답이다.

어휘 CEO 최고경영자 propose 제안하다 restructuring 구조 조정

10.

번역 당신이 프레젠테이션에 포함하기로 결정한 것이 성공에 중요하다.

해설 보통 To부정사, 동명사 및 명사절이 주어 자리에 오면 문장에서 이들 요소가 하나의 단일 개념을 나타내기 때문에 단수 취급을 하고, "~한 것

이(은)"로 해석한다. 여기서 What you decide to include in the presentation에는 명사절로 문장에서 주어 역할을 하므로 단수 동사인 (C) is가 정답이다.

어휘 decide 결정하다 include 포함하다 presentation 발표, 프레젠테이션 critical 중요한, 결정적인

11.

번역 그들이 제안한 것은 우리가 줄곧 고려해 왔던 것이었다.

해설 __________ we had been considering all along는 동사 was의 보어 역할을 하는 명사절이고, 동사 considering의 목적어가 없는 불완전한 절이면서 선행사가 없으므로 선행사를 포함하고 있는 (C) what이 정답이다.

어휘 consider 고려하다, 숙고하다 all along 내내, 줄곧

12.

번역 그 결정은 매니저가 이전 프로젝트에서 관찰했던 것에 의해 영향을 받았다.

해설 __________ the manager had observed in previous projects는 전치사 by의 목적어 역할을 하는 명사절이고, 동사 observed의 목적어가 없는 불완전한 절이면서 선행사가 없으므로 선행사를 포함하고 있는 (D) what이 정답이다.

어휘 decision 결정, 판단 influence 영향을 주다, 영향을 미치다 observe 관찰하다, 목격하다 previous 이전의, 과거의

13.

번역 매니저는 새로운 정책을 시행할지를 결정할 것이다.

해설 __________ to implement the new policy는 동사 decide의 목적어 역할을 하는 명사절이고, 또 "~인지 아닌지"라는 의미로 to부정사와 함께 사용할 수 있는 (A) whether가 정답이다.

어휘 decide 결정하다 implement 시행하다, 실행하다 policy 정책

14.

번역 매니저는 지연이 전체 일정에 영향을 미칠지를 확신하지 못한다.

해설 __________ the delay will affect the overall timeline은 동사 is unsure의 목적어 역할을 하는 명사절이고, 또 완전한 절이므로 (D) whether가 정답이다. 참고로 is unsure는 상태를 나타내는 동사로, 뒤에 명사절이 오면 "~을 확신하지 못한다"라는 의미를 나타낸다. (A) who, (B) which, (C) what은 모두 불완전한 절을 이끄는 관계대명사이므로 적절하지 않다.

어휘 delay 지연 affect 영향을 미치다 overall 전체적인, 전반적인 timeline 일정, 기간

15.

번역 그 결정은 계약 조건이 받아들일 수 있을지에 기반할 것이다.

해설 __________ the contract terms are acceptable은 전치사 on의 목적어 역할을 하는 명사절이고, 또 완전한 절이므로 (A) whether가 정답이다. (B) if는 전치사의 목적어 자리에서는 사용할 수 없으므로 적절하지 않다.

어휘 decision 결정 be based on ~에 기초하다, ~에 기반하다 contract terms 계약 조건 acceptable 수용 가능한

16.

번역 팀은 새로운 프로젝트에 어떤 자원이 필요할지 논의했다.

해설 __________ resources would be required for the new project는 동사 discussed의 목적어 역할을 하는 명사절이고, 또 완전한 절로 명사 resources를 수식하므로 의문형용사 (B) what이 정답이다. (D) which는 선택지가 명확하거나 제한된 경우에 사용되므로, 이 문맥에서는 적절하지 않다.

어휘 discuss 논의하다, 토론하다 resource 자원 require 필요로 하다

17.

번역 팀은 테스트 단계에서 왜 오류가 발견되지 않았는지 분석했다.

해설 _________ the error was not detected during the testing phase는 동사 analyzed의 목적어 역할을 하는 명사절이고, 또 완전한 절이므로 "이유"를 나타내는 의문부사 (D) why가 정답이다.

어휘 analyze 분석하다 error 오류 detect 발견하다 during ~하는 동안

18.

번역 CEO는 누가 그 실수에 대한 책임을 져야 할지를 검토하고 있다.

해설 _________ should take responsibility for the mistake는 동사 reviewing의 목적어 역할을 하는 명사절이고, 또 주어가 생략된 불완전한 절이므로 의문대명사 (A) who가 정답이다.

어휘 review 검토하다, 검사하다 responsibility 책임 mistake 실수

19.

번역 그 보고서는 회사가 추가 자원을 어디에 할당해야 하는지를 자세히 설명한다.

해설 _________ the company should allocate additional resources는 동사 details의 목적어 역할을 하는 명사절이고, 또 완전한 절이므로 "장소"를 나타내는 의문부사 (C) where이 정답이다.

어휘 detail 상세히 설명하다 allocate 할당하다, 배분하다 additional 추가의 resource 자원

20.

번역 질문은 어떤 전략이 가장 좋은 결과를 가져올 것인가이다.

해설 _________ strategy will deliver the best results는 동사 is의 보어 역할을 하는 명사절이고, 또 완전한 절로 명사 strategy를 수식하므로 의문형용사 (B) which가 정답이다. (D) what은 선택지가 명확하지 않거나 제한되지 않은 경우에 사용하므로, 특정 전략 중 하나를 선택하는 맥락에서는 적절하지 않다.

어휘 strategy 전략 deliver 배송하다, 제공하다

21.

번역 당신의 부서를 담당하는 누구에게든 보고서를 제출하세요.

해설 _________ is responsible for your department는 전치사 to의 목적어 역할을 하는 명사절이고, 또 주어가 생략된 불완전한 절이면서 선행사를 포함하고 있는 복합 관계대명사 (A) whoever가 정답이다.

어휘 submit 제출하다 responsible 책임이 있는 department 부서

22.

번역 당신이 프레젠테이션에 유용하다고 생각하는 것은 무엇이든지 가져올 수 있다.

해설 _________ you think will be useful for the presentation은 동사 bring의 목적어 역할을 하는 명사절이고, 또 주어가 생략된 불완전한 절이면서 선행사를 포함하고 있는 복합 관계대명사 (C) whatever가 정답이다. 문맥상 "유용하다고 생각되는 무엇이든지"라는 의미를 나타내기 때문에, 선택지가 명확하거나 제한된 경우에 사용되는 (D) whichever는 적절하지 않다.

어휘 bring 가져오다 useful 유용한 presentation 발표

23.

번역 당신의 필요에 맞는 항목은 어느 것이든 가져가도 된다.

해설 _________ of the items S suits your needs는 동사 take의 목적어 역할을 하는 명사절이고, 또 주어가 생략된 불완전한 절이면서 선행사를 포함하고 있는 복합 관계대명사 (D) whichever가 정답이다. 문맥상 "여러 선택 가능한 항목(items) 중 하나를 선택하는 상황"을 나타내기 때문에, 선택지가 명확하지 않거나 제한되지 않은 경우에 사용되는 (C) whatever는 적절하지 않다.

어휘 item 항목 suit 적합하다 need 필요

24.

번역 그 직책은 채용 매니저가 선택한 사람에게 제공될 것이다.

해설 ________ the hiring manager selects는 전치사 to의 목적어 역할을 하는 명사절이고, 또 목적어가 생략된 불완전한 절이면서 선행사를 포함하고 있는 복합 관계대명사 (B) whomever가 정답이다.

어휘 position 직위, 직책 offer 제공하다 hiring manager 채용 매니저 select 선택하다

PART 6

다음 공지와 관련된 질문 1-4번을 보세요.

> 직원 여러분께,
> 회사의 운영 무결성을 유지하고 민감한 정보를 보호하기 위해, 정보가 조직 내외에서 관리되고 공유되는 방식에 대한 업데이트된 지침을 도입하고자 합니다.
> 첫째, 직원들은 외부로 공유되는 모든 데이터가 회사 정책과 규정을 준수하도록 해야 합니다. 민감한 세부 정보를 전송하기 전에 항상 수신자가 적절한 권한을 가지고 있는지 확인하십시오. 준수를 보장함으로써 직원들은 회사가 법적 및 재정적 문제를 피하는 데 기여할 수 있습니다.
> 둘째, 직원들은 내부 커뮤니케이션이 안전하게 유지되어야 회사가 잠재적인 침해로부터 보호받을 수 있다는 것을 알아야 합니다. 이러한 이유로, IT 부서에서 승인한 암호화 도구만을 사용해 기밀 정보를 공유해야 합니다. 승인되지 않은 플랫폼을 통해 민감한 세부 정보를 공유하면 회사에 심각한 위험이 초래될 수 있습니다.
> 마지막으로, 회사 정보의 오용과 관련된 수상한 활동을 발견하면 이를 신고해 주시길 권장합니다. 즉각적인 신고는 위험을 최소화하기 위해 신속한 조치를 취하는 데 도움이 됩니다.
> 이 지침을 준수하는 것은 안전하고 신뢰할 수 있는 업무 환경을 유지하는 데 필수적입니다. 질문이 있으신 경우, 매니저나 IT 지원팀에 문의하시기 바랍니다.
> 이 사안에 대한 주의를 기울여 주셔서 감사합니다.
>
> 감사합니다,
> 기업 보안 팀

어휘 guideline 지침 share 공유하다 maintain 유지하다 integrity 무결성, 진실성 operation 운영 safeguard 보호하다 sensitive 민감한 introduce 도입하다 update 업데이트하다 manage 관리하다 ensure 보장하다 externally 외부에 policy 정책, 지침 regulation 규정, 법규 confirm 확인하다 proper 적절한 authorization 권한 부여, 허가 transmit 전송하다 detail 세부 사항 compliance 준수 avoid 피하다 legal 법적인 financial 재정적인 consequence 결과 internal 내부의 communication 소통, 통신 encrypt 암호화하다 approve 승인하다 unauthorized 승인되지 않은 expose 노출시키다 serious 심각한 risk 위험 suspicious 의심스러운 activity 활동 immediate 즉각적인 swift 빠른, 신속한 contact 연락하다

정답

1. (A) 2. (B) 3. (A) 4. (C)

1.

해설 직원들이 외부로 공유되는 모든 데이터가 회사 정책과 규정을 준수하도록 해야 한다는 것을 의미하므로 (A) complies with가 정답이다. (B) applies to는 "~에 적용되다", (C) matches는 "일치하다", (D) supports는 "지지하다"라는 의미로 문맥에 맞지 않다.

2.

해설 ________ the recipient has the proper authorization before transmitting sensitive details는 동사 confirm의 목적어 역할을 하는 명사절이고, 또 완전한 절이므로 (B) whether가 정답이다.

3.

해설 confidential은 "기밀의"라는 의미로, 조직 내에서 민감하고 비공개적으로 보호되어야 할 기밀 정보를 다루는 맥락과 가장 부합하므로 (A) confidential이 정답이다. (B) creative는 "창의적인", (C) informal은 "비공식적인", (D) general은 "일반적인"이라는 의미로 문맥에 맞지 않다.

4.
(A) 암호화된 플랫폼을 통한 정보 공유는 필수적입니다.
(B) 즉각적인 보고는 위험을 효과적으로 최소화하는 데 기여합니다.
(C) 이 지침을 준수하는 것은 안전하고 신뢰할 수 있는 업무 환경을 유지하는 데 필수적입니다.
(D) 직원들은 안전한 커뮤니케이션 실천에 대한 워크숍에 참석할 것을 권장 받고 있습니다.

해설 지문의 마지막 부분은 회사의 보안 지침 준수의 중요성을 강조하고 있으므로, 문단 마지막에 추가될 문장은 지침 준수를 통해 회사가 목표로 하는 "안전하고 신뢰할 수 있는 업무 환경"을 유지할 수 있다는 점을 재강조하는 것이므로 (C)가 가장 적절하다.

PART 7

다음 이메일과 광고와 관련된 질문 1-5번을 보세요.

보낸 사람: Brian Lee
(b.lee@techsolutions.com)
받는 사람: Sarah Kim
(s.kim@innovateworks.com)
날짜: 9월 10일
제목: 연례 컨퍼런스 스폰서십 문의

Kim님께,
안녕하세요. 저는 Tech Solutions를 대표하여 다가오는 Innovate Works Annual Conference의 스폰서로 참여하고자 하는 저희의 관심을 전하기 위해 이 메시지를 드립니다. 이 행사는 업계의 전문가들에게 저희의 최신 혁신 제품을 소개할 수 있는 훌륭한 플랫폼이라고 생각합니다.
스폰서십 옵션에 대한 자세한 정보를 공유해 주실 수 있을까요? 특히, 비용, 혜택, 그리고 행사 기간 동안 저희 회사의 브랜드와 제품이 어떻게 소개될지에 대해 알고 싶습니다. 또한, 이달 말까지 스폰서십을 확정한 기업에게 제공되는 조기 등록 할인 혜택이 있는지도 확인하고 싶습니다.
답변 기다리겠습니다. 추가로 필요한 사항이 있으시면 아래 번호로 언제든지 편하게 연락 주시기 바랍니다.

감사합니다,
Brian Lee
마케팅 매니저, Tech Solutions
(555) 123-4567

Innovate Works Annual Conference 2024

올해 가장 주목받는 기술 행사에 참여하세요! Innovate Works Annual Conference는 업계 전문가들과 리더들이 한자리에 모이는 행사로, 최신 기술 발전을 배우고, 네트워킹하며, 탐구할 수 있는 독특한 기회를 제공합니다.

스폰서십 등급:
- Platinum Sponsor: $10,000
  - 모든 행사 자료에 귀사의 로고를 프리미엄 위치에 배치
  - 귀사를 소개할 수 있는 독립 부스 제공
  - 개막 키노트 연설 중 특별 언급
- Gold Sponsor: $5,000
  - 행사 자료에 로고 포함
  - 회사 부스 제공
- Silver Sponsor: $2,000
  - 홍보 자료에 로고 포함

특별 혜택: 9월 30일까지 스폰서십을 확정하면 10% 조기 등록 할인을 받을 수 있습니다! 기술 업계에서 가장 영향력 있는 행사 중 하나에서 귀사의 브랜드를 알릴 수 있는 이 기회를 놓치지 마세요.
자세한 내용은 sponsor@innovateworks.com으로 문의하세요.

어휘 sponsorship 후원, 스폰서십 inquiry 문의, 질문 annual conference 연례회의 express 표현하다 upcoming 다가오는 present 제시하다, 발표하다 latest 최신의 innovation 혁신 professional 전문가 across the industry 업계 전반에 걸쳐 kindly 친절히 available 사용 가능한 particularly 특히 benefit 혜택, 이득 highlight 강조하다 confirm 확인하다 registration 등록 discount 할인 commit 약속하다 look forward to ~을 기대하다 further 추가적인 hesitate 주저하다 reach 도달하다, 연락하다 directly 직접 be part of ~의 일원이 되다, ~에 참여하다 prominent 현저한, 저명한 connect 연결하

다 expert 전문가 offer 제공하다 explore 탐구하다, 조사하다 advancement 발전 tier 계층, 등급 placement 배치 material 재료 showcase 전시하다 impactful 영향력 있는 elevate 격상시키다, 알리다

정답

1. (A) 2. (B) 3. (C) 4. (B) 5. (D)

1. Brian Lee의 이메일 목적은 무엇입니까?
   (A) 컨퍼런스 스폰서십 옵션에 대한 정보를 요청하기 위해
   (B) Sarah Kim을 Tech Solutions의 연례행사에 초대하기 위해
   (C) Tech Solutions의 스폰서십 참여를 확인하기 위해
   (D) 컨퍼런스 연사로 참여하는 것에 대해 문의하기 위해

해설 이메일에서 Brian Lee가 "Could you kindly share more information about the sponsorship options available?"라고 요청하며, 행사 스폰서십에 대한 정보를 묻고 있으므로 (A)가 정답이다.

2. Platinum 스폰서십 등급에 포함된 내용은 무엇입니까?
   (A) 컨퍼런스 자료의 독점 사용
   (B) 개막 키노트에서의 특별 언급
   (C) 컨퍼런스 세션에 대한 조기 접근 권한
   (D) 직원용 무료 행사 티켓

해설 광고에 따르면, "A special mention during the opening keynote"는 Platinum 스폰서십 혜택 중 하나로 언급되었으므로 (B)가 정답이다.

3. 9월 30일까지 스폰서십을 확정했을 때 얻을 수 있는 혜택 중 하나는 무엇입니까?
   (A) 무료 홍보 자료 포함
   (B) 부스 배치 우선권
   (C) 10% 조기 등록 할인
   (D) 참석자용 무료 티켓

해설 광고에서 "Confirm your sponsorship by September 30 to receive a 10% early bird discount!"라는 특별 혜택이 명시되어 있으므로 (C)가 정답이다.

4. Brian Lee가 스폰서십 패키지에 대해 알고 싶어 하는 것은 무엇입니까?
   (A) 제공되는 네트워킹 기회
   (B) Tech Solutions의 제품이 어떻게 소개될 것인지
   (C) 키노트 연사를 선정하는 기준
   (D) 참석하는 다른 스폰서의 목록

해설 이메일에서 Brian Lee는 "how our company's branding and products would be highlighted during the event"라고 명시적으로 언급하며, 브랜드와 제품 노출 방법에 대한 정보를 요청하고 있으므로 (B)가 정답이다.

5. Silver 스폰서십 패키지에 포함된 것으로 언급된 것은 무엇입니까?
   (A) 행사에서 회사 부스 제공
   (B) 네트워킹 이벤트에서 스폰서 언급
   (C) 키노트 세션 동안 로고의 주요 배치
   (D) 홍보 자료에 로고 포함

해설 광고에 따르면 Silver 스폰서십에 "Logo featured on promotional materials only"가 포함되어 있으므로 (D)가 정답이다.

Chapter 16 비교

1. 규칙변화와 불규칙 변화

정답

1. (B) 2. (B) 3. (C)

1.

번역 업데이트된 매뉴얼은 이전 버전보다 이해하기에 더 쉽다.

해설 이 문장은 than이 있으므로 비교급이 필요하고, -y로 끝나는 형용사 easy는 -ier을 붙여 easier가 되므로 (B) easier가 정답이다.

2.

번역 진행하기 전에, 우리는 고객 요구 사항에 대해 추가 정보를 수집할 필요가 있다.

해설 이 문장은 정보와 같은 추상적 개념에서 "추가적인"의 의미를 나타내므로 (B) further가 정답이다.

어휘 proceed 진행하다, 계속하다 gather 모으다, 수집하다

3.

번역 모든 지원자들 중에서, 그녀는 마케팅 경험이 가장 적다.

해설 이 문장에서 Among all the candidates은 셋 이상을 비교할 때 사용되는 최상급 표현이므로 (C) least가 정답이다.

어휘 candidate 후보자, 지원자 experience 경험, 체험

2. 원급(Positive Degree)

✔ CheckPoint 1. 원급의 기본 구조

정답

1. (A) 2. (B)

1.

번역 새 사무실은 이전 사무실만큼 넓어서 모든 직원에게 충분한 공간을 제공한다.

해설 이 문장은 as + 형용사/부사의 원급 + as 구조의 동등비교 구문이므로 (A) as가 정답이다.

어휘 spacious 넓은 provide 제공하다, 공급하다 enough 충분한

2.

번역 프로젝트는 경영진이 기대했던 만큼 효율적으로 완료되지 않았다.

해설 이 문장은 not as + 형용사/부사의 원급 + as 구조의 열등비교 구문이므로 (B) as가 정답이다.

어휘 efficiently 효율적으로 management 경영진 expect 기대하다, 예상하다

✔ CheckPoint 2. 원급으로 최상급을 나타내는 표현

정답

1. (A) 2. (B) 3. (D)

1.

번역 모든 직원들은 가능한 한 철저히 훈련을 완료할 것을 권장 받는다.

해설 이 문장은 as + 형용사/부사의 원급 + as possible이라는 구조로 "가능한 한 ~하게"라는 의미를 전달하므로 (A) as가 정답이다.

어휘 encourage 격려하다, 장려하다 thoroughly 철저하게, 완전히

2.

번역 부서 내에서 Sarah만큼 업무를 제시간에 효율적으로 완료하는 사람은 없다.

해설 이 문장은 부정주어 as + 형용사/부사의 원급 + as 구조를 사용하여 Sarah가 부서에서 가장 효율적임을 강조하므로 (B) as가 정답이다.

어휘 department 부서, 학과 efficient 효율적인

3.

번역 이 해결책은 업계에서 개발된 어떤 해결책과 비교해도 혁신적이다.

해설 이 문장은 as + 형용사/부사의 원급 + as any 단수 명사 구조를 사용하여 이 해결책이 가장 혁신적임을 강조하므로 (D) any solution이 정답이다.

어휘 solution 해결책, 해법 innovative 혁신적인, 창의적인 develop 개발하다

✔ CheckPoint 3. 원급 관련 관용표현

정답

1. (C) 2. (C) 3. (A)

1.

번역 새 시스템은 이전 시스템보다 세 배 더 효율적으로 데이터를 처리한다.

해설 이 문장은 배수사 + as + 형용사/부사의 원급 + as 구조를 사용하여 두 대상을 비교하고 있으므로 (C) as efficiently가 정답이다. 참고로 (D) as efficient는 부사 자리에 올 수 없으므로 적절하지 않다.

어휘 process 처리하다, 가공하다

2.

번역 회사는 증가하는 업무량을 처리하기 위해 올해 작년만큼 많은 인턴을 고용했다.

해설 이 문장은 as many + 가산 복수 명사 + as 구조를 사용하여 두 대상을 비교하면서 가산 복수 명사 interns를 수식하고 있으므로 (C) as many가 정답이다. (D) as much는 불가산 명사와 사용되므로 적절하지 않다.

어휘 hire 고용하다, 채용하다 intern 인턴, 실습생 workload 업무량, 작업량

3.

번역 팀은 원래 예상했던 것만큼의 절반의 시간 안에 작업을 완료했다.

해설 이 문장은 as much + 불가산 명사 + as 구조를 사용하여 두 대상을 비교하면서 불가산 명사 time을 수식하고 있으므로 (A) as much가 정답이다. (B) as many는 가산 복수 명사와 사용되므로 적절하지 않다.

어휘 in half 절반으로 originally 원래, 본래

3. 비교급(Comparative Degree)

✔ CheckPoint 4. 비교급의 기본 구조

정답

1. (D) 2. (A) 3. (B)

1.

번역 새로운 관리자는 갈등 해결에서 이전 관리자보다 더 경험이 많다.

해설 이 문장은 than the previous one이 사용되어 비교급 구조임을 알 수 있으므로 "더 경험이 많다"는 의미의 비교급 형용사 (D) more experienced가 정답이다.

어휘 previous 이전의, 과거의 resolve 해결하다 conflict 갈등, 충돌

2.

번역 이 제품은 이전 모델보다 덜 비싸서 고객들에게 더 접근 가능하게 만든다.

해설 이 문장은 expensive than the previous model이 사용되어 비교급 구조임을 알 수 있으므로 비교 대상 간의 열등비교를 나타내는 (A) less가 정답이다. (C) very는 강조 부사로 형용사를 수식하지만, 비교 구조에서 사용되지 않다.

어휘 expensive 비싼 accessible 접근 가능한, 이용 가능한

3.

번역 직원들은 새로운 정책이 처음 예상했던 것보다 더 효과적이라고 생각했다.

해설 이 문장은 more effective라는 비교급 형용사가 사용되었고, 비교급 뒤에는 비교 대상을 연결하는 than이 필요하므로 (B) than이 정답이다.

어휘 effective 효과적인 initially 처음에

✔ CheckPoint 5. 비교급으로 최상급을 나타내는 표현

정답

1. (A)　2. (D)　3. (A)

1.

번역 그녀는 복잡한 프로젝트를 관리하는 데 있어 다른 누구보다 더 능력 있다.

해설 이 문장은 형용사/부사의 비교급 + than anyone else 구조를 사용하여 그녀가 다른 어떤 사람보다 더 능력 있음을 강조하고 있으므로 (A) anyone else가 정답이다.

어휘 competent 능숙한, 유능한 complex 복잡한

2.

번역 이 프로젝트는 경쟁사들이 시도한 다른 어떤 것보다 더 빠른 결과를 얻었다.

해설 이 문장은 형용사/부사의 비교급 + than anything else 구조를 사용하여 이 프로젝트가 다른 어떤 것보다 더 빠른 결과를 얻었음을 강조하고 있으므로 (D) anything else가 정답이다.

어휘 achieve 성취하다, 달성하다 competitor 경쟁자 attempt 시도하다, 노력하다

3.

번역 새 레스토랑은 이 지역의 다른 모든 레스토랑보다 더 인기가 많습니다.

해설 이 문장은 형용사/부사의 비교급 + than all the other + 복수 명사 구조를 사용하여 새 레스토랑이 지역 내 모든 다른 레스토랑보다 더 인기가 많음을 강조하고 있으므로 (A) all the other restaurants가 정답이다.

어휘 popular 인기 있는

✔ CheckPoint 6. 비교급 관련 관용표현

정답

1. (A)　2. (B)　3. (B)

1.

번역 새로운 정책은 검토 중인 두 옵션 중 더 나은 것이다.

해설 이 문장은 the + 비교급 + of the two 구조를 사용하여 두 가지 선택 중 더 나은 것을 지칭할 때 사용되는 표현이므로 (A) the better가 정답이다.

어휘 consideration 사려, 숙고, 검토

2.

번역 회의가 진행되면서 지시사항이 점점 더 명확해졌다.

해설 이 문장은 비교급 + and + 비교급 구조를 사용하여 "점점 더 명확해지는"이라는 뜻의 점진적인 변화를 지칭할 때 사용되는 표현이므로 (B) clearer / clearer가 정답이다.

어휘 instruction 지침, 지시사항 progress 진행하다, 나아가다

3.

번역 새로운 전략의 결과는 우리가 처음 예상했던 것보다 더 효과적이다.

해설 이 문장은 비교급 + than + expected/anticipated 구조를 사용하여 새로운 전략의 결과가 예상했던 것보다 더 효과적임을 나타내므로 (B) more effective가 정답이다. (D) more positively는 부사로, 형용사 자리에 올 수 없으므로 적절하지 않다.

어휘 initially 처음에 expect 기대하다, 예상하다

4. 최상급(Superlative Degree)

✔ CheckPoint 7. 최상급의 기본 구조

정답

1. (A) 2. (C)

1.

번역 이 디자인은 제출된 모든 개념 중에서 가장 긍정적인 피드백을 받았다.

해설 이 문장은 the + 형용사/부사의 최상급 + of all (the) + 복수명사 구조를 사용하여 제출된 개념 중에서 가장 긍정적이었음을 나타내므로 (A) the most positive가 정답이다. (D) the most positively는 부사의 최상급 형태로, 명사 feedback을 수식할 수 없으므로 적절하지 않다.

어휘 receive 받다 concept 개념 submit 제출하다

2.

번역 이 성과는 우리가 팀으로서 지금까지 달성한 것 중 가장 중요하다.

해설 이 문장은 the + 형용사/부사의 최상급 + (that) + 주어 + have ever + 과거분사(PP) 구조를 사용하여 지금까지 달성한 것 중에서 가장 중요하다는 것을 나타내므로 (C) the most significant가 정답이다. (D) the most significantly는 부사의 최상급 형태로, 형용사 자리에 올 수 없으므로 적절하지 않다.

어휘 achievement 성과 accomplish 성취하다, 달성하다 significant 중요한

✔ CheckPoint 8. 최상급 관련 관용표현

정답

1. (A) 2. (D) 3. (C)

1.

번역 이것은 현재 위기에 대한 최고의 해결책들 중 하나로 여겨진다.

해설 이 문장은 one of the + 형용사/부사의 최상급 + 복수명사 구조를 사용하여 최고의 해결책 중 하나임을 나타내므로 (A) one of the best가 정답이다.

어휘 consider 여기다, 고려하다 current 현재의 crisis 위기

2.

번역 팀은 어려운 상황 속에서 가능한 한 최고의 성과를 냈다.

해설 이 문장은 the + 형용사/부사의 최상급 + possible 구조를 사용하여 어려운 상황 속에서 가능한 한 최고의 성과를 냈음을 나타내므로 (D) the best possible가 정답이다.

어휘 deliver 수행하다, 결과를 내다 challenging 어려운 circumstance 상황

3.

번역 그녀는 조직 역사상 단연코 가장 영감을 주는 리더로 평가받는다.

해설 최상급 강조 부사(by far, the very) + the + 형용사/부사의 최상급 구조를 사용하여 그녀가 조직 역사상 단연코 가장 영감을 주는 리더임을 강조하므로 (C) by far the most inspiring이 정답이다.

어휘 regard 여기다, 간주하다, 평가하다 organization 조직

토익 종합 실전문제

정답

1. (D)	2. (B)	3. (C)	4. (D)	5. (B)
6. (C)	7. (A)	8. (B)	9. (B)	10. (C)
11. (C)	12. (A)	13. (D)	14. (A)	15. (A)
16. (D)	17. (A)	18. (C)	19. (B)	20. (C)
21. (D)	22. (B)	23. (A)	24. (A)	

1.

번역 CEO는 예상보다 회사 전략에 대해 더 많은 세부 정보를 제공했다.

해설 이 문장은 than이 있으므로 비교급이 필요하고, many와 much의 비교급은 more이므로 (D) more가 정답이다.

어휘 strategy 전략 expect 기대하다, 예상하다

2.

번역 새로운 지점은 본사에서 이전 지점보다 더 멀리 위치해 있다.

해설 이 문장은 than이 있으므로 비교급이 필요하고, 물리적 거리를 나타내므로 (B) farther가 정답이다. (D) further는 추상적 거리, 추가적 개념, 심화된 의미를 나타내므로 적절하지 않다.

어휘 branch 지점, 지부 locate 위치하다, 자리를 잡다 headquarters 본사, 본부

3.

번역 모든 후보자 중에서 그녀가 가장 뛰어난 자격을 갖추고 있어 그 직책에 가장 적합하다.

해설 이 문장에서 of all the candidates은 셋 이상을 비교할 때 사용되는 최상급 표현이므로 (C) best가 정답이다.

어휘 candidate 후보자, 지원자 qualification 자격, 자격 요건 suitable 적합한 position 직위, 직무, 직책

4.

번역 모든 경쟁자들 중에서, 그녀의 제안이 환경 문제를 다루는 데 가장 심도 깊었다.

해설 이 문장에서 Of all the competitors은 셋 이상을 비교할 때 사용되는 최상급 표현이 필요하고, 또 추상적 개념에서 가장 심화된 상태를 나타내는 최상급인 (D) furthest가 정답이다.

어휘 competitor 경쟁자 proposal 제안, 제의 address 다루다, 처리하다 environmental 환경의

5.

번역 올해의 매출은 작년만큼 높지 않지만, 추세는 개선되고 있다.

해설 이 문장은 not as + 형용사/부사의 원급 + as 구조의 열등비교 구문이므로 (B) as가 정답이다.

어휘 sales 매출 trend 추세, 경향 improve 개선하다, 향상시키다

6.

번역 그녀는 우리가 함께 일했던 어떤 팀원과 비교해도 신뢰할 만합니다.

해설 이 문장은 as + 형용사/부사의 원급 + as any 단수 명사 구조를 사용하여 그녀가 가장 신뢰할 만함을 강조하므로 (C) as가 정답이다.

어휘 reliable 신뢰할 수 있는, 믿을 수 있는

7.

번역 회사의 최신 모델은 에너지 효율 측면에서 이전 모델의 두 배만큼 효율적이다.

해설 이 문장은 배수사 + as + 형용사/부사의 원급 + as 구조를 사용하여 두 대상을 비교하고 있으므로 (A) as efficient as가 정답이다.

어휘 latest 최신의 predecessor 이전 모델 in terms of ~의 관점에서, ~에 관한 한 efficiency 효율성

8.

번역 우리는 예상했던 만큼 많은 서비스 관련 불만을 받았다.

해설 이 문장은 as many + 가산 복수 명사 + as 구조를 사용하여 두 대상을 비교하면서 가산 복수 명사 complaints를 수식하고 있으므로 (B) many가 정답이다. (A) much는 불가산 명사와 사용되므로 적절하지 않다.

어휘 receive 받다, 수신하다 complaint 불평, 불만

9.

번역 내구성 면에서 이 제품보다 더 튼튼한 제품은 없다.

해설 이 문장은 부정주어 + 형용사/부사의 비교급 + than을 사용하여 내구성 면에서 이 제품이 어떤 제품보다 더 튼튼함을 강조하고 있으므로 형용

사/부사의 비교급 (B) stronger가 정답이다.

어휘 durability 내구성, 내구력

10.

번역 이 호텔의 고객 서비스는 다른 고급 호텔에서 제공하는 다른 어떤 것보다 더 낫다.

해설 이 문장은 형용사/부사의 비교급 + than anything else 구조를 사용하여 이 호텔의 고객 서비스가 다른 어떤 것보다 더 좋았음을 강조하고 있으므로 (C) anything else가 정답이다.

어휘 luxury 럭셔리한, 고급의

11.

번역 이 새로운 모델은 우리가 이전에 출시한 다른 어떤 모델보다 더 저렴하다.

해설 이 문장은 형용사/부사의 비교급 + than any other + 단수 명사 구조를 사용하여 새로운 모델이 다른 어떤 모델보다 더 저렴함을 강조하고 있으므로 (C) any other model이 정답이다.

어휘 affordable 저렴한, 감당할 수 있는 launch 출시하다, 시작하다

12.

번역 부서 내에서 갈등을 해결하는 데 Sarah보다 더 나은 사람은 없다.

해설 이 문장은 부정주어 + 형용사/부사의 비교급 + than을 사용하여 Sarah가 부서 내에서 갈등 해결에 있어 어떤 사람보다 더 뛰어남을 강조하고 있으므로 형용사/부사의 비교급 (A) better가 정답이다.

어휘 department 부서 resolve 해결하다 conflict 갈등

13.

번역 이 스마트폰은 같은 가격대의 다른 모든 기기보다 더 나은 성능을 제공한다.

해설 이 문장은 형용사/부사의 비교급 + than all the other + 복수 명사 구조를 사용하여 스마트폰이 같은 가격대의 다른 모든 기기보다 더 우수함을 강조하고 있으므로 (D) all the other devices가 정답이다.

어휘 offer 제공하다 available 이용 가능한 price range 가격대, 가격 범위

14.

번역 회의가 시작되자마자 화재 경보가 울렸다.

해설 이 문장은 no sooner + 조동사/동사 + 주어 + 동사 + than + 절 구조를 사용하여 두 사건이 거의 동시에 일어났음을 나타내고, 본문 시제가 과거이므로 (A) did가 정답이다. 참고로 no sooner가 문장 맨 앞에 올 경우 도치가 발생하여 주어와 조동사의 위치가 바뀌므로 도치 형태가 와야 문법적으로 맞다.

어휘 fire alarm 화재 경보 go off 울리다, 발사되다, 폭발하다

15.

번역 이 소프트웨어는 대용량 데이터셋을 처리하는 데 있어 이전 버전보다 훨씬 더 잘 작동한다.

해설 이 문장에서 far는 비교급 better를 강조하는 강조 부사로서 "훨씬 더 잘"이라는 의미를 나타내므로 (A) far가 정답이다.

어휘 perform 작동하다, 수행하다 previous 이전의 handle 처리하다, 다루다

16.

번역 제품 출시는 예상했던 것보다 더 성공적이었다.

해설 이 문장은 비교급 + than + expected/anticipated 구조를 사용하여 제품 출시가 예상했던 것보다 더 성공적임을 나타내므로 (D) anticipated가 정답이다.

어휘 launch 출시, 출시하다 anticipate 예상하다, 기대하다

17.

번역 새로운 정책은 직원 문제를 해결하는 데

있어 이전 정책보다 더 나을 게 없다.

해설 이 문장은 no + 비교급 + than 구조를 사용하여 두 대상을 부정적으로 비교하고 있으므로 (A) better가 정답이다. (B) more effectively와 (C) less effectively는 부사로, 형용사 자리에 올 수 없으므로 적절하지 않다.

어휘 address 다루다, 해결하다 concerns 걱정, 우려, 문제

18.

번역 계약을 더 신중히 검토할수록 잠재적인 문제를 더 쉽게 피할 수 있다.

해설 이 문장은 the + 비교급 + 주어 + 동사, the + 비교급 + 주어 + 동사 구조를 사용하여 더 신중히 검토할수록 더 쉽게 피할 수 있다는 의미를 나타내므로 (C) the more easily가 정답이다. (A) the easier는 형용사로, 문맥상 부사가 필요한 자리이므로 적절하지 않다.

어휘 review 검토하다 contract 계약서, 계약 avoid 피하다 potential 잠재적인

19.

번역 그 후보의 자격은 다른 지원자들의 자격보다 분명히 열등하다.

해설 이 문장에서 inferior는 라틴어 비교 표현으로 than 대신 전치사 to를 사용하는 형용사이므로 (B) to가 정답이다.

어휘 candidate 후보자, 지원자 qualification 자격, 자격증 clearly 분명히 inferior 열등한 applicant 지원자

20.

번역 이번 세미나는 올해 진행된 모든 교육 세션 중에서 가장 유익했다.

해설 이 문장은 the + 형용사/부사의 최상급 + of all (the) + 복수명사 구조를 사용하여 세미나가 모든 교육 세션 중에서 가장 유익했음을 나타내므로 (C) the most informative가 정답이다. (D) the most informatively는 부사의 최상급 형태로, 보어 자리에 올 수 없으므로 적절하지 않다.

어휘 seminar 세미나, 워크숍 conduct 실시하다, 진행하다 informative 유익한

21.

번역 모든 지원자 중에서 그녀가 프로젝트 요구사항에 대해 가장 깊은 이해를 보여주었다.

해설 이 문장은 the + 형용사/부사의 최상급 + of all (the) + 복수명사 구조에서 of all (the) + 복수명사가 문두로 도치되어 나간 형태이고, 프로젝트 요구사항에 대해 가장 깊은 이해를 보여주었음을 나타내므로 (D) the deepest가 정답이다. (B) the most deeply는 부사의 최상급 형태로, 명사 understanding을 수식할 수 없으므로 적절하지 않다.

어휘 demonstrate 입증하다, 보여주다 requirement 요구사항, 필요조건

22.

번역 올해의 수익은 회사 역사상 기록된 것 중 가장 높은 수익이다.

해설 이 문장은 the + 형용사/부사의 최상급 + (that) + 주어 + have ever + 과거분사(PP) 구조를 사용하여 역사상 가장 높은 수익임을 나타내므로 (B) the highest가 정답이다. (C) the most highly는 부사의 최상급 형태로, 보어 자리에 올 수 없으므로 적절하지 않다.

어휘 profit 이익, 수익 record 기록하다

23.

번역 영업팀은 새로운 캠페인으로 올해 최고의 실적을 달성했다.

해설 이 문장은 the + 형용사/부사의 최상급 + of + 시간 구조를 사용하여 올해 최고의 실적을 달성했음을 나타내므로 (A) the highest가 정답이다.

어휘 achieve 달성하다, 이루다, 성취하다

24.

번역 이 매장은 휴가철 동안 도시에서 가장 큰

할인 혜택을 제공한다.

해설 이 문장은 the + 형용사/부사의 최상급 + in + 장소/집합명사 구조를 사용하여 도시에서 가장 큰 할인 혜택을 제공한다는 것을 나타내므로 (B) the most generous가 정답이다. (D) the most generously는 부사의 최상급 형태로, 명사 discounts를 수식할 수 없으므로 적절하지 않다.

어휘 offer 제공하다, 제시하다 during ~하는 동안 holiday 연휴, 휴가

PART 6

다음 정보와 관련된 질문 1-4번을 보세요.

> 고객 만족도 보고서
>
> 날짜: 2024년 3월 12일
> 작성자: 마케팅 조사팀
>
> 조사 결과 요약:
> 설문조사 결과, 새 제품군이 이전 제품군보다 더 긍정적인 반응을 얻었다는 사실이 나타났습니다. 고객들은 포장이 광고된 만큼 친환경적이라고 언급했으며, 제품의 사용성은 경쟁 브랜드보다 우수하다고 평가했습니다.
> 하지만 배송 시간이 고객이 기대했던 만큼 빠르지 않아서, 전반적인 만족도가 약간 감소했습니다. 그럼에도 불구하고, 새 제품군의 품질은 우리 회사가 출시한 모든 제품 중에서 가장 우수한 것으로 간주됩니다.
>
> 권고 사항:
> 1. 물류 팀과 협력하여 배송 시간을 단축하고 고객의 기대에 부응하십시오.
> 2. 제품의 친환경적인 측면을 강조하여 긍정적인 고객 인식을 유지하십시오.
> 3. 예상보다 더 빠르게 문제를 식별하고 해결하기 위해 제품 수명 주기 초기에 피드백 설문을 실행하십시오.

어휘 survey 설문조사 receive 받다 packaging 포장, 포장재 eco-friendly 친환경적인 advertise 광고하다 usability 사용성, 사용 용이성 superior 우수한 lead to 초래하다, 이끌다 decrease 감소하다, 축소하다 overall 전체적인, 전반적인 satisfaction 만족 consider 간주하다, 여기다 recommendation 추천 사항, 권장 사항 emphasize 강조하다 maintain 유지하다 perception 인식, 인지 implement 실행하다 life cycle 생애주기 identify 식별하다, 확인하다 address 해결하다, 다루다 anticipate 예상하다, 기대하다

정답

1. (D) 2. (B) 3. (A) 4. (D)

1.

해설 이 문장에서는 than the previous one이라는 비교 구문이 사용되어 비교급 형태가 필요하고, 부사 자리이므로 (D) more positively가 정답이다.

2.

해설 이 문장에서는 명사 brands를 앞에서 수식하는 형용사나 형용사 역할을 하는 현재분사가 필요하므로 (B) competing이 정답이다.

3.

해설 이 문장에서 앞부분은 부정적인 요소(배송 시간문제)를 언급하고, 뒤에서는 긍정적인 요소(제품 품질)를 언급하여 역접 관계의 양보를 나타내며, 뒤에 대명사 this를 수반할 수 있는 전치사가 필요하므로 (A) Despite가 정답이다.

4.

(A) 더 나은 고객 참여를 위해 마케팅 전략을 개선하십시오.
(B) 증가하는 수요를 해결하기 위해 생산 속도를 높이십시오.
(C) 환경 기준에 부합하도록 포장을 재설계하십시오.
(D) 물류 팀과 협력하여 배송 시간을 단축하고 고객의 기대에 부응하십시오.

해설 이 문장은 "Recommendations(권고 사항)" 섹션의 첫 번째 항목으로, 이전 내용에서 언급된 문제(배송 시간 지연)를 해결하기 위한 구체적인 행동 방안을 요구하고 있으므로 (D)가 가장 적절하다. (A), (B), (C)는 문맥에서 언급되지 않은 주제를 다루거나 주요 문제와 관련이 없으므로 적절하지 않다.

PART 7

다음 기사와 내부 메모와 관련된 질문 1-5번을 보세요.

TechCorp, 새로운 AI 기반 도구 출시 예정

TechCorp는 인공지능 분야의 선도적인 혁신 기업으로, 새로운 AI 기반 분석 도구 InsightPro의 출시를 발표했습니다. InsightPro는 모든 규모의 비즈니스를 위해 설계되었으며, 데이터 분석을 간소화하고 의사결정 과정을 개선할 것을 약속합니다.
TechCorp의 CEO에 따르면, InsightPro는 대규모 데이터 세트를 실시간으로 분석하여 효율성을 향상시키고 수익을 증대시킬 수 있는 실행 가능한 인사이트를 제공합니다. 이 도구는 또한 사용자들이 인터페이스를 자신의 특정 요구에 맞게 조정할 수 있도록 맞춤형 대시보드 기능을 갖추고 있습니다.
이 제품은 2024년 6월 1일에 공식 출시될 예정이며, 구독 요금제는 월 $49.99부터 시작됩니다. 2024년 5월 15일 이전에 가입하는 초기 사용자들은 10% 할인 혜택을 받을 수 있습니다.
업계 전문가들은 InsightPro가 데이터 분석 시장, 특히 경제적이고 확장 가능한 솔루션을 찾는 중소기업들에게 큰 영향을 미칠 것으로 예상하고 있습니다.

수신: 마케팅 및 영업 팀
제목: InsightPro 출시 준비

팀원 여러분께,
InsightPro의 공식 출시가 다가옴에 따라, 마케팅과 영업 팀이 성공적인 출시를 위해 협력해야 합니다. 아래의 주요 작업 사항을 확인해 주세요:
1. 마케팅 자료
- 2024년 4월 20일까지 제품 브로슈어와 홍보 영상을 최종 완료하세요. 이 자료들은 실시간 분석 및 맞춤형 대시보드와 같은 InsightPro의 고유한 기능을 강조해야 합니다.
2. 교육 세션
- 모든 영업 사원은 2024년 4월 25일에 예정된 제품 교육 세션을 완료해야 합니다. 이 교육은 팀이 잠재적인 고객 질문에 효과적으로 대응할 수 있도록 준비시킬 것입니다.
3. 초기 사용자 캠페인
- 마케팅 팀은 2024년 4월 10일까지 10% 할인 캠페인을 시작해야 하며, 모든 플랫폼에서 최대한 가시성을 확보해야 합니다.

궁금한 점이나 제안 사항이 있으면 marketing@techcorp.com으로 직접 연락해 주세요. 이 출시를 성공적으로 이끌기 위한 여러분의 헌신에 감사드립니다.

감사합니다,
Rachel Lin
마케팅 디렉터

어휘 innovator 혁신자 artificial intelligence 인공지능 AI-powered AI 기반의 analytic 분석의 streamline 간소화하다, 효율화하다 analysis 분석 enhance 향상시키다, 개선하다 real-time 실시간의 actionable 실행 가능한, 실질적인 insight 통찰 efficiency 효율성 customizable 사용자 정의 가능한 tailor 맞추다 specific 특정한, 구체적인 release 출시하다 subscription 구독 adopter 사용자, 수용자 predict 예상하다, 예측하다 significantly 상당히 small and medium-sized enterprise 중소기업(SME) affordable 저렴한, 합리적인 scalable 확장 가능한, 확장성 있는 align 일치시키다 finalize 마무리하다 brochure 안내서 promotional 홍보의 unique 독특한 feature 특징, 요소 representative 담당자 equip 갖추다 address 다루다, 처리하다 visibility 가시성 dedication 헌신, 전념

정답

1. (A) 2. (D) 3. (A) 4. (C) 5. (B)

1. 이 기사의 주요 목적은 무엇입니까?
   (A) 새로운 AI 기반 도구 출시를 발표하기 위해
   (B) AI 기술의 기술적 특징을 설명하기 위해
   (C) 직원들을 위한 새로운 교육 방법을 소개하기 위해
   (D) InsightPro를 경쟁 제품과 비교하기 위해

해설 기사의 첫 문장에서 "TechCorp... has announced the launch of its new AI-powered analytics tool, InsightPro."라고 명시되어 있으므로 (A)가 정답이다.

2. 기사에 따르면, 업계 전문가들이 InsightPro에 대해 예측한 내용은 무엇입니까?

(A) 기존 도구와 강력한 경쟁에 직면할 것이다.
(B) 많은 기업들에게 너무 비쌀 수 있다.
(C) 관련성을 유지하기 위해 빈번한 업데이트가 필요할 것이다.
(D) 중소기업을 위한 데이터 분석 시장을 변화시킬 수 있다.

해설 기사 마지막 단락에서 "Industry experts predict that InsightPro could significantly impact the data analytics market, especially for small and medium-sized enterprises looking for affordable and scalable solutions."라고 언급되어 있으므로 (D)가 정답이다.

3. 기사의 2단락 3번째 줄에 나오는 단어 "customizable"는 의미상 __와 가장 가깝다.
(A) 개인화된
(B) 고급의
(C) 상세한
(D) 일관된

해설 "Customizable dashboards"는 사용자 맞춤형 대시보드를 의미하며, "personalized(개인화된)"가 가장 적절한 동의어이므로 (A)가 정답이다.

4. 내부 메모의 대상은 누구라고 추론할 수 있습니까?
(A) 마케팅 또는 영업에 관여하지 않는 직원들
(B) InsightPro를 제작한 팀
(C) 제품 출시를 준비하는 직원들
(D) AI 분석 도구에 관심 있는 고객들

해설 메모의 첫 문장에서 "we want to ensure that both marketing and sales are aligned in delivering a successful launch."라고 언급하며, InsightPro 출시를 준비 중인 마케팅 및 영업 팀이 주된 대상임을 명확히 하고 있으므로 (C)가 정답이다.

5. 메모에 따르면, 영업 팀이 완료해야 할 작업은 무엇입니까?
(A) InsightPro의 성능에 대한 상세 보고서를 준비하는 것
(B) 2024년 4월 25일에 예정된 교육 세션에 참석하는 것
(C) 2024년 4월 20일까지 홍보 캠페인을 시작하는 것
(D) 제품 브로슈어의 디자인을 완성하는 것

해설 메모의 "All sales representatives must complete the product training session scheduled for April 25, 2024."라는 문장에서 영업 팀이 해당 교육에 참석해야 함이 명확히 언급되어 있으므로 (B)가 정답이다.